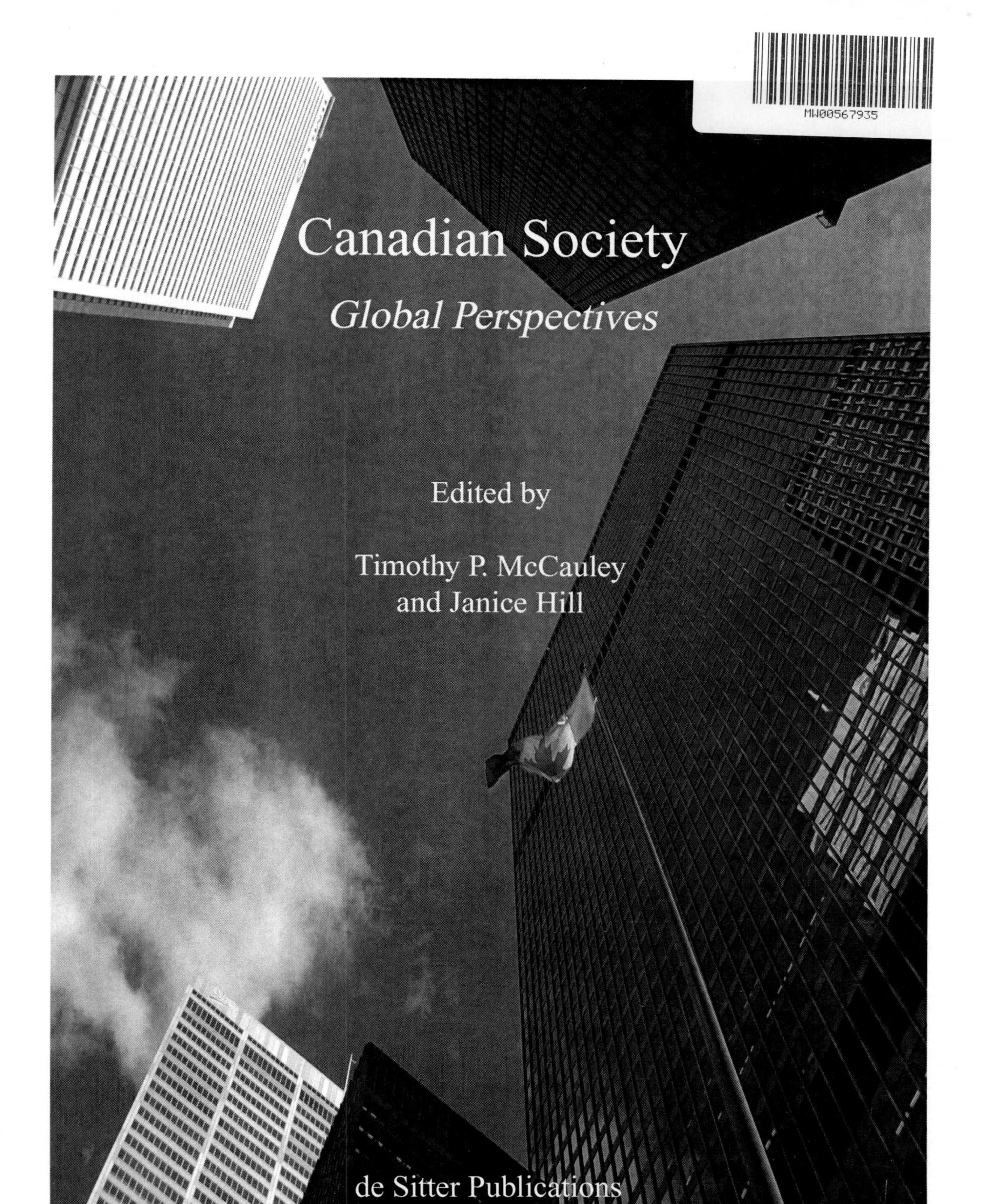

Canadian Society
Global Perspectives
Edited by
Timothy P. McCauley
and Janice Hill
de Sitter Publications

Canadian Society: Global Perspectives

Edited by Timothy P. McCauley and Janice Hill

ISBN 978-1-897160-30-5

Cover and book design by de Sitter Publications

LIBRARY AND ARCHIVES CANADA CATALOGUING IN PUBLICATION DATA

A catalogue record for this book is available from the Library and Archives Canada.

de Sitter Publications
111 Bell Dr
Whitby, ON, L1N 2T1
CANADA

289-987-0656
www.desitterpublications.com
sales@desitterpublications.com

Table of Contents

About the Authors

Dr. Jac J.W. Andrews is a Professor in Educational Studies in Psychology at the University of Calgary. His current research interests are in the areas of childhood psychopathology, psychological assessment, and clinical supervision. Dr. Andrews has published many psycho-educational textbooks as well as scientific articles in peer reviewed journals such as *Adolescence, Journal of Psychoeducational Assessment, British Journal of Educational Psychology, Canadian Journal of Counseling*, and *Canadian Journal of School Psychology*.

Robert M. Bridi is a Ph.D. candidate at the Department of Geography, York University. His research interest revolves around issues related to transnational migrant labour. In the Canadian context, his research focuses on the Seasonal Agricultural Worker Program, and he explores labour related issues that effect the living conditions for migrant agricultural workers.

Dr. Claudio Colaguori is an Assistant Professor at the Department of Equity Studies, York University. He teaches in the Human Rights and Criminology Programs at York University. Dr. Colaguori has twice earned the John O'Neill Award for Teaching Excellence and has been nominated for Television Ontario's Best Lecturer Award. His research is based on Critical Theory and covers issues ranging from social control in the post 9/11 era to social constructions of human culture and the critique of domination.

Wayne Crosby is a Ph.D. Candidate in the Department of Rural Economy at the University of Alberta, Canada. His research interests include environmental sociology, environmental governance, political economy/ecology and social dimensions of environmental change.

Dr. Thomas Fleming is a Professor of Criminology at Wilfrid Laurier University. He is a recipient of the 2007 LIFT Award for Teaching Excellence presented by the Province of Ontario. He has written extensively in criminology including a recently published text on the Canadian criminal justice system. Currently he is conducting research on cross cultural issues in homicidal interactions.

Dr. Heather L. Garrett is a contract faculty member in Sociology at York University in Toronto, Canada where she teaches Research Methods and Population and Society courses. Her research focuses on women's work within a social-historical context; specifically how women in central Ontario contributed to the family economy during the mid-nineteenth century.

Dr. Amal Madibbo is an Assistant Professor in the Department of Sociology at the University of Calgary, Alberta. Her research focuses on race and antiracism, Black Francophone migration to Canada, and race and ethnicity in Sub-Saharan Africa.

Dr. Guida Man received her Ph.D. from OISE/University of Toronto. She currently teaches in the Faculty of Liberal Arts and Professional Studies at York University. Her research interest encompasses the interactions of globalization, transnational migration, women's work, and social inequality, as they are articulated to gender, race and class relations. She has conducted numerous research studies concerning Chinese immigrant women in Canada, and has published extensively in her areas of specialization.

Scott MacLeod is currently completing a Ph.D. thesis at the Department of Political Science at Simon Fraser University, Burnaby, BC, Canada. The tentative title of his dissertation is *Globalization, Social Movements and Democracy in Canada* and stands as a reflection of his research interests in both Canadian Politics and International Relations. Once concluded, the research project will serve as a document of the democratic nature and ideological character of anti-globalization activism in Canada.

Dr. Stephen L. Muzzatti (Ph.D.,York University) is an Associate Professor of Sociology at Ryerson University in Toronto, Canada where he teaches courses in media, crime and popular culture. He's written on the news media's criminalization of youth culture, as well as on terrorism, globalization, consumerism, motorcycle culture and street racing.

Dr. Zabedia Nazim holds a Ph.D. in Education from the Ontario Institute for Studies in Education at the University of Toronto. Her areas of research, teaching and writing include sociology of gender, race and ethnicity, global citizenship, organizational studies, labour relations, social theory and sociology of work and labour. Zabedia has over twenty years of experience working in the Canadian financial services industry. Currently, she teaches at a number of Canadian universities and colleges including Sir Wilfrid Laurier University, Ryerson University, Seneca College and Centennial College. In addition, she works as a consultant specializing in anti-racism and anti-oppression organizational change.

Dr. David A. Nock received his M.A. degree in Canadian Studies from Carleton University in 1973 and his Ph.D. in Sociology from the University of Alberta in 1976. He taught those subjects in addition to Religious Studies at Lakehead University in Thunder Bay, Ontario where he is a Professor Emeritus in the Department of Sociology. He has published four books and about fifty scholarly articles which are detailed at Lakehead's sociology website (see www.lakeheadu.ca and follow the links to David). In a certain sense, "Religion's Changing Face in a Multicultural Canada" is a sequel to his 1993 chapter, "The Organization of Religious Life in Canada," which appeared in *The Sociology of Religion: A Canadian Focus*, edited by W.E. Hewett. The many differences between the two articles indicate the great changes in Canadian society over a brief span of time.

Patricia O'Reilly is a lawyer and activist. She teaches part-time in the criminology law and society programs at Wilfrid Laurier University. She has co-authored and presented papers on aboriginal justice, the Pickton serial murder investigations, and victims' rights.

Dr. John Parkins is an Associate Professor in the Department of Rural Economy where he teaches courses in rural and natural resource sociology. His research explores the changing relationship between natural resource industries and rural communities, social impact assessment, environmental governance, and international development. Recent articles are published in academic journals such as *Society & Natural Resources, Community, Work & Family,* and *Polar Record.*

Dr. David Peat is Executive Director of Research and Innovation for Rocky View Schools in Airdrie, Alberta. Over the past few decades, he has been involved in teaching, teacher training and leadership positions in education and health (e.g., Post-Tsunami training of village workers; Consulting Psychologist) in Canada and in international settings such as Qatar, Kuwait, Singapore and the Maldives.

Dr. Jim Paul is Associate Dean International in the Faculty of Education, University of Calgary. Jim's academic and professional focus is educator preparation and development within local, national and international contexts.

Abigail Salole completed her Bachelors in Criminology at the University of Toronto. She went on to complete her Masters in Social Work also at the University of Toronto. Born in New Zealand, but raised in Burlington, Ontario, her Masters' thesis research involved her revisiting her "hometown" and suburban roots. Currently, she teaches in the Community Outreach and Development Worker program at Sheridan College. She also teaches in the Sociology Department at the University of Toronto. She is completing her doctorate in Criminology at Griffith University in Australia. Her research interests include youth engagement, youth justice policies and community participation/resistance in/to criminal justice polices.

Dr. Alexander Shvarts recently completed a Ph.D. in Sociology at the University of Toronto. His research interests include Russian Entrepreneurs, the Russian Mafia and Russian Jews. Dr. Shvarts teaches various sociology and criminology courses at Humber College, the University of Toronto, and Waterloo University. He has presented papers at several conferences in Europe, Canada, and the United States, and has published articles on the Russian Mafia in *Contemporary Justice Review, International Review of Modern Sociology,* and *Michigan Sociological Review*. He has written articles on Russian Jews in *Diasporic Ruptures: Globality, Migrancy, and Expressions of Identity* and *Studies in Ethnicity and Nationalism*, and he has upcoming book on *Russian Transnational Entrepreneurs: Ethnicity, Class and Capital* published by de Sitter Publications.

Dr. Sharon-Dale Stone is Professor and Chair of Sociology at Lakehead University. She is also affiliated with the Masters of Public Health, the Gerontology programs, the Women's Studies programs, and the Centre for Research in Aging and Health at Lakehead. Her research interests include social gerontology, critical disability studies, gender, sociology of health and illness, and qualitative research methods. She recently published the book, *A Change of Plans: Women's Stories of Hemorrhagic Stroke* (Sumach Press, 2007).

Introduction

Canadian Society: Global Perspectives

Edited by Timothy P. McCauley
and Jancie Hill

York University

This book examines globalization from a Canadian perspective. It is designed to introduce students to key concepts and variables in sociology and to show how they are operationalized in empirical sociological research. This anthology brings together scholars from various disciplines and schools across Canada. They bring fresh insight and analysis to understanding social change.

The sections of this text begin by exploring "Being Canadian" in terms of culture, social interaction and socialization. The chapters progress to cover broader issues including gender, sexuality and health.

Part II looks at how Canadians interact in groups and within bureaucracies. We examine the dynamics of Canadian group life including family, religion, and race and ethinic groups. The overarching theme of this section is that individuals are linked beyond the family to an increasingly complex global community through group life in various institutional frameworks.

Part III deals with social inequalities within Canada and abroad. In this section, the authors delve into racial and ethnic inequality, gender inequality, social stratification and crime and deviance. The chapters illustrate how the unevenness of capitalism leads to conflict within and beyond Canada.

Part IV of the text moves to a discussion of how Canadians operate within a global context. The areas covered include mass media, immigration, globalization and transnationalism. The authors demonstrate that Canada cannot be understood merely as an isolated nation-state; rather we should conceive of our domestic reality in the context of the new world order.

Finally, in Part V the authors explore future trends in Canada's global reality by examining social change, education and environmental issues. To round up the anthology, we included a chapter on research methods to help readers become good "consumers" and producers of social research.

Taken together, the chapters in this anthology will assist undergraduates in their effort to find new ways of understanding and interpreting Canadian society in a global context.

PART I

Being Canadian

Part I seeks to examine how "Being Canadian" involves taking part in Canada's changing culture. Individuals in Canadian society are enmeshed both nationally and internationally in globalization processes and practices.

Chapter 1 by Timothy P. McCauley on **culture** shows how the self evolves from cultural elements. The French Canadian example is then used to show how the forces of social change and globalization in Penetang modify cultures by producing ethnic homogenization and the growth of youth sub-cultures.

Chapter 2 by Parbattie Ramsarran on **social interaction** maps how the Indo-Guyanese community living in Toronto is reconstructing their trans-situational ethnicity via geography and other groups such as South Asians and Afro-Canadians. In Canadian society, the official multicultural discourse promotes differences between groups. Dr. Ramsarran suggests that the unofficial discourse can be one that deconstructs these differences to highlight similarities. These similarities then become anchors for multicultural groups to mobilize in solidarity with each other to tackle inequality.

Chapter 3 by Stephen E. Bosanac and Janice Hill on **socialization** invites us to imagine how Canadians experience ourselves within a global context. The authors identify various values, norms and ideologies that shape the building of communities and the resolution of conflict between communities. This chapter details four possible processes through which socialization occurs and discusses the relevance of family life, schooling, and mass media as important agents of socialization in being and becoming Canadian. Dr. Hill concludes the discussion with an engaging examination of the cultural messages revealed in the "Rant," a Molson Canadian beer commercial that found its way into the zeitgeist of Canadian culture in the spring of 2000.

Chapter 4 by Janice Hill on **gender and sexuality** asks us to question modern liberal education and the social construction of categories such as childhood, adulthood and morality. She asks us to consider how educational systems normalize gender appropriate behaviour both historically and today in the age of globalization. She finds that Western societies like Canada are committed to childhood innocence, but they normalize and Victorianize gender and sexuality.

Lastly, Chapter 5 by Sharon Dale Stone on **health, disability and ageing** provides us with some basic concepts and questions whether health, disability and aging should or should not be conceptualized as being inter-related. She shows how Canadian individuals are fortunate to have an extensive health care system that is enhanced by medicine and technology. Being Canadian is indeed enhanced by its Health Care System, and yet, ageism and capitalism reify the aging process and health issues in Canada.

In all, Part I provides a discussion of the most basic elements of Being Canadian.

Chapter 1

Culture

Canadian Culture in a Global Context

Timothy P. McCauley

York University

INTRODUCTION

The goal of this chapter is to examine Canadian culture as it moves towards a global context. It is argued here that cultures are not hard wired in genes and biology, rather cultures are dynamic, fluid and socially constructed by the interactions of individuals as they live out their daily lives. Culture refers to the sum of practices, values, ideologies and material objects that people create to deal with real life problems (Brym et al., 2010:69). Although cultural variations have been attributed by some scholars to innate characteristics of peoples across the globe, it will shown here that the "biology as destiny" argument is clearly limited compared to Lewontin's (1991:19-37) notion of "biology as ideology." Culture in Canada has moved from an emphasis on ethnic difference to universal values such as inclusion, and within global contexts, sub-cultures emerge to create new forms of identity and belonging, particularly for young Canadians.

To explore the concept of culture and its significance to Canadians faced with globalization, this chapter begins with a discussion of the role of biology in culture and the elements of culture. We demonstrate how biological determinism is a racist ideology and part of xenophobic thinking in support of the status quo. Next, we identify that cultural patterns found within the Canadian context are not fixed or unchanging, rather culture is dynamic and it changes as a result of environmental processes such globalization. Lastly, to show how culture is dynamic and fluid in various social settings, we provide an example of one small town in which two cultures exist within a dynamic produced by the forces of globalization. We show how mass media and globalization modify and homogenize ethnic cultures while at the same they create paths for emerging sub-cultures over time.

BIOLOGY AND CULTURE

Any discussion of cultural differences between races, classes and gender must begin with an analysis of the role of biology in directing and determining cultural variations. In the nineteenth century, for example, evolutionary psychologists developed grand theories of white European cultural superiority by relying upon genetic determinism. Drawing upon Darwin's theory of evolution, they attempted to show that cultural superiority and inferiority of different civilizations with racial and ethnic groups, was the products of genes. These scholars largely ignored environmental influences to demonstrate that "anything good in human evolution was the product of "Northern races" (Lewontin, 1991:27). They also maintained that by looking at the genetic traits of certain individuals they could predict certain behaviours. For example, criminals were more likely to have shifty eyes; red haired people were prone to violence; and black people were likely promiscuous (Brym, 2001:72).

Although evolutionary psychology has been refuted over time, biological determinism continues to be evident in the work of contemporary socio-biologists. Like evolutionary psychology, socio-biologists assert that culture is hard wired in genes. Biological determinism has three fundamental premises. First, that humans differ in their innate capacities. Second, cultural differences derive from these innate characteristics are transferred from generation to generation. Third, differences between races, classes and gender are "inevitable and natural." Although today, most sociologists disagree with this position, the "biology as destiny" argument remains in the work of contemporary socio-biologists (Rushton, 1991). The "biology as destiny" argument is the view that "certain cultural groups" have done more to "modernize" human civilizations through their innate superior genetic capacities. Lewontin, therefore, set out to prove scientifically that biological determinism is the provincial thinking of White Supremacists, Neo-Nazi's, and members of the Eugenics Movement "racists, demagogues and fascist know nothings" (Brym, 2001:73). He contends that most open-minded and scientific scholarship on the issue of biology and culture refutes genetic determinism. Lewontin (1991) argues that "variations among individuals within species are a unique consequence of both genes and environment within constant interaction" (Brym, 2001:76-7). He goes on to say that there is *not one iota of evidence* of any kind that differences in status, wealth and power between races in North America have anything to do with genes" (p.76). In fact, Lewontin's research indicates the important factor in history is "random variation." For example, he finds that 85 percent of all variation is between any two individuals, 8 percent is between ethnic groups and 7 percent between races (p.77). He points to the dangers of adopting notions of "biology as destiny" when exploring cultural patterns and he clearly demonstrates that historically, biology has been used as ideology to maintain systems of inequality around the world. To argue that genes determine cultural responses means that one accepts the status quo and only minimal change to hierarchy, political hegemony and economic inequality is possible. For example, in North America, Europe and South Africa, the biology as destiny argument was embedded in the belief systems of the K.K.K., Nazis and the White Africanners, respectively. These groups over-emphasized biology as the key determinant of culture to maintain their systems of inequality. Thus, to limit cultural analysis to biology is an indication that the individual may be threatened by outsiders, and fearful of social change in the interests of a global community. Clearly, before examining culture, it is important for students of sociology to be aware of the political and ideological implications of certain cultural analyses (Brym, 2010:71).

THE ELEMENTS OF CULTURE

Culture contains a number of important elements and these are at foundation of all human societies through time. The first element of culture is the symbol. Symbols are important ideas that contain meaning for those who recognize them as they interact within particular social contexts (Brym, 2010). Symbolic gestures and cues are part of one's day-to-day processes or going about one's daily routine. For example, nodding one's head to a neighbour or a co-worker is an example of interpersonal communication. Some symbols are accepted with favour, such as smile or a laugh, while other symbolic communication may reflect negativity such as Pierre Trudeau's use of the "finger" in a speech against separatists in Québec politics.

Symbols must be distinguished from signs, which are key components of operational society. Signs are more overt and directive. For example, a STOP sign or the No SMOKING sign carries explicit meanings. Signs can include things from nature such as a crack of thunder, which is a sign that a storm is on the way. It is said that animals, like human beings, react to signs and yet, it is only humans who have the capacity to interpret signs and symbols (Swidler, 1986).

Lastly, language is an extensive and all encompassing component of culture. Language is a "system" of symbols that is learned by members of particular cultural communities. Languages are then incorporated into the thought processes of cultural groups as they carry out their daily routines. Higher education, for example, involves learning, interpreting and processing language as "concepts"–abstract words and ideas (Brym, 2001:66).

Three other very important elements of culture include values, beliefs and norms. Max Weber (1904) was one of the first sociologists to explore the implication of cultural value orientations. Values are "generalized" belief systems about morality and how the world operates. For example, to Weber, Christians, Jews, Muslims, Hindus, Buddhists and Confucians each possess distinctive value orientations that affect their view on politics, economics, and religion (Gerth and Mills, 1946). These values orientations impact greatly upon the economic and political practices in different parts of the world. It has been suggested by some scholars that globalization is simply a homogenization of these cultural differences in political economy (Ritzer, 1993).

Compared to values, "beliefs" are more pragmatic and situational. Beliefs are either prescriptive or proscriptive. A prescriptive belief may be something like "children should be seen and not heard." A proscriptive belief would be children "must be disciplined if they misbehave." It is the case that beliefs derive from value orientations. For example, my own research in Penetanguishene (1991) indicated that Francophone parents originally used strong discipline such as corporal punishment to generate an acceptance of authority and hierarchy. However, these earlier beliefs became more liberal as they were exposed to the larger Canadian society and culture through mass media and transportation (McCauley, 2005).

Another key component of culture is norms. Norms are unwritten rules and they are indeed situation specific. It is normative for an audience to clap in an auditorium and it is an unwritten cultural norm that people look straight ahead in an elevator. One sociological approach that focuses on subtle norms is known as ethnomethodology. This approach, perfected by Harold Garfinkel (1967), utilizes "breaching experiments" to show how interpersonal culture is rooted in social norms. He showed that if one breaks the generalized norms, "others" react in interesting ways. For example, Garfinkel told his students to breach elevator norms by starring at the back of a crowded elevator looking directly at the people. The result of the breach generated interesting responses such as anger, confusing, and doubt (p.37).

Moreover, social norms and group punishments have been studied extensively by anthropologists such as Murdock (1949). Anthropologists often classify normative behaviour with the terms: folkways, mores and taboos. A folkway, such as wearing one's shirt in public, renders the least severe forms of punishment. The breaking of mores, on the other hand, is more severe. This is because mores specify social requirements; they represent core norms that people believe in and are vital to group life. Wearing no cloths in public constitutes a violation of mores. Lastly, taboos are the most severe codes of the society, for example, the taboo of incest.

Norms, values and beliefs are elements of culture that one may observe in various social contexts. Classical sociologists produced studies of both high culture and low culture in their work (Arnold, 1869). High culture was associated with an interest in the opera and the ballet; or an interest in fine art and literature. Taking part in high culture involved wearing proper attire or using correct table manners to follow the normative codes of the upper classes. However, the difference between high and low culture came under scrutiny and criticism beginning in the 1960s. Scholars reviewed earlier interpretations of low cultures; and found them to be elitist and ethnocentric. Thus, today, instead of using the word low culture, they replace it with popular culture (Elliot, 1948). Popular culture refers to the culture produced by trends in the mass media that affects all members of contemporary society.

Moreover, all of the cultural elements above work together in various social contexts and situations to create unique sub-cultures. It is said that sub-cultures have grown in significance within the last 30 years (Hebdige, 1979). Increasingly, group interests and preferences grow through the expansion of technology and communication. The internet, for example, creates a unique and unprecedented platform for new and distinctive sub-cultures to develop. Roland Warren (1963) would classify these communities as vertically created through specialized interests. Examples of vertical communities or vertical cultures might include sporting groups, historical and genealogical societies, dating groups and special interest communities. All of these examples represent vertical community compared to horizontal communities generated by location, for example, people from a small town.

CULTURE: THE CANADIAN CASE

It is important to gain a sense of all the elements of culture and then use them sociologically to develop insight into communities undergoing social change. For example, my research in the small town of Penetanguishene, Ontario showed that cultures are not stagnant. Cultures are modified through time by forces of social change including improvements to transportation, communication, mass media and population growth. The traditional Francophone culture had an emphasis on the values of La Survivance, which meant an acceptance of hierarchy; a strong belief in patriarchy and obedience to authority (McCauley, 1991). This attitude of La Survivance was entrenched in French Canadian culture until the Quiet Revolution of the early 1960s. Only then, and over three decades, did French Canadian culture begin to clearly change in both Québec, and later in French Canadian towns outside of Québec. For example, through the 1960s to the 1980s, the focus of my research in Penetang, French Canadians were influenced by mass media and other sources. Thus, whereas the older Francophones and Anglophones were culturally distinctive in Penetanguishene, the two groups homogenized and became more similar over time. My study was an exploration of three age cohorts: 20 to 30, 30 to 60 and 60 and above.

When researchers study particular cultures in Canada such as French Canadians, one arrives at the realization that Canadian culture on the whole is dynamic and difficult to define. In Canada, various cultural forces influence the political, economic and social practices of Canadians. Canada is said to be unicultural, bicultural and multicultural (McCloud, 1989). Uniculturalism is the product of Canada's colonial heritage and the dramatic impact of the Conquest in 1763 on the Plains of Abraham. The British victory at that time, forced Francophones to generate the ideology of La Survivance. La Survivance meant that French Canada after the Conquest until the Quiet Revolution was sustained by working on the land, respecting the Catholic Church as an authority and by resisting English Canadian materialism (Guindon, 1989). The attitude of La Survivance can be appreciated and understood by reading the classical myth of French Canada, Marie Chapdelaine: (1913) and by observing the video by Roch Carrier called *The Sweater* (1979).

Moreover, during the years in which French Canada maintained La Survivance, roughly 1763 to 1960, English Canadian maintained British institutions and practices as the central components of the

Canadian political economy. Symbols such as Parliament, The King/Queen, the Governor General, Red Ensigns and the Union Jacks embedded within provincial flags, showed that Canada was a colony of the Mother Country, Great Britain. English Canadians felt a strong allegiance to Britain and English Canadians believed that England's battles were Canada's battles too. This produced a "conscription crises" in English and French politics throughout its early history.

Colonialism carried with it the attitude of uniculturalism, strongly emphasized by fraternal organizations such as the Orange Order. The Orange Order stood for beliefs that were pro-Protestant, pro-British connection and anti-Catholic. Consequently, the battle between the Orange and the Green was transplanted to Canadian soil from the Battle of the Boyne in Ireland (1690), and it was symbolized in the Orange parades in cities such as Toronto until mid-1950s. Even today, the unicultural attitude is entrenched in some members of the Royal Canadian Legion and the Scottish Free Masons who feel that over-tolerating cultural variations pulls at the very fabric of Canadian Society. Ten years ago, for example, there was the issue of a Sikh who refused to remove his Turban in a Legion. This year, 2010, the issue of a woman wearing a Burka produced a similar impact in Québec (*Montreal Gazette*, March, 2010). Both are examples of the unicultural attitude found mostly in smaller towns and cities in Canada such as in the Maritimes and across the West. Thus, while uniculturalism has diminished over time, it remains an underlying component of Canadian culture.

The bicultural component of Canadian society was recognized in 1867 through Confederation. Within Confederation, Federal and Provincial powers were differentiated and French Canadians were recognized in areas such as education and religion. Nonetheless, Anglo dominance from 1867 until the early 1960s meant that French Canada would only survive by resisting English Canadian Culture (Guindon, 1989). Only the Quiet Revolution changed the cultural pattern known as La Survivance. Through the 1960s and the Royal Commission on Bilingualism and Biculturalism (RCBB), French Canada emerged with a stronger sense of their basic rights and entitlement. French Canada sought, and achieved, a sense of being "Masters of their own House" through 1960s and 1970s, and while most rejected the violence of the FLQ, the new Francophone ideology included a sense of separation and a distinct society. No longer were French Canadians "*White Niggers of America*" (Valliers, 1971).

Lastly, the multicultural component of Canadian society also emerged from the RCBB. Some contend that multiculturalism was to a large extent, an afterthought (Guindon, 1989). Official multiculturalism became law only through negotiations between 1963 and 1969 and towards *Book Four* of the RCBB in 1969, when multiculturalism was established as Canadian reality. Multiculturalism was entrenched in Canadian culture as other ethnic communities, the Ukrainians in particular, felt left out of the RCBB. Moreover, as a result of this closure, the Other Canadians became The Third Force in Canadian society by the late 1960s. Thus, one might consider that without the emergence of a new Francophone attitude and ideology, Canada might have remained unicultural. For example, Victoria Day, May 24th, could have been established as Canada Day without the Third Force in Canadian cultural politics. However, regardless of the historical circumstances, Canada now is indeed a multicultural nation. Many cultural groups are now recognized and accepted for their distinctiveness. Moreover, the process of becoming a Canadian involves acculturation and not American style assimilation.

CANADIAN CULTURE IN A GLOBAL CONTEXT

Globalization is a force that has only begun to impact Canadian society and culture. Some argue that globalization is simply an extension of modernization (Goode, 1990). It is generally functionalist scholars who subscribe to this adaptive view of social change. Functionalists argue that globalization means that individuals and communities must adapt to changing political and economic circumstances. Conflict theorist and symbolic interactionists are less forgiving. Conflict theorists tend to adopt Dependency Theory or World Systems Theory when exploring globalization (Gunther-Frank, 1969). In this perspective, globalization involves three key forces: universalism, imperialism and capitalism. Conflict theorists use concepts such as "Americanization," "Westoxification" and "homogenization" to describe the impact of globalization on Canadian culture. The three forces of globalization, work simultaneously to produce lasting changes to local communities, societies and cultures. Universalism means that products are produced to a certain standard across the world. Imperialism means that the new system will be maintained by force, if necessary. Lastly, capitalism or the search for surplus value means that capitalists must consistently find ways to make their products cheaper (Brym, 2010). The three forces of globalization above entail that the exploitation of Third World societies to produce cheap labour is justifiable to capitalistic entrepreneurs and their multinational conglomerates. As a result, some scholars critique the unevenness of capitalism by focusing upon immigration between the First and Third Worlds. Richmond (1984), for example, calls the process "global apartheid," insofar as apartheid is a Dutch word meaning separate neighbourhood (Richmond, 1984). Currently, the way in which issues of illegal immigration and the definition and identification of refugees is debated in Canada's parliament is an example of how global apartheid is a significant pattern between the First and Third Worlds.

Nevertheless, some symbolic interactionists and post modernists see the benefits of globalization (Bhagwati, 2004). Globalization brings together people from all over the world. New technologies such as the internet, the Blackberry and the cell phone help to create linkages across the globe. Issues, disasters, sporting events are now global. We see pictures and images from across the world instantly. And over time, it is clear that struggles between the First and Third Worlds, is an improvement in global relations compared to when the Second World or the Eastern Bloc, known as the Soviet Union was a definite threat to freedom. Thus, while globalization may lead to processes such as McDonaldization, which tends to homogenize culture and make humans more similar, unique cultural differences can now be recognized and celebrated as the world moves forward. Some argue that Canada has clearly moved beyond uniculturalism to multiculturalism with events such as Carribana and the Olympic Games of 2009.

GLOBALIZATION AND SUB-CULTURES

The rise in sub-cultures, according to Hebdige (1984), is result of rapid social change combined with alienation. As the forces of globalization prevail and traditional communities lose their importance, the dominant overarching Canadian culture is re-vitalized by unique sub-cultural groups. Individuals, particularly the young, look for meaning in their lives in this context and they discover a sense of belonging by involving themselves in an "in-group" from popular culture. Hebdige, for example, found that in London, England in the 1980s, "Punkers, Mods and Rockers" provided an outlet for alienated British youth. Furthermore, the proliferation of sub-cultures since the 1980s can be attributed to increasing global social media. For while the youth of the 1960s were more monolithic with limited access to radio and television, the youth of today can gravitate to a variety of sub-cultures stemming from the modified mass media. The sub-cultures of today provide individuals with a sense of identity and belonging in an increasingly complex society. Some examples of sub-cultures include Hip Hop, Rasta, Gothic, Skinheads, Ravers, Wiccans, to name a few. With the help of the internet, youth from various towns and cities across Canada can connect with one another, and in the process of interacting within a sub-culture, many symbols, signs and language become important. The symbols may include labels, flags, clothing, music and logos and other paraphernalia that possess symbolic significance and meaning for members as "social insiders." The sub-culture then is formed around important symbolic rituals and practices. Youth sub-cultures thrive in alienating environments such as mass urban settings that are affected by global forces. While in the 1960s, the Hippie sub-culture was a more monolithic group that thrived on the adage "don't trust anyone over thirty," youth sub-culture of today has more specific ideas and interests that grow out of the sense of meaning they derive from their sub-cultures.

GLOBALIZATION AND ETHNIC CULTURE

The growth and modification of ethnic culture as a result of globalization may be understood by focusing upon my research findings in Penetanguishene. Penetang was a small town of 5,400 at the time of my research in the early 1990s. Historically, the relations between Canada's two prominent cultures reflected Weber's notion of social closure. Weber was one of the first sociologists to point out how ethnic hierarchies or "vertical mosaic" (Porter, 1965) are formed and maintained when he developed analysis of social closure. To Weber closure involves:

> A status segregation that transforms the horizontal and unconnected coexistences of ethnically segregated groups into specific political and communal action...the caste structure brings about a social subordination and an acknowledgement `more honour' in favour of privileged status groups. (Cited in Gerth and Mills, 1980:189).

In Penetanguishene, one could easily observe patterns of "social closure" and hierarchy simply by observing the historical and cultural geography of the small town. If one looked to the left, towards the Francophone side of town, one could see small houses and a large Roman Catholic Church. However, looking to the right, up the hill, one could see larger houses of the English Canadian and two smaller Protestant churches. The French side of town was distinct from the English side and historically segregation and hierarchy was evident in ethnic relations in favour of the English. One pattern in this hierarchy involved the Francophone changing their language to English when greeting an Anglophone on the streets of Penetang. According to my respondents, French Canadians in Penetang "would not dare" to use their own French language when an English Canadian approached them.

Furthermore, historical cultural differences between the two ethnic groups became apparent to me by interviewing older inhabitants of Penetang. For example, in interviews with French and English Canadian families I asked some townspeople: What would you do if you won a million dollar lottery? The response of older Francophones was more collectivistic in orientation compared to the English Canadian. The Francophone wanted to spend the money on family or give it the church, whereas the English Canadian, like Ben Franklin, claimed they would put the money in the bank and invest. This significant difference measured with quantitative statistics reflected the Weberian notion of the relationship between the "Protestant Ethic and the Spirit of Capitalism" (McCauley, 1991). The value orientations of the two cultures was at least originally quite distinct. Older French Canadians and Older English Canadian displayed Weber's classical notions of Catholic and Protestant religious value orientations.

However, interviews with younger Francophones and Anglophones in Penetanguishene revealed less difference over time; there was clear evidence of homogenization and similarity between the groups. Both groups reflected more materialistic values; they had more selfish notions of what they would do with one million dollars: It seems that the forces of social change had influenced the two groups. Thus, one only needs to drive through the small town today to see that the influences of media, commercialization, and commodification have homogenized the two groups in a variety of ways. Today in Penetang, the patterns that George Ritzer terms "McDonaldization" are everywhere in the town. Like many small cottage country towns in Southern Ontario, Penetang has homogenized by chain stores like Zellers, Walmart and Canadian Tire and common fast food outlets such as McDonald's, Wendy's and Burger King. These stores and restaurants have levelled the cultural landscape in every small town in Canada, thereby reducing cultural differences between ethnic groups. The small mom and pop restaurants and main street stores are gone and the "locals" in Penetang connect with outsiders via the internet and by discount services on long distance. The citizens of Penetang listen to the same music; watch the same television shows on one hundred channels, and some Francophones see themselves as "moving on up" by purchasing bigger houses on the English side of town. Thus, the forces of globalization, universalism, imperialism and capitalism have increasingly absorbed the ethnic differences in the small town leaving young people to turn to sub-cultures.

In short, the case study of Penetanguishene provides some insight into how two particular cultures became modified and homogenized through time. Material inventions such as the internet, cable television, the cell phone and the Black Berry, changed the patterns of small town, social interaction. Closure between the ethnic groups in Penetanguishene became less noticeable and integration and acceptance of the "others" was clearly evident. Thus, the patterns in Penetanguishene may be viewed as a microcosm of how both ethnic cultures and sub-cultures are formed in the current Canadian global context. Observing the signs, symbols and language of many ethnic groups and the followers of sub-cultures should generate new research into sub-cultures such as Wiccan, Hip Hop, Gothic, Rasta and Rave. These insights may also be helpful in understanding collective behaviours such as the current anti-globalization movement that has raised the level to tension prior to the G20 Summit in late June 2010. All cultures affected by globalization are active and reactive in essence.

In conclusion, this chapter has attempted to define and explore aspects of culture. It initially identified some of the elements that make-up cultures across the globe. Signs, symbols and language are at the foundation of human cultures. Next, a discussion of Canadian culture showed that cultures are not static and fixed by biology; instead they are dynamic and multidimensional. It demonstrated that Canadian society is at one and the same time, unicultural, bicultural and multicultural. Lastly, we demonstrated how French and English cultures homogenized as a result of McDonaldization, a process linked by Ritzer to globalization. Globalization has a tendency to homogenize culture and the proliferation of sub-cultures in this environment is a reaction to globalization's three forces: universalism, imperialism and capitalism.

REFERENCES

Bhagwati, J.B. (2004). *In Defense of Globalization.* NY: Oxford University Press.

Brym, R.J. (2000). *Society in Question: Sociological Readings for the 21st Century,* 3rd ed. Toronto: Harcourt.

Elliot T.S. (1948). *Notes Towards the Definition of Culture.* London: Faber and Faber.

Frank, G.W. (1969). *Capitalism and Underdevelopment in Latin America.* NY: Monthly Review Press.

Freud, S. (1961). *Civilization and its Discontents.* NY: W.W. Norton and Company.

Garfinkel, H. (1967). *Studies in Ethnomethodology.* Cambridge: Blackwell Publishing Limited.

Gerth, H.H., and C. Wright Mills. (1946). *From Max Weber.* London: Routledge.

Guindon, H. (2001). *Québec's Social and Political Evolution Since 1945.* In Daniel Glenday and Anne Duffy (eds.), *Canadian Society: Meeting the Challenges of the 21st Century.* Don Mills: Oxford University Press.

Hebdige, R. (1984). *Subculture: The Meaning of Style.* London: Methuan and Company.

Hemon, L. (1913). Marie *Chapdelaine: A Tale of Lake Saint John County.* Montreal: Le Temps.

Lewontin, R.C. (2003). *Biology as Ideology: The Doctrine of D.N.A.* Toronto: House of Anansi Press.

McCauley, T. (1991). *Family, Religion and Social Change: A Case Study of Penetanguishene.* Thesis (Ph.D). York University Graduate Program in Sociology.

_____. (2005). "French Canadian Families in Penetanguishene." *International Journal of Comparative Sociology* 45(1-2):73-85.

McLeod, Keith. (1984). *Multiculturalism and Multicultural Education: Policy and Practice in Multiculturalism in Canada: Social and Educational Perspectives.* Toronto: Allyn and Bacon.

Murdock, G.P. (1949). *Social Structure.* NY: McMillan.

O'Brian, M. (1971). *The Politics of Reproduction.* Hammersmith: HarperCollins Publishers Ltd.

Ogburn, W.F. (1922). *Social Change: With Respect to Cultural and Original Nature.* Oxford, England: Delta Books.

Richmond, A.H. (1994). *Global Apartheid: Refugees, Racism, and the New World Order.* Toronto: Oxford University Press.

Ritzer, G. (1993). *The McDonaldization of Society.* Thousand Oaks: Pine Forge Press.

Super, R.H. (1965). *Culture and Anarchy with Friendship's Garland and Some Literary Essays*, Volume V of *The Complete Works of Matthew Arnold.* MI: The University of Michigan Press.

Swindler, A. (1986). "Culture in Action: Symbols and Strategies." *American Sociological Review* 51:273-86.

Valliers, P. (1971). *White Niggers of America: The Precocious Autobiography of a Québec Terrorist.* Toronto: McClelland and Steward.

Warren, R. (1963). *Community in America.* Chicago: Rand McNally.

Chapter 2

Social Interaction

The Emergence of Trans-Situational Ethnicity in a Multicultural Space

Parbattie Ramsarran

York University

INTRODUCTION

This chapter seeks to map how the Indo-Guyanese[1] community living in Toronto,[2] Canada is reconstructing their trans-situational ethnicity via geography and other groups, notably the South Asians[3] and Afro-Canadians.[4] The chapter begins with the methodology followed by the conceptual frame. It continues with a brief historically specific introduction of the Indo-Guyanese movements from India to Guyana, (Guyana and British Guiana used interchangeable) and from Guyana to Canada.[5] This is followed with an empirical account of trans-situational ethnicity surfacing. The conclusion suggests strategies on how this discourse can be a catalyst to explore groups' solidarity.

Trans-situational ethnicity as an analytical frame is used to explore Indo-Guyanese attempts to reconstruct their identity and community in the Toronto multicultural space.[6] Conceptually, trans-situational ethnicity reflects the increasingly trans-global ethnicity of immigrants who, at the local level (current country of residency), are reconstructing their ethnicity and community via trans-narratives. For Indo-Guyanese, these narratives are reflective of multiple, geographic centers; the prefix "trans" narrates an ethnicity that is situational but draws upon geography to completely express Indo-Guyanese identity. Accordingly, these narratives are constitutive of their ancestral movement from India to Guyana, and their current movement from Guyana to Canada.

METHODOLOGY

Interviews and participant observation for this chapter were conducted with members of the Indo-Guyanese community residing in Toronto. The Indo-Guyanese community is two generations; the first generation immigrants include the first member of the family to immigrate to Canada, and their senior parents,[7] most of whom were sponsored by their children. Conceptually, second generation refers to the Canadian born children and grand children of the first generation immigrants. The first generation's identity contains elements of three centers, namely India, Guyana and currently Canada. This chapter documents, through participant observation and several in-depth interviews, the multiple discourses of trans-situational ethnicity.

In the Indo-Guyanese community in Toronto, beginning November 2002 to November 2003, for a period of one year participant observation was undertaken at numerous social/community gatherings/events. Sites of participant observations included temples, small and large community/social functions, and social interactions within and outside homes. Additionally, other members of the Indo-Guyanese community provide insights into why they are reconstructing a trans-situational ethnicity.

CONCEPTUAL FRAME

Ethnicity

The word ethnicity is derived from the Greek words *ethnos* meaning people, a company, a nation (Isajiw, 1999; Gordon, 1964). *Ethnikos* is related to *ethnos* but translates to mean people not like us. In its sociological usage, the concept ethnic refers to minority groups, immigrant groups; multicultural groups that share race, culture, tribe, nationality and religion (Weber, 1965).[8]

Specifically, for Max Weber (1965:306), an ethnic group is:

> Those human groups that entertain a subjective belief in their own common descent-because of similarities of physical type or of customs or both, or because of memories of colonization and immigration-in such a way that this belief is important for the continuation of non-kinship communal relationship.

For Indo-Guyanese, their memories of indentureship and their second movement to Canada is what makes them an ethnic group. Like many other multicultural groups, they have a history of migration, and colonialism that have become social markers of ethnic boundaries. However, these social markers are shared with other immigrant groups from Guyana, and other parts of the world. Thus, Indo-Guyanese, in their encounters with other immigrant groups, for example, South Asians, have had to renegotiate their ethnicity beginning with that of their ancestors, and the first generations lived realities grounded in Guyana. It is within the context of reconstructing ethnicity, and community vis-à-vis other groups that Indo-Guyanese trans-situational ethnicity appears.

In sociology, approaches to the study of ethnicity are linked to the assimilationist and cultural pluralist paradigms (Gordon, 1964; Park, 1950). The assimilation paradigm was used by the Chicago School in the 1920s and 1930s to study urban society. This paradigm emphasized stages of contact, accommodation, assimilation and the fusion between immigrant groups' culture and that of the host society. These stages map the reconstruction of ethnicity.

The second paradigm is the cultural pluralist school within which, a similar step-by-step process is articulated in the reconstruction of ethnicity. However, one notable variation in the latter model is the claim that although assimilation occurs, the new identity of the assimilated immigrant group is not wholly constitutive of the host society. For instance, the loss of language and culture might trigger a reawakening of ethnicity. Consequently, the reconstructed ethnicity contains elements of the group original ethnicity fused with that of the host society, for example, hyphenated French-Canadian, Indo-Canadian and Indo-Guyanese. Hence, within cultural pluralism, immigrant groups are directly engaged in the reconstruction of ethnicity

(Glazer and Moynihan, 1963). These two approaches document the lived realities the Indo-Guyanese and many immigrant groups. Moreover, for the Indo-Guyanese, their trans-situational ethnicity is reflective of their multiple movements, and emerges out of social interactions with other groups. These social interactions evoke what is labeled situational ethnicity out of which trans-situational ethnicity surfaces.

Situational Ethnicity

Within the two paradigms of ethnicity are narratives of ethnicity. These are: the subjective/primordialist (herein after referred to as primordialist) and the situational frameworks (Liebkind, 1989). The extreme *primordialist* discourse situates ethnicity in biology, as an ascriptive, inherent, fixed social/biological inheritance (Van den Berghe, 1981). That is, ethnicity is something that humans are born with. Whereas, the social constructionist view of ethnicity, popularly referred to as *situational ethnicity*, focuses on the instrumental, and posits that in social situations opportunistic possibilities prompt the invocation of ethnicity (Geertz, 1963 and Stack, 1986). In the constructive view, ethnicity is one or several socio-cultural characteristics that surface as a result of "a constantly evoking interaction between the nature of the local community, the available economic opportunities and the national or religious heritage of a particular group" (Yancey, Erickson and Juliani, 1976:397). Conceptually, situational ethnicity is located in social relations, context or organizations (Okamura, 1981). Hence, narratives, culture, traditional practices, and symbols are situationally summoned to reconstruct ethnicity and thus, community in new geographic spaces (Hitchcock, 1999; Allen, 1994; Coughlan and Samarasinghe, 1991; Gluckman, 1940).

The Origin of Indo-Guyanese Trans-Situational Ethnicity

For many scholars, including Henry, Tator, Mattis and Rees (2000:76), the category South Asia is applicable to the following groups:

> ...people from India, Pakistan, Sri Lanka, Bhutan, and Bangladesh. It also includes people with roots in South Asia who have immigrated from Kenya, Tanzania, Uganda, the Caribbean Nations, and other countries.

This is a common categorization of Indo-Guyanese people; unfortunately it is incorrect. In substituting South Asian as a label for the Indo-Guyanese, territory and location of origin are given primacy over historical struggles, and lived realities of the Indo-Guyanese and South Asians.[9] Awareness is significant, insofar as it deals with the issues of identity of ethnic/racial minorities in Canada (that is, here in Toronto).

Differences between the mainstream dominant majority and the minorities are recognized, while the differences within minority groups are overlooked. This is because the dominant discourse of majority/minority is one that is controlled and promulgated by the white mainstream community (Bannerji, 2000). Specifically, retaining the concept South Asian to include Indo-Guyanese negates their over one hundred and fifty years of struggle and resistance to colonialism; and other challenges in Guyana that they identify with. It must be recognized that Indo-Guyanese, for over one hundred and fifty years, engaged in and reconstructed their situational ethnicity. Situationally, their ethnicity is rooted in India, hence, South Asian in its origin. As expressed by the Indo-Guyanese, situational ethnicity contains similar (but simultaneously dissimilar) elements from situational ethnicity expressed by South Asians.

It is essentialist to think of Indo-Guyanese situational ethnicity as an extension or an appropriation of the South Asian's ethnicity and identity. The implication of this notion would be a patterning of situational ethnicity and identity that only seeks to reproduce an original sense of belonging and citizenship, thereby negating the two movements that Indo-Guyanese experienced and the transformative potential of these movements. Yancey, Erickson and Juliani (1976:322) refer to this as the "the monolithic treatment of ethnicity." Conceptually, because these two groups look alike, one label can be used to categorize them. However,

> [i]t is…important to undertake a detailed examination of the identities of the ethnic minorities…to unpack the minority groupings distinguishing the religious, linguistic and other cultural components of ethnicity. (Berthoud, 1998:59)

The "Indo" in the label Indo-Guyanese is a social and political identifying tool of distinctiveness. At one end lies an ethnicity that is physically disconnected from India, but nevertheless symbolically, culturally and imaginatively connected. At the other end is a specifically defined Indo-Guyanese situational ethnicity and community that was concretized in Guyana. This is because it was their indentured ancestors who reconstructed situational ethnicity in Guyana. The first and subsequent generations of indentured laborers sustained themselves via this situational ethnicity for "after one hundred years in the colony many regarded India as the 'mother' country,' India had retained ties with East Indians after indentureship" (Narine, 1999:96). After indentureship, the second and following generations continue to have within their consciousness India as their homeland.

India, for the second generation and subsequent generations of indentured laborers, was a mythical land, a faraway place that could only be experienced through the stories that were told and retold, and Indian movies. In Guyana, India was a complete mystery, and became more mysterious as Indo-Guyanese listened to stories from the seniors:

> I remembered as a little boy listening to the stories of my grandfather of what India was like. In India, they are many like us" he said. "Life is simple and India is our own country. I was fascinated with this place called India and remembered asking questions and questions. (Participant # 1, May 12, 2003)

As offspring of Indo-Guyanese listened to stories of India, the mysterious Mother India took on new dimensions and complexities. These stories of mythical Mother India framed their integration and existence in Guyana (Jayawardena, 1963). Anything Indian was superior in comparison to items from other countries.[10] Though miniscule in number, Guyanese who visited India recounted stories of an India that was rich with mystery and glamour, and because they saw a place that others could only imagine; their status was enhanced in the Indo-Guyanese community in Guyana.

> When someone went to India and returned to Guyana, people said with awe, "He went to India. That individual was treated like a god, for he/she walked the soil of India. People sat and listened to him/her as they spoke of that journey to India. What an honor it was to go to India. (Participant # 1, November 16, 2002)

For many senior Indo-Guyanese in Toronto, the myth of return became a desire to see India. In the Indo-Guyanese community someone who visited India achieved a different status because of that visit. There are many tours that are organized to entice Indo-Guyanese to visit their motherland, India. As such, many senior Indo-Guyanese, and others between the ages of thirty-five to fifty visited India. Usually these visits reveal the real India, which does not always match the mythical India that is present in movies and in the imagination of the Indo-Guyanese group. According to one person who visited India:

> India is nasty; the people are poor, very poor. People are begging in the streets, you cannot leave your bag for a second, they will steal it. But some of the places are nice, but the people are very nasty, you cannot drink the water. I am glad I went, but not me again. (Comment overheard at the temple, June 29, 2003)

This is a common sentiment that is expressed by many of the people who visited India.

It is evident that Indo-Guyanese re-appropriated a multiplicity of practices from their ancestors, and these they have transferred and reconstructed in Toronto. To be sure, these reconstructed social and institutional practices have become modes of social exclusion; that is, social boundaries. However, long before immigrating to Toronto, Indo-Guyanese established a social process in their second centre–Guyana.

In Guyana, the process of Indo-Guyanese reconstruction and maintenance of situational ethnicity was in response and reaction to the presence of other groups, including colonialist and Afro-Guyanese. However, it appears that in Toronto, this very process of reconstructing situational ethnicity is being interrupted and questioned. Repeatedly these interruptions and questions arise when Indo-Guyanese interact with South Asians. South Asians do not construct Indo-Guyanese as South Asians; consequently they are not Indians. If South Asians do acknowledge the "Indianess" of Indo-Guyanese, it is that of second-class Indians.

> The embrace by immigrants directly from the subcontinent, when it has been offered to Indo-Caribbean, has never been simple. In it, there was always certain superiority, a sinuous thing that kept eluding the grip, flitting into and out of your hands, giving tenderness a subtle edge... Yet, it still needs to be said that, though [the] attackers didn't know the difference, Indian-looking is not Indian. One-hundred-fifty years of history in Guyana and the West Indies demand that it be said...And that it be said with self-confidence, by an Indo-Caribbean, rather than by a South Asian toting a subcontinental yardstick. (Bahadur, 1998:2-3)

Hence, imposing a South Asian identity on the Indo-Guyanese people presupposes a homogenized unity, transcending ethnicity, class, caste, religion, spatial and temporal differences. This homogenization tends to ignore, among other things, the struggles of indentured South Asians in the Guyana and other regions of the world. These struggles in that geographic space are not part of the experience of South Asians who escaped indentureship.

Indo-Guyanese Trans-situational Ethnicity

In Toronto, many Indo-Guyanese narratives commence or contain geographic references including: "in Guyana" and "back home," "in the Caribbean," "in the West Indies." In a multicultural space, these narratives heighten, not only a geographic boundary but a geographically groundedness of an emerging trans-situational ethnicity. For Indo-Guyanese, these narratives are reflective of the geographic legacies of their indentured ancestors, and speak to their historically specific realities that are rooted in India, and transplanted to Guyana; and are currently, depending on the social interactions, being reconstructed.

Indeed in Guyana, the point of entry into these narratives is India, but in a multicultural Toronto, it is complex. This complexity is because of the multiple narratives that are constructed by other groups that shares similar physiology as Indo-Guyanese, for example, Afro-Guyanese and/or Afro-Caribbean. So as to provide a social context for these narratives of trans-situational ethnicity, the next section chronicles the Indo-Guyanese ancestors' movement from India to Guyana, followed by the Indo-Guyanese movement from Guyana to Canada.

The First Movement

In 1834 slavery ended in the British Empire; several colonies, including British Guiana introduced an apprenticeship period (1844-838) to orient the Blacks to their freedom (Adamson, 1972). After that period, many Blacks despite their "repulsion" to working on sugar estates, so as to survive, were compelled to sell their labor to sugar plantations (Bisnauth, 2000).

However, as with any labor relationship, the two constituents, planters and Blacks had divergent views of the British Guiana post-emancipation labor market. For Blacks, it was a low wage and inconsistent labor market; whereas for planters, it was an un-free, uncontrollable labor market that interfered with sugar production and capital accumulation (Bisnauth, 2000; Jagan, 1997). As a result, planters with political powers that extended beyond British Guiana appealed to the home government in Britain for help in securing a docile, cheap and un-free labor force.

Introduction of the Indenture Contract[11]

Planters used their political and economic power to introduce and institutionalize a signed indenture (Hollett, 1999; William, 1964). The indenture contract sustained the flow of labor and legitimized many restrictive labor practices in British Guiana. For planters the indenture contract was a useful legal instrument to structure labor market participation, thereby fulfilling their production of sugar and profit accumulation needs. The laboring group that contributed to that goal was the indentured laborers from India.

The Arrival of Indentured Laborers in British Guiana

Beginning in 1838 to 1917, close to one million indentured laborers destined for colonial plantations migrated from India to Guyana and the Caribbean. These indentured laborers were distributed to different centers. Emigrating from India to Guyana, indentured laborers took with them the socio-cultural legacies of India. These consisted of their religious beliefs and practices, language, kinship, social institutions, networks, traditional food and clothing. In addition to unique narratives, indentured laborers brought with them a small number of items including religious texts, artifacts, pots, pans, pillows, and blankets. In Guyana, these items, reminders of their lived realities in India, greatly contributed to the reconstruction of their situational ethnicity.

Despite the many differences among indentured laborers (that is, caste, religion, language, and regions), they managed to reconstruct their ethnicity, religion and community.[12] In that social process, many ethnic characteristics and contexts were re-constituted fragments of the originals. For example, in the reconstruction of Caribbean Hinduism,[13] different castes were combined into one.

A regular, intermittent stream of indentured laborers infused and buttressed that social process with narratives and socio-cultural legacies from India. Those "fresh arrivals," as they were called, brought with them new narratives and information about India. In the consciousness of the earlier waves of indentured laborers, these new narratives and information kept alive the memory of India (Mangru, 1993; Rodney, 1981). That social process continued until 1917, when the indentured system ended.

Indentured laborers' collective social responses and social resistance helped to construct, among themselves, what Tonnies (1955) refers to as a *gemeinschaft* type of relationship and community. Although, it was a period of rich and resourceful reconstruction of situational ethnicity and community; it was also a socio-historical period of erecting and maintaining boundaries. That particular social exercise was in response to the other major groups who shared the post-emancipation social space in British Guiana.

In British Guiana, the post emancipation social, political and economic spaces were shared by the three major groups: colonialists freed slaves and indentured laborers. Hierarchally, colonialists dictated social relationships, and those were mediated by labor market demands and the need to generate a profit. Responses to the demands of the labor market had a predictable impact on the nature and format of social boundaries that developed. Hence, many social boundaries erected and maintained were not only of the indentured laborers own making, but instigated by colonialists.

One of the first attempts to erect social boundaries began with assigning labels to the group. Labels that derived from legal infrastructures and norms confirmed assumptions of the status quo. For instance, the label East Indian[14] was a milder form of departure from the category of indentured labor, when compared to the more disparaging label of Coolie.[15]

The second attempt to establish boundaries was the indentured contract (Horowitz, 1976; Lowenthal, 1972). That was a legal and symbolic boundary erected between other groups and indentured laborers.[16] It codified labor by underwriting collective bargaining procedures, the enforcement of labor laws, back to work legislations, subsistence requirements and wages. In comparison to the wages of un-indentured laborers, mostly Blacks, wages stipulated by the indenture contract were low and working conditions precarious. By the 1860s, the demand and compensation for the labor of Blacks declined because they lost most of their bargaining power (Rodney, 1981). Correspondingly, the demand for indentured laborers increased.[17]

Socially, the indenture contract represented a symbolic, as well as an actual breakaway from rooted traditions, for example, religion. In fact, in Guyana religion became an important point of differentiation, not only from the Europeans but more so from Blacks. In the indentured laborers' perception, Blacks were imitating someone else's culture and religion–the European, which indentured laborers perceived to be inferior to their culture and religion.[18] It is within these social, political and economic spheres that indentured laborers reconstructed their situational ethnicity and community.[19] This historically specific social relationship between the Blacks and indentured laborers in colonial Guyana was not one of solidarity. Although, there were few conflicts between these two laboring groups, the Planters fostered the belief that there were actual conflicts. This division along racial line informed all social interactions between these two groups in colonial and post colonial Guyana.

Guyana in the Twentieth Century

The twentieth century heralded many changes in the governance and social relationships in Guyana. Indentureship came to an end in 1917 (Bisnauth, 2000). The former indentured laborers continued in their reconstruction of situational ethnicity, social networks and community. In addition, indentured laborers participated in the social, political and economical institutions of the colony. After several years of political growth and turmoil; Guyana obtained its independence from the British in 1966. From 1957 to 1963, the period leading up to independence, "unprecedented racial turmoil racked [Guyana] and the social relationship between the progenies of Blacks and indentured laborers was cemented in racial conflict. Because of the racial riot and changing political structures, Guyanese from all racial groups began an exodus, many to Toronto, Canada (Jagan, 1997). Indo-Guyanese were among those who migrated.

The Commencement of the Second Movement

At the point of departure, Indo-Guyanese migrated from different areas from pre-industrial, agricultural Guyanese societies: Georgetown (the capital), Berbice, the East Coast and the West Coast of the Demerara River. Once they arrived in Ontario, they became concentrated in the areas of Jane Street and Finch Avenue,

Scarborough or on the outskirts of Scarborough, Pickering, Oshawa and smaller pockets in Brampton, Mississauga and other parts (Birbalsingh, 1997).

Socially, many of the new arrivals to Toronto and elsewhere were helped and supported by close or distant families and/or friends. In this chain migration, the first member of a family migrates, and then encourages others to do so (Lopreato, 1970). Upon arrival, the first arrivals share narratives about the "ins" and "outs" of the new society–meaning, they exchanged ideas about how the new society functions, and how they are socially constructed and located.

For many Indo-Guyanese, narrations of their arrival begin with: "When I came, I had only an address, a phone number and little money" (Participant # 2, May 5, 2003). Usually, this was followed with the comment: "The next day, I had to go and look for work" (Interviewee # 2, May 5, 2003). Through this and other social engagements, Indo-Guyanese trans-situational ethnicity surfaced.

EMPIRICAL ACCOUNTS OF TRANS-SITUATIONAL ETHNICITY

Caribbean/West Indian South America and Indo-Guyanese

The social process of reconstructing ethnicity never stops; it changes as the social world changes (Hall, 1995; Cohen, 1974; Erikson, 1968). In this multicultural space, differences between multicultural groups are visible, but as previously discussed, historically specific realities are often overlooked. . For the Indo-Guyanese there is the erroneous act of labeling them South Asian but this is less harsh in comparison to the label Afro-Caribbean. The colossal mistake of assigning the label Afro-Caribbean to Indo-Guyanese can be located in the geography and generalization of inhabitants of the region.

In local narratives, Guyana as a country is culturally reflective of the Caribbean/West Indies; it follows that Guyanese, be it Indo or Afro (descendants of the Blacks) are frequently identified as Caribbean/West Indians.[20] Factually, Guyana is a country in South America. This was one of the first complexities that Indo-Guyanese encountered, they were considered to be Caribbean/West Indian, that is, Afro-Caribbean.

This is because the early presence of Afro-Caribbean in Toronto has succeeded in creating an identity of the Caribbean as being Afro-Caribbean. If Indo-Guyanese were to "go with the flow," that is, accept that they are from the Caribbean, this acceptance would not be reflective of their presence in Guyana and their situational ethnicity.

Indeed, indentured laborers were distributed to other islands in the Caribbean, and represent twenty percent of the nearly five million inhabitants. The twenty percent Indo-Caribbean inhabitant share, not only a history of migration to the region, but also experiences of marginalization in the region.[21] It must be noted that Indo-Caribbeans have contributed to this marginalization. To illustrate a brief discussion ensues.

Although, Indo-Caribbeans have resided in the Caribbean region for over one hundred and fifty years, "for many, they are not quite of it (Birbalsingh, 1997, 1989; Itwaru, 1989; Lowenthal, 1972).[22] While they have no bridges that connect them with India, the century long process of settling into their 'new' home [the Caribbean and Guyana] still continues" (Israel, 1994:34). This difficulty with "settling in" may be related to their conscious attempt to preserve the connection with India. They continued to believe that they are "temporary sojourners" in the Caribbean (Allahar and Varadarajan, 1994:130).[23]

Undoubtedly, to the Indo-Guyanese person, the Caribbean with its hybridity of race and ethnicity is more reflective of Afro-Caribbean people.[24] This perception is reinforced by the appearance of Caribbean culture as made up of a collage of cultural realities, which displays hybrid features of race and ethnicity. For many Indo-Guyanese, this represents typical Afro-Caribbean culture,[25] seemingly without a center, sensual, and unfocused.[26]

Notwithstanding and to be repetitive, the shared historically specific realities of colonialism mediated relationship between these two groups, regardless of their domicile in the Caribbean or Guyana. In fact, during colonialism many stereotypes constructed by these groups of each other were encouraged by the colonialist; and to this day continues to impact social relationship between them. Specifically,

> [c]olonialism as it was manifest in both Trinidad and British Guiana certainly provided, as a system based in the last resort upon overt coercism, an inherently 'conflictive arena'...Thus a situation was born where stereotypes emerged with greater virulence on all sides and served as they always do to divide further by justifying with an aura of rationality a basically false situation. (Cross, 1996:35-36)

These stereotypes were easily transferred to the Toronto multicultural space and continue to inform the Indo-Guyanese consciousness. Ironically, these stereotypes are once again replicated in a similar social hierarchy, that is, Whites are superior and multicultural groups are inferior. Consequently, Indo-Guyanese resort to articulating their reconstructed situational ethnicity, but with the geographic preface as the following interviewer's response illustrates:

> We (Indo-Guyanese) needed to create our own institutions; we needed to establish ourselves as Indians from the Caribbean. At every opportunity, we pointed out the differences between the Caribbean Blacks and us. Our physiology, our food, our religion and our family these are the differences and these differences are very important. (Participant # 12, March 30, 2003)

Participant # 9, using the differences in physical characteristics, pointed out to his White Canadian boss common physiological differences between the Indo-Guyanese and the Afro-Caribbean:

> I was the only Indian working for my company and they called me 'the Black man.' One foreman used to call me 'Nigger.' He called me Nigger for several months and one day the boss came to the work site and I went to the boss and said "this man (the White foreman) keeps calling me a Nigger,...Why is he calling me a Nigger? (Participant # 9, March 3, 2003)

In the Toronto multicultural space, Indo-Guyanese are determined not to be invisible. Their two movements, reconstructed situational ethnicity and their multiple struggles in Guyana robe their daily lived realities. Unfortunately, their lived realities are grounded in the oppositional stereotype of the Afro-Guyanese/Caribbean.

> We (Indo-Guyanese) quickly established ourselves as law-abiding citizen and hard working. We came for the betterment of our children. We worked hard and purchased houses and sent our children to school. The Blacks created problems, we did not create problems. (Participant # 4, January 23, 2003) We did not get into trouble with the laws; we did not go on welfare. We worked for what we have. (Participant # 3, July 10, 2003)
>
> Blacks are not like us, they are different...Look at how many Black girls are getting pregnant and going on welfare. (Participant # 4, January 23, 2003

For Indo-Guyanese, reconstructing and maintaining their trans-situational ethnicity required the re-erection of familiar boundaries; these boundaries were present in Guyana. Several Indo-Guyanese separate themselves from the Caribbean by pointing out that Guyana is geographically located on the continent of South America. One participant reported that he is regularly asked, "Where are you from?" He would reply:

> I am from South America, I was born in Guyana, the former British Guiana and I am from South American the only English speaking country on the continent of South America. (Participant # 1, June 23, 2003)

Reconstruction of trans-situational ethnicity in Toronto also includes culture, class, geography and race. These social constructs separate Indo-Guyanese community from members of the other Caribbean groups residing in Toronto.

> We don't really like to think of ourselves as Caribbean. The Caribbean has that stigma attached to it. It is a sensual culture…The people from Guyana call themselves Guyanese or South American because they don't want to be associated with the Caribbean. (Participant # 2, May 5, 2003)

> Moving to Canada…I do not tell people that I am from the Caribbean because…Caribbean are seen as Blacks. (Participant # 3, May 23, 2003)

> Since I moved to Canada, I tell people that I am from South America. (Participant # 4, January 23, 2003)

For the following two adolescents, trans-situational ethnicity is scripted with intergenerational influences that are geographically grounded:

> According to my parents, Guyana is located on the continent of South America; therefore we are South American. (Participant # 5, March 8, 2003)

> Guyana is in South America, so I am South American. Guyana is not in the Caribbean, Guyana is in South America and I am South American. (Participant # 6, November 12, 2002)

The next participant is an interesting example of the situationally rootedness of ethnicity, as it relates to other structural discourses, but framed by geography.

> What difference does it make, we are all black in Canada, even if we are Caribbean or South American and refer to ourselves as "brown people, to the [Canadians] we are all Blacks.[27] (Participant # 7, December, 12, 2002)

What the above data reveal is the density of involvement, historical specificities and multiplicity of historical, geographical, racial and ethnic boundaries that are reflected in trans-situational ethnicity.

The next few Indo-Guyanese provided answers to questions that reflected the complexity of their trans-situational ethnicity. A common question posed to many Indo-Guyanese and one that many of them grapple with is: "Are you South American or Indo-Caribbean?" At a social gathering (April 13, 2003), an Indo-Guyanese male's clear-cut response gave a raw and revealing insight to his group's thinking in this area: "Indo-Guyanese who call themselves South American in Canada want to be another race." Participant # 8 privileged the British domination in the Caribbean and the English language as visible modes of trans-situational ethnicity:

South America is Spanish with Spanish people and Spanish culture, do you see Indo-Guyanese having any Spanish culture? Do they speak Spanish? If the ship that brought them from India landed in Mexico, then it is a different story, but it landed in Guyana. Guyana was British and so were many other Caribbean/West Indian islands, so Guyanese are Caribbean or West Indian people, not South American. (Participant # November 16, 2002)

Participant # 9, who referred to himself as West Indian, sarcastically demarcated residency in a country, as opposed to an island, as constructing a geographic hierarchy:

Indians from Guyana...they are from South America. Me! I am a West Indian; I was born in the West Indies. I am not a South American. (Participant # 9, March 3, 2003)

Several adolescents, in comparing themselves to people from India used the category East Indians, and in reference to themselves used the label West Indian. Further inquiry into these two labels, reveals the practicalities of these labels via the cardinal points of the compass:

The East Indians are from India, the East, and we are from the West, therefore, we are West Indians. (Participant #10, February, 9, 2003)

It is interesting to note that in the original proposal for this study, the concept of labeling the adolescents born in Canada became a topic of discussion. Originally, adolescents were categorized as Indo-Canadian; they objected to this label. Instead they suggested Indo-Guyanese as a label for themselves. That particular discussion was revealing because the prior assumption was that the Canadian born adolescents (second generation) would respond to the label Indo-Canadian. Wanting to be specific, adolescents were informed that they do not have the experiences of those born in Guyana, and as such, cannot label themselves Indo-Guyanese. They were nonplussed and stated that their parents were from Guyana. The adolescents went as far as to use their circle of friends as evidence that they are Indo-Guyanese. The majority of their friends are from the Indo-Guyanese or Caribbean group.

While Indo-Guyanese were not identified as authentic Indians, they certainly did not want to be identified as Afro-Caribbean. Thus, they redefined their negative encounters with South Asians into a newly constructed trans-situational ethnic identity. Depending on the social context and social interaction, the newly constructed trans-situational ethnic identity is reflective of their own interests. For example, when the Indo-Guyanese encountered Afro-Caribbean people, they tend to stress the Indian elements in their trans-situational ethnicity. Whereas, when they encounter South Asians, Indo-Guyanese emphasize Guyana as the demarcating ethnic variable.

CONCLUSION

This chapter explores how the Indo-Guyanese are constructing their trans-situational ethnicity in a multicultural space. Within this multicultural space a colonial hierarchy is evident. The Canadian state dominated by White males dictates social, political and economic access to resources. This is achieved via the political manipulation of immigrant groups vis-à-vis legislations such as the Multiculturalism Act. According to Bannerji (2000), this deliberate strategic manipulation prevents acts of solidarity from occurring across multicultural groups, for example, group solidarity based on race.

Indo-Guyanese and South Asians, for instance, can organize in solidarity with each other using their marginalization in Canadian society. As with South Asians, Indo-Guyanese, with their historically specific experience of divisive colonial social technique, can seek to align themselves with both Afro-Guyanese and Afro-Caribbean. Collectively, as one group, they can respond to their marginalized status by drawing upon their shared historically specific realities of colonialism and migration.

In Canadian society, the official multicultural discourse promotes differences between groups. It is the suggestion that the unofficial discourse can be one that deconstructs these differences to highlight similarities. These similarities then become anchors for multicultural groups to mobilize in solidarity with each other to tackle inequalities, despite the Multicultural Act. Hence, the conceptualization of ethnicity being put forth is not that there are no differences in ethnicity, but that these differences in a multicultural space become highly politicized (Bannerji, 2000). Multicultural groups, in politicizing ethnic differences, limit their ability to mobilize. Frequently, it appears that race and class are used to construct multicultural groups in comparison to Whites with the outcome being one of superiority (the Whites) and inferiority (multicultural groups).

Members of this multicultural society need to become involved in trying to effect social change. Many generations of immigrant/minority groups have not experienced other social, political or economic realities, hence, they need to become critically engaged. Critical engagement begins by questioning the accepted lived realities. We ask, whose ordinances are you socially, politically and economically situated? Who has harnessed power and by what means? How is this power used to manacle you and your critical consciousness? What is the social institution that provides or impacts your learning? Who are the owners? Who or which group benefits if the majority of the masses languish on the beds of reality television shows?

Seek out your fellow progressive members of the mainstream group and reach out in solidarity with each other and become engaged.

NOTES

1 The label Indo-Guyanese is used in the plural; these are the people whose ancestors who moved to Guyana from India; Afro-Guyanese refers to the people who are of African ancestry.

2 The Indo-Guyanese community in Toronto has a history of two movements that includes three centers, and two movements, the first movement involuntary and the second voluntary. Indentured laborers' involuntary migration (1839-1917) from India (the first center) to British Guiana (the second center, hereinafter referred to as Guyana); their voluntary movement from Guyana to North and South America and Western Europe. There were 240,000 people who migrated from India to Guyana, of which 84% were Hindus and 16% were Muslims (Bisnauth, 2000). In Guyana the second center, the group reconstructed ethnic identity and community. This chapter focuses on the Indo-Guyanese who immigrated to Toronto, Canada. As no official statistic is available, the Indo-Guyanese population in Canada is estimated to be about 150,000 to 200,000, approximately 60,000 of whom reside in Toronto (Discussion with a member of the Guyana Consulate: February 12, 2003; Ramcharan, 1999).

3 In this study, the label South Asian as used by the Indo-Guyanese is in reference to people from India, Pakistan and Bangladesh. The Sri Lankans are not included in this category, the Indo-Guyanese often referred to them as "Sri Lankan."

4 Contextually, Afro-Canadian refers to Blacks who migrated or were born in Canada; the emphasis is on Blacks from the Caribbean/West Indies and Guyana.

5 In 1492, Christopher Columbus discovered the New World; specifically, in 1498, on his third voyage he discovered the Guianas. This area included British Guiana, now Guyana, Dutch Guiana, now Suriname and French Guiana. The Guianas were not rich in the gold that was found in countries like Mexico and Peru, consequently these countries were not occupied by the Spaniards. In 1815, one of the Guianas became a colony of Britain, hence the name British Guiana.

6 In 1988 the Federal Government introduced Bill C-93 – the Canadian Multicultural Act. This Act fosters Canada's immigrant population attempts to maintain their ethnic and racial identity. Expressly, the Act promotes an understanding that Canada is a nation of many racial and cultural groups, and recognizes the freedom of all of these racial and cultural groups to main-

tain and practice their culture in Canadian society. This Act promotes tolerance for differences. (For a critique of this Act see Bannerji, 2000, *The Dark Side of a Nation.*)

[7] It is quite common for the children to migrate and then sponsor their parents.

[8] In the context of this chapter, the concept ethnicity is not used interchangeable with race. Although, there is occasionally an inclination for ethnicity to be used interchangeable with race; to do so deflect attention away from the social, political and economic inequalities that result from discrimination based on race. However, alongside the dominant discourse of race, is the discourse of ethnicity that occurs in the highly politicized multicultural space of Toronto. Sanctioned by the state, the latter discourse is common within multicultural groups and governs their access to resources (Bannerji, 2000). Frequently, this discourse underlines conflicts between these multicultural groups, and regularly it is in these discourses of multiculturalism that race is used interchangeably. For example, the myth of Canada being a raceless society, in that, it allows people of many cultures to live by side. However, tolerance for other cultures or differences does not translate to mean equal access to social, political and economic resources (Wallis, 2009; Bannerji, 2000).

[9] According to Grosfoguel (1999), Jamaican and Haitian immigrants that migrated to the United States of America between 1965 to 1980 were unnoticed because of the multicultural environment and the presence of Afro-American. It appears that this is one of the fears of the Indo-Guyanese community is that politically they will not be recognized as distinct from South Asians. Hence, the need to cling to their distinctiveness as a community.

[10] "...Feelings of nostalgia experienced by the first generation of indentured Indians –their desire to return to India and sentimental extolling of all things Indian-continue to be felt to some extent by many Indo-Caribbean who have come to Canada" (Dabydeen, 1989: 252).

[11] It must be noted that the indentured contract, despite provisions that allowed for the negotiation of personal and employment relationships exemplify a labor relationship that was similar to slavery. In the former the servitude of the person that was purchased, whereas for the latter it the person that was bought. (Galenson, 1984). A form of 'un-free' labor, *paramone – debt bondage,* closely resembling indentureship existed in Greek and Roman times (de Ste. Croix, 1988). Human labor was leased with a claim to their future earnings. The indenture contract existed in the 1600s, it was used to transport and contract European workers to the New World. Those European workers were replaced by slaves (Galenson, 1984; Tinker, 1977).

[12] The Blacks were denied this privilege.

[13] This is not unique to indentured laborers, studies of other groups (Thomas and Znaniecki, 1918; Writh 1928; Zorbaugh, 1929) have documented that the social context of the host society impacts on the reconstruction of immigrant groups social, political and economical institutions. What is unique to indentured laborers as a group is the socio-historical period, indentured contract and social context of their reconstructed identity and community.

[14] Originally, the group was and continues to be labeled East Indian because they originated for the East Indies.

[15] An unskilled Asian laborer – Hindi and Telegu: Kuli – day laborer, perhaps from Kuli – a tribe in Gujarat or Urdu Kuli – slave. (http://www.wmic.edu/dialogue/themes/indian words.htm). The term also traces its origin in Japanese and Chinese laborers to mean common laborer. This is as a result of trading that occurred between India and China years ago, the label traveled aboard the ships.

[16] The indenture contract as a labor retention warranty was regulated by colonial statutes and binding upon both parties. It required laborers to sign a legal document, i.e., an indenture that covenanted away their freedom for a specific time period (in that instance five years) and for a stipulated wage and other amenities. Moreover, as a recruitment instrument, it shifted the financing of migration from the planters to the laborers.

[17] In fact, for similar tasks performed by the Blacks, indentured laborers were paid less. Moreover, the indenture contract as an instrument to control the movement of laborers away from, and off plantations, stipulated that laborers needed a special pass. As an indentured laborer he/she was physically bounded to the plantation, consequently, his/her labor was easily accessible and obtainable to planters (Bisnauth, 2000). Indentured laborers in the late 1800s to early 1900s earned sixteen cents per day, compared to freed slaves who earned thirty-two cents per day's labor. Indentured laborers worked longer hours and their most desirable quality was their dependent, contractual status on the plantation (McLewin, 1987). In fact, indentured laborers were very much aware of the harsh conditions and low wages they were being paid; however, their ac-

ceptance of the conditions was because of the indentured contract that bound them to plantations. Hence, for indentured laborers, plantation labor provided opportunities, as well as constraints. Labor was opportunistic, in that it provided a means of subsistence; a passage back to India and the ability to remit funds to families in India. These opportunities informed the consciousness of indentured laborers, and heavily influenced their migration to Guyana. Labor was constraining because it was contractual, different legal sanctions were imposed for violations and a 'pass' was needed to exit the plantation; therefore, movements from plantation was restrictive.

[18] During slavery, the slaves had little freedom to reconstruct their culture, although they did achieved minimum success. The culture that the freed slaves practiced might have been a synthesis of African culture and the white man's culture. This produced a synthetic culture that became the culture of the freed slaves.

[19] Blacks and indentured laborers had a limited social relationship based on labor and later became intermingled by limited cultural exchanges in the areas of food and burial practices. According to Jagan (1997), Rodney (1981), and Adamson (1972) the social relationship between Blacks and indentured laborers must be located in plantations' economy. For as Rodney (1981: 174) notes, "the two main groups of involuntary immigrants-African and Indian-having arrived at different times, had developed competing interests. More important still was the conviction by each group that their interests conflicted." Factually, planters recognized the conflicting interests, the racial, religious and cultural differences, and promoted those; thereby, as previously noted instigating the erection and maintenance of boundaries between these two groups.

[20] For this brief discussion, Caribbean and West Indies are used interchangeable.

[21] In the Caribbean and other parts of the world, the history of slavery is well documented, whereas the history of indentureship is an under-researched area of study.

[22] A word of caution as I employ the concept Indo-Caribbean to categorize the ancestors of the indentured laborers in the Caribbean, it must be noted that the "Indo-West-Indians [Caribbean] constitute multiple presence of complex laboring, religious, political, economic, intellectual and other relationships. They adhere to differing forms of Hinduism and other religions of India, differing Islamic perspectives, a multiplicity of Christian denominational orientations, forms of atheism, many labor and are exploited by entrepreneurs from their own race, many have adapted practices which are Afro-West-Indian, British, American, Canadian, and many share in indigenous cultural phenomena which speak of the burgeoning of a consciousness unique to the socially polyglot nature of their existence (Itwaru, 1989: 204).

[23] This view of them as sojourner was also popular in Malaysia (Kaur, 2001).

[24] Afro-Caribbean have lost many of their social, political and cultural institutions due to centuries of slavery, but this is not acknowledged by many members of the Indo-Caribbean population.

[25] In comparison to the Indo-Caribbean population, Afro-Caribbean appears to have integrated more into the dominant culture. That is, Afro-Caribbean with their fragmented cultural forms from Africa successfully crossed with European cultural forms to inscribe the Caribbean landscape. When the Indo-Caribbean migrated to Toronto, they were mistaken for Afro-Caribbean, thus, regarded as not having a distinct ethnic culture.

[26] Notwithstanding, Indo-Caribbean people, despite their invisibility in history, literature, cultural and, to a lesser extent, political spheres of the Caribbean, have made several distinguishing contributions. Due to their high numbers in Guyana, Trinidad and Tobago and Suriname they have secured the highest political office. In addition, several world famous cricketers and writers are from this group. Yet, juxtaposing the success of Indo-Caribbean people in politics with other historical and social successes, Indo-Caribbean people's accomplishments in the region are practically invisible.

[27] Many first generation Indo-Guyanese in being asked where they are from would often reply "I am East Indian but I was born in Guyana or the Caribbean."

REFERENCES

Adamson, A.H. (1972). Sugar *without Slaves: The Political Economy of British Guiana, 1838-1904.* London: Yale University Press.

Allahar, A.L., and T. Varadarajan. (1994). "Differential Creolization: East Indians In Trinidad and Guyana." *Indo-Caribbean Review* 1(2):123-140.

Bahadur, G. (November 1998). "Indian Looking: It Still Need to Be Said That, Though Maharaj's Attackers Didn't Know the Difference, Indian Looking is not Indian." http://206.20.14.67/achal/archive/nov98/looking.htm.

Bannerji, H. (2000). *The Dark Side of the Nation: Essays on Multiculturalism, Nationalism and Gender.* Toronto: Canadian Scholars' Press.

Berthoud, R. (1998). "Defining Ethnic Groups: Origin or Identity." *Patterns of Prejudice* 32(2):56-63.

Birbalsingh, F. (1997). *From Pillar to Post: The Indo Caribbean Diaspora.* Toronto: TSAR.

Bisnauth, D. (2000). *The Settlement of Indians in Guyana 1890-1930.* England, Leeds: Peepal Tree.

Cohen, A. (1976/1974). *Urban Ethnicity.* NY: Tavistock Publications.

Coughlan, R., and S. W. R. De A. Samarasinghe (1991). *Economic Dimensions of Ethnic conflict: International Perspectives.* (Introduction). London: Inter Publishers.

Cross, M. (1996). "East Indian-Creole relations in Trinidad and Guiana in the late Nineteenth Century." *Journal of Caribbean Studies* 14(1-2):14-38.

Dabydeen, C. (1989). "The Indo-Caribbean Imagination in Canada." In *Indenture and Exile: The Indo-Caribbean Experience,* edited with an Introduction by Frank Birbalsingh. Toronto: TSAR (Published in Association with the Ontario Association for Studies in Indo-Caribbean Culture).

Erikson, E.H. (1968). *Identity: Youth and Crisis.* NY: W.W. Norton.

Geertz, C. (1963). "The Integrative Revolution: Primordial Sentiments and Civil Politics in the New States." In *Old Societies and New States: The Quest for Modernity in Asia and Africa,* edited by Clifford Geertz. NY: Free Press.

Glazer, N., and D.P. Moynihan. (1963). *Beyond the Melting Pot: The Negroes, Puerto Ricans, Jews, Italians and Irish of New York City.* MA: M.I.T. Press.

Galenson, D.W. (1984). "The Rise and Fall of Indentured Servitude in the Americas: An Economic Analysis." *The Journal of Economic History* 44(1):1-26.

Gluckman, M. (1940). *Economy of the Central Barotse Plain.* Livingstone, Northern Rhodesia: The Rhodes-Livingstone Institute.

Gordon, M. (1964). *Assimilation in American Life: The role of Race, Religion and National Origins.* Oxford: Oxford University Press.

Grosfoguel, R. (1999). "Puerto Ricans in the United States: A Comparative Approach." *Journal of Ethnic and Migration Studies* 25(2):129-140.

Hall, S. (1995). "Negotiation Caribbean Identities." *New Left Review* 209(January-February):3-14.

Henry, F., C. Tator, W. Mattis and T. Ress. (2000). *The Colour of Democracy: Racism In Canadian Society.* 2nd ed. Toronto: Harcourt Brace.

Hitchcock, M. (1999). "Tourism and Ethnicity: Situational Perspectives." *International Journal of Tourism Research* 1:17-32.

Hollett, D. (1999). *Passage from India to El Dorado: Guyana and The Great Migration.* Cranbury, N J: Associate University Presses.

Horowitz, D.L. (1975). "Ethnic Identity." In N. Glazer and D.P. Moynihan (eds.), *Ethnicity: Theory and Experience.* MA: Harvard University Press.

Isajiw, W.W. (1999). *Understanding Diversity: Ethnicity and Race in the Canadian Context.* Toronto: Thompson Educational Publisher.

Israel, M. (1994). *In the Further Soil: A Social History of Indo-Canadians in Ontario.* Toronto: University of Toronto Press Inc.

Itwaru, A. (1989). "Exile and Commemoration." In F. Birbalsingh (ed)., *Indenture and Exile: The Indo-Caribbean Experience.* Toronto: TSAR Publications.

Jagan, C. (1997). *The West On Trial: My Fight For Guyana's Freedom:* Antigua: Hansib Caribbean.

Jayawardena, C. (1963). *Conflict and Solidarity in a Guianese Plantation.* London: University of London: The Athlone Press.

Kaur, A. (2001). "Sojourners and Settlers: South Indians and Communal Identity in Malaysia." In Crispin Bates (ed.), *Community, Empire and Migration South Asians in Diaspora.* Hampshire: Palgrave.

Liebkind, K. (ed.). (1989). *New Identities in Europe: Immigrant Ancestry and the Ethnic Identity of Youth.* Aldershot Gower.

Lopreato, J. (1970). *Italian Americans.* NY: Randon House.

Lowenthal, D. (1972). *West Indian Societies.* NY: Oxford University Press.

Mangru, B. (1987). *Benevolent Neutrality: Indian government Policy and Labor Migration to British Guiana.* London: Hansib Publishing Limited.

Narine, D. (1999). "Children of the Ganges: Migration, Mobility, and Identity in the Diaspora." In M. Gosine (ed.), *Sojourners to Settlers: Indian migrants in the Caribbean and the Americas.* Windsor Press.

Okamura, J.Y. (1981). "Situational Ethnicity." *Ethnic and Racial Studies* 4:452-65.

Park, R.E. (1950). *Race and Culture. Collected Papers V.1.* Glencoe: Free Press.

Rodney, W. (1981). *A History of The Guyanese Working People 1881-1905.* MD: The John Hopkins University.

Stack, J.F. (1986). *The Primordial Challenge: Ethnicity in the Contemporary World.* California: Greenwood Publishing Group.

Thomas, W.I., and F. Znaniecke. (1927). *The Polish Peasant in Europe and America.* NY: Alfred Knopf.

Tonnies, F. (1955). *Community and Association: Gemeinschaft und Gesellschaft.* Translated and Supplemented by Charles P. Loomis. London: Routledge and Paul.

Van den Berghe, P.L. (1981). *The Ethnic Phenomena.* NY: Elsevier.

Weber, M. (1965). "Ethnic Groups." In T. Parsons, E. Shils, K.D. Nagele, and J.R. Pitts (eds.), *Theories of Society: Foundations of Modern Sociological Theory.* NY: Free Press.

Williams, E.E. (1966). *Capitalism and Slavery.* NY: Capricorn Books.

Wirth, L. (1965). "The Problem of Minority Groups." In T. Parsons, E. Shils, K.D. Nagele, and J.R. Pitts (eds.), *Theories of Society: Foundations of Modern Sociological Theory.* NY: Free Press.

Yancy, W., E. Erickson and R. Juliani. (1976). "Emergent Ethnicity: A Review and Reformulation." *American Sociological Review* 41:319-403.

Zhou, M., C. Bankston III and R. Kim. (2002). "Rebuilding Spiritual Lives in the New Land: Religious Practices among South East Asian Refugees in the United States." In P.G. Min and J.H. Kim (eds.), *Religion in Asian America: Building Faith Communities.* CA: Altamira Press.

Zorbaugh, H. (1929). *The Gold Coast and The Slum: A Sociological Study of Chicago's Near North Side.* IL: University of Chicago Press.

Chapter 3

Socialization

Being and Becoming Canadian: Socialization in National Context

Stephen E. Bosanac
and Janice Hill

York University

INTRODUCTION

When sociologists study culture and social groups, they make inherent assumptions about the processes through which culture develops and is experienced by community members. That is, sociologists make assumptions about *socialization*, or the many intricate ways that individuals learn how to belong to the various groups they are a part of. Today, it is increasingly important to understand culturally-specific socialization processes, as multi-national and globalizing forces enhance opportunities for both multi-cultural alliances and conflicts. The study of socialization in Canada invites us to imagine how we, as Canadians, experience ourselves within a global context, and enables sociologists to identify various values, norms and ideologies that shape the building of mutually respectful communities, the creation of effective alliances amongst communities, and the resolution of conflict between communities. This chapter details four possible processes through which socialization occurs, and discusses the relevance of family life, schooling, and mass media, as particularly important agents of socialization in being and becoming Canadian. We conclude our discussion with an examination of the cultural messages revealed in the "Rant," a Molson Canadian beer commercial that found its way into the zeitgeist of Canadian culture in the spring of 2000.

AN INTRODUCTION TO SOCIALIZATION

Socialization is a term widely used throughout the various disciplines that constitute the social sciences. However, for sociologists, the term has a very specific meaning, with a very particular theoretical origin. The term socialization refers to the various social processes through which community members learn the rules of social interaction and integrate into society (Clausen, 1968). The concept of socialization grew out of micro-sociology, or the study of interpersonal and intrapersonal processes that occur when people socially interact with one another. To study socialization, sociologists must look outside the individual to examine the ways in which social structures and interpersonal dynamics with others shape shared traditions, customs, social roles, symbols and languages, while examining the inherently intimate, and somewhat unique experience of group belonging, where socially-learned norms, values and ideologies are internalized by individuals. In this way, self-identity, feelings, desires, and fears either reify or challenge the communities we belong to.

Socialization is a life-long, dynamic process that permeates all aspects of society. It requires interaction between individuals, their communities' social systems, and the larger organizations they are part of. The dynamic enmeshment of these three realms can be imagined this way: Each individual, with his or her own unique intrapersonal concerns, exists at the centre of his or her own life, around which concentric circles of influence are formed. From this individualized centre-point, all individuals integrate into communities of increasing size and personal distance. Typically, the most immediate community is the nuclear family or an individual's intimate partnerships where individuals share the experiences of daily life. Slightly more removed from this immediate community is their extended family, consisting of cousins, uncles, aunts and their nieces and nephews. While individuals may share a common family history with other group members, they may not always feel fully integrated into their extended family. Their behaviour may maintain the norms, values and ideologies of the extended family, although they may hold strong intrapersonal desires to behave otherwise. The extended family may exist as part of a larger community sharing ethno-cultural traditions or spiritual beliefs, where group members do not all know each other but share the assumption of common values and beliefs. Even larger communities may share a common language such as English that is spoken with regional dialect around the world. Alternatively, global communities may share a religious identity, despite acknowledging disparate beliefs about specific particular religious practices. For example, Catholic communities around the world share a presumption of foundational uniformity, despite debating the role of women in the church, abortion, and the alleged "sinfulness" of homosexuality. As community organizations grow in size and personal distance, the individual must increasingly imagine their connection to others in these larger communities. Our capacity to so effectively imagine this connection is the effect of interdependent socialization processes that occur throughout the many communities to which we belong (Anderson, 2003).

For sociologist studying contemporary global culture, this imaginary sharing of identity helps explain the distinctly modern phenomenon of nationalism, where members of specific nations embrace the moralities and character traits associated with being part of a particular nation. Their personal identity embodies the qualities generally associated with their national identity (Anderson, 2003). For example, the Swiss are generally thought to value punctuality. And so, we nod our heads in knowing appreciation of the accuracy and orderliness of their train systems, imagining this to be a reflection of their national character. In more extreme cases, hatred, oppression and genocide may be the result of popular views that imprint undesirable national stereotypes on individuals (Turner, 2010).

The dynamic nature of these various interdependent socialization processes enables society to remain stable from generation to generation, while adapting to the inevitable shifts in historical circumstance that affect it. Group members will embrace morals and characteristics they value, or find instrumental in daily life. History demonstrates that more traditional aspects of community norms, values and ideologies typically remain fairly consistent, providing continuity of culture and predictability to community members over longer periods of time. Similarly, group members will likely reject morals and characteristics that challenge their individual identity and personal choices. On a social level, the rejection of certain morals and characteristics, and the corresponding presentation of alternatives, creates the capacity for change within societies–social and material innovations are introduced and may be adopted by the mainstream over time. The intensity with which societies are exposed to these alternatives has increased dramatically with globalization and enhanced access to knowledge. So "being and becoming" a member of a human community, or a nation, is related entirely to what is culturally expressed and personally experienced.

FOUR POSSIBLE PROCESSES OF SOCIALIZATION

While theorists continue to debate the relevance of some specific elements of socialization, they generally agree upon four key ideas. First, socialization processes enable individuals to integrate into their social world. This may be seen as a positive function of socialization in that it creates possibilities to fulfill the human need for belongingness. Alternatively, integration may be seen as a negative aspect of socialization, creating compliance and shutting down non-normative human potentials. Second, socialization processes are culturally and historically specific, arising from the social and material conditions within each culture. Third, the study of socialization continues to include the investigation of the role of biology in shaping human behaviour. For example, a growing body of research suggests, among other things, that children demonstrate innate tendencies towards empathy. These findings challenge assumptions that all human behaviour is learned (Decety, Michalska and Akitsuki, 2008). And fourth, socialization processes involve the interplay between the internal self, and the exterior world. How this interplay occurs is the focus of various theories of socialization. Four of the most widely influential views about the process of socialization will be explored.

Erving Goffman (1959) is widely known for his theoretical perspective called dramaturgy. Dramaturgy utilizes the concepts of Role Theory to create a deeper understanding of social interaction. For Goffman, individuals adopt behaviours consistent with the role they wish to perform in their communities. Roles are constituted by a collection of norms, attitudes, self-images, values and behaviours that are regarded as consistent with each other within a shared, cultural context. For example, one would expect a fitness trainer to eat healthily, exercise regularly, sleep sufficiently, and avoid abusing his or her body with drugs or alcohol. A fitness trainer who does not behave this way may be perceived as lacking personal morals and values consistent with their professional role, and the fitness-centred lifestyle that is assumed to accompany it. In extreme cases, community members who step outside the normative boundaries of their role risk being labeled immoral, deviant or pathological. A police officer that steals evidence or accepts bribes, for example, could be considered immoral or manifest a "criminal personality type." In this way, socialization is a conservative force that enables social stability by perpetuating existing social organization.

In 1969, Herbert Blumer introduced the term "symbolic interactionism" to the sociological community and coalesced a community of theorists studying human interactions on a micro-level. For Blumer, human behaviour and social interaction are shaped by the meanings these behaviours and interactions are infused with. Specific behaviours, such as a kiss, may symbolize a feeling, idea, or relationship which is context and culturally specific. For example, giving your great-aunt a kiss at a family gathering conveys a different meaning and connotes a different kind of a relationship, than a kiss between lovers saying goodbye at the airport. Since maturation allows for a deepening of insights about the subtle, and appropriate use of behavioural symbols, the self is constantly formed and re-formed through a continuous and lifelong process of symbolic, social interaction with other community members. So, socialization processes occur through continuous feedback from the social world, where symbols are consciously used to represent an individual's identity in their various communities.

B.F. Skinner (1974) introduced the idea of radical behaviourism to the study of the dynamics of socialization, where human behaviour is the sole effect of learning. Behavioural learning occurs through the simple processes of positive and negative reinforcement. When behaviour is rewarded, we repeat it. When behaviour goes unrewarded, or is punished, we are less likely to repeat the behaviour, and eventually the behaviour is lost from our behavioural repertoire. Skinner's approach assumes humans are utilitarian in our social orientations–wanting to achieve maximum benefit with a minimum of effort. Behavioural patterns that achieve this are maintained, until they are replaced by more effective strategies. Even acts of apparent altruism lack a moral imperative. For example, a young person may give up their seat on the bus to an elder. At first glance this may appear altruistic, that the youth has chosen to stand while the elder, who is presumably less physically capable of standing, sits for the remainder of the trip. However, Skinner suggests that hidden rewards motivate behaviour we consider altruistic. In this case, the young person may experience increased self-esteem by giving up his or her seat to the elder, and in so doing ultimately acts out of self-interest. For Parsons, socialization occurs through the rational process of decision-making, where we choose to display socially-appropriate behaviours that are rewarded by other community members.

Talcott Parsons is also widely recognized for his contributions to the understanding of socialization. Popularly labeled a "functionalist," Parsons (1982) stresses the concept of internalization in shaping human identity and social behavior. Social order and behavioural hierarchies are experienced first through various institutional structures such as those found within the family, and educational and religious communities. Children internalize these orders, creating cognitive maps that indicate how social order and human interactions are "supposed" to be. These maps combine with a shared system of expressive symbolism and a collective moral conscience to ensure social stability within social groups. For Parsons, the imprinting of individuals with templates for the ordering of the social world is a key aspect of socialization.

For many sociologists, Parsons found a way to merge the study of the internal processes of identity construction popularly discussed by psychologists, with the study of social structures, particularly those endorsing clear and totalizing identities (Douglas, 1987). Marxists, and others interested in the shaping of social power dynamics could investigate the oppressive way that "agents of socialization" construct modern identities, and shape individual social interactions. While this "top down" approach emphasizes the restrictive nature of forces of socialization, it is important to acknowledge the constitutive role that we play, as community members, in creating and recreating the very symbolic meanings, identities, and behaviours that we exhibit. A deeper understanding of the key agents of socialization in contemporary Canadian culture will assist us in our exploration of what it means to be and become Canadian in a global context.

AGENTS OF SOCIALIZATION IN CANADA: FAMILY, EDUCATION, MEDIA

In contemporary Canadian society, popularly identified "agents of socialization" include the family, the educational system, and mass media. These are sites where a shared sense of identity or common agenda is internalized–to use Parsons' term. When placed within a national context, these sites are where we learn how to be Canadian, and the social meaning behind those behaviours that make us Canadian.

The Canadian Family

Many well-respected Canadian sociologists such as Margrit Eichler (1981, 1988, 1997) and Nancy Mandel and Ann Duffy (2000) maintain that the family is a foundational, or primary agent of socialization in contemporary Canadian society. The family is widely believed to be our first source of socialization, where the needs of young infants and children are tended to, and the first experience of group membership is felt. In fact, the primary socialization of children is often identified as the most important responsibility of the child's family. Families that fail in this regard may be considered "dysfunctional" and the source of the various consequential social problems affecting children as they mature (McDaniel and Tepperman, 2000).

The family is regarded as a key institution in the transmission of culture from generation to generation, and is therefore a vital institution in shaping social stability and reproducing society. For example, children learn gendered habits of behaviour, that reflect notable differences in communication styles, household task assignment, personal grooming habits, leisure pursuits, and later, occupational choices. For many individuals, occupational choices are also shaped by class-based expectations of work and income, and specific labour skills that are learned within the family. Many working class children learn to become a worker just like their parents, while middle class and upper class children are encouraged towards professional careers, or inherit the financial means to secure future resources (McDaniel and Tepperman, 2000.)

Shifts in the daily realities of family life influence the nature of our socialization. The burgeoning of single-parent families, falling birth rates, immigration trends, and changing gender roles and labour markets are reflected in popular views about families, and our own experiences of family life. In 2005, Canada became the fourth country in the world to legalize same-sex marriage on the basis that denial of marriage rights to same-sex couples was a violation of their rights under the Canadian Charter of Rights and Freedoms. This indicates a dramatic shift in mainstream views of marriage, which historically evolved as a religious sacrament sanctioned by the state, to a state protected right of individual expression (Larocque, 2006). These cultural shifts in family life are of particular interest to sociologists for whom the family structure provides a template that shapes the desires, values, expectations, and social sensibilities of those within it.

The presumed importance of the family in reproducing society is underscored in an examination of the history of Canada's Aboriginal peoples, where the dissolution of the Aboriginal family, and its greater communities was the aim of government programs throughout the 1900s (Kimayer and Valaskakis, 2009). Attempts to dismember Aboriginal families served as a means of genocide, where the destruction of culture-sustaining family ties meant the loss of traditional language, spirituality, and perspectives of human society. In 1920, the Canadian federal government mandated attendance of Aboriginal children in residential schools, designed to house and educate Aboriginal children and facilitate their assimilation into colonial, industrial Canadian society. Children were forcibly removed from their families and contained in these boarding schools, where the sharing of Aboriginal cultures, knowledge, and languages was strictly punished. Canada's last residential school closed in 1996. Since this time, the extent of abuse Aboriginal children suffered at the hands of "well-intentioned" educators has been increasingly revealed (Furniss, 1995).

The long-term cultural impact of separating generations of children from their families, and denying them cultural knowledge and expression is witnessed in the on-going realities of Aboriginal poverty, drug and alcohol abuse, intergenerational violence, suicide, and the lack of access to health care and education. As children, residential school survivors had severely limited opportunities to learn behavioural codes and cultural values from their elders, and so, were not able to integrate into their communities when they returned home. While the stated goal of the residential school system was to facilitate the assimilation of Aboriginal peoples into white culture, most residential school survivors found assimilation into racist, anti-Indian society impossible. Today, generations of Aboriginal peoples have lived without the stabilizing influence of family, predictability of daily life, and personal existential meaning facilitated by the sharing of norms, values and ideologies. Aboriginal leaders emphasize the need to re-enculturate their young people, to teach them the ways of their elders, as a means to heal their communities and bring an end to their personal disempowerment and systemic oppression. For many, this is done through the reintegration of multi-generational Aboriginal families (Kimayer and Valaskakis, 2009).

The historical targeting of Aboriginal peoples for assimilation into white culture demonstrates the pervasive nature of Canada's English and French populations in shaping normative views of Canadian family life. Aboriginal assimilation meant abandoning more communal and extended family organizations for the modern, nuclear family sanctioned by the state and church through "official" marriage rituals. Ideally, parents would abandon traditional hunting, trapping, and trading, subsistence based living for waged employment in more industrialized, urban areas. These ideals reflect popular views that privilege modernization, and the various institutions that support it (Francis, 1993).

Ironically, mainstream Canadians appear to take pride in presentations of the cultural remnants of Aboriginal traditions on the world stage. The opening ceremony of the 2010 Olympics in Vancouver, for example, featured Aboriginal dancers from communities across Canada. Representatives from the four host First Nations welcomed visitors to the games, and to their territories upon which the games were held, even while Aboriginal peoples outside the Pavilion protested unresolved land claims issues, as well as state-endorsed impoverishment and abuse.

Like all other agents of socialization, family values, structures, and ideologies are historical and culturally-specific. This is apparent in the differing values and behaviours encouraged by English Canadian, French Canadian, Aboriginal, and multi-cultural families that currently constitute Canadian family life. While Canada's tri-cultural, and now multi-cultural nature is frequently identified as an inhibitor to the formation of a distinct Canadian way of life, the history of colonial rule, and the legacy of English, Protestant values in shaping Canadian family life can certainly be observed. Today, the exploration of Canadian families as a primary agent of socialization often acknowledges the challenges of Canada's multi-cultural population in acclimating to our colonial cultural legacy.

Canadian Education

Another key agent of socialization is our educational process. Most Canadians spend about 20 years in schooling institutions. Schools are miniature societies where we learn skills like attentiveness, punctuality, and obedience to authority figures. From the functionalist perspective, educational institutions teach students to be productive members of a society, promote the transmission of culture, instill social control, encourage personal development, and mark the first place where we really experience selection, training, and placement of individuals in social ranks. Children's varied experiences in school depend upon their class, race, gender, and ethnicity. The acknowledgment of the different treatment of children based on race, class, gender, ethnicity and other categorical distinctions within the school system has come to be known as the hidden curriculum. Children learn the capitalistic system in school including the valuing of competition and materialism, the importance of work over play, and obedience to authority (Gillborn, 1992).

Today, mainstream concerns about the role of the Canadian school system include the impact of schooling on the development of children's values. Research indicates that family socialization goals differ from those of the school system. This is particularly apparent in schools that encourage discipline and respect for authority, or openly teach birth control techniques (Berns, 2010). Canadian parenting trends continue to indicate growth in "permissive parenting," where children are encouraged to explore the world around them, communicate their needs, and question authority when appropriate (Corsaro, 1997). Despite the contemporary focus on children's expression and personal freedom, sex education and exposure to birth control techniques remain the contested terrain of the family.

The growing support for Afro-centric schooling in Canada suggests increased concern for the impact of historical, race-based policies in the social construction of race within the educational system. Separate schools dedicated to teaching Afro-centric history to Black children is considered a vital first step in helping children and youth of African descent gain a greater sense of self-esteem, while deepen their understanding their own cultural history (Johnson and Joshee, 2007). For symbolic interactionists, socialization results from daily interactions between teachers and other students as well as administrators, so ethno-centric schools intensify student's exposure to positive role models, from whom they receive culturally-sensitive feedback about their behaviour (Schofield, 1999).

Support for ethno-specialized schools continues to be the topic of much debate, specifically in light of Canada's official policy of Multiculturalism (1988). Canadian national identity has long been associated with an alleged appreciation for cultural diversity, a quality that distinguishes Canadians from their assimilation-focused, American neighbours. According to some, establishing Afro-centric schools throughout Canada supports the viability of other ethno-specific schools under the Charter of Rights and Freedoms. Networks of ethno-specific schools, each with ethno-focused curriculum and ethno-isolated student bodies poses a challenge to the underlying premise of multi-culturalism, where the simultaneous intermingling of distinct cultures is regarded as ideal.

Canadian Mass Media

The third agent of socialization that will be discussed here is mass media, which includes: books, newspapers, magazines, film, radio and sound recording, television, cable and other multichannel services, videogames, the internet and the world wide web. Thorough discussion of all these forms of mass media in the socialization of Canadians clearly lies outside the scope of this chapter, however, acknowledgment of the vast and various modalities through which Canadians are exposed to ideas about who they are, is certainly appropriate. The widespread use of mass media to socialize Canadians is clearly an effect of historical circumstances where technological innovation and access shapes the very nature of socialization.

In contemporary Canadian society, the integration of media into our daily lives is ubiquitous. Mass media informs us about events, introduces us to a wide variety of people with differing viewpoints, exposes us to products and services, and entertains us. The potential of mass media to shape Canadian identity and the world around us is enormous. Estimates of Canadian children's daily exposure to mass media suggest that 2.5 hours are spent watching TV, and 7 hours involve the use of computers, ipods, video games, or a DVD player. In total, our children spend over 3,500 hours a year engaged with some form of mass media. In contrast, they spend 1,200 hours a year in school.

While mass media has the potential to widely educate Canadians, research supports the fact that children know more about media figures than current events. Parents and educator have concerns about the loss of traditional learning skills associated with high levels of exposure to mass media. Research in the United States confirms a decrease in reading skills among school aged children in the last 10 years, and a related decrease in school grades, book reading, physical exercise and fitness. The use of technology and exposure to mass media may serve as an indicator of social status among Canadians, and reflect the very real challenges to cultural integration that are posed by the "digital divide" (McLuhan, 2003). Poor, isolated, or disenfranchised segments of the Canadian population, such as many of the Northern Aboriginal communities, become increasingly distanced by their lack of access to computer knowledge and the various resources that mass media can provide.

The role of mass media in socialization processes is particularly interesting given the distinctly modern capacity to belong to larger and larger social groups. In his book *Imagined Communities* (2003), Benedict Anderson claims that nations, such as the Canadian nation, are largely imagined, where members of the national community adopt the cultural values, mores, folkways and concepts of normality that are imagined by the collective identity. These imagined identities are disseminated throughout Canada, and the rest of the world through the many forms of mass media. We collectively create an identity where being a particular kind of Canadian is reinforced, and we as Canadians recreate this identity through acting out these distinctly Canadian behaviours in books, television shows, films, and throughout the internet. With the imaginary nature of Canadian national identity in mind, we can now consider the instrumental role of media in shaping what it means to be or become Canadian.

BEING AND BECOMING CANADIAN

In April 2000, Molson's Brewery released what was to become Canada's most widely celebrated beer commercial, called "The Rant." This commercial was part of a larger campaign to sell Molson Canadian beer using the popular, nationalistic slogan "I AM Canadian." In "The Rant," an "average" Canadian named Joe, dressed in jeans and a flannel shirt, stands in front of a video screen depicting various images of Canadian culture, and announces with increasing fervour:

> Hey. I'm not a lumberjack, or a fur trader, and I don't live in an igloo or eat blubber, or own a dog sled, and I don't know Jimmy, Sally or Suzy from Canada, although I am certain they're really, really nice. I have a Prime Minister, not a President. I speak English and French, not American. And I pronounce it "about" not "aboot." I can proudly sew my country's flag on my backpack. I believe in peacekeeping not policing; diversity, not assimilation; and that the beaver is a truly proud and noble animal. A tuque is a hat. A chesterfield is a couch. And it is pronounced "zed": not "zee"–"zed"! Canada is the second largest land mass! The first nation of hockey! And the best part of North America! My name is Joe. And I am Canadian!...Thank you.

The immense popularity of this campaign inspired numerous parodies, where Newfoundlanders, Albertans, British Columbians, Quebec sovereignists, and many others, including Canadian cultural icon William Shatner similarly declared their acceptance or rejection of stereotypes associated with their public identity. Although Molson's retired the slogan "I AM Canadian" shortly after its merger with the American company Coors in 2005, the legacy of Joe Canadian continues, as the character and his rant remain widely recognized within contemporary Canadian culture (Seiler, 2002).

For a sociologist, the phenomenon of Joe Canadian's "I AM Canadian" rant provides fertile soil for a rich discussion of the concept of "socialization." What was it about this commercial that caught the attention of so many Canadians? What does the widespread enthusiasm for this commercial, and its parodies, tell us about Canadian nationalism, and our sense of group membership?

The search for a distinctly Canadian identity has been the topic of much discussion over the last 200 years. This is due in part to the historical rise of the United States, with their War of Independence and subsequent proclamation of state sovereignty in 1776. In contrast, the Canadian colonial state, Canadian identity and Canadian nationhood is described as something that took shape within America's shadow and, according to many researchers, Canadians have struggled ever since to establish our own distinct, separateness from the United States. This struggle is apparent in the present day antipathy of mainstream Canadian culture for all things American, and constitutes the overt thrust of the "I AM Canadian" Rant, where Canadian identity is celebrated as that which is clearly "not American" (Millard, Riegel and Wright, 2009).

The overtly patriotic nature of the rant is itself a statement about the image of Canadians in popular culture. Canadians are internationally stereotyped as quiet, unassuming, polite, and diffident in their patriotism. The fervour with which Joe Canadian celebrates his nationhood, and the swelling crowds of Canadians that applauded Joe's rant, provide Canadians with another way of seeing themselves–as people actively reclaiming Canadian ways, and besmirched Canadian symbols, and as people more patriotic than perhaps even they imagined. Canadian hockey prowess is declared near the conclusion of the rant, and alludes to a long-standing, national passion for the distinctly Canadian sport that grew along side of, and reflected cultural rivalries between English and French Canadians.

Other historically pertinent stereotypes of Canadians as either fur-trading colonizers or Aboriginal in dissent are dispelled in the Rant, and underscores the distinctly English-Canadian focus of Molson's beer commercial. The reality is that some Canadians do own a dog sled, live in an igloo, eat blubber, and trade fur. While the multicultural focus of Canadian policies is described as a belief in diversity, the image of Joe Canadian that is portrayed in the Rant is not multicultural in orientation. Rather, Joe Canadian is a jeans and flannel shirt wearing hoser. Portraying the typical Canadian as a hoser adds another layer to the parody of this commercial, where Canadians both celebrate and reify the very stereotype that they simultaneously wish to undermine. The success of this commercial as part of the Canadian cultural zeitgeist lies in its capacity to play upon images, icons, stereotypes, and values that are an effect of widespread processes of socialization, where interplay between the internally experienced self and the externally experienced social environment is noted.

CONCLUSION

The importance of the family, education and mass media in shaping individual identity, and the norms, values, and ideologies of communities cannot be understated. For many researchers, these agents of socialization represent powerful forces for social stability and for social change. In an increasingly globalizing world, the relevance of national identities, with their corresponding stereotypes is acknowledged. The development of positive, life-enhancing alliances between very different kinds of communities often depends on the capacity of each community to understand the other. With this goal in mind, the study of socialization processes and their relevance to imagined Canadian identity and nationalism continues to be appreciated.

REFERENCES

Anderson, Benedict. (2003). *Imagined Communities: Reflections on the Origin and Spread of Nationalism*, 13th ed. London: Verso Press.

Berns, R. (2010). *Child, Family, School, Community: Socialization and Support.* Belmont: Wadsworth Press.

Bong, M., and Clark, R.E. (1999). "Comparison between Self-Concept and Self-Efficacy in Academic Motivation Research." *Educational Psychologist* 34(3):139-153.

Clausen, J.A. (ed.). (1968). *Socialization and Society.* Boston: Little, Brown and Company.

Corsaro, W.A. (1997). *The Sociology of Childhood.* Thousand Oaks: Pine Forge Press.

Decety, J., J.K. Michalska and Y. Akitsuki. (2008). "Who Caused the Pain? An fMRI Investigation of Empathy and Intentionality in Children." *Neuropsychologia* 46(11):2607-2614.

Douglas, M. (1987). *How Institutions Think.* London: Routledge & Kegan Paul Limited.

Duffy, A., D. Glenday and N. Pupo. (eds.). (1997). *Good Jobs, Bad Jobs, No Jobs: The Transformation of Work in the 21st Century.* Toronto: Harcourt Brace & Company Canada.

Duffy, A., and N. Mandell. (2000). *Canadian Families: Diversity, Conflict and Change.* Toronto: Harcourt Brace Canada.

Eichler, M. (1981). "The Inadequacy of the Monolithic Model of the Family." *The Canadian Journal of Sociology* 6:(3):367-388.

_____. (1988). *Families in Canada Today: Recent Changes and Their Policy Consequences.* Toronto: Gage.

_____. (1997). *Family Shifts: Families, Policies and Gender Equality.* Toronto: Oxford University Press.

Francis, D. (1993). *The Imaginary Indian: The Image of the Indian in Canadian Culture.* Vancouver: Arsenal Pulp Press.

Furniss, E. (1995). *Victims of Benevolence: The Dark Legacy of the Williams Lake Residential School.* Vancouver: Arsenal Pulp Press.

Gillborn, D. (1992). "Citizenship, 'Race' and the Hidden Curriculum." *International Studies in Sociology of Education* 2(1):57-73.

Goffman, Erving. (1959). *Presentation of Self in Everyday Life.* NY: Doubleday Books.

Grant, K., C. Amaratunga, M. Boscoe, A. Pederson and K. Willson. (eds.). (2004). *Caring For/Caring About: Women, Home Car, and Unpaid Labour.* Aurora: Garamond Press Ltd.

Johnson, L., and Reva Joshee. (2007). *Multicultural Education Policies in Canada and United States.* Vancouver: University of British Columbia Press.

Kendall, D., J.L. Murray and R. Linden. (2007). Sociology in Our Times.,4th ed. Canada: Thomson Nelson.

Kimayer, L. and G.G. Valaskakis. (2009). *Healing Traditions: The Mental Health of Aboriginal Peoples in Canada.* Vancouver: University of British Columbia Press.

Larocque, S. (2006). *Gay Marriage: The Story of a Canadian Social Revolution.* Toronto: James Lorimer and Company Ltd.

Macionis, J.J., J.N. Clarke and L.M. Gerber. (1994). *Sociology.* Canadian Edition. Scarborough: Prentice-Hall Canada Inc.

McDaniel, S., and L. Tepperman. (2000). *Close Relations: An Introduction to the Study of Families.* Scarborough: Prentice Hall Allyn and Bacon Canada.

McLuhan, M. (2003). *Understanding Media: The Extensions of Man.* Edited by Terrence W. Gordon. Corte Madera, CA: Gingko Press.

Millard, G., S. Riegel and J. Wright. (2009). "Here's Where We Get Canadian: English-Canadian Nationalism and Popular Culture." *American Review of Canadian Studies* 32(1):11-34.

Parsons, T. (1982). *On Institutions and Social Evolution,* edited by Leon Mayhew. Chicago: Chicago University Press.

Pierson, J. (2002). *Tackling Social Exclusion.* London: Routledge.

Schofield, K. (1999). *The Purposes of Education.* Australia: Queensland State Education.

Seiler, R. (2002). "Selling Patriotism/Selling Beer: The Case of the "I AM CANADIAN!" Commercial." *American Review of Canadian Studies* 32(1):45-66.

Shavelson, R. J., and R. Bolus. (1982). "Self-Concept: The Interplay of Theory and Methods." *Journal of Educational Psychology* 74:3-17.

Skinner, B.F. (1974). *About Behaviorism.* NY: Vintage Books.

Smith, S.W., and S.R. Wilson. (eds.). (2010). *New Directions in Interpersonal Communication Research.* Los Angeles : Sage Publications.

Williams, B.K., S.C. Sawye and C.M. Wahlstrom. (2005). *Marriages, Families & Intimate Relationships.* Boston, MA: Pearson.

Chapter 4

Gender and Sexuality

Morality, Gender, and the Sexual Regulation of Children: The Roots of Canadian Ideals

Janice Hill

York University

INTRODUCTION

At the turn of the twentieth century, Canadian children occupied a special place in building the Canadian nation, consolidating the collapsing British Empire, and bringing "civilization" to even the least "modernized" areas of the world. State-sanctioned schools, Protestant religious communities, and philanthropic organizations like the Boy Scouts and the Girl Guides, portrayed children as the embodiment of Canada's imagined future as world leaders, and targeted them for moral education (Hill, 2000). First Nations children and others identified as a threat to Canadian's moral stability were the special concern of reformers whose regulatory programs in residential schools and orphanages used harsh, disciplinary measures to acculturate children to late Victorian ideals of social and moral propriety (McConnell, 2010). Strategies for teaching gender-appropriate and sexually normative ideals were shaped by repressive, sexist views typical of this time, and were enmeshed with issues relating to race and class. While acknowledging the historic complicity of these prevalent social indicators, this chapter explores the spread of gender appropriate, heterosexist ideals within Canadian children's culture in the early 1900s. The cultural, psychological, economic and social legacy of late Victorian ideals of gender and sexuality is discussed in terms of its continued presence in Canadian global perspectives.

BECOMING MODERN

Within the larger global context, contemporary Canadian society is regarded as "modern." This term paints a very clear picture of Canadian society in the minds of the "mainstream." Its an image of integrated technology, accessible resources, a stable market economy, and a governmental ideology rooted in Liberalism. However, the term "modern" has a much more specific meaning for sociologists. To be "modern" is to embody distinct ideologies and technologies arising out of the unique historical process of "modernization."

Coterminous processes of rationalization, industrialization, liberalization, and urbanization, to name a few, were experienced throughout Western populations from the 1600s onwards, and fuelled the colonization of non-Western populations. For sociologists, to be modern is to live in a society, like Canada, where the mainstream cultural forces and material realities of people align with these distinct ideologies and technologies. A brief exploration of a few of these social contingencies will deepen our understanding of the historical connections between the concerns of Canada's moral reformers for the gender and sexual development of children and Canada's current global perspective as a "modernized" nation.

When sociologists study modernity, we study ourselves–the way we live, what we think, how we define truth, and make sense of who we are, either individually or collectively. We are "modern" because we share common ideas about the way that life is, and we see the world and contemporary Canadian society as somehow different from that which came before us. Modernity, then, is a historical process whose various aspects have culminated in our distinctly Canadian culture (Hall, 1996. For an alternate perspective on the "modern-ness" of modern societies, see Latour, 1993). As such, the study of modernity requires sociologists to take a wide-lens approach that acknowledges many interwoven social contingencies within the modernizing process, and reveals their intricate interplay.

Commitment to three distinct and contingent concepts contributed to the rise of Canadian modernity and fuelled the commitments of social reformers in the early 1900s. The concepts are: *individualism, self actualization* and *rationality.* These concepts form the basis of the Liberal mindset, reinforcing one another to create tautological justification for wide scale moral reform. Underlying each concept is the shared belief that modernization is a marker of social and moral progress, and progress is both desirable and evolutionarily imminent.

The first concept is that of *individualism*, where members of society are regarded as distinctly unique from one another. They are encouraged to develop greater autonomy within their communities and enhance their special abilities. When fully developed, these abilities will bring about personal success, community appreciation, and facilitate a society based on social meritocracy, where the best and the brightest rise to their natural positions as leaders in their fields. The thrust of liberalism lies in the idea that social progress comes through individual development and personal excellence. Individualism is the foundation for modern, civil government that embodies the notion that a state is stable when its individual citizens are self-identified.

The second concept is that of *self-actualization* where individuals shape their life through the exercise of personal choice. Taking a utilitarian approach, modern, liberal individuals weigh potential risks against potential benefits of actions, and govern themselves accordingly. In this way, modern individuals, and their collective embodiments, can be said to "choose" their life trajectories, and to suffer the punishments of "bad choices" knowingly and in a self-conscious manner. This means that individuals are fundamentally desire driven–wishing to exercise their free will without limits. However, this desire is mediated by powerful cognitive skills of discernment that successfully over-ride those desires most likely to lead to punishment. Rationality, delayed gratification, and self-discipline are key to modernization and social progress.

These two concepts fit nicely into the third concept described here. *Rationality* is regarded as the primary means for revealing truth and so, is thoroughly supported by the scientific worldview increasingly popularized throughout the 1800s and normalized in the early 1900s. Systematized within the rational scientific process, deductive and inductive techniques of reasoning were thought to reveal the foundations of the physical world, exposing humanity's evolutionary past while providing insights into it's future. When linked to modernity, the acquisition of scientific knowledge is equated with "progress." After all, scientific knowledge generated technologies that increased material productivity, enhanced the lived realities of citizens, and expanded the spheres of influence of modernized nations. For social reformers, modernization was equated with social evolution that manifested as technological progress and cultural expansion. The ideological commitment to "progress" fuelled nineteenth and twentieth century colonization of Aboriginal cultures across Canada, and around the world.

Today, *postcolonial theorists*[1] such as Anne McClintock and Chandra Talpade Mohanty are highly critical of this view of modernization, which defines social change within non-Western cultures according to Western ideals. Within a colonizing context, modernization refers to the process by which non-industrialized, traditional nations adopt the ideologies and technologies of industrialized nations. Adoption involves the shifting of cultural values, family structures, economies, and religious communities, among other things. Modernization requires such radical shifts, that movement towards modernization is often measured in terms of the loss of traditional cultures that embody a competing, non-rational worldview. Since traditional culture is typically transmitted through intergenerational rituals and the interdependent sharing of material resources, modernization then, necessitates the breakdown of communities. When transmission of traditional culture from generation to generation is inhibited, social change is more readily facilitated. Individualism, with its focus on autonomy and independence, offers community members several alternative lifestyle possibilities. The promise of self-actualization and material gains often leads community members in "modernizing" nations to travel far from their families, enter a waged labour economy, and adopt non-traditional, westernized behaviours that better align with industrialization. Social change brought about by modernization is accompanied by shifts in gendered and sexual behaviour. So, the material modernization of a nation is contingent upon the modernization of it's people. The creation of modernized people, often begin with their children.

MODERNITY, CHILDREN, NATION

Social reformers saw themselves as a modernizing force in Canadian society, and believed their commitment to creating a generation of morally superior Canadian children would secure Canada's political power on a world scale. If "the 20th century belonged to Canada" (Berger, 1970:3), as Prime Minister Sir Wilfrid Laurier claimed in 1904, then Canadian children would be the means to achieve this goal. Moral reformers were greatly concerned with the gendered and sexual behaviour of Canadian children. Gender appropriate behaviours that reified heterosexuality were foundational for the maintenance of the nuclear family structure. Continuity of the family structure was thought vital to social stability, moral propriety, and the creation of a strong and politically empowered Canadian nation. The interplay between these various social factors and their relationship to Canadian national identity is the focus of sociological investigation.

While many factors encouraged moral reformers to focus on the behaviour of Canadian children between 1900-1920, three key shifts in perspective about children and childhood were particularly influential within the modernization process, and relevant to moral reformers. These shifts include increasingly popular views encouraging the "naturalization of childhood," the conflation of religious duty with national responsibility, and the suitability of the scientific process in normalizing gender appropriate and heteronormative behaviours–the behaviours believed typical and natural of male and female heterosexual people. Deeply rooted in Canada's colonial past, these views continue to shape contemporary ideas about the importance of appropriately gendered behaviour and heteronormative sexual development in children.

The first significant shift is characterized by a growing naturalization of childhood,[2] wherein children are regarded as innocent beings in the process of becoming self-aware contributors to Canadian society. This means that specific behaviours of children that challenge predominant moral codes of social propriety, result from children's social ignorance. Gender inappropriate behaviours or sexual improprieties, like public genital touching or masturbation, for example, are regarded as innocent acts of natural expression. This marks a big shift in thought, where earlier religiously based views regarded such behaviours as indicative of man's inherent tendencies to sinful wrong-doing. Naturalized views of childhood reframed these behaviours as "misguided" or even "explorative and playful" (Arnup, 1994).

The contemporaneous rise of child psychology and the introduction of the lifespan perspective, as characterized by the work of G. Stanley Hall[3] and later Jean Piaget,[4] popularized the view that as innocents, children must be protected. Adults were to guide them through the various stages of their development so they would reach adulthood as rational, appropriately mannered citizens and family members. Moral reformers and community leaders were keen to take on this role, considering this to be of honourable service to developing the Canadian nation. The importance of adult guidance in the gendered and sexual development of children is clearly acknowledged by Sigmund Freud who claims in 1929 that the capacity of adults to successfully engage in a heteronormative society directly results from their experiences as children (Freud, 1930/1961).

Throughout his vast body of work, Freud suggested that all children move through stages of development that are psycho-sexual in nature, where children encounter a new desire, and the potential to fulfill that desire. They also learn to repress that desire, and comply with social norms. For example, all infants recognize a desire for oral satisfaction. The mother's breast fulfills this desire until the child is weaned, when the infant experiences betrayal–they desire the breast but can not have it. Demands on their part do not make the breast reappear. Eventually, they cope with their feelings of betrayal and disappointment by repressing their desire for the breast deep within their subconscious. Individuals learn to control their desire, especially those desires that cannot likely be fulfilled, through the psychological mechanism of repression. This means that individual repression makes collective society possible, since all members of society learn to repress their most compelling desires. In this way, social control and order is linked to the collective abandonment of desire, and the appropriate resolution of each psycho-sexual stage of development generates individuals whose behaviour reifies the moral, social order.

Conversely, Freud suggested, children who do not learn to successfully repress their desire at each stage of development, will manifest compulsive attachment behaviours as adults. For example, their unrepressed desire for the breast will be transferred to another object, perhaps a blanket, stuffed animal, or their thumb. In more extreme cases, unrepressed desire may result in object fetishism, where sexual gratification is achieved only with the help of the object. Most notably, if repression is not achieved in the Oedipal stage where desire for the mother is paramount, children will become "inverts," or homosexual. They may form same-sex attachments, and display gender-confused behaviour considered problematic in the early twentieth century, such as whistling in women, and excessive primping in men.

While Freud's ideas may sound ridiculous to our twenty-first century ears, these examples underscore the sociological view that gender and sexuality are both individually experienced and culturally understood. Further, Freud's ideas act as precursors to popular present-day views that gender appropriateness and heteronormativity in adults is learned through their personal experiences as children. Today, just as in the early 1900s, parents, moral leaders, institutions, and government are called upon to diligently protect children, whose development towards gender-appropriate and heteronormative adulthood is at risk. Since adult gendered behaviours and sexual preferences are markers of previous experiences, those concerned with child welfare place great importance on child protection. With this in mind, educational and philanthropic programs designed to guide children towards greater self-discipline, thereby encouraging the repression of desire in children, fit nicely within the larger, social context of Canadian liberalism.[5]

The second significant shift in social perspective concerns religion. Religion contributed to the changing views of gender, sexuality and childhood in the early 1900s. Historically, Canadian state formation was strongly influenced by Methodism–a form of Protestantism emphasizing the doing of daily Christian acts that would be rewarded by earthly prosperity and heavenly recognition. By 1910, popular perspectives of one's Christian duty to God merged with ideas that one was also duty-bound to the Canadian nation. Conveniently, one's duty to God could be achieved through dutiful support for the Christian Canadian state. This was possible since the expansionist agenda of the Protestant church could be achieved through the "building of God's kingdom on earth"–right here in Canada.[6] The conflation of the Methodist agenda with the state agenda is especially overt in representations of mothers, fathers, and children at this time, just as Canada entered into the First World War to defend and support Britain as the self-proclaimed most valuable colony in Britain's dwindling empire.

Gender appropriate and heteronormative men, women, and children ensured social and moral stability within Canada, secured the sanctity of the nuclear family, and encouraged the growth of political and economic presence outside of Canada. As such, men, women, and children became agents of Canadian moral fortitude and national showmanship. The expression of appropriately gendered behaviour became increasingly hegemonic as ideas about masculinity and femininity became more firmly entrenched in the story of Canadian national identity. As soldiers, men represented the hyper-masculinized, male–the officer and gentleman who would fight to bring colonial values, and modern civilizing culture to even the darkest corners of the world. As mothers, women represented the hyper-feminized female–the nurturer who supported her soldier-husband as he bravely defended the values embodied by her, his family, and his nation. She was morally pure and physically fecund, birthing many children who would in turn become the mothers of the nation, and the soldiers that defended her (Comachio, 1993). Children represented the future of the Canadian nation–the greatest resource to be managed with care, and with great attention to their moral upbringing (Davin, 1978).

The shift from overt duty to God, to duty to nation is illustrated in the rise of para-military organizations that instilled gender appropriate and heteronormative values and behaviours within its group members. Both the Canadian Girl Guide and the Boy Scout movements formed between 1905 and 1910 as para-military organizations for children. The Girl Guides encouraged girls and young women to form character consistent with Christian values of moral purity, modesty, and dedication to the caretaking of others. For example, Girl Guides were typically called upon to project a more "natural" image of womanhood in the *Gazette*, the official magazine of Girl Guide movement:

> Girl Scouts ban using powder, rouge, lipstick, eyebrow pencil,...no scout [is] allowed to die [sic] her hair or use peroxide or other bleach...short skirts and high heels must go. Each Scout must convert at least three girls from appearing in public with a flour face. (National Girl Guide Headquarters, 1917)

Similarly, Boy Scouts were to shape their character around the Christian values of temperance, sexual discipline, and dedication to God and the defence the nation (Curtis, 1990). For the organization's creator Lord Baden-Powell, sexual abstinence laid the foundation for character development, and relinquishing masturbation would stabilize the British Empire's looming dissolution (Barclay, 1923).

While it can be convincingly argued that the Canadian nation was more overtly Christian in the early 1900s than today, the remnants of this Christian perspective is clearly apparent in the Canadian state's interest in the character development of children–being a Canadian child meant preparing for future service to Canada, a nation foundationally rooted in Christian values and morals. Today, Canadian concerns with gender and sexuality continue to be linked to Christian views of moral propriety, and state policy continues to encourage gender appropriate, heteronormative values. State policies that censor both public and private sexual expression encourage "erotophobia," and resist the sexualization and queering of Canadian culture

(Ince, 2005). Laws criminalizing solicitation, restricting access to pornography, censoring sexually explicit materials such as sex toys limit sexual interaction and supposedly protect Canadians from dangerous acts of immorality. Ironically, notions about the sexual innocence of children are reified when the lived experiences of children who are sexually trafficked, sexually abused, and sexually "precocious" remain invisible, even at a time when mass media increasingly sexualizes representations of children (Postman, 1994). Changes to Canadian laws that now permit same-sex marriage and recognize the rights of gay couples in many social capacities marks a recent shift in state sanctioning of sexuality and heteronormativity.[7] The legacy of this shift in terms of its capacity to engender real and meaningful equality in the lives of Canadians has yet to unfold.

The third significant shift in social perspective contributing to changing views of gender, sexuality and childhood in the early 1900s is related to the rise of scientific discourses dedicated to cataloguing human physiology and evaluating gendered behaviour. Cataloguing combined with statistical aggregation enabled the creation of ideal, "normalized" types.[8] The bell curve expressed the distribution of qualities and characteristics across selected populations, normalizing aspects of individual and group behaviour consistent with the existing social order, and with the general principles of liberalism (Davis, 2006). Normalized behaviours were equated with preferred social behaviours including rationality, a sense of independence, thriftiness, temperance, among others. Demographic analysis became the tool of statesmen and reformers seeking to validate their desire to align the Canadian colonial state with more liberal ideologies, and support Canada's emergence as a world leader in the twentieth century (Valverde, 1991).

Initially, bell curving human physiology by sex was undertaken. Numerous studies produced data focusing on the comparative measurement of male and female bodies. Organ size, location, and arrangement were catalogued and their significance to gendered behaviour was imagined (Winton, 2001). Measuring the commonality of gender appropriate behaviours made normalization possible and legitimated the view that gendered behaviour was innate. Men and women were depicted as occupying distinct behavioural arenas that reflected "natural," complimentary realms. As competitors, men could focus their physiologically determined propensities for aggression and leadership in the waged labour force, where effective breadwinning was a sign of masculine prowess. Similarly, women's innate abilities to nurture and homemake made the on-going reinvigoration of the nuclear family possible. Women's domestic work sustained both current and future generations of workers. The belief that gendered behaviour was innate in origin encouraged social reformers to focus on teaching "dangerous" children gender appropriate behaviour. For example, the growth of the residential school system in the nineteenth century was solely designed to instruct First Nations children in the ways of White society, thereby enabling their assimilation. Tutelage included gendered etiquette classes that focused on, among other things, pouring tea and child-minding for girls. Boys were instructed in skills related to their eventual role as breadwinners and fathers. The adoption of White proprieties was contingent upon the loss of First Nations' cultures and languages. The harshness with which this agenda was applied is well documented in numerous accounts of residential school survivors who faced beatings, sexual abuse, disease and humiliation at the hands of their teachers.[9]

Finally, researchers such as Alfred Kinsey in the United States turned their attention towards the distribution of human sexual behaviours along the bell curve. Two publications by Kinsey, *Sexual Behavior in the Human Male* (1948) and *Sexual Behavior in the Human Female* (1953) were particularly influential in North America, including Canadian discussions of human sexuality. Kinsey's mammoth data collections created the research base required to challenge lingering Victorian ideals of gender and sexuality that were still restricted by strict codes of propriety. Kinsey, and later researchers like Masters and Johnson are charged with invalidating conservative views of human sexuality and upsetting mainstream perceptions of gender appropriate sexual behaviour.[10]

The social relevance of this mathematical exercise of bell curving lay in the perceived importance of reforming all those whose qualities and characteristics scored beyond the bell curve's mid-range, thereby identifying them as "abnormal" and in need of special treatment, or "deviant" and in need of criminal intervention (Chenier, 2008). In the early 1900s, "dangerous" children became the targets of normalization strategies that, by the 1950s, evolved into more malignant techniques for conformity (Brock, 2003). Social regulation in schools, community groups, family, and the workplace evolved in response to increasingly popular ideas about the need to control gendered behaviour and sexuality (Adams, 2003). Despite the centrality of individualism to liberal political ideology, the need to control and discourage gender inappropriate and non-hegemonic sexual behaviours was justified by the belief that conformity to social norms would enhance life satisfaction for those troubled by non-conformist desires. In this neo-Freudian view, non-normativity created personal conflict, and prevented social acceptance and self-actualization. This view fuelled the use of electro-shock therapy, forced sterilization, and drug therapies for politicized women, exceptional children, lesbians and gay men, among others, across North America (see, for example, Krasnick, 2010; Feldberg et al., 2003).

THE LEGACY OF LATE VICTORIAN IDEALS OF GENDER AND SEXUALITY

While the early 1900s might seem like quite a while ago, socially-speaking it is not. Rather, the belief that we are nothing like the reformers of 100 years ago is a trick of modern discourse, which stresses our separation from things that have come before. We rush towards our future, and away from our past, propelled forward by the promise of social change and life enhancement. With our attention firmly placed on technological advancement, we barely notice the cultural, psychological, economic, and social legacy of late Victorian ideals of gender and sexuality still apparent in contemporary Canadian society and relevant to Canadian global perspectives.

In situating the liberal subject at the centre of Canadian social propriety, and normalizing this subject's behaviour and appearance, "otherness" is created. This means that all those who do not fit this normalized ideal are relegated to another category constituted around their difference. Once labelled "other," differentness tautologically becomes the indicator of non-normativity.[11] For example, heterosexuality is regarded as normative and calls to mind the sociological view of modernity as a historical process. The hegemony of heterosexuality is enabled by the network of mutually supportive contingencies that reinforce social ideologies and governmental technologies so thoroughly that they are seemingly unnoticed by those in compliance. So, gender appropriate and normative sexual behaviours appear self-evident, rather than culturally constructed.

Within our current discussion, several "others" can be identified. For example, the liberal framework assumes the liberal subject is adult, since individualism, self-actualization and rationality can only be fully grasped by a sentient, adult being. Therefore, children are "others." Similarly, the Canadian liberal view assumes the Canadian subject is best represented by Whites of English descent, as historically this group held formative social and economic power. Despite the presence of Canada's French and First Nations cultures, and the participation of countless immigrant populations to Canadian nation-building, these groups are relegated to the category of "other." Further, those who are not gender-appropriate in behaviour and appearance, or who demonstrate non-hegemonic sexuality are considered "other." Finally, on a global scale, all non-Canadians are "othered" within the Canadian national context, represented by those who lie beyond the immediate borders of Canada but within its sphere of cultural influence. Post-colonial social theorists note the racialization of "othering" as part of continued colonial power dynamics. Despite the diversity of all those considered "other," one common idea lies at the heart of the process of "othering"–that is, "othering" is rooted in the presumption that western society is inherently superior to non-western society. And just like the reformers of 100 years ago, contemporary interests in the modernization of traditional cultures presume western cultural superiority and legitimize views that gender appropriate and heteronormative values and behaviours are to be encouraged in modernizing cultures.

The creation of "otherness" supports the modernizing agenda as it encourages political, cultural, and economic shifts in more traditional communities around the globe. For children, this means encouraging the development of protectionist views aimed at naturalizing their childhood and repressing sexuality. This agenda is so infused with moral conviction that to suggest otherwise seems inhumane–after all, children need to be protected from sexual knowledge and experiences, we claim. These claims are made with good intention fuelled by the belief in superior western morality, but do not acknowledge the lived realities of many children as they themselves experience their own lives. For example, research with child prostitutes in Thailand exposes the hegemony of western ideals. According to Heather Montgomery (2009), when child prostitutes were asked how they perceive the work they do, exploitation and abuse was never mentioned. In fact, children saw themselves as vital contributors to their family's economy. Montgomery concludes that foreign policies that advocate the protection of children, especially from employment in the sex trade industry, are too simplistic. They do not fully grasp the complex social relations underpinning prostitution and the lack of alternatives for many children (Montgomery, 2009). Rather, Western concern for the sexual exploitation of children often overshadows the views of children themselves, rendering children's experiences as wrong, misguided, pathological, or the result of abuse itself. So firmly committed are we to the view that children must remain sexually innocent, that to suggest otherwise often invokes sexual perversion. Ironically, Western sexual protectionism has intensified with increases in sexual access to non-Western children, through the sex tourism and the use of the internet.

Western views about gender and sexuality, particularly with respect to children, are thought to reflect the moral superiority of modernized nations. Canadian mainstream views that focus on the naturalization of childhood, protectionism, and the repression of sexuality, especially in children, poignantly illustrate this presumption. Contemporary views emerge out of late Victorian thinking about the relationship between gendered and sexual behaviours, and social normalization. Ideals and morals of the early 1900s are still foundational in contemporary attitudes towards gender and sexuality. As a modern nation, contemporary Canadian views of childhood as naturalized, reify beliefs that children are a valuable national resource, best protected through restrictive sexual regulation. Views about childhood, the need to protect and educate children, and the role of children in nation-building, constitute a significant aspect of Canada's global identity. This perspective shapes Canadian identity and Canadian perspectives of global change.

NOTES

1. Most notably, seminal postcolonial theorists include Spivak (1999); Lewis (2004), Mohanty (1984).
2. This concept is first explored in Aries (1998). For a more contemporary review of the ambivalence underscoring views of children and childhood, see Zelizer (1994).
3. Most notably in Hall (1901/1924).
4. Arguably, the most significant of his lengthy list of publications embodying these principles were published between the years of 1965 and 1989.
5. For a current discussion of the impact of the age of consent laws on child sexuality and its relationship to heteronormativity, see Hunt (2009).
6. Considerable evidence suggests that the impact of Methodism in English Canada is ubiquitous–the state does not become less religious but rather the state hides its religious agenda behind discourses of citizenship. This is the thrust of Christie and Gauvreau (1996).

[7] For Michael Warner (1999), the move to same-sex marriage is problematic since it continues to stigmatize those engaged in relationships outside of sate sanctioned marriage, and invalidates all other forms of relationships.

[8] According to Ian Hacking (1992), the expression of reality through demography is strongly linked to modernity.

[9] A thorough look at the residential school experience is discussed in Furniss (1995).

[10] Most notably, this was the focus of sexology. See Bland and Doan (1994).

[11] This has been most thoroughly discussed in post-colonial genres where whiteness forms the basis of normality, and all "non-whiteness" is relegated to the realm of other.

REFERENCES

Adams, M.L. (2003). *The Trouble with Normal: Postwar Youth and the Making of Heterosexuality.* University of Toronto Press, Toronto.

Anonymous. (1917). "Scrapbooks," located in Miscellaneous file, unpublished collection, Toronto: National Girl Guide Headquarters, November 7.

Aries, P. (1998). "From Immodesty to Innocence." In H. Jenkins (ed.), *The Children's Culture Reader.* NY: New York University Press.

Arnup, K. (1994). *Education for Motherhood: Advice for Mothers in Twentieth-Century Canada.* Toronto: University of Toronto Press.

Barclay, J. (1923). *Character Training in the Wolf Cub Pack.* London: The Faith Press Limited.

Berger, C. (1970). *The Sense of Power: Studies in the Ideas of Canadian Imperialism, 1867-1914.* Toronto: University of Toronto Press.

Bland, L., and D. Laura. (eds.). (1994). *Sexology in Culture: Labelling Bodies and Desires.* Chicago: University of Chicago Press, Chicago.

Brock, D. (2003). *Making Normal: Social Regulations in Canada.* Toronto: Nelson Education Ltd.

Chenier, E.R. (2008). *Strangers in our midst: sexual deviancy in postwar Ontario.* Toronto: University of Toronto Press.

Christie, N., and G. Michael. (1996). *A Full-Orbed Christianity: The Protestant Churches and Social Welfare in Canada 1900-1940.* Montreal: McGill-Queen's University Press.

Comachio, C. (1993). *Nations are Built of Babies: Saving Ontario's Mothers and Children, 1900-1914.* Montreal: McGill-Queen's University Press.

Curtis, S. (1990). "The Son of Man and God the Father: The Social Gospel and Victorian Masculinity." In M. Carnes and C. Griffen, (eds.), *Meanings for Manhood: Constructions of Masculinity in Victorian America.* Chicago: University of Chicago Press.

Davin, A. (1978). "Imperialism and Motherhood." *History Workshop* 5: 9-11.

Davis, L. (2006). "Constructing Normalcy: The Bell Curve, the Novel, and the Invention of the Disabled Body in the Nineteenth Century." In L.J. Davis, (ed.), *The Disability Studies Reader.* NY: Routledge Press.

Feldberg, G., M. Ladd-Taylor, A. Li, and K. McPherson. (2003). *Women, Health and Nation: Canada and the United States since 1945.* Montreal: McGill-Queen's University Press.

Freud, S. (1930/1961). *Civilization and Its Discontents.* NY: W.W. Norton and Company.

Furniss, E. (1995). *Victims of Benevolence: The Dark Legacy of the Williams Lake Residential School.* Vancouver: Arsenal Pulp Press.

Hacking, I. (1992). *The Taming of Chance.* Cambridge: Cambridge University Press.

Hall, G.S. (1901/1924). *Adolescence: Its Psychology and its Relation to Physiology, Anthropology, Sociology, Sex, Crime, Religion, and Education.* Vol. 2. New York: D. Appleton and Company.

Hall, S. (1996). "Introduction." In S. Hall, D. Held, D. Hubert and K. Thompson (eds.), *Modernity: An Introduction to Modern Societies.* Massachusetts: Blackwell Publishing.

Hill, J. (2000). "Politicizing Canadian Childhood Using a Governmentality Framework." histoire social - *Social History* 33(65).

Hunt, K. (2009). "Saving the Children: (Queer) Youth Sexuality and the Age of Consent in Canada." *Sexuality Research and Social Policy* 6(3):15-33.

Ince, J. (2005). *The Politics of Lust.* Vancouver: Pivitol Press.

Latour, B. (1993). *We Have Never Been Modern.* Massachusetts: Harvard University Press.

Lewis, R. (2004). *Rethinking Orientalism: Women, Travel and the Ottoman Harem in 2004.* New Jersey: Rutgers University Press.

McConnell, J. (2010). *Analysis of Documents Related to Residential Schools in Canada.* NY: VDM Verlag.

Mohanty, C.T . (1988). "Under Western Eyes: Feminist Scholarship and Colonial Discourses." *Feminist Review* 30 (Autumn):61-88.

Montgomery, H. (2009). "Are Child Prostitutes Child Workers? A Case Study." *International Journal of Sociology and Social Policy* 29(3-4):130-140.

Postman, N. (1994). *The Disappearance of Childhood.* NY: Vintage Books.

Spivak, G. (1999). *A Critique of Postcolonial Reason: Towards a History of the Vanishing Present.* Boston: Harvard University Press.

Valverde, M. (1991). *The Age of Light, Soap, and Water: Moral Reform in English Canada, 1885-1925.* Toronto: McClelland and Stewart.

Warner, M. (1999). *The Trouble with Normal: Sex, Politics, and the Ethics of Queer Life.* Massachusetts: Harvard University Press.

Warsh, C.K. (2010). *Prescribed Norms: Women and Health in Canada and the United States since 1800.* Toronto: UTP.

Winton, M.A. (2001). "Paradigm Change and Female Sexual Dysfunctions: An Analysis of Sexology Journals." *Canadian Journal of Human Sexuality* 10(1-2). Available at http://www.sieccan.org/cjhs.html.

Zelizer, V. (1994). *Pricing the Priceless Child: The Changing Social Value of Children.* New Jersey: Princeton University Press.

Zilney, L., and L. Anne. (2009). *Perverts and Predators: The Making of Sexual Offending Laws.* NY: Rowman and Littlefield.

Chapter 5

Health, Disability and Ageing

Health, Disability and Ageing: Are they Related?

Sharon Dale Stone

Lakehead University

INTRODUCTION

Do you think of yourself as healthy? How can you tell? Do you think of yourself as disabled? Why do you think you are or are not? Who said and under what authority? And if you think of yourself as healthy but at the same time disabled, how can that be? Isn't that a contradiction in terms? Finally, are you looking forward to growing old? Why or why not? Do you see old age as a time of declining health and encroaching decrepitude? Where did you get these ideas?

This chapter uses these questions as a starting point for discussing the topics of health, disability and ageing. The goal is to review some basic information that will help you to provide informed answers to the questions posed above. In particular, we will see the ways in which the subjects of health, disability and ageing are popularly constructed as highly inter-related, when in fact they have little to do with each other. Explaining why this is the case is a complex matter but as you will see, an enormous piece of the puzzle can be found in recognizing the dominance of scientific medicine. Let's begin there.

Health and Medicine: Are they Related?

Canadians tend to be proud of living in a country that provides free healthcare to all citizens. Canada instituted state-funded healthcare back in the 1960s based on the belief that the provision of free healthcare will improve people's health status (Dickinson and Bolaria, 2002). It makes sense, doesn't it? If you want to improve health, improve people's ability to have access to ways to care for their health. Indeed, it does make sense to improve access to healthcare. The problem is that governments tend to define healthcare quite narrowly. Healthcare tends to be defined solely in terms of services provided by accredited medical professionals. These are the people who have a degree from a recognized degree-granting university, such as the degree of MD, a degree as a nurse, or a degree as a physiotherapist. Without a university degree in a recognized medical specialty, the government will not officially recognize what someone does as providing healthcare services.

If you want to go to a Chinese herbalist for your health, you will have to pay for it yourself. Similarly, if you want to argue that you need to get your yoga sessions paid for by the government because yoga keeps you healthy, you're not going to get anywhere (unless, of course, your MD is the one providing the yoga session). Even more problematic, however, is that you are not going to get your nutritional needs met by applying to the government for money to purchase what you need to stay healthy. You might be able to get counseling from a nutritionist, who will help you tailor Canada's Food Guide to satisfy your taste buds, but you won't get the food paid for. For that, you are on your own. Amazing, isn't it? Without adequate nutrition we will die. Guaranteed.

It is well-documented that nutrition is a vitally important factor determining health. Other determinants of health include access to safe housing, safe neighbourhoods, transportation, and secure employment (for more on the social determinants of health, see Raphael, 2009). The Ottawa Charter for Health Promotion (WHO, 1986) says that prerequisites for health include peace, shelter, education, food, income, a stable ecosystem, sustainable resources, social justice, and equity. As well, Health Canada (a branch of the federal government) says that health is determined by a variety of social factors including income and social status, social support networks, education, employment, working conditions, the physical environment and the social environment.

Note that in these lists of the determinants of health, there is no mention of access to medical care. Indeed, there is little population-based evidence to show that people's health improves when they have access to medical professionals. In fact, critics such as Ivan Illich have mounted impressive evidence to show that "medical professional practice has become a major threat to health" (1976; 2003:919). There is even some evidence, albeit controversial, which suggests that people are less likely to die when doctors go on strike (as they did, for example, for 23 days in 1962 in Saskatchewan, for 25 days in 1986 in Ontario, and for all of January 1976 in Los Angeles County, California; see James, 1979; Meslin, 1987). When doctors withdraw their services, however, any decline in the number of deaths can be largely explained by the fact that fewer people undergo surgery, and as any surgeon should tell you, surgery is always risky.

The growth in access to medical professionals has led to a growth in the incidence of iatrogenic disease (from the Greek *iatros* which means healer, and *genesis* which means origin). Iatrogenic disease can be defined as including any adverse reaction or outcome resulting from medical treatment. It is difficult to get accurate statistics on the prevalence of iatrogenesis, but estimates based on hospital data in the United States suggest that iatrogenic disease is responsible for 250,000 deaths annually (Starfield, 2000; see also Leape, 2000). This makes iatrogenic disease the third leading cause of death in the U.S., after heart disease and cancer. All of this leads to the question of why governments narrowly focus on services provided by accredited medical professionals. The answer has a lot to do with the power that MDs have in contemporary society.

The medical profession, which is dominated by people who have an MD, has tremendous power in our society (see Lupton, 2003). MDs get to decide who is well and who is not and they get to decide what to do in order to make someone well. Their pronouncements are listened to and seriously considered by governments. MDs are a self-regulating profession, which means that they do not allow non-MDs to monitor or otherwise police their activities. Each Canadian province has a College of Physicians and Surgeons (CPS) and doctors need to register with the provincial CPS to get and maintain a license to practice medicine. Each CPS also requires members to follow a code of ethics in order to maintain their license. From an outsider's perspective, though, there is a serious problem with the fact that each CPS gets to decide on its own whether ethical standards have been breached and if so, what to do about it. With no independent watch-dog, the public must take the word of physicians that as they go about their business they always have the public's best interests at heart.

Medical Training

Since the early twentieth century, the capstone of training to become an MD has been to spend time training in a hospital. What is interesting about hospitals is that they are institutions set up for the convenience of MDs. The hospital is the epitome of a modern, rational institution in the Weberian sense (Weber had a lot to say about institutions and bureaucracies). For example, there is an emphasis on standardization and a focus on how to do things efficiently (see Hewa 2002 for a discussion of the rationalization process in medicine).

There is also an emphasis on technology–whereas diagnosis was once regarded as an art, increasingly doctors rely on machines to diagnose disease (e.g., stethoscope, x-ray, EEG, ECG, CT scan, MRI, etc.). More troubling is that these machines tend to be regarded as though they can infallibly produce objective, clear and reliable information when in fact they cannot (see Butler, 1993; McKinlay and McKinlay, 1981). Moreover, the reliance on technology serves to reinforce the idea that if the doctor cannot see, feel, taste or hear evidence of pathology, then there is not in fact a problem. This is obviously not helpful for the large numbers of people who have illnesses that doctors cannot see, feel, taste or hear (to read about women with invisible illnesses that are nevertheless significantly disabling, see Dreidger and Owen, 2008). These people have a very difficult time being taken seriously by doctors.

The Biomedical Model

All accredited medical professionals in Canada are trained in scientific medicine, which is founded on the assumptions of a biomedical model of disease (see Hewa, 2002). Key assumptions of this model are: 1) mind-body dualism; 2) physical reductionism; 3) the doctrine of specific etiology; and 4) the machine metaphor. Let's examine these assumptions.

Mind-Body Dualism. This assumption can be traced back to the philosophy of René Descartes (famous for saying "I think, therefore I am"). The idea is that the mind and the body are separate entities: one does not influence the other. Thus, the physician can (and should) observe disease without having to consider the person inhabiting the body. This allows for abstract clinical observation, which Michel Foucault (1973) has termed "the clinical gaze." Doctors learn to view patients as docile bodies which can be observed, manipulated and transformed.

Physical Reductionism. This is the assumption that disease can always be understood in terms of disordered bodily functions. That is, disease is the property of an individual body and has nothing to do with the context in which that body exists. With this assumption, there is no room for a recognition or consideration of the social determinants of health. Consider, for example, the case of workers injured while performing their workplace duties. It is well documented that some occupations are hazardous to health, typically because employers do not have adequate safeguards in place (see Smith, 2000, also see the Institute for Work and Health website: http://iwh.on.ca). Coal miners, for example, take their life into their hands when they go to work. In 1992, 26 workers lost their lives in the Westray mining disaster in Nova Scotia, and in April 2010, at a coal mine owned by Massey Energy, 29 lost their lives in a mining disaster in West Virginia. Those who spend decades working in coal mines, meanwhile, are at risk of contracting black lung disease, thanks to constantly breathing in coal dust. Physicians, however, are not trained to treat and eliminate the social conditions that cause so much disease. They are trained to treat the individual body.

Doctrine of Specific Etiology. This is the assumption that each disease is caused by a specific, potentially identifiable agent. The doctrine grew from the nineteenth century discovery of germs and the role they can play in disease. As René Dubos (1959) points out, however, the doctrine of specific etiology cannot completely explain the cause of disease. That is, most of us are constantly in contact with potentially harmful germs, yet only some of us get sick, and we do not even get sick each time we are in contact with germs. The search for a specific cause, nevertheless, continues unabated. Typically, it leads medical researchers to search for a "magic bullet" treatment that will cure disease. This justifies our ever-growing reliance on pharmaceutical drugs (for a hard-hitting analysis of the pharmaceutical industry in Canada, see Lexchin, 2006).

The Machine Metaphor: This is the assumption that the body is best understood as a collection of mechanical parts that can break down. This justifies specializations such as cardiology or orthopedics. A cardiologist is trained to focus on the heart and not consider the body's bone structure, while an orthopedist is trained to focus on bones, joints, ligaments and muscles and not consider how the heart works. This leads to the belief that non-working parts (for example, a "bad" heart; a "bad" knee) can be fixed or even replaced without affecting another part of the body, just as we replace, for example, a door hinge that no longer works.

The biomedical model is hegemonic in our society, which is to say that it is widely taken for granted as the only reasonable way of understanding illness and disease (see Lupton, 2003); also it is so pervasive that alternate explanations of the causes and cures for illness and disease are treated as nonsensical and/or unthinkable. Thus, those experiencing illness or disease are expected to take on what sociologist Talcott Parsons (1951) called "the sick role."

The sick role

No one in their right mind is supposed to want to be sick. Modern physicians are ostensibly dedicated to treating/curing sickness, and sickness is viewed as a kind of unwanted deviance. Physicians, moreover, are the only people who are granted the legitimate authority to treat and (one hopes) cure sickness. Consequently, people who are sick are expected to place themselves under the care of a physician and assume "the sick role."

The concept of the sick role remains very useful for understanding societal expectations regarding sickness. The concept fundamentally relies upon an understanding of physicians as all-powerful experts, and the contrasting understanding of patients as passive. When people are sick, they are expected to take up the sick role. This allows them certain privileges, but there are also certain responsibilities they must fulfill:

Privileges

1. the sick person is exempt from usual social role responsibilities (e.g. working, going to school, etc.);
2. the sick person is exempt from responsibility for his/her condition.

Responsibilities

1. the sick person must view being sick as undesirable and want to get well;

2. the sick person is obligated to seek technically competent help and co-operate in the treatment process.

The idea of the sick role works reasonably well when someone is experiencing an acute illness–for example, appendicitis which is an emergency, or a broken leg which can be set and which will heal in good time. People with acute illness usually do want to get well and usually do consult an accredited medical professional for treatment. Moreover, most onlookers are sympathetic and accordingly willing to exempt the sick person from usual responsibilities, *provided that* the sick person seems genuinely interested in getting better. As well, most people are willing to agree that no one should be blamed for getting sick. There are exceptions to this general state of affairs, however. As we will see in a later section, it does not make sense to apply the sick role to people with chronic illness or disabled people. As a society, we tend to understand what is going on when people experience acute illness but we tend to be mystified by people with chronic illness or impairment. First, though, we will examine access to health care in Canada, and the extent to which people can get treatment for illness and disease.

The Canada Health Act

In 1957, as a result of the pioneering efforts of Tommy Douglas, the Canadian government passed an *Act* to give Canadians access to free hospital stays and in-hospital treatment. By 1961, all provinces had a hospital insurance plan for residents. In 1966, the federal government passed the *Medical Care Act* to give Canadians access to free out-of-hospital physician visits, and by 1971 all provinces had a health insurance plan for residents, to cover physician care. This meant that physicians would bill the government for their services, and there was a set fee that they could receive from the government. Over time, each province added to the kinds of services that the government would pay for, such as physiotherapy, chiropractic treatment, or ambulance rides (but, especially over the past decade, many provinces have been gradually de-insuring services that were previously covered, such as physiotherapy, chiropractic treatment, or ambulance rides). Until 1984, however, when Canada passed the *Canada Health Act*, physicians in some provinces were free to bill their patients directly, and/or charge their patients over and above the fees they received from the government. Specialists were especially likely to "opt out" and "extra bill" their patients. The *Canada Health Act* was designed to put an end to this practice, and it identified five principles that provinces had to follow in order to get federal help with funding health insurance:

1. Universality: all Canadians must be covered on an equal basis.

2. Accessibility: all Canadians must have equal access to health care services provided by accredited medical professionals (this principle disallows extra billing).

3. Comprehensiveness: there must be coverage of a broad range of services provided by accredited medical professionals.

4. Portability: Canadians can carry their insurance between provinces.

5. Public administration: health insurance must be administered by a non-profit agency responsible to provincial or territorial government.

Problems with the *Canada Health Act*

There are numerous problems with the *Canada Health Act*, and in this section we will look at two. One huge problem is that it defines health care in terms of services provided by accredited medical professionals, and physicians in particular. Thus, it supports the hegemony of a biomedical understanding of health and illness. Moreover, given that most physicians are still paid on a fee-for-service basis (rather than, for example, paid a salary that is unrelated to the number of patients seen), and given that physicians are trained to focus on treatment and cure, there is no incentive for physicians or other medical professionals to promote or otherwise focus on the prevention of sickness (for more on this, see Armstrong and Armstrong, 2008). For this reason, it is often said that Canada funds a sickness care system rather than a health care system.

Equally problematic, the *Canada Health Act* defines accessibility quite narrowly and without consideration for geographical distances. That is, it does not seem to matter that many Canadians reside far away from service providers. This is a particular problem for those living on remote aboriginal reserves or in other remote areas of the country. Those outside densely populated urban areas are, for all practical purposes, denied service on an equal basis with urban dwellers. Those who live in large cities can get to a doctor or hospital relatively easily, and they may even be able to shop around for a physician they like. Others, however, have either no access to a physician or hospital without travelling great distances, or they have limited access to shrinking numbers of family physicians (for more on this problem, see Pong and Pitblado, 2005; also Crooks and Andrews, 2009).

Increasingly, we are seeing calls for privately funded health services because more and more people are having trouble getting an appointment to see a physician, or are having to wait longer and longer times for elective hospital procedures. As Armstrong and Armstrong (2008) point out, however, there is little evidence that wait times are either unreasonable or dangerous to heath. They also argue convincingly that for the great majority of people, privately funded health services alongside publicly funded services would actually work to lengthen rather than shorten wait times. With privately funded health services, those with the most money would be able to "jump the queue" to buy instant access, and the rest of us would have to wait longer. This would clearly be a two-tiered system of health care.

Arguably, we already have two-tiered access to many health care services. For example, consider the point made earlier in this chapter, that according to the *Canada Health Act*, only the services provided in hospitals and by physicians must be covered by a governmental insurance plan. Consequently, many services that are important for preserving health or restoring health after sickness are not actually covered by governmental insurance plans. In Ontario, for example, if you have a musculoskeletal injury, there are restrictions on whether you are entitled to free physiotherapy to treat your injury. Generally, if you are aged 20-64 you can only get free physiotherapy either while you are in the hospital or immediately upon discharge from the hospital. Otherwise, you will be on your own regarding payment (for more information on what is or is not covered by the Ontario Health Insurance Plan, see the website: http://www.health.gov.on.ca/en/public/programs/ohip/default.aspx). In effect, it is already the case that those who can afford to pay (or who have generous private insurance plans) can more easily have access to services and products (such as prescription drugs) that can preserve or restore health. Along with those who live in remote areas, those who are impoverished do not have the same access.

Chronic Illness

As mentioned in the discussion of the sick role, it can be difficult to make sense of people with chronic illness. By definition, a chronic illness is an illness that does not ever get better. People living with chronic illness cannot simply take a drug, have an operation, or engage in some other time-limited behaviour to rid themselves of disease. Some common examples of chronic illnesses are auto-immune diseases such as arthritis, multiple sclerosis, or myalgic encephalomylitis (M.E., also known as chronic fatigue syndrome). Heart disease also qualifies as a chronic illness. These conditions may temporarily respond to treatment, but will never completely go away. Moreover, the consequences of chronic illnesses are often invisible to onlookers (see Dreidger and Owen 2008; Stone, 1993, 2005).

Common consequences of chronic illness include ongoing pain or extreme fatigue, but because sufferers typically look "just fine," others may have difficulty believing that they are truly ill. This, indeed, is probably the worst part about having a chronic illness: that others often do not believe that there is a problem. In other words, the attitudes of others can be much harder to deal with than whatever bodily symptoms someone may be experiencing. It is common for people with chronic illness to spend years looking for a physician who will agree that there is a physical problem, and even when a physician agrees, other people may remain skeptical regarding their claims of illness (see Moss and Teghtsoonian, 2008; for a discussion of women and chronic illness, see Dreidger and Owen 2008; for experiences of low back pain, see Vroman, Warner, and Chamberlain, 2009). The invisibility of much chronic illness can be a particular problem in the workplace, as Vickers (2001) discusses with reference to Australia, as Crooks, Stone and Owen (2009) discuss with reference to Canadian academics, or when injured workers attempt to re-enter the workforce as Stone et al. (2002) discuss with reference to northern Ontario.

Disability

The subject of disability is typically understood as related to health, and disabled people are typically assumed to be in need of medical care above and beyond what the non-disabled population needs. These assumptions flow from the hegemony of the biomedical model of disability–a model that sees disability in terms of individual tragedy (see Oliver, 2009; Thomas, 2007). From this perspective, disability is an undesirable medical problem that an individual can have, and which needs to be treated or fixed with professional knowledge and expertise. Thus, rehabilitation is important to make the disabled person as "normal" as possible.

From the perspective of the social model of disability, however, disability has nothing to do with health, and there is no reason for medical professionals to take charge of the lives of disabled people. As Davis (1997) explains, the idea of "normal" is a relatively recent invention, not to mention an unfortunate invention. As Stone (1995) argues, biomedicine works to perpetuate the belief that bodily perfection is possible, and this harms all of us.

The social model of disability offers a perspective that stands in stark contrast to the biomedical model. The social model makes a distinction between *impairment* (a bodily condition which is what most people understand as disability) and *disability*, which is socially created, rather than something objective that an individual can "have." From this perspective, what needs to be fixed is not the individual body, but a social and built environment that was designed for the convenience of people with a narrow range of bodily types and abilities. To be disabled, then, is to be socially disadvantaged on account of living in a world that is either unwilling or unable to flexibly adapt to individuals' different needs, whether those needs include ramps or workplace policies that will allow access to employment for all who are willing to work. As many social model theorists have argued, disability is social oppression (for example, see Abberley, 1987; for comprehensive commentary see Thomas, 2007). To address disability, therefore, there is no need to seek help from medical professionals. Rather, there is a need to change the social and built environments.

Growing Old in Canada

Are you looking forward to growing old? If you're like most people in Canada, then chances are good that you fear getting old. After all, we're constantly inundated with the message that getting old sucks, youth is where it's at. At least, that's the message we seem to be hearing just about everywhere we turn. Growing old is commonly yet erroneously equated with increasing disability and decrepitude (Stone, 2003). Turn on the TV and you're likely to see a commercial for anti-ageing cream to protect your skin and keep you from getting wrinkles or age spots (yes, the decline into old age apparently starts around age 25, so be prepared!), or maybe you'll be treated to an advertisement about the wonders of a particular retirement community which, we are told, is where you will need to go if you want to have a good time when you're old (hmmm, maybe you should talk to grandma and gramps about how great it would be if they could reinvent themselves somewhere else-—where they can be with "their own kind.")

Most Canadians buy into these sorts of ideas because the anti-ageing industry has done a pretty good job of selling us the idea that ageing brings poor health and a decline into decrepitude, while the mass media have pretty effectively focused our attention on what's not so fun about getting old, thus deflecting our attention away from what is really wonderful about getting old. If you don't have access to alternative sources of information, it's impossible to fight against these messages.

Ageing: What's It Like?

Just as disability has been medicalized (that is, discussed as though medical professionals ought to be in charge of decisions about what to do), so has ageing been medicalized (Katz, 1996 discusses the medicalization of ageing at length; also see Cole, 1994 for a fascinating discussion of historical ideas about ageing). Given the legitimate authority that physicians enjoy in our contemporary society, it can be extremely difficult to challenge this medicalization. As is the case with disability, however, there is no compelling reason to think that ageing means an inevitable decline into poor health and decrepitude.

The experience of growing old depends on who you ask and what kind of life experiences they've had. Most generally, if you ask someone who is basically an unhappy person, then you're likely to hear about the losses that ageing can bring. But if you ask someone who is basically a happy person, then you're likely to hear that getting older feels just the same as being young. You might even be treated to the platitude "you're only as old as you feel." (Kaufman 1986 interviewed elders about their self-understandings and based on this research developed the term "the ageless self.")

Keep in mind the fact that all of us are ageing–we begin ageing from the moment of birth. It is interesting, therefore, that in contemporary society we tend to think of the subject of ageing as something that is relevant only to those past a certain age–typically 50+. This is actually a major problem because it encourages all of us to deny our own personal experiences of ageing, and we are encouraged to identify and reify differences between younger and older people. Thus, we treat older people as "other" – not part of the mainstream. This, of course, profoundly colours the experience of ageing.

Ageing across the entire life course is a huge topic. In this chapter I can only draw your attention to this fact and encourage you to ponder your own experience of ageing–even if you have yet to reach the ripe old age of 20! For the rest of the chapter, I will focus on discussing ageing issues that are relevant to those who are aged 65+.

The experience of ageing is undoubtedly different in these first decades of the 21st century than it was 100 years ago. Back in 1921, only 4.8% of the Canadian population was aged 65+, so it was not that common to see old people around. Fast forward to the present day, and we find that according to 2009 statistics, 14.9% of the Canadian population is over the age of 65 (Statistics Canada, 2009). By 2025, the projection is that 20% of the population will be over the age of 65. With so many old people around, we have turned old age into a social problem to be solved (for more on this, see Hazan, 1994).

As you can probably imagine, the experience of living to age 65 would have been quite different back in 1921 than it is today, when it is not seen as anything special. Back then, living to age 65 or beyond was considered an achievement–something to be celebrated. These days, people tend to moan about turning 65. They might even get a sympathy card on their 65th birthday–a person has to live to 90 or 100 to find others celebrating their age. An interesting change! Today, it is the rare person who does not dread their 65th birthday. What happened?

The Social Production of Ageing as a Problem

Sometime around the end of the nineteenth century, in countries that had their economies and social traditions transformed by the industrial revolution, old people began to be talked about as a social problem (for a discussion of how and why this happened, see Katz, 1996). The problem of ageing seemed to become even more acute as the twentieth century progressed, so that now in the early twenty-first century, there is widespread concern over what we are going to do about our ageing population.

To a large extent, concerns about growing numbers of elders stem from the unfounded belief that old people need more health care services than young people (Gee, 2002). The evidence suggests, however, that to the extent that old people use more health care resources than young people, it is not necessarily because they are less healthy but because doctors send them for more tests based on the belief that the health of old people needs to be closely monitored (cf. Gee, 2002). This is one of the consequences of the production of old age as a medical problem–with physicians being widely perceived as the appropriate people to solve the problem of old age, it is not surprising that there is little questioning of decisions made by physicians about the need to routinely send old people for medical tests. As well, old people are more likely to be taking multiple prescription medications, again not because there is clear evidence that they need these medications, but because physicians are more likely to prescribe multiple drugs to their elderly patients (Carey et al., 2008).

We have come to believe that old people are somehow different from the rest of us, and ignored the ways in which ageing is socially produced. Unfortunately, there seems to be little interest in mainstream society in deconstructing old age or celebrating the presence of elders in society. Instead, we seem to be quite happy to segregate old people in specially created retirement communities or nursing homes, or encourage them to hang out at seniors' centres (i.e., away from young people) or in RV parks. We do not have laws about age segregation, but we are mostly very happy to self-segregate. As such, there is little opportunity for young people to get to know old people in meaningful ways. Sometimes, young people spend time with grandparents but they are unlikely to see their grandparents as typical old people–for many it seems, their grandparents are not like other old people. Segregation, however, allows stereotypes about "the other" to flourish. An important stereotype is that old people are not healthy. We can hang on to this particular misconception only as long as we cling to the belief that the "problem of old age" is first and foremost a medical problem. So long as we do that, we will fail to see old people for who or what they really are: a heterogeneous group of ordinary people just like the rest of us.

Globalization

The discussion of issues in this chapter has focused on the Canadian context, and the chapter closes by turning briefly to the world stage, to focus on two salient considerations. First, Canadians are not alone in living with a culture that privileges scientific medicine as a panacea for treating the body (for a critique of the tendency to view scientific medicine as panacea, see Evans and Stoddart, 1994). The World Health Organization (WHO) has from its beginnings in 1948 been based on scientific medicine. This is highly significant, because the WHO directs and coordinates health for the United Nations and:

> It is responsible for providing leadership on global health matters, shaping the health research agenda, setting norms and standards, articulating evidence-based policy options, providing technical support to countries and monitoring and assessing health trends. (WHO n.d.)

The hegemony of the WHO when it comes to matters of health means that local ways of understanding the issues of health, disability and ageing, when they are contrary to biomedical views, cannot compete on the world stage. Around the world, people are being encouraged to look to westernized versions of health care as the route towards good health (for a discussion of differing cultural conceptions of health and illness, see Corin, 1994). Similarly, as anthropological work shows, the WHO's interest in defining disability means that local knowledges and practices are increasingly eclipsed (see Ingstad and Whyte, 2007). Even the ageing process is coming to be seen in similar ways around the world, thanks to the export of westernized ideas (for a discussion of beliefs about ageing in India, see Cohen, 2000; for an international discussion of the western version of ageing as encompassing only decline and loss, see Graham and Stephenson, 2010).

A second consideration is that globalization means not only the spread and increasing reach of ideologies such as reverence for capitalism and values that support a capitalist economy, it also means that diseases can easily and quickly spread around the world. The ubiquitousness of air travel means that once a disease appears in one location, it is highly likely to appear far away a short time later. You may recall the SARS epidemic from early 2003. This deadly respiratory illness seems to have originated in China, but despite the containment efforts of health officials worldwide, SARS quickly spread to other countries (see Lau et al., 2010). Also consider the spread of HIV/AIDS around the world, due in large part to international travel (see Bastos, 1999 for a discussion of worldwide responses to HIV/AIDS). The same argument could be made about the H1N1 flu epidemic of 2009. Then there is the threat of contracting the potentially deadly West Nile Virus from a mosquito bite–this virus was first identified as such in the West Nile area of Africa and has since spread worldwide. The list of infectious diseases could go on and on. The point is, it is difficult if not impossible to stop the spread of infectious diseases, so that even if you live in a wealthy country in the industrialized world, you are not necessarily protected. Moreover, it is becoming increasingly clear that scientific medicine is not the answer to infectious disease. Rather, we need to address the social determinants of health, and this is precisely what biomedicine is not good at doing (for a discussion of this point, see Usdin, 2007).

Considerations such as these will, one hopes, lead you to critically question and investigate the efficacy of scientific medicine and the medical model for solving global problems related to the disparate issues of health, disability, and ageing. This chapter has argued that health, disability, and ageing are huge topics that ought not be constructed as inter-related. Now it is up to you to do your own research to decide these matters for yourself.

REFERENCES

Abberley, P. (1987). "The Concept of Oppression and the Development of a Social Theory of Disability." *Disability, Handicap and Society* 2:5-20.

Armstrong, P., and H. Armstrong. (2008). *About Canada: Health Care.* Halifax: Fernwood.

Bastos, Cristiana. (1999). *Global Responses to AIDS: Science in Emergency.* Bloomington, IN: Indiana University Press.

Butler, I. (1993). "Premature Adoption and Routinization of Medical Technology: Illustrations from Childbirth Technology." *Journal of Social Issues* 49(2):11-34.

Carey, I.M., S. De Wilde, T. Harris, C. Victor, N. Richards, S.R. Hilton, and D.G. Cook. (2008). "What Factors Predict Potentially Inappropriate Primary Care Prescribing in Older People?" *Drugs and Aging* 25(8):693-706.

Cole, T.R. (1994). *The Journey of Life: A Cultural History of Ageing in America.* Cambridge: Cambridge University Press.

Cohen, L. (2000). *No Ageing in India: Alzheimer's, The Bad Family, and Other Modern Things.* CA: University of California Press.

Corin, E. (1994). "The Social and Cultural Matrix of Health and Disease." In R.G. Evans, R.G. Morris, L. Barer and T.R. Marm(eds.), *Why Are Some People Healthy and Others Not? The Determinants of Health of Populations.* NY: Aldine de Gruyter.

Crooks, V.A., and G.J. Andrews. (2009). "Thinking Geographically about Primary Health Care." In V.A. Crooks and G.J. Andrews (eds.), *Primary Health Care: People, Practice.* Vermont: Ashgate Publishers.

Crooks, V.A., S.D. Stone, and M. Owen. (2009). "Multiple Sclerosis and Academic Work: Socio-Spatial Strategies Adopted to Maintain Employment." *Journal of Occupational Science* 16(1):25-31.

Davis, LJ. (1997). "Constructing Normalcy: The Bell Curve, the Novel, and the Invention of the Disabled Body in the Nineteenth Century." In Lennard J. Davis (ed.), *The Disability Studies Reader.* NY: Routledge.

Dickinson, H.D., and B.S. Bolaria. (2002). "The Canadian Health Care System: Evolution and Current Status." In B.S. Bolaria and H.D. Dickinson (eds.), *Health, Illness, and Health Care in Canada*, 3rd ed. Scarborough: Nelson Canada.

Dreidger, D., and M. Owen (eds.). (2008). *Dissonant Disabilities.* Toronto: Canadian Scholars' Press.

Dubos, R. (1959). *The Mirage of Health.* NY: Doubleday.

Evans, R.G., and G.L. Stoddart. (1994). "Producing Health, Consuming HealthCare." In R.G. Evans, R.G. Morris, L. Barer and T.R. Marm(eds.), *Why Are Some People Healthy and Others Not? The Determinants of Health of Populations.* NY: Aldine de Gruyter.

Foucault, M. (1973). *The Birth of the Clinic: An Archaeology of Medical Perception.* NY: Tavistock.

Gee, E. 2002. "Misconceptions and Misapprehensions about Population Ageing." *International Journal of Epidemiology* 31:750-753.

Graham, J.E., and P.H. Stephenson (eds.). (2010). *Contesting Aging & Loss.* Toronto: University of Toronto Press.

Hazan, H. (1994). *Old Age: Constructions and Deconstructions.* NY: Cambridge University Press.

Hewa, S. (2002). "Physicians, the Medical Profession, and Medical Practice." In B.S. Bolaria and H.D. Dickinson (eds.), *Health, Illness, and Health Care in Canada*, 3rd ed. Scarborough: Nelson Canada.

Illich, Ivan. (1976). *Medical Nemesis: The Expropriation of Health.* NY: Random House.

_____. (2003). "Medical Nemesis." *Journal of Epidemiology and Community Health* 57:919–922.

Ingstad, B., and S.R. Whyte (eds.). (2007). *Disability in Local and Global Worlds.* CA: University of California Press.

James, J.J. (1979). "Impacts of the Medical Malpractice Slowdown In Los Angeles County: January 1976." *American Journal of Public Health* 69(5):437-443.

Katz, S. (1996). *Disciplining Old Age: The Formation of Gerontological Knowledge.* VA: University Press of Virginia.

Kaufman, S. (1986). *The Ageless Self: Sources of Meaning in Late Life.* WI: University of Wisconsin Press.

Lau, E.H.Y., C.A. Hsiung, B.J. Cowling, C-H. Chen, L-M. Ho, T. Tsang, C-W. Chang, C.A. Donnelly, and G.M. Leung. (2010). "A Comparative Epidemiologic Analysis of SARS in Hong Kong, Beijing and Taiwan." *BMC Infectious Diseases* 10: 50. Available at: http://www.biomedcentral.com/1471-2334/10/50.

Leape, L.L. (2000). "Institute of Medicine Medical Error Figures are not Exaggerated." *Journal of the American Medical Association* 284(July 26):95-97.

Lexchin, Joel. (2006). "Pharmaceutical Policy: The Dance between Industry, Government, and the Medical Profession." In D. Raphael, T. Bryant, and M. Rioux (eds.), *Staying Alive: Critical Perspectives on Health, Illness, and Health Care.* Toronto: Canadian Scholars Press.

Lupton, D. (2003). *Medicine as Culture*, 2nd ed. London: Sage Publications.

McKinlay, J.B., and S.M. McKinlay. (1981). "From Promising Report to Standard Procedure: Seven Stages in the Career of a Medical Innovation." *Milbank Memorial Fund Quarterly* 59:374-411.

Meslin, E.M. (1987). "The Moral Costs of the Ontario Physicians' Strike." *The Hastings Center Report* 17(4):11-14.

Moss, P., and K. Teghtsoonian (eds.). (2008). *Contesting Illness: Processes and Practices.* Toronto: University of Toronto Press.

Oliver, M. (2009). "The Social Model in Context." In T. Titchkosky and R. Michalko (eds.), *Rethinking Normalcy: A Disability Studies Reader.* Toronto: Canadian Scholars' Press Inc.

Parsons, T. (1951). *The Social System.* NY: The Free Press.

Pong, R.W., and R. Pitblado. (2005). *Geographic Distribution of Physicians in Canada: Beyond How Many and Where.* Ottawa: Canadian Institute for Health Information.

Raphael, D. (2009). *The Social Determinants of Health,* 2nd ed. Toronto: Canadian Scholar's Press.

Smith, D. (2000). *Consulted to Death: How Canada's Workplace Health and Safety System Fails Workers.* Winnipeg: Arbeiter Ring Press.

Starfield, B. (2000). "Is US health care Really the Best in the World?" *Journal of the American Medical Association* 284(July 26):483-485.

Statistics Canada. (2009). CANSIM, Table 051-0001.Available online at http://www40.statcan.gc.ca/l01/cst01/demo10a-eng.htm.

Stone, S.D. (2005). "Reactions to Invisible Disability: The Experiences of Young Women Survivors of Hemorrhagic Stroke." *Disability and Rehabilitation* 27(6):293-304.

_____. (2003). "Disability, Dependence and Old Age: Problematic Constructions." *Canadian Journal on Aging* 22(1):59-67.

_____. (1995). "The Myth of Bodily Perfection." *Disability and Society* 10(4):413-424.

_____. (1993). "Must Disability Always Be Visible?" *Canadian Woman Studies* 13(4):11-13.

Stone, S.D., M.E. Hill, K. Kawchuk, E. Lefrancois, K. Maki, S. Mantis, and B. Pilato. (2002). *Connecting for Change: Injured Workers in* Northwestern Ontario *and The Effectiveness of Peer Support.* Final report to the Workplace Safety and Insurance Board (Ontario).

Thomas, C. (2007). *Sociologies of Disability and Illness: Contested Ideas in Disability Studies and Medical Sociology.* Basingstoke: Palgrave Macmillan.

Usdin, S. (2007). *The No-Nonsense Guide to World Health.* Toronto: Between the Lines.

Vickers, M.H. (2001). *Work and Unseen Chronic Illness: Silent Voices.* NY: Routledge.

Vroman, K., R. Warner, and K. Chamberlain. (2009). "Now Let Me Tell You in my own Words: Narratives of Acute and Chronic Low Back Pain," *Disability & Rehabilitation* 31(12):976-987.

WHO [World Health Organization]. No date. "About WHO." Available online at http://www.who.int/about/en/.

_____. (1986). *Ottawa Charter for Health Promotion.* Geneva: WHO. Available online at www.who.dk/policy/ottawa.htm.

PART II

Group Interactions

In the second section, we examine the dynamics of Canadian group life beginning with the family. The overarching theme of this section is that individuals are linked beyond the family to an increasingly complex global community through group life in various institutional frameworks.

Chapter 6 by McCauley on **families** explores the relationship between family definitions and theories to social change. It argues that these definitions of family need revision to suit a global context.

Chapter 7 by David Nock on **religion** examines the changing face of religious affliation in Canada. He shows that religious affliations and practices are affected by "new source immigration" and a secularized Canadian culture. His findings indicate that among the more established Canadians, the "Nones" have grown as the most significant religious category.

Chapter 8 by Amal Madibbo on **racial and ethnic communities** deals with ethnic identity with the Francophone diasopora in Alberta and Ontario. The author shows how the groups have empowered themselves within the larger Canadian society.

Lastly, Chapter 9 by Colaguori and Jacobs on **bureaucracy** shows how group life is affected by bureaucracy and red tape in a complex social structure. The National Hockey League is then provided as an important example of bureaucracy and Weber's formal rationality.

In sum, the chapters in Section II introduce students to Canada in an institutional framework, which is influenced by the forces of globalization.

Chapter 6

Families

Family Definitions and Theories: Towards A Canadian Global Agenda

Timothy P. McCauley

York University

INTRODUCTION

The purpose of this chapter is to introduce students to the nature and variety of definitions that direct the sociological study of the Canadian family in the second decade of the new millennium. For over two centuries, sociologists have developed definitions and utilized a variety of theoretical perspectives to study family life in social contexts such as Canada. Definitions and theories direct current research as well as provide a foundation for assisting future scholars to understand the perseverance of the family as a collective ideal.

The central argument of this chapter is that definitions and theories of the family have been products of the level of social change in the societies from where sociological research derives. Studies of the family reflect key stages in Western history including colonialism, urbanism, Fordism and feminism. Each of these stages has played a significant role in how sociologists define and conceptualize family. Moreover, as Canadian society moves towards a global context, more dynamic definitions of family are required to understand the role of family in a society that is always changing. This chapter seeks to generate a definition of family that explains how it continues to have meaning for individuals in spite of social change and globalization.

EVOLUTIONARY THEORIES OF THE FAMILY

The earliest sociologists to study "the family" were highly influenced by the colonial economic patterns of the nineteenth century. The colonial attitude was by and large ethnocentric and Euro-centric. To theorize about the institution of family, scholars in universities such as Oxford, Cambridge, Paris and Berlin often relied upon "accounts" of sojourners who traded back and forth with the mother countries of Europe. Scholarship at the time was often limited to aristocrats and eccentric intellectuals who often isolated themselves within elitist university settings. It was in these surroundings that they tended to generate ethnocentric and grand narratives of family and cultural patterns. To construct their accounts, they relied heavily upon Charles Darwin's works including: *Origins of the Species* (1859) and the *Decent of Man* (1871). Darwin showed how human evolution is tied to natural selection and a struggle for survival of the fittest. Scholars of the family, in turn, wove Social Darwinism into their analyses of family patterns across the globe.

Three of the most noteworthy scholars of family patterns during this stage included Johanne Brachofen (1862), Lewis Morgan (1871) and Edward Westermarck (1925). Brachofen, for example, developed a uni-linear theory of family history in his text entitled, *The Mother Right* (1862). Within the *Mother Right*, he depicted the history of family as a three stage progression from sexual promiscuity, to gynaecocracy, and finally to patriarchy. Brachofen theorized that the stages in family history represented a movement toward more civilized human behaviour. As such, he regarded the Victorian patriarchial family form as the most ideal family form, and a progression away from the barbarism that he believed was pervasive in the colonies. A similar analysis of family development was found in the work of Lewis Morgan in his text entitled, *Systems of Consangunity and Affinity of the Human Family* (1871). Like Brochofen, Morgan offered a three-stage conception of history characterized as Savagery, Barbarism and Civilization. He demonstrated how human societies evolved towards civilization and decency as evidenced by Victorian monogamy. In particular, his work emphasized the fact the woman's sexuality must be controlled in civilized society to ensure consanguinity or ties by blood. Lastly, Edward Westermarck (1925) offered a bridge between evolutionary theory and structural functionalism by suggesting that many primitive societies were not necessarily promiscuous, rather they had some family patterns reflective of a modern society. Nevertheless, even Westermarck maintained that European and English cultures demonstrate higher morality and development.

It is important for Canadian sociology to reflect upon the early evolutionary scholarship into family life and social development. An examination of these early works supports the ideas of Canadian postmodernists who maintain that early theories of the human family were grand narratives lacking in historical specificity and context (Baudrillard, 1987). And while the evolutionists did demonstrate that family is a collective ideal and at the root all human societies across the globe, their research was macro-structural and lacking in historical detail. For instance, all the scholars above seem to have influenced Durkheim and his notion that collective patterns (i.e., family) occurs *sui generi* and are at the heart of human society.

A specific evolutionary scholar worth mentioning who focused directly upon the importance of family in Victorian England was Lord Schaftbury. Shaftbury held that

> there can be no security to society, no honour, no prosperity, no dignity at home, no nobleness of attitude towards foreign nations, unless the strength of people rests upon the purity and firmness of domestic system. Schools are but axillaries. At home the principles of subordination are planted and the man is trained to be a good citizen. (Wohl, 1978:9)

Shaftbury was convinced that Victorian society at large could only be sustained through patriarchal family and the subordination of women and children. Clearly then, theories, concepts and definitions of family developed from evolutionary family theorists were broad meta-narratives showing a uni-linear path of family development towards patriarchy, monogamy and morality.

FAMILY, SOCIAL REFORM AND THE CHICAGO SCHOOL

The next group of scholars to impact on the study of family were the Chicago School symbolic interactionists of the 1920s and 1930s. It is important to note that although Canadian urbanization occurred later than in the United States or Europe, the studies of symbolic interactionists found their way into Canadian social research largely from the Chicago School. Unlike the broad linear theories of the evolutionary theorists, the symbolic interactionists were responding to key factors in social change in Europe and North America through the late nineteenth and early twentieth century, namely, industrialization and urbanization. Urbanism represented the mass movement of families from the feudal countryside into cites characterized by over-crowding, competition and crime (Wirth, 1938). At the turn of twentieth century, families in American cities such as Chicago were without progressive social legislation such as The New Deal - Baby Bonus, Welfare and Unemployment Insurance. Consequently, the Chicago School's focus was upon real families struggling within cities with overcrowded accommodations, pollution and crime. The University of Chicago generated scholarship concerned with social reform and the day-to-day lives of families in the often chaotic, social order of the early twentieth century. The most noteworthy sociologists of the Chicago School included Robert Park (1928), Ernest Burgess (1925), C.H. Cooley (1928), and G.H. Mead (1934). Each of these influential sociologists believed that social life should be observed through "interpretative sociology" of natural ecological communities. For example, Robert Park maintained that community itself is a major factor influencing human behavior in the way that the city functions as a microcosm. He argued that

> [i]n these great cities, where all the passions, all the energies of mankind are released, we are in a position to investigate 'the process of civilization', as it were, under a microscope. (1928:890)

The Chicago School applied sociological research to families that reflected Max Weber's interpretative approach to sociology, particularly Weber's notion of vershetein. Vershestein was an interpretive approach emphasizing "empathetic understanding" to study social life in cities such as Chicago, where the population grew in exponential leaps at the turn of the twentieth century. The Chicago school approach was often referred to as an ecological approach insofar as

> [i]t seeks to unify intelligent thought and *logical method with practical actions* and appeals to experience. (p. 227)

The influence of the Chicago School upon contemporary Canadian family sociology cannot be underemphasized. The Chicago School represented an important transition in research from observing macro-institution changes in family history–"institutional approach," towards viewing "family as a social group" with unique dynamics and interpersonal characteristics and interaction. Ernest Burgess, for example, defined family as simply "a unity of interacting personalities" (Burgess, 1926:109). For Burgess, every family exists within a social context (i.e., neighbourhood, social class, and ethnicity composition). Burgess's, thinking then assisted Canadian sociologist Horace Miner to study French Canadian family functions from participant observation studies of their "daily round" (Miner, 1939). The micro study of the "family as a group" gained predominance across North America, particularly during the Great Depression.

Many other sociologists from United States and Canada adopted the Chicago style of sociology through the mid-twentieth century including Lloyd Warner (USA), Horace Miner (Canada and USA), Everette Hughes (Canada) and K. Ishwaran (Canada). Warner, for example, studied families in his series of studies known as *Yankee City* (1935). In these works, he observed families in terms of internal power dynamics, kitchen table conversations, division of family tasks, and child rewards and punishment. Then, using Warner's approach, Everette Hughes in his *French Canada in Transition* (1943) showed how French Canadian families adapted to industrialization during the War Years within the transitional Parish Town of Cantonville, Québec. Lastly, another study by K. Ishwaran in the 1960s and 1970s, used emphathetic understanding to demonstrate how the Calvinist religious values help to construct the Holland Marsh north of the city of Toronto (Ishwaran, 1977). Ishwaran noted that his methodology included "a genesis of involvement" (1977:2). In other words, the research done in the Chicago style in Canada and the United States examined families, not as institutions adapting over large periods of time, but rather as groups situated within social contexts where the sociologist could appreciate and understand individuals on the level of the families themselves. Thus, the Chicago style withholds value judgements of human participants while at the same time strives for objectivity in social research. Clearly, their emphasis reflects the Weberian notion of vershestein or "emphathetic understanding"–a distinctively qualitative, sociological approach.

FAMILY AND FORDISM: THE FACTORY MODEL

The next phase in defining and theorizing about families came about as a result of Fordism. Henry Ford's assembly line in 1910 revolutionized the relationship between work and family. Ford rationalized North American production and consumption patterns not only in the workplace but also in the realm of family life. The notion of the public sphere as a "man's world" and the private home as the domain of women was the norm of middle-class families during this time. Traditional notions of family inspired by the "factory model" included the "cult of domesticity" or the "cult of true womanhood"–a movement of white middle-class women who argued that the traditional family is the best place to rear children. However, the cult of domesticity, a prevailing view among upper and middle class white women during the late nineteenth century, was in fact a tool of capitalistic ideology. Thus, according to Barbara Welter (1966), an unintended consequence of this ideology was its support for capitalism and patriarchy through presumption of women's invisible labour inside the home. The cult of domesticity was a cult of "true womanhood" in which women needed to be pious, pure, submissive and domestic in order to generate families that were "havens in a heartless world" (Welter, 1966:151-174). Fordism, in other words, helped to solidify the split between the male sphere of work in the public realm and the female sphere in the private realm. Men in the age of Fordism were expected to earn the "family wage" in exchange for woman's care of children.

Moreover, emergent definitions and theories of family during the time of Fordism highly regarded "privatized nuclear family" as key to functional, industrial society. One major theorist who unintentionally lent support to this notion emerged from the discipline of anthropology. George P. Murdock (1949) studied 250 different societies and found that although there may be variations in the nuclear form, the two parent family was indeed the "nucleous" of the atom. The heart of all human societies.
Murdock defined family as

> a **social group** characterized by common residence, economic cooperation, and reproduction. It includes adults of both sexes, at least two of whom maintain a socially approved sexual relationship, and one or more children, own or adopted, of the sexually cohabiting adults. (1949:2)

In turn, Murdock's definition supported his anthropological predecessor, Bronislaw Malinowski, who in 1913 stated that the nuclear family "must be universal" since it filled a basic biological need—caring for and protecting infants and young children (Malinowshi, 1913:11).

In addition, Murdock's definition seemed to be reflected in the work of Talcot Parsons who refined

Durkheimian structural functionalism during the mid-twentieth century. Parsons' investigation of family, found proof of an "isolated nuclear family" (Parsons and Bales, 1955). For Parsons, the smallest and most functional family structure in an industrial society was the "nuclear form"–consisting of mother, father and their children. And the nuclear family was made functional by its "role complimentarity"; its clear definition of complimentary roles. And, although Parsons did not directly assign gender to these roles, he implicitly assumed that males should perform the "instrumental role" outside the family setting, while women should assume the "expressive role" inside the home. In Parsonian family analysis, men were "the producers" in the public realm and women were caregivers and "the nurturers" in the domestic sphere. The nuclear family was the ideal family type" insofar as it served the needs of industrial societies and it functioned best in isolation. An isolated nuclear family exists independently of the kin network, and it is free to move as the economy demands. Furthermore, the intimate nuclear family can specialize in stabilizing adult personalities in a "competitive, impersonal and heartless world" (Lashe, 1988).

Three examples of functionalist research in the early 1960s "the height of Fordism," included Blood and Wolf (1960), Goode (1963) and Litwak (1960). Blood and Wolf, for example, refined the "resources theory of power" (1960) within the family, which showed how power is operationalized in nuclear family settings. They hypothesized that family power may be determined by observing how the family deals with important life changes such as buying a home, buying a car, or decisions on moving the family. They found the males, therefore, held more family power since men generally have more "resources." Thus, unintentionally it seemed that Blood and Wolfe's resources theory advocated in favour of the instrumental and expressive roles in the family. Thus, it is clear to see how theory was highly criticized by feminist scholars of the emerging Second Wave.

Another Fordist study of family was Litwak's (1960, 1965) critique of the Parsonian notion of the isolated nuclear family. Litwak found that it was incorrect to assume that as families move from the countryside to the city, they maintained themselves in isolation. In fact, Litwak found that families tended to gravitate to their own extended relatives in urban contexts. From this observation, Litwak defined the term "modified extended" family:

> The modified extended family structure...consists of a coalition of nuclear families in a state of partial dependence. Such partial dependence means that nuclear family members exchange significant services with each other, thus differing from the isolated nuclear families as well as retain considerable autonomy, (that is, not bound economically or geographically), therefore differing from the classical extended family. (Litwak, 1965:291)

Thus, Litwak's notion of modified extended family was an improvement upon Parsonian functionalism in that it reflected the reality of many ethnic families in Canadian cities, such as the Italians, Jews and Chinese. These ethnic groups historically lived near relatives in the same neighbourhoods. They interacted for purposes such as cordial relations, work and income. For example, Bossaivain (1970) studied the Italians in Montreal by operationalizing Litwak's notion of the modified extended family.

Another illustrative example of family theory to emerge from Parsonian functionalism was W. Goode's (1963) study of families across the globe. Goode developed the approach known as convergence theory. His argument was that all families in many global contexts were converging on the Western model in matters such as family power, mate selection and kinship. For Goode, modernization was a uniform process and that all societies sooner or later, would move toward conjugal–as opposed to consanguinous–family relations. For as societies modernize, family relations become more liberal, rational and less traditional.

In summary, it is clear that the Parsonian notion of the isolated nuclear family, provided a basis for many more functionalist studies of family in the 1940s, 50s and 60s. Functionalism validated Fordism–the factory model that viewed family as a system functional to industrial society. Families often moved to the suburbs to live out this industrial American and Canadian dream.

Two prominent Canadian sociologists who advocated functionalism include S.D. Clark and K. Ishwaran. Clark's focus was uniquely Canadian in that he saw interconnection between economics, history, family and community. His theory supported the notion that family was one of the most basic social institutions of Canadian society. Next, K. Ishwaran's research in 1970s and 1980s focused upon the issue of families in Canada versus the Canadian family (Ishwaran, 1971). In 1983, he provided a precise definition of family that raised concern for Canadian feminists at York University:

> Family is a group defined by a sex relationship, involving members of the opposite sex, sufficiently precise and enduring, to provide for procreation and upbringing. (York Seminar, 1983)

In Ishwaran's view, family was a precise institution as well as a vital social group for the functioning of societies such as Canada. Moreover, G.N. Ramu classified the research above as "standard family theory" (1989:20). He noted that the problem with standard family theory was that other alternative family forms in Canada were viewed as ignored or viewed as deviant and dysfunctional. These definitions excluded family forms such as same-sex families, single parent families and childless families (Veevers, 1975). Thus, by the late 1960s, the social and political implications of functionalism became clearly apparent and outdated and thus a new stage in family studies emerged in the West known as "second wave feminism." The second wave of feminism was borne from the dissatisfaction with the proto-typical nuclear family reality, and it was indeed the invention of the birth control pill that helped to liberate women's thinking about reproduction and production.

FEMINISM AND FAMILY DEFINITIONS

The feminist movement has produced three clearly defined "waves" to date and each has contributed to our understanding of family power and gender relations in familial settings. The first wave began in the late nineteenth century, characterized by the Suffragettes. The Suffragettes were a movement of women committed to having women accepted as equal human beings in society with voting rights. The first wave suffragettes drew their strength from the first feminist, Mary Wollenstonecraft, the earliest feminist known for the *Vindication of the Rights of Women* in 1792. Next, the second wave of feminism began in the 1960s; and the third wave in the 1990s is generally considered as an extension of the second wave. Second and third wave feminism were both reactions to Parsonian functionalism and while the second wave focused on women's oppression in general, the third wave sought the inclusion of oppressed women from all racial and class backgrounds. Finch (1989), for example, maintains that Parsonian functionalism serves as a backdrop to this feminist research in that Parsons was a white middle-class scholar whom "feminists loved to hate" (p.12).

To date, the second wave of feminism is more sophisticated than the first wave in that it involves both feminist political action combined with feminist scholarship. For example, it is theoretically divided into five branches including Marxist/Socialist, Liberal, Radical, Post modernist and Anti Racist. All of the Branches above view the family as a social construction not a monolithic, unchangeable, reality. First, an excellent example of a Marxist/Feminist text is Barret and MacIntosh's work entitled, *The Anti Social Family* (1982). Their book is a re-orientation of the debate on the nature of the family in contexts such Canada and the United States. To Barret and MacIntosh, the family is a construction of the owners of the means of production who are predominantly men. Capitalism functions with an ideology of familialism that promotes the nuclear family as an ideal. Capitalism entrenches patriarchal relations between men and women and it limit's women's capacity for labour in the public realm. Women, who are single, divorced or who live alternative arrangements must deal with an ideology of familialism in office settings. For example, even if a woman were to "make it to the boardroom," she would likely be the one who gets coffee. The system according to Barret and MacIntosh rejects alternative lifestyles. Consequently, the only solution to women's oppression must be the radical transformation of the state in capitalistic society. Thus their vision of transformed society mirrors Fredrick Engels' concept in his famous essay, "Family, Private Property and the State" where he wrote:

> Along with [the classes] the state will inevitably fall. Society, which will re-organise production on the basis of a free and equal association of the producers, will put the whole machinery of state where it will then belongs: into the museum of antiquity, by the side of the spinning-wheel and the bronze axe. (1884:110)

Clearly, Barrett and MacIntosh were inspired by Engels' notion of the family and the state. The state and the family to these feminist scholars is anti-social.

Next, an example of a liberal feminist is Margarit Eichler who coined the concept of monolithic bias. Eichler is a "liberal" who does not believe capitalism will be transformed in the interest of women and the proletariat. Rather, Eichler accepts capitalistic society in her text entitled, *Families in Canada Today* (1989). In this text, she seeks only to improve women's reality by generating grounded analysis of family diversity and change. Eichler basic thesis is that traditional studies of family such as the work of Parsons, reflects, "monolithic, sexist, conservative and micro-structural thinking" (Eichler, 1989:12). Structural functionalists, she argues, fail to recognize the ideological nature of their writing. The functionalist develops an "is" orientation instead of an "ought" and they rarely question the status quo. Eichler, therefore, develops a definition of family classifying its spheres of influence. She asks us to consider when defining family: Who is included and who is not? Which type of family benefits from the state? Which families are left behind? She is, therefore, a liberal feminist who supports incremental, piecemeal changes in legislation to reflect the diversity and variety of families today.

The third branch of feminism deemed "radical" is an approach that emerged from the colleges and universities of the 1960s; a period of upheaval created by the Vietnam War and the Civil Rights Movement. Feminists such as Keller (1971) and O'Brian (1981) reflect this "radical orientation." Keller (1971) wrote an essay in 1971 entitled, "Does the Family Have a Future?" Her answer to that basic question was that family *does not have a future* since mankind has reached a point in time when babies can be born in test-tubes and raised in public institutions. O'Brian, on the other hand, talked about family power in terms of the "alienation of the male seed" (O Brian, 1981). Her key finding was that family *does not* have a future since women and men are vastly different in their nature. Destroying the family, she maintains, would liberate women from an oppressive society.

Fourth, an example of post modern feminist is Jane Flax's book, *Thinking in Fragments* (1981). This text is clearly post-modernist in orientation insofar as it seeks to deconstruct basic family typifications such as "nuclear," "extended" and "modified extended." Flax views families as fragmented and rich in diversity, plurality and chaos. Flax points to the limitations of traditional family concepts and she believes family scholars should re-think their "grand narratives" and think in fragments.

Finally, the fifth and most recent branch of feminism, is the anti-racist approach. Anti-racist feminism combines the variables, race, class and gender when developing their rich, multivariate sociological analyses. The anti-racist approach is both novel and reactionary. Anti-racist ideas began in the early days of the second wave of feminism when some scholars saw the need for feminist studies that were more contextual and group specific. Theorists such as Dorothy K. Smith realized that feminism was largely dominated in the late 1960s by white middle-class women who were financially able to attend universities and colleges in Canada and the United States. Anti-racist feminists, therefore, adopted a multivariate approach. By combining the variables, race, class and gender, they were able to illustrate equity issues in family power, authority and minority relations.

One of the earliest second wave feminists who adopted an anti-racist slant was Carol Stack. Stack's text, appropriately entitled, *All Our Kin Strategies for Survival in Black* (1974), studied poor Black families in the Southern United States. Through her research, Stack came away with an inclusive definition of family. She holds that family may be defined as

> the smallest, organized durable network of kin and non-kin who interact daily, providing domestic needs of children and assuring survival. (1974:111)

The definition above demonstrates that among Blacks of the Old South, family was a unique structure. Black families emerged in many oppressive contexts such as the Reconstruction Stage following the Civil War. Often the men would leave their biological families in search of employment, while other men might come along to join particular families. In this sense, the Black family was "inclusive and situational." Black families would adopt lone children and would include outside individuals into the family mix. It is interesting to note that even today, Black families have higher rates of adoption compared to White and Hispanic communities (Tipton, 2005). Clearly, Stack's work helped to develop the anti-racist feminist approach to the study of the family. Anti-racist feminism is an inclusive perspective. It seeks to uncover the realities of family life among minority groups as they struggle with capitalism and social inequality.

Some interesting texts from Canada that reflect the anti-racist branch of feminism include Henry and Tatem (1994) and Das Gupta (2007). These texts show that the feminist orientation is not monolithic and, in fact, there are an abundant variety of feminists in Europe, United States and Canada that attempt to develop a historically detailed and situational understanding of the variety and diversity of family forms today. Canadian examples of anti-racist feminism can be understood through gleaning texts such as Nancy Mandel and Duffy. Mandel and Duffy's first edited text was entitled, *Reconstructing the Canadian Family* (1988) and it was later complimented and enhanced with *Canadian Families: Diversity, Conflict and Change* (2004). Both texts are rich in their analyses of women's realities with family in the latter stages of the twentieth century. They both adopt a Socialist/Marxist feminist approach combined with some anti-racist feminist analyses.

In summary, the feminist perspective on the family has moved the discussion into the twenty-first century. As a result of their work, students of sociology can ponder how to correctly define family in a rapidly changing society. Is family about blood ties, gender roles, ethnicity, religion, emotions or power? The issues of family are highly political as society continues to grow on global dimensions.

FAMILY: A NEW DEFINITION IN A GLOBAL CONTEXT

Given the abundant variety of definitions of family to date and to define family in a global context, sociologists may be well served by returning to August Comte who believed that sociology may be called social physics. In Comte's *Early Essays* he suggested that, "scientists could direct society–from biology to social system–since there are many laws to be discovered by scientists that may be used for social betterment" (Comte, 1877:10). Thus, with Comte's basic premise in mind we borrow from natural science and consider

Einstein's theory of relativity from the discipline of physics and his equation, $E=MC^2$ combined with the concept of symbiosis from botany. Could it be that E equals Family Energy, which is equivalent to a mass of individuals symbiotically connected and moving at the speed of light–a unit of measurement related to time, space and motion.

We seek a definition of the family that applies within countries of both the First and Third World in this age of globalization characterized by universalism, imperialism and capitalism. In spite of the existing perspectives and previous definitions of family, it is clear that they are each lacking in some respect in understanding the totality of human families in and across societies and social contexts. Thus, below we consider that family is at the heart of human society while it is also a domain of issues regarding power and social interaction. Therefore, our definition of family is as follows:

> Family is a unit of energy that equals a mass of individuals symbiotically linked in time, space and motion.

As a result of globalization, families in Canada are no longer limited to one space; as Burgess suggested, in his notion that families are a "unity of interacting personalities." Family is also more than simply a "gendered institution" as feminists contend. And the family is more than the unequal roles, instrumental and expressive, found in Parsonian theory. Family is a dynamic unit in time, space and motion and all of these components make-up who one considers a global definition of family.

First, families are about **TIME.** New family members born through reproduction and newborns make us think about past generations of our family. We say things such as "the baby looks like Aunt Mary or Uncle Fred" and we register our children with the state at birth with our family name. Thus, families today are at least "three generational" even though they live apart. TIME holds children, parents, and grandparents together. And one only needs to check internet hits on genealogy to know that human identity is formed and solidified by knowing families past, present and future. Second, families are also about **SPACE** and spatial issues. Although family members may live across the globe from one and another, they continue kinship ties through technology and communication. Notice how long distance rate charges and postage have become increasingly a part of everyday Canadian culture. Third, families are also about **MOTION** either positive or negative. Positive motion occurs in families when family members assist one and another in growth and development. While negative motion is caused by disorders in the family such as alcoholism and drug abuse. It is found, for example, that alcohol is a disorder of the past whereas stimulants create disorders of understanding future motion (Bennet et al., 1987).

The key term in our definition of family above, therefore, is symbiosis from natural science. Symbiosis is a concept developed from the Swiss botanist, Simon Schwendener. Botany studies the relationship of flowers and plants. In simple terms, symbiosis reflects the dynamic of the pine tree and moss. Thus, "as the moss is to the pine," human family members are a unity of individual characters symbiotically linked in TIME, SPACE AND MOTION. Regardless of micro-physical, physical and meta-physical dimensions of self, human collectivistic needs are provided by the family, no matter how complex, differentiated and individualistic society becomes. As Durkheim has shown,

> the species that the designates the clan collectively is called its totem. The totem of the clan is also that of each of its members. (2006:254)

In this age of global connectedness we struggle with our identity in a global context. Canadian students studying the family might be well advised to remember that under conditions of mechanical solidarity, there is no need to reflect upon the tribe as against other tribes. It is a given. Primitive man only needs to look upon the totem for a sense of identity and belonging to the family and the group. Ken Morrison states in his analysis of Durkheim that

> think of **the clan** as a large family unit; members of the clan are united by bonds of kinship and such mutual duties as mourning of the dead, taking revenge on their enemies, and not marrying fellow members of the clan. Moreover, the clan is united by beliefs and practices that centre on the clan's totem–a sacred object or creator that serves as the collective emblem of the group. (2006:258)

In conclusion, definitions of family and their theoretical perspectives have undergone vast changes over the past three centuries. Research moves from macro-institutional approaches to more dynamic and contextual frames. The work of the early evolutionists helped to recognize the importance of families across societies. The interactionists and functionalists of the early to mid-twentieth century focused our attention on family structures, power and interaction in various contexts. Next, the feminists of the 1960s showed how family is a gendered social institution designed for and by men, particularly capitalists. Lastly, the anti-racist approach shows how the study of the family can be multivariate and multi-situational and further definitions are needed. Thus, we argue here that to find new ways of studying families, sociologists should perhaps return to the roots of the discipline by adopting Comte's notion of social physics for it seems that as globalization intensifies, families are increasingly about TIME, SPACE AND MOTION in a global framework.

REFERENCES

Barrett M., and M. MacIntosh. (1982). *The Anti-Social Family.* London, Versa.

Bennet, L.A., D. Reiss, and S. Wolin. (1987). *The Alcoholic Family.* New York: Basic Books.

Best, S., and D. Kellner. (1998). "Exploring Modernity." In A.A. Berger (ed.), *The Postmodern Presence.* London: Sage.

Blood, R.O., and D.M. Wolfe. (1960). *Husbands and Wives: The Dynamics of Marital Living.* NY: The Free Press.

Boissevain, J. (1970). *The Italians of Montreal: Social Adjustment in a Pluralistic Society.* Ottawa: Queens Printer.

Clay, K., and J. Holah. (1999). "Fungal Endophyte Symbiosis and Plant Diversity in Successional Fields." *Science* 285(5434):1742-1744.

Comte, A. (1848). *A General View of Positivism.* London.

Darwin, C. (1871). *The Decent of Man.* London: John Murray Publishing.

_____. (1859). *Origin of the Species.* London: John Murray Publishing.

_____. (1859). "On the Origin of Species by Means of Natural Selection, or the Preservation of Favoured Races in the Struggle for Life."

Durkheim, E. (1893/1960). *The Division of Labour in Society.* Translated by G. Simpson. NY: The Free Press.

_____. (1912/1954). *The Elementary Forms of Religious Life.* Translated by J. Swain. NY: The Free Press.

Eichler, M. (1983). *Families in Canada Today: Recent Changes and their Policy Consequences.* Toronto: Gage Publishing.

Flax, J. (1990). *Thinking Fragments: Psychoanalysis, Feminism, and Postmodernism in the Contemporary West.* Berkeley: U California Press.

Henry, F., and C. Tator. (1996). *The Colour of Democracy.* Toronto: Nelson Thompson Learning.

Ishwaran, K. (1977). *Family, Kinship and Community: A Study of Dutch Canadians.* Toronto: McGraw Hill Ryerson.

Keller, S. (1974). "Does Family Have a Future?" In Rose Laub Coser (ed.), *The Family: Its Structure and Functions.* Stony Brook: Macmillan.

Lashe, C. (1977). *Haven in a Heartless World: The Family Besieged.* NY: Basic Books.

Litwak, E. (1960). "Geographic Mobility and Extended Family Cohesion." *American Sociological Review* 25(3):385-394.

Malinoski. B. (1915). *The Trobrian Islands.* London: Routledge and Kegan Paul.

Mandell, N., and A. Duffy. (1988). *Reconstructing the Canadian Family: Feminist Perspectives.* Toronto: Butterworths.

Mandell, N., and A. Duffy. (2000). *Canadian Families: Diversity, Conflict, and Change*, 2nd ed. Toronto: Harcourt Brace.

Morgan, L. (1871). *Systems of Consanguinity and Affinity of the Human Family.* Washington: Smithonian Institution.

Morrison, K. (2006). *Marx, Durkheim and Weber: Formations of Social Thought.* London: Sage Publishing.

O'Brian, M. (1981). *The Politics of Reproduction.* NY: Routledge and Kegan Paul.

Parsons T., and R.F. Bales. (1955). *Family Socialization and Interaction Process.* Glencoe Illinois: Free Press.

Ramu, G.N. (1979). *Courtship, Marriage, and the Family in Canada.* Toronto: Macmillan.

_____. (1989). *Marriage and Family in Canada Today.* Toronto: Prentice Hall.

Stack C. (1974). *All Our Kin: Strategies for Survival in a Black Community.* NY: Basic Books.

Tipton, S. (2005). *Family Transformed: Religion, Values and Family in American Life.* Georgetown: Georgetown University Press.

Welter, B. (1966) "The Cult of True Womanhood 1820-1860." *American Quarterly* 18(2): 151-174.

Wirth, Louis. (1938). "Urbanism as A Way of Life." *American Journal of Sociology* 44:1-24.

Wohl, A.S. (1978). *The Victorian Family: Structure and Stresses.* NY: Taylor and Francis.

Chapter 7

Religion

Religion's Changing face in a Multicultural Canada

David A. Nock

Lakehead University

CONTINUITIES AND DISCONTINUITIES IN CANADA'S RELIGIOUS PAST AND FUTURE

Quite often predictions are made on the basis of extending (or extrapolating) the trends of the present into the future. Generally speaking such predictions are based on the assumption that factors now taken for granted will continue into the future (extrapolation). If we assume that inflation will continue at or about the level it has recorded in recent years, then our retirement assumptions would be quite different than if we anticipated years such as the 1980s when inflation was up to ten times more than recent figures. Some forecasters reject predicting major changes out of distaste for speculations which seem "apocalyptic" and turn the future upside down from the present.

If one looks at data from the1961 census, the portrait of Canadian religion looked like this: Roman Catholics constituted about 47% of the population, 41.5% belonged to Mainline Protestants (defined as the Anglican, United, Lutheran and Presbyterian churches), 6.4% belonged to Conservative Protestant churches such as Baptists, Pentecostals and Salvation Army; Other Christian churches accounted for 2.2%; 1.5% belonged to Non-Christian World Religions, mainly but not entirely comprised of Jewish adherents, and a very few, 0.5% professed "no religion affiliation," also known as the "None" category (Bowen, 2004:24).

If one simply made forecasts on the basis of extrapolation forty years into the future, such predictions would have been in error. It is true that Roman Catholics had remained quite a strong presence in 2001 at 43.2% but Mainline Protestants had taken a severe decline to less than 20% (19.9), non-Christian World Religions had seen a noticeable rise to 6.4% and the None category had jumped from half of one percent to 16.5%. The category of Other Christian had taken a jump to 7.1%. This bare statistical summary may hide more than it reveals.

For Canada's first century from 1867 to the 1960s, religious ethos had been built on Roman Catholic and Protestant dominance, outside of Québec mainly the mainline Protestants previously indicated. Even the mainline Protestant level of 41.5% in 1961 had seen percentage declines from previous decades when mainline Protestants had comprised almost a majority of the entire Canadian population. For example, in 1911 (one hundred years prior to the forthcoming Canadian census), mainline Protestants had accounted for 48.4% of the Canadian population (Mol 1985:175). Although Roman Catholics accounted for an important percentage of the Canadian population (39.4% in 1911 and 46.8% in 1961), their distribution was regionally skewed with about 90% of Québec residents identifying as Catholic.

In addition, mainline Protestants had tended to be more economically prosperous than the average in Canada (Heaton, 1986:63) and tended to dominate boards of directors of the largest business corporations (Porter, 1968:290). Such dominance by mainline Protestants was also evident in Canadian Parliaments (Laponce, 1958:253-58) and among Prime Ministers (see Nock, 1993 for details). From 1867 until 1968, all Canadian Prime Ministers (and years of tenure) were Protestant with the exception of three Roman Catholics (Thompson, Laurier, and St-Laurent). Thus, Protestants held the Prime Ministership for three-quarters of those years, Roman Catholics for one-quarter. From 1968 until 2005, Roman Catholics dominated as Prime Minister (Trudeau, Turner, Clark, Mulroney, Chrétien, Martin with only a brief exception in Kim Campbell). Recently, there has been a trend to Conservative Protestant (Evangelical and Fundamentalist) affiliations among Conservative Party Parliamentarians including Prime Minister Harper himself (McDonald, 2006:44-61; 2010).

Obviously someone who made predictions in 1961 about forty years into the future on the basis of extrapolations would have been quite wrong. It is the aim of this chapter to explore why such predictions have proven to be so inaccurate as we enter the second decade of the twenty-first century.

Moreover even when things look the same in matters of religion, that is often not the case. Although Roman Catholicism has remained fairly stable as measured by the Canadian census, we must always remember that Canadian census religious data measure affiliation, not actual membership or identifiable commitment. So looking closer, we find that although Roman Catholic affiliation had only fallen 3.6% in the forty years between 1961 and 2001 and remained the choice of over 43 percent of Canadians, the *active* commitment of Catholics has fallen much more dramatically. Thus, weekly attendance at mass has fallen from over 80% in the 1950s down to the low to mid-20% level in the 1990s and the twenty-first century (Bowen, 2004:32).

Moreover, the nature of Catholicism has changed somewhat over the years. Catholicism used to be characterized by a very hierarchical, non-democratic, and patriarchal nature that held to a notion of absolute truth that was defined by the "magisterium" (the teaching hierarchy of Roman Catholic leaders as symbolized in the proclamation of the Pope's infallibility in matters of faith and morals). This notion of absolute truth as defined by the church led naturally to judgements of other churches as falling short of divine truth whether these be other Christians groups or rival world religions. In the 1960s Pope John XXIII called the Second Vatican Council in which he challenged the Catholic Church to throw open the windows of the church to a greater openness to modern ideas, and many Catholics took this invitation up with open arms. In short order, notions which previously had been unthinkable such as a married rather than celibate clergy, female priests, greater democracy and involvement of the laity (those not ordained to the priesthood or members of religious orders) became entertained by Catholics including many who are active or core (Bowen, 2004 includes data on such matters: see page 259).

Despite the election of the conservative John Paul II in 1979 followed by the subsequent election of another conservative pope (Benedict XVI), it does not seem that the rank and file will simply revert to beliefs and practices that were taken for granted up until Vatican II. Or to put it differently, the conservative hierarchy may continue to adhere to traditionalistic beliefs and practices while many Catholic laypeople and lower clergy exhibit varying degrees of resistance even while continuing to identify as Catholics (some may find themselves completely alienated or even expelled from the church). The Catholic world now seems a house divided in a way that was not the case with the monolithic church before the 1960s.

However, another trend identifiable in Canadian Catholicism is its growing ethnic pluralism and multiculturalism. Since this mirrors the official Canadian ideology and growing demographic trends in the Canadian population toward "visible minorities," this may be a source of strength to Canadian Catholicism if fostered in a strategic fashion. Thus, it is not without significance that the first bishop of Asian descent (Vincent Nguyen) has recently been named to the Canadian Catholic episcopate (Laidlaw, 2010), a refugee immigrant from Communist Vietnam in 1984 who risked pirates, Vietnamese government patrols and the natural elements to make his escape. (A significant percentage of the Vietnamese population shares a Catholic identification.)

This trend in Canadian Catholicism to greater ethnic pluralism and multiculturalism is somewhat recent in its implementation. Not so long ago, the majority of Catholics in Canada as a whole (and not just in Québec) were from the Francophone charter group with a minority of Irish and Scottish adherents. These groups dominated the episcopate, and in fact, much of the story of Catholicism had to do with tensions between the Francophones outside of Québec and British or Irish immigrants (see Mol, 1985:204 for some of the conflicts in Manitoba and elsewhere on the Prairies and on Bishop Michael F. Fallon of London and his arguments against French Canadian church leadership in Ontario, see Fay, 2002:169).

Although Canada had been open to immigration since its birth in 1867 (and in Upper and Lower Canada before that), the ethnic predominance in the country comprised the French and those from the diverse British groups (Irish, Scottish, English, Welsh). Up until the late1890s, very few immigrants came from non-British or non-French origins. Starting with the Laurier government from 1896 on, many of the large new wave of immigrants came from Other European origins such as Ukrainians and Finns. Such Other European origins of immigrants became even more predominant after 1945 with the end of World War II. Robert Choquette points to Catholicism's expanding multiculturalism when he states, "So it was that Catholic Christianity in Canada was strongly French Canadian, then Irish Canadian in the nineteenth century, before becoming progressively more multicultural in the latter half of the twentieth century" (2004:401-402).

THE IMPACT OF NEW SOURCE IMMIGRATION

Canadian society expert Harry H. Hiller (2006) has drawn attention to the rapid and dramatic dichotomy between what he refers to old source immigration and new source immigration to Canada (a complete description of Canada's population would also require discussion of Canada's significant aboriginal populations). As indicated above, the first waves of settlement and colonization after the British Conquest of 1759 added an essentially British population to the earlier settler-colonists provided by the French Empire. The British were much more likely to be Protestant and the French Roman Catholic (although as indicated, there were Catholic populations amongst the British, especially among the Irish and Scots). Later, and especially after 1896, Canada started to attract immigrants from northern and eastern Europe such as Germans, Finns, and Ukrainians. Later on still, after World War II, many immigrants came from southern Europe such as Italians, Portuguese, and Greeks.

This is what Hiller refers to as "old source" immigration. Old source immigration racially was characterized as "Caucasian," meaning white and European. Almost all of the "old source" immigration was Christian but with significant divisions between the Roman Catholics, Protestants, and Eastern Orthodox and a variety Christian sects with distinct lifestyles and cultures (such as Hutterites and Amish or

Doukhobors). This diversity was quite significant enough to create social tensions in Canada over a period of decades despite the racial and religious homogeneity (white and Christian). As late as the 1960s, British-Canadians tended to be Protestant as a majority and oriented to a definition of Canada that retained symbolic loyalty to the British Empire and its successor, the Commonwealth (just look at the portrait of the Queen on our coins and her continuing status as Canada's Head of State, with the Governor-General acting as her "stand-in"). There existed a strong tendency for the British-descended majority to look on British ethnicity as a truer symbol of Canadianism (see Igartua, 2006 for details), and others of diverse European origin, whatever their citizenship, to be foreigners or aliens (this was common in Canadian English speech until recently). Although Catholicism has had a long constitutional recognition in various Canadian jurisdictions (even today, Ontario is characterized by a system of taxpayer-supported "separate" or Catholic schools that goes back to the Province of Canada in 1841), Protestants were inclined to look at such arrangements with distrust and dislike, and to regard other Christian religions such as Orthodoxy and the minority sects as "ethnic religions."

It was only in the 1960s that resentment began to build against this vision of Canada. In 1963, the Liberal government of Lester Pearson set up the Royal Commission on Bilingualism and Biculturalism to investigate and rectify the lagging political, economic, and linguistic status of francophones within Canada and Québec. The prevailing definition of Canadian society can be seen in the terms of reference which called for "an equal partnership between the two founding races" (Hiller 2006:194). This was an already archaic use of the term "race" to refer to those of English (or British) and French ethnicity. It disregarded the presence and significance of both other immigrant groups and their contributions to Canadian society, and also aboriginal peoples and nations. It was protests from a number of these Other European immigrant groups to the "B and B" Commission that their contributions were being overlooked that led in the end to the mandate of the Commission being expanded to include multiculturalism. Ukrainian-Canadians are often singled out as having been the most militant and most effective in calling for this change. At the time, however, most immigration to Canada still came from Europe and thus consisted of Caucasian Christians. Multiculturalism was defined formally as a Canadian doctrine in 1971 and with this went the final remnants of the notion that British-Canadians were inherently more authentically Canadian than others.

In the long record of history we see some long periods when little seems to change. In others, change occurs quickly and dramatically. This process or rapid change is evident in the 1960s and 1970s. No sooner had the conception of Canada identity changed to multiculturalism so as to recognize the contributions of mainly Other European groups such as Ukrainians, than a dramatic shift in Canadian immigration policy began to take place. As Europe recovered from the devastation of World War II, fewer Europeans wanted to emigrate; also the racial leanings of Canada's immigration policy was terminated in favour of an "objective" and non-discriminatory points system. The consequence was that immigration from Europe became a minority, and the majority of immigrants started to arrive from Asia, Africa, the Middle East, and Central and South America. As late as the years from 1956-60, 85.5% of Canada's immigrants came from Europe and only 2.6% from Asia; between 1998-2002,S only 19.1% came from Europe (including the United Kingdom), and 51.47% from Asia (Hiller 2006:181).

The result has been increasing representation of the various world religions in Canada. A second point not directly related to the first but as a consequence of Canada's commitment to multiculturalism, has been the effort to ensure that at least some of these "new source" immigrants or their second and third generation offspring find places in Canada's economic and political elites. This has been evident in appointments as Canada's de facto Head of State (standing in for the Queen), the Governor-General. Recent appointments have included a Chinese-Canadian and a Haitian-Canadian, both of them immigrants and members of visible minorities (the Right Hons. Adrienne Clarkson and Michaelle Jean).

In the Canada that existed leading up to Canada's recognition of multiculturalism in 1971, the only significant religious minority was Judaism. Essentially this was because one prominent stream of Jews (the Ashkenazy) had found their way to Europe after their historic expulsion from ancient Judea by the Roman Empire after two failed revolts against their Roman occupiers in the first two centuries of the Common Era. In Europe, Jews were often persecuted, sometimes violently. In other cases they were simply not recognized as "real" citizens of the nation in which they lived (citizenship was often extended only in the nineteenth century in the spirit of the egalitarian values and ideals of the French Revolution). As a result of this treatment, many Jews were happy to emigrate to North America (some of these themes can be seen in the popular musical and movie "Fiddler on the Roof"). By 1921, Jews represented 1.4% of the Canadian population and this percentage remained at 1.5% for several decades through 1951 (Mol, 1985:175).

Despite obstacles and barriers, Jews were able to become Canada's first large religious minority vis-a-vis the Christian majority, primarily because of their European provenance. Although a few immigrants from other world religions also made it to Canada during this time, their numbers were small and their social recognition minimal. This all started to change quickly in the years after 1971.

The *Canadian Global Almanac 2005* included a useful article on "Changes in Religious Practice." It pointed to the continuation of a long-term downward trend in the population who report Protestant denominations, a marginal falling-off for Roman Catholics, but a substantial increase for religions such as Islam, Hinduism, Sikhism and Buddhism. The article reports, "Much of the shift in the nation's religious make-up during the past several decades is the result of the changing sources of immigrants, which has contributed to a more diverse religious profile" (2005:81) and specifically to "changing immigration patterns from regions outside of Europe, in particular Asia and the Middle East" (2005:83).

The article goes on to emphasize the relatively recent immigration pool as resulting in this new diversity:

> Immigration was a key factor in the increases for all these groups. The proportion of immigrants entering Canada with these religions increased with each new wave of arrivals since the 1960s. Of the 1.8 million new immigrants who came during the 1990s, Muslims accounted for 15%, Hindus almost 7 percent and Buddhists and Sikhs each about 5 percent. (2005:83)

The article also reports that "in terms of age, each of these religions had relatively young populations" and this may bode well for their continuation as contrasted with some of the Christian denominations and the "greying" of their flock. As a result of immigration patterns and birth rates, the Jewish population no longer represents the largest non-Christian population being surpassed by Muslims somewhere between 1991 and 2001. The Jewish percentage itself dropped from 1.2% to 1.1% while the Muslim percentage rose from 0.9% to 2% between 1991 and 2001. In 2001, the Jewish population at 1.1% was very closely followed by Buddhist, Hindu, and Sikhs at about 1% each (2005:81). Many of the adherents of these new world religions carry with them a designation by the Canadian government as "visible minorities."

Despite the characteristics of the new source immigration the change in Canada's religious composition is not dictated solely by changing immigration streams. Reginald Bibby especially has emphasized the large percentage of new source immigrants coming from Christian affiliations (1993 and 2002). Some of these come from historic Christian minorities in their homelands. Examples would include South Asians from the Indian state of Kerala and the Christian Coptic minority in Egypt (both of these are ancient Christian populations claiming to apostolic conversion at the hands of St. Thomas and St. Mark respectively); other such populations may come about from Asian, African, and other populations converted by European Christian missionaries in the course of the last several centuries (such as the Catholic Vietnamese). Bibby

(1993) comments: "despite the rise since the 1980s in the number of people coming from Asia and other Third World countries, what is often not recognized is the fact that large numbers of these people *also* have been arriving as adherents to the Christian faith, rather than other world religions" (p. 23). Not only that, but Bibby found evidence that "[f]or all the talk about having a multicultural society," religious assimilation *to* Christianity by new source immigrants or their offspring can still be observed. At least in 1993, Bibby concluded that: "Put bluntly, when it comes to religion in Canada, the mosaic is largely a myth" (p.26), a finding he reiterated in his more recent *Restless Gods* (2002:22-23).

Despite putting his finger on a significant feature that should not be overlooked about the new source immigration (continuing significant Christian affiliation percentages), the increase in Canadians reporting a non-Judeo-Christian religion cannot be ignored and the rises we have seen in such affiliation since 1961 will no doubt jump further after the 2011 census returns are released.

According to a 2005 Statistics Canada projection, the members of non-Christian world religions will increase from 6.3 percent in 2001 to between 9.2 and 11.2 percent in 2017 (Seljak, 2008:13). In the meantime, Canadian scholarship is beginning to take note and Paul Bramadat and David Seljak's *Religion and Ethnicity in Canada* (2005) represents a landmark with its detailed chapters and statistics on the non-Christian world religions in Canada. In his 2002 book *Religion in Western Society*, English sociologist Stephen J. Hunt commented: "No discussion of religion in Western societies would be complete without a survey of the faiths of ethnic minority groups. In the 1980s such an overview would not have warranted a separate chapter of a book on contemporary religion. Today the extraordinary ethnic diversity which has developed in the West now makes this imperative" (p.178). In 1993, I myself published a chapter entitled "The Organization of Religious Life in Canada" in which I ignored the growing presence of the world religions' presence in Canada. I justified this on the basis of their still-small overall statistical presence and a desire to keep the chapter clear and uncomplicated. Even in 1993 that was a questionable decision; today I would agree with Hunt that the growth of the world religions of ethnic minorities is one of the major new stories in religious adherence in the West even as Christianity suffers from a prolonged decline.

With the new source in immigration and consequently the rise of Canadians reporting non-Christian affiliations, a new set of questions has arisen about to what degree Canadian society and Canadians should accommodate religious practices associated with these world religions. Just about each of the newly grown world religions in Canada has created questions on this score:

1. Issues from Sikhs have often centred on the dress of devout male Sikhs which should include a turban and a small dagger in the under-clothing, known as a "kirpan" (this kirpan is not intended for self-defence or for violent behaviour but a symbol of divine truth).
2. Hindus have raised the issue of whether it is permissible to distribute the ashes of cremated remains in rivers and waterways such as is done in India.
3. Ultra-orthodox Jews (often called Hassidim or Haredim) have raised issues such as whether gyms should have frosted glass to shield their males from women dressed for gym and exercise classes.
4. Muslims have raised a number of issues which extend from expecting public and semi-public institutions such as universities to make available a prayer space for their five times daily prayer ritual to the preference of some Muslim women who wish to wear the burka or niqab which go far beyond hijabs (head scarves) to cover virtually the entire face and body. Even the wearing of the hijab has led to certain controversies such as in organized sport.

As I write these lines just such a debate is brewing in Québec focusing on a Muslim woman who was ejected from a French-language class on the grounds that the teacher could not see her and that she could not expect to benefit from the instruction. In the past when such cases have come to the Supreme Court of

Canada, the rights of religious minorities have often been protected as a result of the courts applying the Charter of Rights and Freedoms with its protection of religious freedom (Jehovah's Witnesses instigated the protection of religious minorities into Canada's two original charters of rights after a prolonged period of persecution by Québec governments in the 1940s and 1950s).

Thus several years ago, considerable controversy erupted in Québec when a Sikh boy was ejected from school for wearing a kirpan, on the grounds that it was a dangerous weapon. The Supreme Court of Canada decided in favour of the Sikh boy, finding that the danger posed was minimal or non-existent. Local residents of Hérouxville, a small Québec town, raised controversy by wanting to teach new immigrants that they should acclimate to Québec and Canada and not expect their religious and cultural observances to be given protection. The controversy spread to Montréal where most new source immigrants actually reside. It was here that the controversy between Hasidic Jews and YM-WCAs erupted. Many women took offense at being told by ultra-religious Jews that their gym apparel was offensive. Commentators noted the irony that Québec itself had made major moves to shed its once-fervent Catholicism in the 1960s for a secular way of life, only to have the new-source immigrants clambering for recognition of their particular religious practices in the public square. In the wake of this controversy, a commission on "Reasonable Accommodation" was set up under the leadership of Anglophone Canadian philosopher Charles Taylor and Québecois sociologist Gérard Bouchard. Despite its findings, the controversy about what constitutes reasonable accommodation continues with both the federal Conservative and Liberal parties saying they may support a Québec government decision to bar Muslim women from wearing the niqab or burka in accessing public and semi-public services (such legislation is proceeding in France and Belgium).

The concern about "reasonable accommodation" of the non-Christian world religions is greater in Québec because of the feeling of many Québecois that their distinctive Francophone culture is potentially under threat if undermined by excessive Anglicization and globalization. In the Rest of Canada (ROC), such greater identity concerns have waned. First of all, Canada's self-definition as "British" very quickly faded in the 1960s (Igartua, 2006). This had to do with the decline of the United Kingdom, and the UK's decision to pay more attention to the European Union; it also had something to do with the renaissance of Francophone Canadians in the 1960s and 1970s for whom the British tie had been objectionable (as seen by riots whenever Queen Elizabeth or other royalty visited the province). English Canada, later rebranded as Anglophone Canada or ROC (the rest of Canada) increasingly accepted a redefinition of Canada as multicultural, multiethnic, and multiracial and with that redefinition has come some acceptance of accommodating the practices of the world religions.

However, that is not to say that religious accommodation is as easy as acceptance of these other three "multi" aspects of Canada's modern self-identity. Lest we in Anglophone Canada feel smugly superior to the controversies in Québec, let it be said that there have been a number of such controversies dating back many years in ROC. Just as in Québec, there was a movement toward secularism and secularity in the ROC, at least in the public square. Judicial rulings no longer can appeal to the Christian origins of the country, which is why the laws against polygamy passed in 1891 to confront polygamous Mormon immigrants to Alberta, have been regarded as unenforceable in recent years because the basis of these laws had come from a Christian sensibility. Another series of rulings in the 1980s and 1990s had struck down laws banning businesses from being open on Sundays (the Christian holy day) on the same grounds.

BELIEVING WITHOUT BELONGING?: THE CANADIAN NONES

If Canada has become an increasingly secular nation in the public square, that must result from a greater number of Canadians who accept that transition. The most noticeable grouping consists of the so-called "Nones" (No religious affiliation). You will remember that this has grown from 0.5% in 1961 to 16.5% in

2001. However, we should note that in 1961, those who wanted to identify with this response had to write it in. The category for Nones was only provided in 1971 when there was a significant leap to 4.3%, caused in part by this clerical change (supported as it was by the burgeoning critique of religion and Christianity in the 1960s). In only thirty years, this response has jumped almost four hundred percent.

It is quite likely that this census material based on religious affiliation underestimates the ranks of those who are best categorized as Nones. There are many Canadians who may still indicate a religious affiliation on the Canadian census but for whom religious membership, involvement, and attendance are so minimal as to be almost invisible. In this regard, Kurt Bowen's typology of Canadian religiosity bears examination. He identifies the "Very Committed" as those who attend weekly and define themselves as religious; the "Less Committed" attend one to three times a month but not weekly or who attend once a week but say religion is not important to them (one imagines some spouses and partners as fitting in this latter category); on the other hand are "Seekers" who state that religion is important to them or who self-identify as religious but who rarely or never attend religious services; then there are the avowedly "Non Religious" who say religion is not important to them and who rarely or never attend. According to Bowen, as many as 40% of Canadians fit the Non Religious Category and another 28% the Seeker category; only 32% count among the religiously Committed (20% for the Very Committed, and 12% for the Less Committed).

This system of classification would essentially raise the Nones to a much higher level than the Canadian census's method. Bowen's typology provides some justification for seeing Canada as far along the path to secularization and secularity. In fact his book bears the title, *Christians in a Secular World: The Canadian Experience (*although only 7% of Canadians actually endorse atheism; Bibby, 2006:187).

However the growing percentage of Nones in Canada should not in itself imply that Nones lack supernaturalistic, spiritual, or metaphysical beliefs. British sociologist Grace Davie (1994) has caught this very well in her book *Religion in Britain Since 1945: Believing without Belonging.* American sociologist Robert Bellah and his associates recognized this as far back in the 1980s in their interview with nurse Sheila Larson in their best-selling and often-reprinted book *Habits of the Heart, 1985.* She indicated that she couldn't remember the last time she had gone to church. Nevertheless she had constructed her own faith which she herself defined as "my own Sheilaism," which included loving yourself and showing compassion for others. It also included mystical experiences which included an experience of hearing God reassure her that all would be well with a patient undergoing surgery; in another experience also involving her nursing profession, she felt that Jesus Christ was visible in the mirror (Bellah et al., 1986:235). The evidence provided by Davie and Bellah et al. refutes the view that the growth of Nones has something to do with Enlightenment thinking and its rejection of anything not immediately confirmed by the materialistic five senses.

In Canada it has been sociologist Reginald W. Bibby who has explored most thoroughly the spirituality and supernatural experiences of the Nones. Bibby likes "reminding people [that] these kinds of findings illustrate the reality that Canadians have not exactly gone the rational route that some wise men of old, led by the likes of Sigmund Freud, anticipated. We continue to supplement so-called rational explanations with explanations that are anything but scientific in nature" (2006:188).

Rather than accepting the preferred explanation of reductionistic materialists that humans have become more "rational" and thus are able to do without the realm of the supernatural, it may simply be that people today have less time for involvement in groups. It is now a commonplace observation that involvement in a wide array of organized groups has suffered from the fast-paced modern lifestyle. Indeed, American social scientist Robert Putnam made this the central point of his lengthy but riveting book *Bowling Alone* which pointed out the decline in membership numbers for an array of organized groups. No one who has seen the book's front cover will forget it, highlighting as it does the picture of a solitary, wistful and lonely bowler, bowling neither with family or friends nor bowling in a league competition with others.

CONCLUSION

It has been almost fifty years since the 1961 Canadian census as we await the forthcoming census for 2011 (typically it takes several years for the release of the new data to the public). If we had extrapolated the data from the 1961 census fifty years into the future, our predictions would have been quite wrong. Canada then was primarily Christian (Protestant and Roman Catholic especially), with only small numbers of Nones. The main minority world religion was Judaism with quite small representations from the others. Christianity, as then understood, provided a general framework to the values, norms, and laws in Canada.

Today, we find that the percentage of Christians is declining; in some cases as with mainline Protestantism this decline has been dramatic (this decline was emphasized as long ago as 1987; see Roof and McKinney). Evangelicals have not declined, but remained at their historical numbers of about seven percent. However, despite their persistent hopes for dramatic gains, the reality seems to be that just as many people leave as enter their doors (Bowen identifies this as the "revolving door syndrome"; 2004:37-38). Roman Catholicism has suffered declines, especially in the number of truly committed Catholics but remains a vibrant force outside Québec in ROC. The question remains of whether questioning lay Catholics will stay within a church ruled by a hierarchical, non-democratic celibate male magisterium, which is in such great disjuncture with the values, norms, and practices of the wider society (such as the almost universal acceptance of women in public leadership roles within Canadian society).

The distrust of groups in modern society and the unwillingness of many to be joiners have led to a situation where the Nones comprise a still-increasing category. Understanding their spiritual, metaphysical, and supernatural needs should become a priority for all faith communities as Reginald Bibby has reminded us. Because most Nones, Seekers and the Non-Religious are *not* hard-core atheists or reductive materialists (remember that only seven percent of Canadians endorse atheism, Bibby, 2006:187), they remain an important constituency capable of being wooed by the organized faith communities. However, encouraging them to "join" will go against the Nones' core principle of believing without belonging. Faith communities will have to become adept at a range of options which encourage Nones to participate without leading them to feel like lobsters caught and trapped in a boiling pot.

As far as the major World Religions, their adherents are likely to grow. It is hard to see an end to the pattern of the new source immigration to Canada, especially as Canada needs immigration to make up for the deficient Canadian birth rate which falls well beneath the "replacement rate" of 2.1 children per woman (at present, the average Canadian woman bears about 1.5 children). However, it is possible that sources for the new patterns of immigration might change as some areas of the Third World or Global South become more prosperous. Just as Europe ceased to provide the bulk of immigration after prosperity was restored in the 1970s, some of the new-source countries from Asia which have provided the majority of immigrants in recent decades might contribute fewer migrants if their economies continue to boom. If that were to happen, then African and Latin American immigration might provide new Christian communities. Islam might continue to thrive with its strength in Africa and the Middle East. If this scenario came about, the populations of Sikhism, Buddhism, and Hinduism might report slower growth rates. However, such a changeover from within the new source immigration still remains a hypothetical change from current patterns. Muslim, Sikh, Hindu, and Buddhist populations are likely to grow in percentage terms for some time to come. The CBC "hit comedy" *Little Mosque on the Prairie* is more than just a fable as mosques and similar religious meeting houses can now be found outside the largest census metropolitan areas (CMAs).

REFERENCES

Anon. (2005). "Changes in Religious Practice." *Canadian Global Almanac.* Toronto: John Wiley and Sons Canada, 81-83.

Bellah, R.N. et al.(1986). *Habits of the Heart: Individualism and Commitment in American Life.* NY: Harper and Row.

Bibby, R.W. (1993). *Unknown Gods: The Ongoing Story of Religion in Canada.* Toronto: Stoddart.

_____. (2002). *Restless Gods: The Renaissance of Religion in Canada.* Toronto: Stoddart.

_____. (2006). *The Boomer Factor: What Canada's Most Famous Generation is Leaving Behind.* Toronto: Bastian Books.

Bowen, K. (2004). *Christians in a Secular World: The Canadian Experience.* Montréal and Kingston: McGill-Queen's University Press.

Bramadat, P. and D. Seljak (eds.). (2005). *Religion and Ethnicity in Canada.* Toronto: Pearson Education Canada Inc.

Choquette, R. (2004). *Canada's Religions: An Historical Introduction.* Ottawa: University of Ottawa Press.

Davie, G. (1993). *Religion in Britain Since 1945: Believing without Belonging.* Oxford: Basil Blackwell.

Fay, T.J. (2002). *A History of Canadian Catholics.* Montréal: McGill-Queen's University Press.

Heaton, T. (1986). "Sociodemographic Characteristics of Religious Groups in Canada." *Sociological Analysis* 47:54-65.

Hiller, H.H. (2006). *Canadian Society: A Macro Analysis,* 5th ed. Scarborough: Prentice-Hall.

Hunt, S.J. (2002). *Religion in Western Society.* NY: Palgrave.

Igartua, J.E. (2006). *The Other Quiet Revolution: Nationalist Identities in English Canada, 1945-71.* Vancouver: UBC Press.

Laidlaw, S. (2010). "Vincent Nguyen to become Canada's first bishop of Asian descent." TheStar.com (Toronto Star). January 13.

Laponce, J.A. (1958). "The Religious Background of Canadian M.P.s." *Political Studies* 6:253-274.

McDonald, M. (2006). "Stephen Harper and the Theo-Cons: The Religious Right's Mission in Ottawa." *The Walrus* 3:8:44-61.

_____. (2010). *The Armageddon Factor: The Rise of Christian Nationalism in Canada.* Toronto: Random House Canada.

Mol, H. (1985). *Faith and Fragility: Religion and Identity in Canada.* Burlington, ON: Trinity Press.

Nock, D.A. (1993). "The Organization of Religious Life in Canada." In W.E. Hewitt (ed.), *The Sociology of Religion: A Canadian Focus.* Toronto: Butterworths.

Porter, J. (1968). *The Vertical Mosaic: An Analysis of Social Class and Power in Canada.* Toronto: University of Toronto Press.

Putnam, R.D. (2001). *Bowling Alone: The Collapse and Revival of American Community.* NY: Simon and Schuster.

Roof, W.C., and W. McKinney. (1992). *American Mainline Religion: Its Changing Shape and Future.* New Brunswick: Rutgers University Press.

Seljack, D. et al. (2008). "Secularization and the Separation of Church and State in Canada." *Canadian Diversity/Diversite* 61:6-24.

Chapter 8

Racial and Ethnic Communities

The African Francophone Identities within the Francophone Diaspora

Amal Madibbo

University of Calgary

INTRODUCTION

Various forms of encounters, including processes of identification, political resistance and cultural creativity as well as trends of racialization and marginalization, have occurred between and within the African Diaspora and the Francophone Diaspora. These encounters are a result of numerous processes of slavery; French and Belgium colonialism, and neo-colonial patterns of migration, displacement and dislocation. They were produced across places in Africa, the Caribbean, Europe and the Americas within a Black Atlantic that adds to Gilory's (1993) notion of this space–which refers to the United Kingdom, the Caribbean and the USA–Africa, Black France and Black Canada sequence.

In this chapter, using interviews and documents collected in Ontario and Alberta,[1] I explore a collective group identity that has emerged in the context of the encounters between the African Diaspora and the Francophone Diaspora in Canada. It is a form of identity developed by Sub-Saharan African Francophone immigrants aged 18-35, and termed "Une identité africaine francophone / An African Francophone identity." I explore two relevant identification processes: the identity construction and the identity negotiation. In terms of the identity construction, which refers to "[the] creation, formulation, and expression of…identities" (Rummens, 2003:22), I address the salient markers that determine the creation of this identity, its social, political and cultural expression as well as the social resources used to formulate it. Identity negotiation is concerned with "the political nature of…identification...between or among, and by or within groups, via the interactions of individuals" (Rummens, 2003:22). In this regard, I examine the various strategies developed by subjects to empower themselves in order to better negotiate their social and political position within the Francophone Diaspora and enhance their claims for collective group rights. In addition, I discuss what the construction and negotiation of this phenomenon reveals about the power dynamic and social relations within the Francophone Diaspora. Finally, I suggest that an intersection between the African Diaspora Studies and the Francophone Diaspora Studies could provide a space to conceptualize the complex identity processes that emerge in the context of Diaspora, migration, racialization and linguistic minoritization. This venture will also allow for rethinking the potential of the Francophone Diaspora to accommodate diversity and the multiplicity of identities, and for capturing the relationship between the African Francophone immigrants and one of their major sites of settlement in Canada: the Francophone Diaspora. As Diasporas refer to the dispersion of a people that share a common ethnic identity outside their homeland, this chapter also reiterates the link between the Canadian Diaspora Studies and globalization. As a social phenomenon associated with the movements of peoples around the world, globalization is relevant to the migratory movements of Africans and the creation of African Francophone communities in Canada, topics that constitute a field of interest for the Canadian Diaspora Studies.

THE CONSTRUCTION AND NEGOTIATION OF THE AFRICAN FRANCOPHONE IDENTITY

Scholars concerned with the construction and negotiation of the identity of newcomers and immigrants within diasporas in pluralist multicultural societies such as Canada underwrite multiple ways in which these subjects are incorporated into their host society (Hébert, 2003; Isajiw, 1999; McAndrew, 2001; Tettey and Puplampu, 2006; Walters et al., 2006). They indicate that some immigrants identify solely with the host society, others develop distinct ethnic identities–choosing not to participate in the larger society, while others become active members of the host society and, at the same time, maintain a unique ethnic identity or develop a diasporic identity.

The multiplicity of the identity strategies is also apparent within Canada's Francophone Diaspora particularly in the case of the African Sub-Saharan immigrants who are significantly diverse along ethno-racial, gender, age, geographic, religious and political lines. Some of these immigrants leave the Francophone space to associate themselves with the larger Anglo Canadian and/or Black/African identities. Others remain within the Francophone communities, taking on various forms of identification such as a sense of belonging to multi-racial/ethnic groups which consist of Caucasians, Métis or Asians, notably Vietnamese. The identities developed by these subjects also include a collective group identity described as an "African Francophone identity," which will be the focus of this chapter.

The formulation of the collective African Francophone identity is engendered by the subjects' consciousness about the ambivalent social and political position in which Francophones find themselves as a linguistic minority in predominantly Anglo Canadian spaces. This leads the immigrants to foster identification and attachment with the Francophone Diaspora's collective histories, cultures, struggles and aspirations. Additionally, the subjects seem to develop overtime a collective identity among themselves as African Francophones, based on: an awareness of their African common histories and struggles relevant to slavery, colonialism and racism; the desire to support democratization and development processes in their shared place of origin–Africa, and the desire to integrate themselves successfully with Canada's Francophone Diaspora. The subjects' collective allegiances both to the Francophones and among themselves as Africans mirror a diasporic characteristic feature that Cohen (2008) describes as the tendency of members of diasporas to develop a collective identity with "co-ethnic members" in their country of settlement.

The construction of the collective African Francophone identity is also determined by particular practices produced within the Francophone Diaspora. Subjects have feelings of alienation and non-belonging triggered by numerous forms of racism and racialization. These latter trends are depicted, at the subjective level, by the prominence of a racially, religiously and culturally homogeneous understanding of "a Francophone identity." As Knight (2001) points out, there still exists in the dominant imaginary a fixed

Francophone identity, whereby being Francophone is synonymous with being white, Catholic, Québécois or French-Canadian. These ideas are represented by notions such as "Un francophone de souche / A Francophone of French-Canadian origin" and "Un francophone pure laine / A racially pure French-speaking person" (see also Dallys, 2002). The notion of "Un francophone de souche" refers to an individual who is constructed as a white French speaker who has been in Québec for generations and has roots from France. The concept of "Un francophone pure laine," which describes the Quebecers of Franco-Catholic ancestry, "confirms what many Québécois have always believed," that "they, the descendants of original French settlers, are the only true Québécois" (Tandt, 2009). These two notions are, therefore, politically and culturally charged in that they reiterate "racial purity" and posit recognition given to individuals and groups that the dominant culture conceives as the legitimate Francophones. Meanwhile, these notions other non-white racialized Francophones including Sub-Saharan Africans that are perceived of as "immigrants," hence "outsiders" (see Dei, 2005; Shahsiah, 2006), placed outside the Francophone space of belonging.

The ideas about who is and who is not imagined to be a legitimate Francophone are portrayed, at the level of the institutional practices, by access, or lack thereof, to material and other social resources within *la francophonie*. African Francophone immigrants face unemployment and under-employment that result in significant socio-economic gaps between white Francophones and racialized minorities whereby the latter group experiences severe poverty. Additionally, the lack of open discourse about racism and racialization faced within *la francophonie* and the lack of appropriate measures that could counter these discriminatory practices contribute to impeding the African Francophones' sense of belonging to *la francophonie*. (For a thorough analysis of the racism that African Francophones immigrants face within *la francophonie* see Ibrahim, 2003; Madibbo, 2006, 2008.)

The research participants are also concerned about particular forms of racism that resurface in the larger Canadian society such as the very existence and practices of an Alberta-based neo-Nazi group named *The Aryan Guard* (http://www.aryanguard.net). This group, which is primarily located in the city of Calgary, held in that city in 2007 and 2008 a series of rallies as well as hate and racially charged flyering in their campaign targeted at immigrants. Furthermore, subjects also raise concerns about the findings of recent statistics that reveal that, while some diasporic groups in Canada like the Chinese and Japanese have thrived economically and that they experience significant economic mobility, Blacks "fare worse from one generation to the next" (Jiménez, 2008) and that third-generation of Black immigrants earn less than the newcomers. It can be argued that the above examples relating to the practices of Alberta's neo-Nazi group and the lack of economic mobility for Blacks illustrate features of diaporas that Cohen (2008) terms the immigrants' "troubled relation with the host society." These practices unveil discrimination in the labor market, hostility towards racialized immigrant groups and racial stereotyping–factors that could jeopardize the immigrants' attachment to and identification with the host society. However, even though these processes relate to the African Diaspora and the country of settlement (Canada) in general, they also concern the Francophone Diaspora in a number of ways. Whether or not the Francophone Diaspora contributes to these practices directly, the African Francophones are one of the groups that face these processes and these subjects feel the need to counter these discriminatory practices from within many sites including the Francophone Diaspora.

Additionally, existing tensions and divisions within the African Francophone community receive particular attention in the subjects' discourse about their identity. These tensions are caused by factors such as the competition for scarce financial resources associated with funding through community organizations and are augmented by the loyalty to particular ethnic groups at the expense of the general economic, political and social interests of the larger African Francophone community. These tensions hinder opportunities for development among African Francophones–a point stressed by a Congolese woman in Calgary who states that "Ce sont ces luttes qui font que la communauté africaine francophone n'avance pas / It is because of these fights that the African French-speaking community does not advance." In this regard, the construction of the collective African Francophone identity is seen as a way of rectifying these divisions and strengthening solidarity among the African Francophones. This collective identity would co-exist with other individual identities–such as a Senegalese identity or a Rwandan identity–and would be perceived of as an empowering strategy that could lead to balancing intra-community divisions; it would also help situate the African Francophones in a stronger political and social position within *la francophonie.*

Therefore, the African Francophone identity is formulated to deconstruct dominant ideas about Francophone identities; to rectify particular forms of racialization encountered both within *la francophonie* and the larger Canadian society, and to resolve tensions and conflicts within the African Francophone communities. It portrays the subjects' desire to belong, and asserts multiple ways in which the Francophone identity could be construed.

Subjects express their affiliation with the African Francophone identity by their engagement in and commitment to *la francophonie* and by participating in its social, political and cultural events and organizations. The expression of this identity also entails making and supporting claims for French language rights and services–an issue which represents one of the major collective demands of Francophones in Canada. In addition, the African Francophone identity embodies Blackness both as a skin color and as a signifier of African continental and diasporic cultures and histories of oppression and resistance. It is also expressed by cultural, social and political activities associated with Blackness and African-ness such as anti-racist activities, artistic and musical events and the celebration of Black History Month. These social and political forms of activities assert the relevance of slavery, anti-racism, and immigrants' integration to the Francophone identities and could, therefore, lead to conceptualizing these identities in numerous ways that could reflect the increasing diversity within the Francophone Diaspora.

As Kelly (1998) reminds us, in the Canadian context, resources such as films, music and community sources serve as bases for the construction of Black identities. As some of the resources needed for the development of the African Francophone identity–notably those that are relevant to Black history and culture and anti-racism–are not readily available within *la francophonie*, subjects strategize to acquire these resources from other spaces including the larger African community. Canadian cities like Toronto contain many sites of African social and political productivity, as illustrated by the existence of established African communities, festivals, cultural and economic networks, and antiracist materials and events. Cities in Alberta, such as Calgary are increasingly recognized as focal centers of African social and political activity. Events like *Afrikadey*, a festival of African cultures, music and arts celebrated in the city of Calgary in August of every year (www.Afrikadey.com), provide subjects with empowering spaces of resistance and creativity. Subjects enter these spaces to acquire and benefit from the social networks and the expertise that these African communities have developed with regards to anti-racist education and African/Black history and culture, and use the resources to develop and affirm their African Francophone identity.

This process also tells us that African communities and cultures in Canada have become important *points of reference*–in Sudbury's (2004) language–in the construction of the African Francophone identity. The concerned process allows for centering the Canadian context and de-centering what Silvera refers to as the "dominant positioning of African Americanism as a totalizing signifier of black identities in the Americas" (cited in Davis, 2004: 65). However, it is important to note that the Black American culture, notably its hip-hop music, receives particular attention in some of the African Francophones' identity discourse. As a Cameroonian male in Toronto points out, this form of music and culture embodies "un fort message socio-culturel / an empowering socio-cultural message" that provides subjects with social and political agency and encourages them to identify with the Black/African struggles and aspirations. This position affirms Ibrahim's (2003) contention about the key role that Black American culture plays in the formulation of the African Francophone identities in Canada. It also echoes Kelly's (2001) notion of "borrowed identities," which reveals that the Black (i.e., African) identities in Canada are largely built on American popular culture and that African-Canadians adopt Afro-American meanings and interpretations of Blackness. However, it is important to point out that the Black American culture is not the only salient source that impacts on the creation of the African Francophone identity analyzed in this chapter. This identity is also discussed in relation to other cultural and political forms such as the Caribbean reggae, continental African music, ideological discourses relevant to Pan-Africanism and *la négritude,* along with experiences subjects face in their migratory trajectories in numerous African countries, in Canada, France and Belgium or other sites of settlement in Asia or Europe. These experiences constitute the set of values and ideas that enable subjects to develop their collective African Francophone identity.

In this sense, the linguistic minority status of Francophones in Canada, particular forms of racialization the Sub-Saharan African immigrants face within the Francophone Diaspora and the larger Canadian society, along with these immigrants' desire to rectify tensions within their community, are some of the salient factors that determine the formulation of the collective African Francophone identity. Subjects negotiate this identity by developing strategies such as building alliances among themselves as African Francophones and by navigating racial and linguistic spaces–both French and English speaking spaces–and the larger African sites. These strategies are adopted in order to: acquire resources that would enable the subjects to assert their cultural heritage; to empower themselves in order to better negotiate their political and social position within *la francophone*; to make and gain demands for the collective linguistic and racial equity rights, and to enhance the inclusion of racialized immigrant groups within *la francophonie.*

The construction and negotiation of the African Francophone identity reveal tensions for social resources, political power and recognition of the multiple identities within the Francophone Diaspora. Meanwhile, these identification processes also assert social agency whereby subjects take on new forms of identities in order to accomplish what Cohen (2008) portrays as the possibility for members of a Diaspora to achieve "a distinctive creative, enriching life" in their host society. This invites us to conceptualize the Francophone Diaspora both as a site of contested and competing identities, and also as a location that could provide its immigrants with successful socio-economic inclusion. An intersection between the African Diaspora Studies and the Francophone Diaspora Studies could provide a space to explore these issues.

THE POTENTIAL OF THE INTERSECTION BETWEEN THE AFRICAN DIASPORA STUDIES AND THE FRANCOPHONE DIASPORA STUDIES

Bringing together the African Diaspora Studies and the Francophone Diaspora Studies could allow for fostering an integrated intersection between multiculturalism and bilingualism in the Canadian context. On the one hand, multiculturalism and bilingualism are seen as competing ideologies. As Taylor (cited in Couture, 2002: 147) remarks, in Canada multiculturalism enforces "une certaine insécurité / a particular kind of insecurity" for Canada's national minorities, notably for the French-Canadians. This position mirrors reluctance to endorse multiculturalism within *la francophonie* based on the assumption that the achievement of the bilingual project–the building of a bilingual Canada from Coast to Coast to Coast–can solely be achieved by the promotion of French-language rights. In this sense, addressing multiculturalism-related issues such as racial equity rights and racizalization (Fleras and Elliott, 2002) is perceived as a process that could jeopardize the accomplishment of the bilingualism project (see Dallys, 2002).

On the other hand, multiculturalism and bilingualism are increasingly considered complementary ideologies (Adam, 2005; Cardinal, 2002; Lafontant, 2007). This approach promotes the incorporation of studies on bilingualism and French-language rights into the multiculturalism and immigrant integration scholarship. The approach could, therefore, allow for exploring the Francophone Diaspora both as a site of multiple, contested (or complementary) identities and as a location that could provide its immigrants with the possibility of achieving a "distinctive enriching life." The merger between the Francophone Diaspora Studies and the African Diaspora Studies could further enhance this latter approach by providing conceptual tools that bring together the notions of language and linguistic rights with those of race, racism, racialization and the immigrant status, in the study of the formulation and negotiation of the multiple identities within the Francophone Diaspora. It could also lead to stressing the critical and antiracist forms of multiculturalism that challenge Euro-centric perspectives on identities (Dei, 2000; James, 2003), assert the re-distribution of socio-political power within societal institutions and affirm the relevance of racism, African-ness, Blackness, and racial equity to the bilingualism project. Additionally, the proposed merger between multiculturalism and bilingualism could affirm that turning the experiences of African Francophone immigrants into a "distinctive enriching life" within the Francophone Diaspora necessitates increasing the awareness surrounding racism and racialization, augmenting anti-racist educational material, and implementing appropriate diversity and employment equity programs and policies within *la francophonie.*

For example, more specifically, these processes will situate *la Francophonie* in a better position to counter the forms of racism that are of concern to African immigrants such as the Alberta-based new-Nazi group anti-immigrants' campaign. *La francophonie* could then join the anti-racist activities and rallies that are being held in cities like Calgary in opposition to racist movements and in support of Alberta's growing diversity and multiculturalism (Schneider, 2007). The proposed processes could also enable the Francophone Diaspora to contribute to reducing the economic immobility experienced by Black immigrants in Canada by improving and enhancing the socio-economic inclusion of the African immigrants within *la francophonie.* In this sense, providing the necessary resources and policies for the elimination of racism and discrimination and the enhancement of socio-economic inclusion could allow the African immigrants to accomplish successful lives within *la francophonie* and strengthen their sense of attachment, identification and belonging to the Francophone Diaspora (Breton, 2005).

As Dib (2006) remarks, the number of visible minority immigrants will grow to 20-25 percent of the total Canadian population by 2017. Additionally, immigration will become the source of all population growth by 2025 where the majority of immigrants will consist largely of visible minorities. This leads us to assert that African immigrants will continue to constitute significant proportions of the Francophone population. In this context, the intersection between the African Diaspora Studies and the scholarship on the Francophone Diaspora could potentially be quite beneficial for elucidating important issues such as understanding the relationship between the Francophone Diaspora and the African Francophone immigrants as these immigrants engage themselves in the processes of negotiating their multiple identities, defining their collective struggles and aspirations, building their communities and shaping the future of *la francophonie* in Canada.

NOTES

[1] The analyzed data in this chapter are part of the project *the Racial and Ethnic Identity of African Francophone Immigrants* (2007-2010), which is funded by the University of Calgary Starter Grants and *le Centre canadien de recherche sur les francophonies en milieu minoritaire* of the University of Regina. The project's principal investigator, Dr. Amal Madibbo, owes grateful acknowledgements to the research's participants, and to the research assistants, Chinelo Pnwanke and Josée Couture, for their excellent work and their many helpful suggestions. Acknowledgements also go to Jan Hill, York University and Shivu Ishwaran, de Sitter Publications, for their constructive feedback.

REFERENCES

Adam, D. (2005). "L'immigration et la francophonie canadienne." *Francophonies d'Amérique* 16:27-35.

Breton, R. (2005). *Ethnic Relations in Canada: Institutional Dynamics.* Montreal: McGill-Queen's University Press.

Cardinal, L. (2002). "Droits linguistiques, droit des minorités, droits des nations: de quelques ambiguïtés à clarifier avant de parler d'avenir." In C. Couture, J. Bergeron and C. Denis (eds.), *L'Alberta et le multiculturalisme francophone : témoignages et problématiques.* Edmonton: Le Centre d'études canadiennes de la faculté Saint-Jean.

Cohen, R. (2008). *Global Diasporas: An Introduction.* NY: Routledge.

Couture, C. (2002). "L'immigration et le malaise des sociétés dominantes au Canada." In C. Couture, J. Bergeron and C. Denis (eds.), *L'Alberta et le multiculturalisme francophone: témoignages et problématiques.* Edmonton: Le Centre d'études canadiennes de la faculté Saint-Jean.

Dallys, P. (2002). "Le multiculturalisme et l'école de la minorité francophone au Canada." In C. Couture, J. Bergeron and C. Denis (eds.), *L'Alberta et le multiculturalisme francophone: témoignages et problématiques.* Edmonton: Le Centre d'études canadiennes de la faculté Saint-Jean.

Davis, A. (2004). "Diaspora, Citizenship and Gender." *Canadian Women Studies: Women and the Black Diaspora* 23(2):64-69.

Dei, G. (2000). "Towards an Anti-Racist Discursive Framework." In G. Dei and A. Calliste. (eds.), *Power, Knowledge and Anti-Racism Education.* Halifax: Fernwood.

Dib, K. (2006). "Canada's 150th Anniversary, Multiculturalism and Diversity: Vehicles for Sustainable Socio-Economic Progress." *Canadian Ethnic Studies* 38(3):143-159.

Fleras, A., and J. Elliott. (2002). *Engaging Diversity: Multiculturalism in Canada.* Toronto: Nelson Thompson.

Gilroy, P. (1993). *The Black Atlantic: Modernity and Double Consciousness.* London: Verso.

Hébert, Y. (ed.). (2003). *Citizenship in Transformation in Canada.* Toronto: University of Toronto Press.

Ibrahim, A. (2003). "Marking the unmarked: Hip-hop, the gaze and the African body in North America." *Critical Arts Journal* 17:52-71.

Isajiw, W. (1999). *Understanding Diversity: Ethnicity and Race in the Canadian Context.* Toronto: Thompson Educational Publishing.

James, C. (2003). *Seeing Ourselves: Exploring Race, Ethnicity and Culture.* Toronto: Thompson Educational Publishing.

Jiménez, M. 2008. "Immigrants Face Growing Economic Mobility Gap." *Globe and Mail.* Accessed on June 1, 2010 from *http://www.theglobeandmail.com/servlet/story/RTGAM.20081006.wcensus0610/BNStory/National/.*

Kelly, J. (2001). *Borrowed Identities.* NY: Peter Lang Publishing.

_____. (1998). *Under the Gaze: Learning to be Black in White Society.* Halifax: Fernwood Publishing.

Knight, M. (2001). "The Negotiation of Identities: Narratives of Mixed-Race Individuals in Canada." MA Thesis, University of Toronto.

Korazemo, C., and R. Stebbins. (2001). "Les immigrants francophones de Calgary." *Cahiers Franco-canadiens de l'ouest* 13(1):37-50.

Lafontant, J. (2007). *L'intégration en emploi, à Winnipeg, des immigrants Francophones racisés: une étude exploratoire.* Les cahiers du CRIEC No. 32. Montreal: Université du Québec à Montréal.

Madibbo, A. (2008). "L'intégration des jeunes immigrants francophones de race noire en Ontario: défis et possibilités." *Thèmes canadiens* Spring:50-54.

Madibbo, A. (2006). *Minority within a Minority: Black Francophone Immigrants and the Dynamics of Power and Resistance.* NY: Routledge.

McAndrew, M. (2001). *Immigration et diversité à l'école.* Montreal: Les Presses de l'Université de Montréal.

Rummens, J. (2003). "Conceptualising Identity and Diversity: Overlaps, Intersections, and Processes." *Canadian Ethnic Studies* 3:10-25.

Schneider, K. (2007). "Racists Interrupt Rallies." *The Calgary Sun*, August 26.

Shahsiah, S. (2006). "Identity, Identification and Racialization: Immigrant Youth in the Canadian Context." CERIS Working Papers No. 49. Toronto: The Joint Centre of Excellence for Research on Immigration and Settlement.

Sudbury, J. (2004). "From the Point of No Return to the Women's Prison." *Canadian Women Studies: Women and the Black Diaspora* 23(2):154-163.

Tandt, M. (2009). "Federal Campaign will be Nasty." Accessed on March 20, 2009 from www.stan(dard-freeholder.com/ArticleDisplay.aspx?e=1179181&auth=MICHAEL%20DEN%20TANDT

Tettey, W., and K. Puplampu. (2006). *The African Diaspora in Canada: Negotiating Identity and Belonging.* Calgary: University of Calgary Press.

Walters, D., K. Phythian, and P. Anisef. (2006). "The Ethnic Identity of Immigrants in Canada." CERIS Working Papers No. 38. Toronto: The Joint Centre of Excellence for Research on Immigration and Settlement.

www.Afrikadey.com. Accessed on June 1, 2010.

www.aryanguard.net. Accessed on June 1, 2010.

Chapter 9

Bureaucracies

Understanding Bureaucracies

Claudio Colaguori
and Merle A. Jacobs

York University

INTRODUCTION

This chapter examines bureaucracy and addresses the specific interactions that take place in social organizations in Canadian society. It will provide the reader with an overview of bureaucracy by examining its positive and negative aspects. We will also consider the sociological perspective of Max Weber (1864-1920) who studied bureaucracy in detail. Bureaucracy is a sociological concept that refers to an aspect of social reality with which many of us are quite familiar and it has been extensively studied. One encounters bureaucratic type organizations virtually everyday of life. In today's world the term bureaucracy means "red tape," "long lines," "government rules," and centralized administrative decisions where the person we are talking about claims to be "just following the rules." We live in a world where many rules abound and the characteristics of hierarchy control the interactions that take place. Bureaucratic administration is part of the process of maintaining social order and social control. These formal procedures and rules produce an environment where the rule enforcer has power based on administrative authority within a power structure that is designed to maximize organizational efficiency. "Bureaucracy" implies a less personal relationship than traditional forms of social interaction and the encounter is often one of calculation and control. Think of being in a line-up to get your passport renewed or to pay a traffic ticket–when you finally get "served" are you greeted with a smile and genuine concern for your needs or are you treated with coldness and impatience? Bureaucracies often tend to make their officers act in impersonal ways because the nature of bureaucratic administration is so *rationalized* and calculating that it teaches its officers to treat people as abstractions or tasks to be completed. People often refer to this impersonalized experience as "being treated like a number," and indeed we are often asked to take a number and wait for it to be called-out to be served.

As Canadians we are members of a complex and diverse society and we often clearly recognize the difference between being treated with openness and respect or with coldness and disrespect. Bureaucratic ways of organizing social life emerged in the shift that arose when traditional agrarian society was replaced by modern institutionalized industrial society. In the traditional society which started to disappear in Europe and North America in the 1800s, people mostly dealt with other people they knew. There were formal and informal networks of relations that members of the society relied upon to get things done. Many parts of the world still retain this agrarian, village style of interaction although it is quickly giving way to globalization. The advent of the new industrial society instituted a great number of changes such as the training of an entire population into workers. This new society was based on various institutions such as school, workplace, government, law and prisons, social services and many more. This complex institutional reality we are describing is the reality of bureaucratically organized society. Bureaucracy was identified by the classical sociologist Max Weber as a central feature in the organization and functioning of modern societies.

Human societies were not always bureaucratic. The significant transformation that occurred when people moved away from rural life into highly populated cities formed by the industrial revolution a few centuries ago meant that the way people engaged with each other had to shift from interactions based on *community* to interactions based on *association* (Tonnies, 1957). In this formation of modern society human populations grew in size and became concentrated in urban centres, and as a result many new bureaucratized social institutions were formed to service and control these new populations. Things that are familiar to us and that we take for granted such as schools, centralized government, and the separation between family and the workplace, are recent inventions only a few hundred years old, and they became part of the rational organization of the new modern society. The modern society needed to be organized in a way that maximized the capacity of dealing with large numbers of people in a calculated and organized way. Bureaucratic forms of organization are ideally designed to get things done fast and efficiently. They are based on centralized decision making with various levels of management and the detailed coordination of tasks among bureaucratic officials. If one thinks of a machine one can imagine how all of its parts working together make the machine function properly. In this sense a bureaucracy is like a machine made up of human decision makers who implement rules and guidelines in order to get tasks done. A bureaucracy is thus a form of *social technology,* just as in tribal societies humans make decisions on the basis of small groups under the leadership of an honoured official who mediates discussion and keeps order. It would be incorrect, however, to compare human bureaucracies with naturally occurring hierarchies such as ant colonies. There is a big difference between ant societies and human bureaucracies: ants are consistent in their behaviour and are guided by instincts, whereas human bureaucracies are based upon the following of orders, and are subject to the follies of human actors such as self-interest and absence from work. Furthermore, bureaucracies are often plagued with inefficiencies because of personal bias among its members, behavioural inconsistency and power struggles. This is why the term *bureaucracy* has a double meaning. In the ideal sense it means the efficient delivery of convenient services to the individual and the rational organization of administrative tasks, but it also means inefficiency, corrupt abuses of power, and "getting the run-around" by people in control. Bureaucracy is nevertheless very much a part of Canadian life and as global networks expand, it is indeed becoming more a part of our increasingly globalized world.

Domestically we can identify bureaucratically run organizations in our schools, our hospitals and health care systems, our mobile phone providers, our workplaces and in our various levels of government. Globally we can identify bureaucratic organizations such as The United Nations, The World health Organization, The World Trade Organization, multinational corporations, and many other powerful institutions that shape human lives in tremendously powerful ways. These institutions along with many others affect the ways we live due to the fact that more and more decisions which shape our realities about communications, banking and finance, work, careers, lifestyle, health, environment and education, and where we choose to settle down and make a life, are made by global organizations that are bureaucratic in nature.

DEFINING BUREAUCRACY

Not all institutions are bureaucratic in nature. The family is an institution with which the vast majority of us are quite familiar, and although it has a power structure where children live under the authority, rules and guidance of parents, it is clearly not defined as bureaucratic. Parents do not implement family decisions by creating committees and getting managers to realize the goals of the committees and then wait for all of these processes to be completed in order to proceed with a task or decision. If that were the case then a simple matter of what to have for breakfast might be an onerous task! Now imagine a hospital instead of a family – how would a hospital decide on what to serve for breakfast? This may seem simple but let's look at it a bit more carefully. There has to be a health and nutrition committee that decides what the menu items will be and things like allergies and food safety need to be considered. And then there is the matter of which companies will provide the food ingredients to make the meals and how it will be delivered and how left over food will be discarded. The hospital bureaucracy will also have to follow health and safety guidelines along with legal labour practices in the kitchen operation and much, much more all so that a patient can get a nice little omelette and some orange juice for a morning meal. Bureaucracies are designed to simplify things but they can also complicate things. This is because bureaucracies are made up of people and humans are often fallible and self-serving. This point was quite apparent to Max Weber, the sociologist who undertook the most detailed sociological analysis of bureaucracy. For Weber a bureaucracy is an organization of *power.* It is not necessarily the most efficient way of doing things within organizations but it is the best way to ensure power and control remains in the hands of those who occupy positions of authority. For Weber, bureaucracy is "formally the most rational means of exercising authority over human beings" (Weber, 1968: 223). Bureaucracy is clearly a paradoxical way of organizing social structures since it has both positive and negative aspects:

Positive Aspects of Bureaucracy	**Negative Aspects of Bureaucracy**
- organized records keeping	*- potential for corruption by officials*
- potential for efficiency	*- potential for inefficiency*
- system for accountability	*- inherent anti-democratic tendencies*
- positions of power can be rotated	*- concentrates control in the hands of a few*
- tendency for institutional stability over time	*- resistant to institutional change and renewal*

Max Weber pointed out the negative effects of bureaucracy and the productive aspects, the rules and the way in which it organized society. In his study of formal organizations, he suggested that bureaucracy as a rational-legal system that promoted the rationalization of organization in their task and goals. Max Weber (1946) outlined some of the key characteristics of a bureaucracy as follows:

- specification of jobs with detailed rights, obligations, responsibilities, scope of authority
- system of supervision and subordination
- extensive use of written documents
- training in job requirements and skills
- application of consistent and complete rules
- assignation of work and hire personnel based on competence and experience

Weber established fundamental criteria to the ideal of bureaucracy and that it had rational-legal authority defined as "authority resting on a belief in the legality of patterns of normative rules and the right of those elevated to authority under such rules to issue commands" (1946:196-198). Weber maintained that bureaucratization was a powerful social force within social life. In modern institutional organizations such as hospitals, bureaucratic management in everyday life can be traced through committees, policies, standards and rules, which plan, implement and manage the day-to-day affairs of the organization.

Modern theorists of bureaucracy base their views on Weber's (1947) ideal type. He formulated it mainly with the administrative apparatus of the modern state in mind. Bureaucracy (Weber, 1947:329; 1946:196-198) and its rules have determined and helped define authority. In formal organizations norms and beliefs concerning social relationships are replaced with administration based power and control. As Weber noted, legitimacy is a form of power relations that allows those in power to influence and decide on the allocation of resources and to make it appear just and impartial. With authority and power comes the ability to control resources. Rules and procedures become areas of control that can be used in the maintaining of behaviour and communication through procedural means. The rules that define the tasks and responsibilities of each participant are entrenched in written documents as well as the formal mechanisms such as daily conferences or team meetings. The concentration of decision-making at the top of the hierarchy (Weber, 1947: 329-341) provides authority that appears legal and regulated in the best interest of those they serve.

It is important to note that Weber's understanding of bureaucracy is inseparable from his view of modern society as a whole. In his analysis of modern industrialized society, Weber believed that social life and subjective experience was becoming increasingly "disenchanted" and that humans were becoming increasingly disconnected from nature and more and more becoming processed by the mechanization of the modern world of industrial capitalism. Weber emphasized the *rational* organization of modern society. By "rational" he did not necessarily mean logical or sane or correct, or even the best way of doing things. Rationalization is a type of order and there can be many different types of rationalization. The way a painter organizes her brushstrokes on a canvas in comparison to the way a graffiti artist sprays the side of a building have different types of rationalization in their manner of expression. Rationalization for Weber meant that as society grew more complex, decisions and plans for its maintenance had to be technically calculated, even to the point of mathematical or scientific calculation. Since human societies do not follow the laws of nature (as in the animal kingdom), human societies needed to be planned out according to human legal rules created and enforced by the political state. The bureaucratic rationalization of society means organizing a system of administration that allows for maximum planning, calculation and control over the processes that are the responsibility of each organization or institution. A key element of the operational mentality or rationalization is the bureaucratic system of control. Since bureaucracy was becoming a central feature of social life that replaced traditional forms of human association with impersonal, institutional and alienating ways of life, Weber went so far as to say that life in the modern bureaucratized and administered world was akin to living in an "iron cage."

Authority and power are bureaucratic when they are attached to the position of individual officers and define the position in terms of rights and obligations, which create a field of influence within which the individual can legitimately operate (Morgan, 1986). The authority structure usually holds positions within the power structure and is seen as flowing from top-down in a pyramidal hierarchical structure. These leaders within the organization become the elite and their interests may not coincide with those whom they employ or serve. Oftentimes their primary interest is to maintain their power, even if so doing would be detrimental to the organization as a whole. As Weber stated: "Once it is fully established, bureaucracy is among those social structures which are among the hardest to destroy" (Weber, 1968: 987).

This is due to the fact that people who work at the upper rungs of the bureaucracy have much to gain by retaining their positions as the organization is the place which provides them with a career, social status, authority and a sense of security through their power over others. It is no surprise then that those who occupy senior positions in organizations often do so because of their own interests rather than an interest to serve the wider community. Of course this is not always the case, and many institutions are staffed by dedicated and well-meaning officers who struggle against the inherent power imbalances that bureaucratic institutions tend to foster.

According to Weber, traditional authority is viewed as legitimate since social institutions often have the legal right to control and exercise their authority. Rational authority is the rule of law. Bureaucracy exists within this framework as the rules and policies are authorized and are implemented because it coincides with the power created by the state (otherwise known as the government). Bureaucratic rules justify behaviours, decisions and interactions by those who run the bureaucracy. As alluded to above, the bureaucratic system is not without serious faults. Thus, Weber also argued that bureaucratization would lead to alienation that was similar to Marx's notion of alienation (Marx, 1984), which implied feelings of a loss of self or of being socially excluded. Both Karl Marx and Max Weber agreed that the increased efficiency of production and organization would lead to more alienation and depersonalization. People put up with these negative aspects of social life because they do so for a pay cheque or because they are forced to cooperate with the bureaucracies that structure their lives.

Bureaucracy can help to reduce uncertainty and increase the way we can predict outcomes. The "empowerment" of workers, a buzz-word that exist today, has to exist within a formalized system with constraints and rules. We are not stating that workers may not exercise any autonomy. It is simply that autonomy is constrained within a formalized workplace. Autonomy has to be exercised within their job description that originates from management. Autonomy is an outcome shaped by bureaucracy's characteristics. The search for meaning in signs and symbols used to express rules has to be understood by the employee within her\his work place and is a means of understanding how bureaucracy exist in their environment. A key concept is social identity, an individual's sense of who she or he is within a group so that one's action in a particular situation depends on the way that situation is perceived. Workers are aware of the rules. Ritualism that exists within companies; and employees modify their social identity to "fit in" and not be called "a trouble maker" (Jacobs 2008, 2007, 2000).

When studying group life within organizations we study the ongoing drama of action, some visible, while other actions are behind closed doors. The shared understanding of the situation and the development of that understanding is viewed as the formation of conduct as each human situation is located within the specific context of a group. In bureaucratic organizations they can be coded in policies or unwritten codes of conduct. Since human beings are not born with social symbols in their brain, it then must arise out of social interaction from reference groups. The group helps mould human personality (Cooley, 1956) and instil human ideas. Cooley states:

> communication here is meant the mechanism through which human relations exist and develop… all the symbols of the mind, together with the means of conveying them through space and preserving them in time. (1956:61)

Understanding communication within groups (Lewin, 1948; Blumer, 1969) is to understand the interdependence in the goals of group members where the group's task is such that each member's performances have implications for her\his fellow members' performances, with human conduct as a product of situated social interaction (Prus, 1996). These implications may be positive or negative. Group life within organizations needs to be addressed as it relates to the structures and the culture that produces behaviours such as collegiality, racism and abuse. Shared meaning and understanding is a way of describing culture within an organization. We cannot understand bureaucracy without acknowledging the interactions that take place within formal organizations.

Rules of conduct are part of social interaction for the self and others to interact within a specific interaction. Interaction, when viewed as a game or a theatre stage, has rules of conduct. When we play games, individuals need the rules of the game to understand the acts of others and what plays are allowed and not allowed within the game (Goffman, 1959). There are broader rules for determining and sometimes for negotiating whether the situation is a game, a job interview, a flirtation, or a life or death matter. When rules in a society or in a religion are codified they become laws in that society or religion. In an organization the rules of the "game" can be seen as company objectives, goals, and\or standards. It is interesting to note that the bureaucratic model in organizations is increasingly governed by professional standards or government regulations that are designed toward against inefficiency or abuse of power.

One of the ways in which Canadian workers are affected by the forces of globalization has much to do with bureaucracy. The Weberian sociologist George Ritzer (1993) coined the concept of *McDonaldization* to illustrate the way that an increasing number of social institutions, especially workplaces, are following the model of a McDonald's fast food restaurant where there are highly ordered and rationalized management and control systems in place to ensure that work tasks are clearly set out and that management, production and service models are the same whether the restaurant is in Ottawa or Moscow. The globalization of capitalism has had a profound effect on labour practices around the world. It has had the effect of streamlining and coordinating business practices so that domestic particularities or local ways of doing things are starting to give way to more universalized and standardized modes of organization. This is all an effect of bureaucracy that stretches across national borders. We see similar examples of corporate globalizing bureaucracies in the spread of Walmart across the world, and also the form of cultural globalization where local tastes and food consumption preferences are increasingly shaped by corporate giants such as Coca-Cola, in what some refer to as "Cocacolonization." Clearly, business corporations use interconnected global bureaucracies to run their entrepreneurial operations, thus demonstrating how bureaucracies are excellent at consolidating administrative power and re-defining national identities to fit with foreign cultural consumption choices and tastes. It is important to note that labour unions and non-governmental organizations also use bureaucratic forms of management and administration, and they also reflect the positives and negatives of bureaucracy.

CANADIAN BUREACRACY

Let us now turn to some examples that help clarify some of the contradictory features of bureaucracy and also help us examine how bureaucracies can reflect national identity. Canadian identity is a difficult thing to define clearly. Canada is a nation of immigrants settled on Native land and continues to be a population heavily composed of immigrants and their progeny. Thus the question of Canadian identity is not clear-cut since Canada is a multicultural society and many Canadians identify with different aspects of culture. Although Canada is a mosaic of cultures it is also a nation, and thus there are some elements about Canadian *national* identity which are perhaps more easily identifiable. Organized competitive sports such as The Olympic Games illustrate how national identity can often merge with or even supersede ethnic and cultural identities. During The Olympics many Canadians banded together in support of Canadian athletes in the hopes of gaining medals which would contribute to national pride. The Olympics, however, are not exclusively a Canadian event. They represent the quintessential example of a bureaucratic type of organization that is international in scope. You may recall how during the 2010 Winter Olympics there was a controversy regarding the inclusion of women's ski jumping category. Ski jumping is the only sport in the Winter Olympics that is not open to both men and women and this anomaly was rightly challenged at the legal level. The Vancouver Olympic Organizing Committee claimed this exclusion of women to be a case of discrimination and took this claim to the British Columbia Supreme Court and lost. In this case the International Olympic Committee, a non-Canadian bureaucratic institution, had the power to override Canadian politics and culture. Clearly this case represents how bureaucratic decisions made at a larger international level can also have an interplay and effect on the institutions that are shape Canadian culture and identity

Hockey is another competitive sport that many people associate with a distinct Canadian identity. Many young boys and girls grow up playing, watching or cheering hockey and it is readily identified as something that belongs to Canada whether this is official or not. But is hockey truly Canadian? National Hockey League hockey is experienced by many as an engaging form of entertainment and for many that is all it remains, however, if we look behind the scenes there is much more to hockey than meets the eye. NHL hockey is an example of a bureaucratically organized institutional structure that spans both national and international boundaries. Each team is associated with a particular city. (In Olympic hockey teams are designated for countries.) One would think that the Toronto team is somehow owned by Toronto or that the players are from Toronto, but that is hardly the case. The patriotic connection drawn between geographical areas and their designated teams is a social construction. NHL hockey teams are first and foremost a form of corporately owned private property that is designed primarily as a way to earn profits for their owners. The NHL does this by generating fanfare and revenues from games and video broadcast sponsorship. NHL players are also workers since they get paid for providing a service to team owners. Some may argue that they are really entrepreneurs insofar as they earn relatively high amounts of money, however, the 2004-2005 labour dispute lockout of professional hockey players by the NHL that caused the cancellation of what would have been the 88th season shows us that bureaucratic decision making and corporate conflicts between owners and workers can come into effect to reveal the true sociological/bureaucratic structure of institutions whose inner workings we often think little about until their effects are publicly revealed.

Another recent case illustrates how NHL hockey system is a very bureaucratic organization that contains a number of separate but interacting bureaucratic organizations and is not free of controversy and conflict. Even though NHL teams are private property commodities, the case of a wealthy corporate entrepreneur to buy a hockey team shows how bureaucratic decision-making can complicate and prevent business transactions within the so-called free-market system our society claims to uphold. Canadian entrepreneur Jim Balsillie has attempted to buy a hockey team on three occasions but each time his efforts have been blocked due to factors such as territorial concerns over moving teams from one city designation to another. In the case of his attempt to purchase the bankrupt Phoenix Coyotes, a deal which was approved by the then owner of the team, the deal never happened because the NHL bureaucracy intervened and decided to exercise its control by claiming team owners do not have the right to re-designate teams to another host city–in this case from Phoenix, Arizona to Hamilton, Ontario.

In yet another example of how bureaucratic decisions are not always made in the best interest of the institution or its lower level employees we have the case of former head of the National Hockey League Players' Association, Alan Eagleson, to illustrate flagrant corporate corruption. Eagleson held various conflicting positions of power within the world of hockey and used them to bolster his own fortunes. He was involved in player disability and insurance scams, and infamously bankrupted the great Boston Bruins defenceman Bobby Orr by misrepresenting him to the Bruins and lying to the Bruins about Orr's true professional wishes. While Bobby Orr was desperate to finalize a deal with the Bruins team, Eagleson prevented Orr from knowing about lucrative offers that were sent his way. Eagleson is now a convicted felon in two countries and has been removed as a member of The Order of Canada (Hagan in Linden, 2004: 493).

What is the *rationality* that guided each of these separate events in the bureaucratic practice of the NHL? How did bureaucracy serve to uphold or destroy fair practices? How is it that an organization that is designed to fulfil one function ends up becoming a mechanism for personal gain or corporate profits? Is this potential for power and corruption something endemic to the nature of bureaucracies or is it a matter of "a few bad apples" in an otherwise functional system?

CONCLUSION

Individuals who hold positions of power within organizations are entrusted to act in the best interest of those whom they serve but oftentimes the nature of bureaucratic organizations is such that accountability is thwarted and certain self-seeking individuals can damage the efficiency and integrity of an organization. Nevertheless, the bureaucratic form of social organization is very much with us. Most people work within them, get their education within them, receive social services from them, and there is an increasing level of bureaucratization across society that we must contend with.

Bureaucratic organizations are made up of individuals who interact and communicate with each other to produce goods, or provide services or social resources. When these individuals interact they have a shared understanding of the organization based on rules, professional standards, and hierarchy. Efficiency is brought about through cooperation based on power and authority. The constraint placed on employees in these organizations can be traced to the organization's mission statement, goals, objectives, policies and procedures, and outcomes. Bureaucracies have rituals and rules where authority is lead by administrators requiring compliance. In sum, although aimed at efficiency, this type of organization is often experienced as dehumanizing, impersonal and can be unaccountable when mistakes are made that affect individual lives.

REFERENCES

Blumer, H. (1969). *Symbolic Interactionism: Perspective and Method.* NJ: Prentice Hall Inc.

Cooley, C. (1956/1902). *Human Nature and the Social Order.* NY: Charles Scribner's Sons.

Goffman, E. (1959). *The Presentation of Self in Everyday Life.* NY: Doubleday Anchor.

Habermas, J. (1976). *Legitimation Crisis.* London: Heinemann.

Hagan, John. (2004). "Corporate and White-Collar Crime." In Rick Linden (ed.), *Criminology: A Canadian Perspective,* 5th ed. Toronto: Thomson Nelson.

Jacobs, M. (2000). "Staff Nurse Collegiality: The Structures and Cultures that Produces Nursing Interactions." Unpublished doctoral dissertation. York University, Sociology.

_____. (2007). *The Cappuccino Principle: Health, Culture and Social Justice in the Workplace.* Toronto: de Sitter Publications.

_____. (2008). *Women's Work: Racism and Trauma.* Toronto: APF Press.

Lewin, K. (1948). *Resolving Social Conflicts.* NY: Harper and Row.

Mouzelis, N. (1967). *Organisation and Bureaucracy: An Analysis of Modern Theories.* London: Routledge and Kegan Paul.

Marx, K. (1984/1845). *Selected Writings.* T. B. Bottomore (ed.). NY: McGraw-Hill.

Prus, R. (1996). *Symbolic Interaction and Ethnographic Research.* Albany: State University of New York Press.

Ritzer, George. (1990). *Frontiers of social Theory: The New Syntheses.* NY: Columbia University Press.

_____. (1993). *The McDonaldization of Society.* Newbury Park: Pine Forge Press.

Tonnies, F. (1957). *Community and Society.* NY: Harper and Row.

Weber, M. (1946). “Class, Status and Party.” In H. Gerth and C. W. Mills (eds.), *From Max Weber: Essays is Sociology*. NY: Oxford Press.

_____. (1968). *Economy and Society–An Outline of Interpretative Sociology*. NY: Bedminster Press.

_____. (1969/1947). *The Theory of Social and Economic Organization*. Translated and edited by A.M. Henderson and T. Parsons. NY: Free Press.

PART III

INEQUALITIES

This section explores some areas of social inequality within Canadian society as a result of globalization.

Chapter 10 by Abigail Salole examines **social inequality** within a specific Canadian context. A suburb of Toronto is used as a key research site from which to explore specific social interactions that reflect inequality within the day-to-day activities of suburban Canadians.

Chapter 11 by Zabedia Nazim on **racial and ethnic inequality** follows the experiences of restructuring (during the mid-1980s to early 2000) of twenty-three ethno-racial women bank workers from one of Canada's big banks. She provides a unique perspective of the workings of Canadian banks by centering the voices of ethno-racial women bank employees who constitute a growing segment of retail bank workers.

Chapter 12 by Guida Man on **gender and inequality** focuses upon immigrant women who have been devalued by neoliberal policies and practices. Guida provides documented research showing that gaps in racial, gender and social class have increased over time. She scientifically demonstrates how immigrants' with previous credential and work experience are not recognized by Canadian public institutions. Licensing bodies and professional associations operate as "labour marker shelters" that reduce competition by placing more emphasis on "Canadian experience."

Finally, Chapter 13 by Patricia O'Reilly and Thomas Fleming provides a comprehensive analysis of **crime and deviance** in Canada. They effectively show how mass media provide images of the rise in violent crime when in fact these crimes are fewer in Canada compared to previous decade. The author finds that television documentaries such *The First 48* from the United States have a tendency to produce fear and outrage. They are the "ideological tools" of neo-liberal strategy makers.

In summary, Part III of this anthology is devoted to the key issues of social inequality in Canada in the context of globalization.

Chapter 10

Social Inequality

"Keeping up Appearances": Social Inequality in Suburbia

Abigail Salole

Sheridan Institute of Technology and Advanced Learning

INTRODUCTION

> *What developed was a society of families turned inward to themselves… How the recreation room should be finished, where the baby should be fed, or where the best place to shop were the kinds of problems which came to occupy the attention of the population.*
>
> *–The Suburban Society (Clarke, 1966:194)*

The sentiment expressed by Clarke in the above quote was a popular observation made by sociologists in the nineteen sixties (see, for example, Jacobs, 1961; Mumford, 1961). The concern at the time was that suburban structure and urban sprawl was conducive to a "loss of community" and a general widespread unawareness of social problems like inequality (Warren, 1963). This concern about the disconnection of those living in suburbs continues today, and yet, the suburb has changed as an entity. The vast expansion of suburban areas has created a variety of places that exist outside of urban areas and therefore the study of cities that are not urban is actually quite complex and varied (Oliver, 2001). One distinction of present day suburbs is that they are more self-contained. Indeed, suburbs are more like cities unto themselves, rather than dormitories of the metropolitan areas. This chapter examines social inequality in the suburbs from the perspective of young people living in Burlington, Ontario, a suburb of Toronto. On the surface, Burlington is a city that is regarded as a prototypical suburb. It has a bastion image of being home to the nuclear family and is made synonymous with the symbol of the white picket fence.

This chapter demonstrates how social inequality is often perpetuated by cultural norms that minimize difference. Cultural norms that encourage a certain homogenization of people perpetuate social inequality insofar as differences are glossed over with a veneer of neutrality. Using personal narratives and experiences, this research examines the pervasiveness of "intentional sameness" and how social inequality is "culturally managed" in suburbia. The commercial reconstitution of "normal" and consumer culture are two social forces that perpetuate this minimization of difference.

LOCATING BURLINGTON

There is not one unified homogenous entity called "Burlington." Rather, there are multiplicities of experiences of Burlington based on social location (i.e., race, class, gender, sexual orientation, and age). Importantly, Burlington, like most modern cities (and other geographical entities), was not fashioned out of thin air. This city is a product of a White settler society in which Indigenous peoples were dispossessed from their land. The colonization of Native peoples in Canada is a historical experience that is often suppressed and erased from mainstream knowledge. Lawrence (2002) explains that

> in order to maintain Canadian's self-image as a fundamentally 'decent' people innocent of any wrong doing, the historical record of how the land was acquired–the forcible and relentless dispossession of Indigenous peoples, the theft of their territories, and the implementation of legislation and polices designed to effect their total disappearance as peoples–must also be erased. It has therefore been crucial that the survivors of this process be silenced–that Native people be deliberately denied a voice within national discourses. (Pp.23-24)

As a result of this silencing, it is difficult to find a non-Eurocentric historic account of the area from archival data. Indeed, it is a little known fact that the Mississauga Nation is currently negotiating a land claim with the Government Specific Claims Branch for the lakeshore and bay area of Burlington (Mississauga Nation, 2005).

Burlington is home to 164,500 people. In terms of race, Burlington remains predominantly White, with less than 10% of the population identified as belonging to a "visible minority" group.[1] Burlington's land-use structure is what many have come to know as "typically suburban." There are mostly single-family residential neighbourhoods that are demarcated from places of employment and consumption. This land use structure is most amenable to transportation based on car travel. Of course, individuals connect with people across time and space and, therefore, social networks or "community" cannot be assumed based on geography (Wellman, 1998). Despite this increasing fluidity, geographical boundaries and identities remain important for a multitude of reasons for the purposes of this study.

METHODOLOGY

The research presented here is part of a larger research project that examined the social inclusion of youth in Burlington (Salole, 2005). In this participatory research I used a number of different methods to engage the participants (n=22). I attempted to triangulate my research methods in order to ensure that youth participants were a part of both data collection and the data analysis of the experiences of living in Burlington. Research participants are not merely acquiescing providers of information, but they are also actively reflecting on their lived experience and consciously communicating this to the group.

A number of different data collection methods were used including focus groups (dialogue), photovoice, and journals. The study involved young people, aged 16-18, coming together once a week for a total of thirteen weeks from March to June 2005. Participatory Action Research (PAR) literature operates under the supposition that liberation occurs through critical pedagogy in which participants achieve greater self and community awareness through dialogue and heightened social awareness. Park (1993) states:

> [D]ialogue produces not just factual knowledge but also interpersonal and critical knowledge, which defines humans as autonomous social beings. This is an essential reason for the people's participation in research. It is not just so they can reveal private facts that are hidden from others but really so they may know themselves better as individuals and as a community. (p.12)

In contrast to traditional methodologies, an advantage of PAR is the value of liberation embedded within the research process. In this study, our data analysis was constant in the sense that we were always asking ourselves why Burlington was experienced in a particular way. There were also distinct moments in our discussions of social inclusion where each group would pause and engage in open coding in order to establish categories for our experiences of social inclusion.

The youth participants also engaged in a "Photo-voice" process in which participants take photographs informed by their lived experience and use these images as a way to communicate to others. Youth participants were asked to prepare "free-writes" for at least 2 of the pictures that they chose. The mnemonic "SHOWeD" (Wang et al., 2004) was used in order to provide a framework for the freewrite. This mnemonic stood for: What do you See here? What is really Happening? How does this relate to Our lives? Why does this problem or strength exist? What can we Do about it? In addition, fifteen youth participants maintained journal entries about the research experience. I also kept a personal reflection log to document my "action-reflection cycle" (Maguire, 1987).

"NORMAL" IN BURLINGTON

> *If you're not white, rich, straight in Burlington you're gonna spend pretty much all your time trying to be–or at least look like it. – Natalie*

The most salient finding from this research was this local definition of what is "normal." People who are normal in Burlington are those who are white, middle-class, university educated (or university bound), and heterosexual. This notion of normal permeates everyday lived experience and is equated with neutrality or the minimization of difference. Kenny (2000) found the same "neutralness" in her examination of whiteness in a suburban American town. She explains, "This is a community of intentional sameness. The tropes of difference are held at bay, disavowed, avoided, or at the very least disguised, translated into less direct vocabularies …" (p. 117).

Many of the youth participants explained that "everyone" believes Burlington to be a "perfect" place to live and raise their children. As Natalija describes:

> People move here well because they think that everyone here is friendly, it is safe there are good schools and like people can compare their gardens and stuff. People come here to…I don't know…forget about the rest of the world and its problems.

I also asked youth participants who they think lives in Burlington; who they think feels the greatest sense of belonging in Burlington; and whether a sense of belonging or inclusion in Burlington differed based on social identity like race, class, gender, occupation or migration status.

Some youth participants explained that people in Burlington are simply ignorant and are not aware about inequality. Research participants explained that they thought that many people in Burlington had no real desire to learn about social issues and were quite content in the illusion that there is no inequality in

Burlington. Many of the youth participants described this code as something that is pervasive and harmful but at the same time polite and ambiguous, resulting in a silencing of the existence of marginalization. Collins (2000) contends:

> within a rhetoric of color-blindness that defends the theme of no inherent differences among races, or of gender-neutrality that claims no difference among genders, it becomes difficult to talk of racial and gender differences that stem from discriminatory treatment. (p. 279)

Indeed, an important feature of the cultural code in Burlington and a feature that sustains this code is the perceived need to avoid conflict. If people raise disturbances they run the risk of being further alienated because it breaks with the norm of "minimizing our differences." This means anyone identifying or speaking about inequality runs the risk of being described as over-reacting. While these accusations are not exclusive to Burlington, the level of intolerance for anti-oppressive language (described by the youth participants as "political language") is a part of the "avoidance culture" in Burlington. In our discussions about Burlington, many of the youth participants noted that it is widespread to avoid mentioning race, sexual orientation or ethnicity at all. Under this regime of silence it is taboo to describe someone as Black, Muslim, or Lesbian. According to these pervasive rules, many Burlingtonians argue that "people are people" and to describe someone by their social identity is offensive. Brown (2003) in her study also identified this practice as being prevalent within Oakville (a city which borders Burlington). In her study of Oakville, she writes: "One of Shelly's classmates wanted to tell her that she looked like a particular black soccer player, but she couldn't bring herself to use the word 'black'" (p.61). A particular occurrence that highlighted the discomfort that youth participants felt when social identity or oppression was discussed occurred when Marcel, Natalie (youth participants) and I attended a workshop in Toronto that sought to raise awareness about the construction of a new youth jail in Brampton, Ontario. One particular exercise involved all participants gathering on one side of the room, with the word jail posted on the other side of the room, intended to symbolize a metaphorical prison. The facilitator read out particular social characteristics which statistically increased one's likelihood of incarceration and then informed participants who met that particular characteristic how many steps to take toward prison. For example, if you were under 18 years of age, you were asked to take a step forward, or if you were a Black person you were asked to take a step forward, and so on. At the end of the exercise, Marcel, a young Black man from a low-income family was the only person who remained in the metaphorical jail, based on the fact that his social characteristics represented an over-represented identity in Canadian prisons. Natalie (a young White woman from a middle-class family) rushed to Marcel after the exercise and gave him a hug explaining she "didn't know he was poor" and this made her "so sad." Natalie, being close friends with Marcel, explained in an embrace, "I just want us to be equal...we are equal and I don't care what they say I am always going to treat you like we are equal."

This illuminated that the code in Burlington is not necessarily to strictly avoid talking about oppression or social characteristics. Rather, what people seemed most uncomfortable with was a unit of analysis that is not individualistic. Twine (1996) had a similar analysis in her study of bi-racial or mixed race women of African descent in her study of the construction of White identity in suburbia. Twine explains that the suburban location worked against racial identification because, first, residents were predominately White and there were few experiences that allowed identification as non-White. Secondly, the middle-class ideology of liberal individualism discouraged racial identification. She describes: "Being raised white and middle-class emerged as being linked to learning to privilege specific ideological positions, namely the tendency to self-identify as first 'an individual' with no links to a specific racialized or ethnic community" (p.214). This "Race to Incarceration" exercise, therefore, directly counters the Canadian notions of meritocracy and equality in which an individual's destiny is the result of the effort or the merits of what they put forth. Marcel was the only person in this metaphorical prison because he was black, male, low-income and young–all of which are not illegal and, therefore, should not, according to merit-based myths, make him more likely to be incarcerated. The youth of colour in this research also reported feeling comfortable in predominately white settings. In a conversation about racial identity in Burlington, Marcel described that, "Yes, my skin is black. But all my friends are White and pretty much everyone around me is White–so like…I don't know it is just different–I am very comfortable in room of White people because I am always in a room of White people." Twine (1996) describes similar phenomena of White identity being a comfort zone for the "brown skinned white girls" in her study. While I did not specifically ask youth of colour in this research whether they identify culturally as White, they certainly described feeling comfortable immersed in whiteness in Burlington. However, it would be an overstatement to conclude that the youth of colour participants in this study always felt comfortable in White culture and that White culture was always "accepting" of everyone. Indeed, in contrast to the widely held belief that Canadian racism is subtle and discreet, many of the youth of colour participants had experienced overt racism. Consider the following three experiences from youth participants:

> In grade nine my teacher couldn't say my name so she just called me "number four'And I can't even tell you how many times I explained to her how to say my name I even asked her to call me Katrina–but she still called me number four for the whole semester. – Jihyang
>
> One time I said to someone that I don't celebrate Christmas on December 25 because I follow a different calendar. They told me that as a Canadian I had to go by their calendar. – Natalija
>
> I had one teacher who always tries to talk like a rap guy with me and I think he thought it was funny but it was like only with me because I'm the only one[2] in the class and he would just say stupidness like 'hey gee my shorty has two booties, what's the deal yo'? and then he would make jokes in front of the whole class like when like when I was talking to someone in class…so he would make jokes that I was making drug deals in class. – Marcel

These overt incidences of racism were seen as isolated and did not formulate part of the everyday experience for youth in Burlington. However, as we further discussed manifestations of racism it was clear that there was a significant level of normalized racist incidences experienced by the youth participants. While racism can be quite overt, the difference with this type of racism is that it is not expected to lead to any sort of conflict. In fact, it appears that what is normalized is the fact that people are not supposed to take offence to the insults. Therefore, the most shocking aberration to this system of "normal" would be for a person to call someone a racist. These intentions of "not meaning to cause harm" do not, however, apply when it comes to gay or lesbian youth. Indeed Max, a gay youth, explained that he had been ostracized since he was a young boy in Burlington. As a self proclaimed "effeminate gay man" he is routinely harassed in public spaces and was also harassed while in elementary and high school. This harassment was constant and no argument was made that "fag" was meant to be taken lightheartedly. Meanwhile, Max reports that a number of his friends (especially his young male friends) know that he is gay but just try to ignore it or not talk about it. A socialized pattern in Burlington emerges from these narratives: It is acceptable for friends to identify and make "jokes" about race and ethnicity, but it is not acceptable for friends to talk openly about a gay friend's sexual orientation. In contrast, it is not acceptable for an "outsider" to use racial slurs or to make racial comments but it is not unheard of for a complete stranger to ostracize a gay person and for this to be tacitly accepted by many.

Perpetuating Forces

How has this hegemonic concept of "normal" remained so pervasive for these youth participants? The culture seems to maintain a narrow concept of "normal" and this conception of normal minimizes differences, which mask social inequality. The commercial reconstitution of normal and pervasive consumer culture were two perpetuating forces identified by youth participants.

Commercial Reconstitution of Normal

We recognized a number of ways that commercial spaces reconstituted "normal" by their supposed neutrality. Consider the following dialogue about positive spaces for the Burlington LGBT (Lesbian Gay Bisexual and Transgendered) community:

> Facilitator: Okay so there is no gay bar in Burlington. Not only is there no gay bar…I can hardly think of any stores that have the gay pride triangle on their door? Oh wait, do y'know what that is?
> Conversation diverges to what the Safe space triangle represents is.
> Facilitator: Okay but for real why do you all think there is no gay bar or gay coffee shop in Burlington. Hamilton has a Gay Village, Toronto has a Gay Village, we all know that but like, cities like Windsor and Welland also have gay bars. Why is it that there are none–no for sure safe spaces for gays and lesbians to go to in Burlington?
> Eliza: It's because if there was a gay bar in Burlington everyone would know that we are not perfect. And well there goes our whole idea of perfect.
> Murmur of agreement from a group of youth participants.
> Kate: Burlington is too reserved.
> Trisha: And I think well, I think that gay people in Burlington…they know that yeah maybe that store might be like an okay place to go for them but so what? The city is not safe…So you're much better just going to Toronto to go out. I mean you may as well it's so close.

In another conversation Eliza indicated that she thought that if more stores displayed the safe space triangle in their front window, they might suffer a loss of business because of the pervasiveness of homophobia in the community.

The research participants became "cultural anthropologists" in identifying when this "normal" or "fakeness" was present. Brendan, for instance, took a picture of the magazine section in the Burlington Chapters store. The picture was of a section of magazines that had lesbian, gay, and marijuana magazines as well as anti-consumerist magazines like Adbusters. This section of magazines was labeled "Alternative Viewpoints." In his freewrite Brendan wrote:

> This relates to my life because I am always being told what to think. With this I'm supposed to think that being gay is a viewpoint and that marijuana is what lowlifes do because no one normal would do this stuff unless they were alternative. This problem exists because big time corporations love to tell us how to think.

Out of curiosity I visited Chapters in Toronto, investigating what the titles on the magazine racks were there. Interestingly, there was no such thing as an "Alternative Viewpoints" section. Gay and lesbian magazines were displayed based on their appropriate subject matter. For instance, gay and lesbian health magazines were in the health and wellness section with heterosexual health and wellness magazines, while

Adbusters could be found with other current affair magazines. Is the Burlington social code so pervasive and powerful that even Chapters follows their rules by marginalizing these identities? Or are Toronto consumers just more politicized and would find the managing of "difference" insulting? Why would a large corporation whose success is built on mass production and uniformity throughout their stores create this difference?

A prominent feature of this "sameness" that the youth reported was with respect to the aesthetic of Burlington. Many neighbourhoods, especially new suburban neighbourhoods, look the same. Some youth described this feature of Burlington as an organizing structure of Burlington, while other youth participants thought that this aesthetic nature of Burlington was a symptom and representation of the culture of Burlington:

> Yeah like when I go to one of my friends houses they do not even have to tell me where anything is. I know where everything is because their house is the same as mine, and the same as everybody else's–everything is the same. – Sam

> What I see in this picture is a street of houses with perfectly mowed lawns, and perfectly paved driveways. This is the typical Burlington street. It's a representation of how suburbia is created. All the houses are exactly 2 metres apart, making sure that their flowers are equally watered. Moreover, it relates to the typical Burlingtonian life, since everyone is perfect. If your [sic] not normal than you're not perfect, you don't live here. You live in Warwick Drive where the real life takes place.[3] Where you can be different and no one cares. These houses represent how everyone and everything is the same in Burlington. This problem exists in our lives because since no one is courageous enough to speak up; and if you do, you're told that those problems don't exist in Burlington.
> – Natalija, Photovoice Freewrite

> Of course people feel disconnected and like they are not a part of the community in Burlington. People just drive from place to place and have no real interaction with each other–even though we are living the exactly the same life. We live in a bubble. – Jihyang

All three of these narratives make observations about the homogeneity of the community. Sam is referring to the similarities in the floor plans of the houses of his friends. Natalija emphasizes a number of sources of homogeneity that are captured in her picture: the distance between the houses, the amount of water that the flowers receive. She links the "equality" in aesthetics to the homogenizing or perfect image of living in Burlington. Meanwhile, Jihyang points to how the structure of Burlington has created a community of people with many similarities but who nevertheless do not interact with one another in a meaningful way.

Consumer Culture and Consumerism

> *The branded multinationals may talk diversity, but the visible result of their actions is an army of teen clones marching–in "uniform," as the marketers say–into the global mall. Despite the embrace of polyethinic imagery, market-driven globalization doesn't want diversity; quite the opposite. Its enemies are national habits, local brands and distinctive regional tastes. – (Klein 2000:129)*

An important feature of what is considered "normal" in Burlington is the culture of consumerism. This consumerism is fueled by a materialism that presupposes that "keep up appearances" means the accumulation of material good and trends relative to others. Youth participants recognized this consumer culture and described it as "fake." Similarly, participants pointed to the mass production of merchandise and cookie-cutter development as a way of describing this fakeness. As a sustaining force of what is considered normal in Burlington, a pervasive consumer culture prescribes that the most important role that people have in Burlington is the role of consumer. Moreover, this consumer culture is related to the hegemony of big corporations who dominate the suburban market and limit the diversity of products available to people living in these communities. While this mass-production is something that is felt everywhere as a product of globalization, Klein (2000:140) notes that large metropolitan areas like Toronto still have competitive small business "while the suburbs, small towns and working class neighbourhoods get blanketed in–and blasted-by–the self replicating clones [the big-box stores and mega corporations]." Everything is mass-produced and mass-marketed, leaving the impression on the youth participants that they are a product of this super-sized scheme. This journal entry from a research participant explains:

> Everywhere you go everyone is wearing the exact same thing because the popular clothing stores do purchase merchandise in bulk. I know that it is only clothes but at the same time, that is all that most people have to represent themselves. – Stacey, Journal Entry

A symbol of this consumer driven culture is the commercialization of public space as represented in the fact that the shopping mall has become the de facto town square where youth spend a lot of their social time (Harris, 2004). With this new space for young people to occupy under the condition that they look and act like potential consumers comes increased surveillance of young people. This consumerism is described as a place of belonging for some. For example, one youth used only positive words to describe a Burlington mall in her Photo-voice free-write:

> This is a picture of the mall. This is my favourite mall because they let you just hang out here and this is a real positive place for teens to be. It is safe and you can pretty much stay here all day and even meet new people sometimes. There are lots of places for everyone to shop. They have a store for people who are plus sized and they even have a store for pregnant people. This relates to our lives because we need somewhere to go when it is not nice outside. This strength exists because the other mall was getting too old. We can continue to shop in this mall!

A number of youth disagreed with the sentiment that these spaces were necessarily a positive place for youth. Many participants reported experiences of youth getting kicked out of commercial spaces for being in "too big" of a crowd, of youth being accused of stealing, and of youth having to find alternative places to hangout because the mall was cost-prohibitive. These alternate experiences leave the impression that experience in commercial space is directly linked to how much you appear to be a consumer to the governing forces. Harris (2004), for example, writes:

> It has been well documented that young people are not considered to be citizens within their communities with equal rights to the public domain. However, what is also becoming apparent is that the public domain is itself a contested site, and with privatization much of it has been rezoned as commercial. Consequently, for youth to rightfully enter into these spaces they must demonstrate their viability as consumers. (p.121)

One's viability of being (or appearing to be) a consumer is directly linked to important social characteristics like income level and race. Therefore, one's experience in these new public spaces greatly depends on who you are and how well you fit into the consumer mould.

CONCLUSION

> *Suburbia is a landscape that is ubiquitous, a backdrop to life so commonplace that few take conscious notice of it. Freeways, shopping malls, commutes, lawns, detached homes, soccer games, mortgage payments, and the home fix-it jobs define the texture of life for many of us, as we go through our daily routines shaped by a suburban framework of life. Yet few of us stop to think critically about this backdrop, the spatial organization that shapes out lives, how we spend our time, where we go, and even how we interact with–and think about–other people.*
> *– The Suburb Reader (Nicolaides and Wiese 2006: 4)*

In contrast to the above quote, this chapter documented the experiences of youth "stopping to think" about the ways that social inequality is avoided in Burlington by failing to appreciate difference and by perpetuating an individuation of social problems. This chapter examined the local cultural of minimization in Burlington. While this "minimization of difference" certainly exists outside of the city limits of Burlington, it is useful to consider how these norms can be localized and experienced from a shared city experience. How ignorance of social inequality is perpetuated also examined in this chapter. Specifically, the commercial reconstitution of normal and pervasive consumer culture were identified as important social forces that perpetuate this pattern.

NOTES

1 The term "visible minority" is commonly thought to be a state-created term. Bannerji (2000) explains how the term "visible minority women" is "a categorical child of the state, cradled by the Ministry of Multiculturalism and the Secretary of State, this expression underpins and is the mainstream counterpart notion of the woman of color" (p.545). I use the term with reservations and only to refer to state-based research in which the term "visible-minority" is a part of the research question.

2 When Marcel explained the he was the "only one" he meant that he was the only Black person in the school.

3 The Warwick Court that Natalija is referring to is a well-known low-income area of Burlington with low rent apartments.

REFERENCES

Bannerji, H. (2000). "The Paradox of Diversity: The Construction of a Multicultural Canada and 'Women of Colour.'" *Women Studies International Forum* 23(5), 537-560.

Brown, M. (2003). "Growing up Black in Oakville: The Impact of Community on Black Youth Identity Formation and Civic Participation." Burlington: Community Development Halton. Available on-line at www.cdhalton.ca.

Clarke, S.D. (1966). *The Suburban Society.* University of Toronto Press: Toronto.

Collins, P. (2000). *Black Feminist Thought: Knowledge, Consciousness and the Politics of Empowerment.* NY: Routledge.

Harris A. (2004). *Future Girl: Young Women in the Twenty-First Century.* NY: Routledge.

Jacobs, J. (1961). *The Life and Death of Great American Cities.* NY: Random House.

Kenny, L.D. (2000). *Daughters of Suburbia: Growing Up White, Middle-Class and Female.* NJ: Rutgers

University Press.

Klein, N. (2000). *No Logo: Taking Aim at the Brand Bullies.* Toronto: Vintage.

Lawrence, B. (2002). "Colonization and Indigenous Resistance in Eastern Canada." In S. Razach (ed.), *Race, Space and the Law: Unmapping a White Settler Society.* Toronto: Between the Lines Press.

Maguire, P. (1997). *Doing Participatory Action Research: A Feminist Approach.* Amherst: University of Massachusetts Press.

Missisaugas of the New Credit Nation (2004). "Mississauga Nation Treaties." Retrieved August 1, 2005 from http://www.newcreditfirstnation.com/topur2.htm.

Mumford, L. (1961). *The City in History.* NY: Harcourt.

Nicolaides, B., and A. Wiese (eds.). (2006). *The Suburb Reader.* NY: Routledge.

Oliver, J.E. (2001). *Democracy in Suburbia.* Princeton: Princeton University Press.

Park, P. (1993). "What is Participatory Research? A Theoretical and Methodological Perspective." In Peter Park et al. (eds.), *Voices of Change: Participatory Research in the United States and Canada.* Toronto: Ontario Institute of Studies in Education Press.

Salole, A. (2005). "Behind the Picket Fence." Unpublished Masters Thesis. University of Toronto: Toronto.

Statistics Canada. (2006). "Community Profiles." Retrieved May 1, 2010 from http://www12.statcan.ca/census-recensement/index-eng.cfm.

Twine, F.W. (1996). "Brown Skinned White Girls: Class, Culture and the Construction of White Identity in Suburban Communities." *Gender, Place, and Culture* 3(2):205-224.

Wang, C.C., and S. Morrel-Samuels, P. Hutchison, L. Bell and R.M.P Pestronk. (2004). "Flint Photovoice: Community Building Among Youth, Adults, and Policy Makers." *American Journal of Public Health* 94(6):911-913.

Wellman, B. (1998). "From Little Boxes to Loosely-Bounded Networks: The Privatization and Domestication of Community Center for Urban and Community Studies, University Of Toronto." Retrieved May 1, 2010 from http://www.chass.utoronto.ca/~wellman.

Chapter 11

Racial and Ethnic Inequality

Reflections on Globalization, Multiculturalism and Diversity: The Power and Politics of Ethnic Market Staffing and Credit Scoring in Canadian Banks

Zabedia Nazim

Wilfrid Laurier University

INTRODUCTION

Canada is a country widely recognized for its pluralistic framework of multiculturalism. Distinct ethnic groups are able to maintain their differences while peacefully and respectfully coexisting with one another. In a globalizing world, countries are looking to Canada in an effort to deal with the increasing diversity within their societies. But is Canadian multiculturalism as democratic, humane and equitable as we are led to believe it is, or is there more to this multiculturalism than meets the eye?

There is very little social research exploring Canada's big banks and almost none from the perspective of ethno-racial employees. When these perspectives are examined, interesting contradictions in the "multicultural focus" of Canada's banks are revealed. This chapter demonstrates how the practices of ethnic market staffing, that is, staffing organizations with employees to reflect the ethnic communities they serve, in conjunction with a computerized system of credit scoring, support the domestic and global financial goals of the institutions themselves. Canadian banks use ethnic market staffing and computerized credit scoring strategies to simultaneously target profitable segments of the Canadian population and their global connections, and exclude marginalized individuals within these communities (ACORN, 2004; Dreier, 2003; Dymski, 2001, 2004; Nazim, 2007). Disenfranchised individuals, marginalized by poverty related to race, gender, language, immigration status and so forth, are denied access to banking resources by ethno-culturally diverse, front-line staff intentionally placed to convey the institution's support for diversity.

This chapter is part of a larger study examining the experiences of restructuring (during the mid-1980s to early 2000) of twenty-three ethno-racial women bank workers from one of Canada's big banks.

This chapter provides a unique perspective of the workings of Canadian banks by centering the voices of ethno-racial women bank employees who constitute a growing segment of retail bank workers.

CANADIAN MULTICULTURALISM: A TEMPLATE FOR ETHNIC MARKET STAFFING

In Canada, multiculturalism emerged as a federal policy in response to three major factors: the Québec separatist movement, the shift towards a more non-discriminatory immigration policy that allowed for greater immigration of "non-Europeans," and the concerns of representation in Canadian society by non-British, non-French and non-First Nations Canadians. The Quiet Revolution in Québec and increased French-Canadian nationalism threatened the political and cultural dominance of Canada's British-origin Canadians. The official response was the creation of the Royal Commission on Bilingualism and Biculturalism in 1963. However, the French/British bicultural and bilingual model of Canada generated anxiety among non-British and non-French groups as to what their status would be in Canadian society. The result was increased pressure from these groups, in an effort to secure symbolic recognition and cultural equality in Canada (Abu-Laban and Stasiulis, 1992; Barnes and Nazim, 2004). The 1971 ruling Liberal Party under the leadership of Prime Minister Pierre Trudeau attempted to balance individual freedom with national unity by introducing the policy of multiculturalism.

Since its inception, Canadian Multiculturalism has been critiqued mainly for its symbolic approach to difference, particularly race and ethnicity. Critics have pointed to Canada's social hierarchy, which operates to differentially position people along axes of race, class, gender and ethnicity within Canadian institutions and society at large. Hence, despite this policy's various shifts since the 1970s, the underlying framework remains firmly intact. The problematic nature of the multicultural framework is well noted. At the heart of multiculturalism policy and discourse are concepts of tolerance, accommodation, sensitivity, harmony, and diversity that Henry et al. (2000:29-30) argue, "conceal the messy business of structural and systemic inequality and the unequal relationship of power that continue to exist in a democratic liberal society." Meanwhile, Bannerji (2000) points out that multiculturalism acts as an administrative and ideological tool of the state. It rearranges questions of social justice, unemployment and racism into politically neutral issues of cultural diversity. Cultural diversity is then limited to discussions of religious and traditional expression, which renders invisible the structural inequalities of the Canadian state.

For example, Canadian banks are spearheading the economic benefits of multiculturalism. The frontlines of these institutions mirror the ethnic diversity of Canadian society. In an effort to attract the business of Canada's ethnically diverse population, banks have sought to reflect the communities they serve, which has meant an increase in the number of ethno-racial employees. However, the relationship between Canada's big banks and racialized communities reflects the larger history of exclusion and marginality that have plagued successive waves of immigrants. Racism, patriarchy, sexism, and colonialism have shaped Canada's economic, social and political policies; leaving ethno-racial peoples largely on the fringes of the Canadian financial services industry (Bolaria and Li, 1988; Razack, 2002). In fact, it is no secret that Canada's political economy is built on a system of immigration that is racially stratified with certain ethno-cultural groups emigrating to Canada as cheap sources of manual labour (Walker, 2008; Galabuzzi, 2005).

Since the introduction of the point system in 1967, Canada's immigration policy has changed so as to attract skilled labour and professionals, wealthy immigrants, entrepreneurs and investors (Barrington, 2008; Li and Lo, 2008; Nash, 1997). Today, Canada's banks realize the opportunity and potential profit to be made from these communities in Canada and globally. For example, the greater movement of people around the globe has meant that remittances are a growing and lucrative business for banks (Bose, 2007).

However, banks have failed to garner the trust of minoritized peoples. For example, current American research suggests that Latin American immigrants possess not only a general distrust of banks but also fear requests about documentation (e.g., pertaining to their legal status), product complexity and fees (Blair, 2003). Suspicion and distrust between banks and Muslim, Middle Eastern and South Asian communities has been heightened "post 9/11" as the financial activities of these communities have come under intense scrutiny and suspicion (Nazim, 2007). This lack of trust amongst ethno-racial communities has created a dilemma for Canada's financial sector as it re-imagines Canada's multi-racial population containing potentially profitable enclaves. In an effort to attract consumers from these groups, Canadian banks recognize the obsolescence of the traditional image of the European, elite/middle-class white male banker.

The work of Scott Lash and John Urry (1994) on postmodern society highlights the blurring of economic and cultural factors when it comes to work. Their use of the term "economy of signs" refers to the increasing importance of image, signs and symbols embodied in individuals and products in a postmodern society. In interviews with bank workers, many stressed the importance of images, signs and symbols embodied in individuals when it comes to shaping the relationship between ethno-racial communities and banks. They argued that banks started to hire people from ethno-racial communities in an effort to attract consumers from these communities, knowing that ethno-racial consumers would more likely trust and conduct their financial business with someone from their own community rather than from the traditional middle-class, white male bank worker (Nazim, 2007).

The recent expansion of foreign banks in the Canadian market illustrates the attempt to capitalize on this general distrust between ethno-racial communities and Canada's banks. Foreign banks have attracted consumers from ethno-racial diasporas by garnering trust through ethno-cultural connectedness. For example, ICICI (Industrial Credit and Investment Corp. of India) caters primarily to Canada's large South and East Asian new immigrant communities. Nicholas Keung, immigration and diversity reporter for the *Toronto Star* (2005:A21) writes, "Trust and connection with Canada's newcomer communities is what the ICICI is banking on in establishing a footing in Canada." Further, Keung (2005:A21) cites K. Vaman Kamath, managing director and CEO of ICICI Bank as saying, "We identified Canada as it has a significant South Asian population, the segment that's largely familiar with and identified with the brand."

Since their establishment, Canadian banks have not built trust and connectedness with Canada's ethno-racial communities. In fact, these institutions originally served the business interests of elite European men. Despite the shift towards mass banking during the post-war era, which saw the inclusion of female and working-class as customers, Canada's immigrant population and racialized communities in particular, were still largely excluded. In the 1940s and 1950s, ethnic credit unions arose to serve the interests of ethnic communities members (mainly from Eastern Europe) unable to access mainstream banks. Communal trust and informal rules of conduct underscored the cultural connectedness of trusted union members (Li and Lo, 2008). Today, Canadian banks attempt to mirror the growth of ethnic credit unions by appealing to ethnic diversity and cultural commonality through the use of ethnic market staffing (Nazim, 2007).

ETHNIC MARKET STAFFING AND THE POWER AND POLITICS OF DIFFERENCE

Ethnic market staffing focuses on the strategic placement of racialized and ethnicized bodies on the frontlines of financial institutions, where they are visible to the public, and able to attract the business of ethnoracial customers. Considering the long-standing exclusion and under-representation of ethno-racial people in this industry, ethnic market staffing can be viewed as an inclusive organizational restructuring practice. However, many bank workers in the study dispute its inclusive nature. They argue that this organizational practice operates to construct diversity along a horizontal axis, diverting attention from the ways it maintains and reinforces existing hierarchical relations of power and privilege (see Nazim, 2007).

There is a general consensus expressed among the workers in this study that they have very little input or voice when it comes to the articulation and positioning of difference and diversity in the organization. Instead, they point to men and women from privileged organizational positions who have little or no knowledge of the histories of those individuals and groups they are charged with positioning, but rather rely on essentialist and static notions of identity. A common practice noted by bank workers in the study was the use of the phrase "the right fit" to determine the boundaries of where racialized employees can and cannot work in the organization. For example, one worker told of a story where a black female manager was told in an interview that she would not be the *right fit* for the predominantly Italian area where the branch she was applying to was located (Nazim, 2007).

Social differences and their intersections are important indicators of who is allowed to work where in the organization (Booth, 2001). This is particularly important at the frontline where social differences are visible to the wider society. Where service is linked to issues of accessibility, which include language, it becomes more difficult to see how practices such as the use of the term "right fit" are exclusionary. For example, the organization can argue that a black woman who does not speak Italian will not be able to communicate with many of the clientele in this area, affecting the quality of customer service. Hence, explanations of service and accessibility divert attention away from the ways that social differences organize relations of power and privilege between and within "communities." Instead, talk of *service* and *accessibility* become an acceptable way of keeping in place exclusionary and oppressive organizational practices.

The exclusionary nature of ethnic market staffing is more visible when issues of service and accessibility are not linked to language barriers. For example, Bina, a Muslim female manager who wears the hijab (headscarf) revealed that the organization would never place her in a branch manager position downtown because the dominant "white yuppie clientele" would not want to deal with a Muslim woman of colour, who they would view as a "hindrance on management" (Nazim, 2007).

There are often differences when it comes to where racialized people see themselves in the organization and where those with the power to position them see them. For example, Bina is aware that she will never be assigned to the branch manager position downtown. This is a position that is associated with power, knowledge, authority, privilege and status, traditionally reserved for middle-class/elite heterosexual, ablest white men. Bina's skin colour, ethnicity, gender and religion not only distance her from this dominant image, but also stand as the antithesis to what it represents (Nazim, 2007).

When marginalized people pursue employment opportunities in places where their presence disrupts and challenges the dominant social order, it is expected of them to explain the necessity of their presence in these places. For example, when Bina applied for a management position at a branch where a there is a large Jewish clientele she was asked how she would deal with customers who were not comfortable with her hijab (Nazim, 2007). Meanwhile, there is no concerted attention paid to the positioning of whiteness in the organization. Similar questions are not asked of the dominant bodies simply because their presence in these institutions is viewed as normal and natural. Concerns around "fit" are never an issue for dominant bodies. Rather, the onus is on racialized peoples to explain and justify how their presence will "fit" into the existing order of a particular space/place in the organization, and by extension the wider society.

Ethnic market staffing operates as an administrative and ideological practice which functions to position ethno-racial employees in ways that keep in place the existing social order of the organization and the wider society it mirrors. It is only when these employees attempt to move out of these assigned spaces that the social relations of power that mark them and the larger society are rendered visible (Nazim, 2007).

Ethnic market staffing is premised on a framework of Canadian multiculturalism and constitutes the model on which mainstream organizations including banks staff their frontlines. However, the emphasis on expressive and descriptive notions of culture where it comes to ethnic market staffing hides and disguises issues of power, privilege, identity, knowledge and entitlement that underlie its practice. At the heart of ethnic market staffing are critical questions such as, who has the power to articulate and position difference? How is difference being articulated and positioned? And, in whose interest is difference being articulated and positioned?

While it has been argued that that the main aim of ethnic market staffing has been to attract consumers from ethno-racial communities, it also serves a more insidious purpose, which is to mask the ways in which organizational practices marginalize and exclude poor ethno-racial consumers, those who are considered to be a "risk."

NEUTRALIZING RISK: CREDIT SCORING AND THE POWER AND POLITICS OF IDENTITY

In order to maximize profit, the financial services industry worldwide has paid particular attention to the management and reduction of risk[1] (Clarke et al., 2001; Dymski, 2001, 2004; Lipuma and Lee, 2004; Maroney, Naka, and Wansi, 2004). Globally, financial institutions have focused their attentions on middle-class and affluent segments of societies. For example, in recent years wealth management has been the fastest growing sector of Western financial institutions (Johnson, 1995; Rose, 1992; Trott and Sjogren, 1997). These institutions are interested in individuals with higher than average levels of capital that can purchase investment services, on which the banks earn fee income. In fact, fee income has become a major way for financial institutions to generate profit. Prior to deregulation of the industry in the 1980s, banks earned their profits largely from the interest rate spread (the difference between interest paid on deposits and the higher interest charged on loans). As the profit emphasis shifted away from interest rate spread towards the generation of fee income, banks have become involved in selling riskier financial products and services (Johnson, 1995). At the same time they have attempted to exclude lower socioeconomic segments of society, those considered high risk (Dymski, 2004; Leyshon and Thrift, 1993; Squires, 2003).

Globally, financial organizations have made it increasingly difficult for the growing mass of poor to use mainstream banks. One way to exclude the poor has been to withdraw services from economically depressed areas (ACORN, 2004; Dreier, 2003; Leyshon and Thrift, 1993). In their work on the 1990s restructuring of the UK financial services industry, Andrew Leyshon and Nigel Thrift (1993) coined the term "flight to quality" to describe the industry's abandonment and retreat to a more affluent client base through the process of financial infrastructure withdrawal, by which services and operations are withdrawn from certain social groups and localities.

In Canada, a similar pattern of "flight to quality" has taken place. While there are obvious regional differences, there are also patterns of income disparities in many of Canada's major urban cities. As a result, these cities have also experienced the withdrawal of financial infrastructure. For example, branch closures have occurred in some of Canada's most disadvantaged neighbourhoods, such as the Pointe St-Charles neighbourhood of Montreal, the Regent Park area of Toronto and the Downtown Eastside area of Vancouver (CCRC, 1997:4). The Financial Consumer Agency of Canada (FCAC) reported more than seven hundred branch closures across Canada between 2001 and 2003 (ACORN, 2004: 15).

One reason that banks have been prepared to close branches is due to the growth of more cost-effective distribution channels (e.g., ATMs, telephone and computer banking). In his work on community reinvestment in America, Peter Dreier (2003) argues, "the accelerating decline of bank branches and the increase of ATMs and on-line banking appear racially neutral, but they have significant racial implications. Because poor and minority households are less likely to have computers, they are even more likely now than before to be served by pawnbrokers, check-cashing stores, predatory lenders, and other forms of fringe banking" (p.207). Bank workers in the study also argue that automated channels do not work for those customers who the industry already marginalizes. Many note that computers are a luxury for lower-income individuals and language issues are often a barrier for new immigrants. However, risk is also structured into these automated channels and functions to disadvantage those individuals and groups who are already marginalized (Nazim, 2007).

The withdrawal of financial infrastructure from economically disadvantaged areas is linked to the rise in check cashing and payday lending stores that charge between 300% and 900% in annual interest once all the different charges, fees and insurance costs are tallied. It is estimated that there are more than 1,200 payday lending stores across Canada, which generate more than one billion in annual revenue (ACORN, 2004:5). ACORN Canada (2004) found that bank branch closures in Toronto and Vancouver have been concentrated in lower-income neighborhoods and payday lenders are moving aggressively into this vacuum. The location and distribution of payday lending operations is closely, although not perfectly, related to significant concentrations of low-income families. The pattern closely follows the residential concentration of those without knowledge of one or both official languages and also follows concentrations of single parents (p.15).

Canadian banks have continued to resist pressure to adopt anti-discrimination legislation, despite growing poverty and racism in Canada. For example, over the past two decades, the percentage of poor women in Canada has increased to almost 19 percent of all adult women. Among these women, Aboriginal women, those from visible minority groups and those with disabilities are over-represented (Neal, 2004: 32). Meanwhile, new immigrant households continued to record among the weakest income gains and sharpest increases in low-income rates during the 1990s (Enns, 2005; Farrell, 2005; Klodawsky et. al., 2005).

Access to credit is one of the most important financial instruments for people. Credit is important to people since it allows them to build their current resources by borrowing from their future earnings (Hollis, 2001:73). For example, taking out a mortgage on a house allows someone who can't afford to pay for the entire house immediately, to purchase the house over time from the bank. Financial institutions worldwide are now relying on computer software programs to create more pervasive monetary networks of inclusion and exclusion, particularly when it comes to access to credit. Computer software now enables banks to create geographically specific marketing programs where the residential areas of desirable clientele are identified and targeted. Through "financial super-inclusion," banks could target only the most desired clientele, and limit their recruitment programs to the appropriate size and scope. One result of this process is the exclusion of those poorer, marginalized groups who do not purchase financial products or services and who are regarded as costly and unwelcome consumers (Leyshon and Thrift, 1999:447).

Centralized computerized credit scoring systems are heralded as a cost-effective way of processing large volumes of credit applications. This centralized system of financial lending, more commonly referred to as credit-scoring, is a computer-based management tool, which relies on multivariate statistical analysis to predict the credit performance of consumers. Credit-scoring software attempts to overcome information asymmetries by enabling firms to discriminate between *good* and *bad* customers "at-a-distance," based upon the analysis of occupational, demographic, geographic and other data provided directly by the consumer or from other databases (Leyshon and Thrift, 1999:436).

The central element to all credit-scoring systems is the "scorecard," which is the basis for analyzing the responses contained on the specifically designed application forms that banks require customers to complete. Each response is weighted according to the perceived likelihood of debt being repaid or an account being used responsibly. The lending decision is then reduced to a summed score, a comparison between the derived score and the current threshold for acceptance or rejection. These scores, more commonly called *risk scores,* are generated by risk-based computer software and serve as the basis for granting credit (Leyshon and Thrift, 1999:444).

Critical social research on computerized lending and credit-scoring systems, particularly in the United States (Cloud and Galster, 1993; Dreier, 2003; Dymski, 2001, 2004; Golinger and Mierzwinski, 1998), reveal the ways in which these systems structure social inequality along axes of race, class, gender and their intersections. This research is quite consistent with earlier findings when it comes to patterns of social inequality and access to credit. Essentially, those groups historically marginalized (e.g., women, African-American, Hispanic, Latino, and new immigrants) continue to experience difficulties when it comes to gaining access to credit. In Canada, the relationship between social inequality and access to credit is limited and less conclusive, given the fact that financial institutions do not collect statistics on race when it comes to credit. However, the findings of existing Canadian social research that attempts to address the relationship between social inequality and access to credit, point to trends and patterns similar to the American research when it comes to race, gender, immigrant status, language and class (ACORN, 2004; CCRC, 1997; Gravenor, 2001; Novac, Darden, Hulchanski, Seguin, Berneche, 2002).

Computerized credit-scoring systems function to redistribute power and decision-making from the margins towards the center of financial organizations (Bowker and Star, 1994; Grint and Woolgar, 1997; Shaoul, 1989; Star, 1991; Woolgar, 1998). This centralization of credit-scoring systems operates to standardize lending policy, enabling senior management to exert power "at-a-distance" more effectively than in the past. The simultaneous operations of dispersal and centralization have become part of the landscape of globalization (Sassen, 2001).

In his work on credit-scoring, Shaoul (1989) argues that decision-making power increasingly resides with large credit-scoring consultancies like Equifax, who developed the automated credit-scoring and behavioural score cards that distinguish "good" and "bad" customers and supply data on consumers. The rise of credit-scoring has yielded a new form of praxis within the financial services industry, founded primarily upon computer software. Software including credit-scoring software can be viewed as constituent of a new set of information practices, which through the agency of software houses and consultancies are spreading across economies. Embedded in software are schemas or protocols about the world. These protocols are reifying standards that emphasize selection and control. This software installs relatively unchangeable, taken for granted protocols in the day-to-day information practices of organizations, providing unified ways of interpreting events, influencing the ways in which decisions are made and standardizing such decisions over time and space (Grint and Woolgar, 1995; Leyshon and Thrift, 1993, 1999; Woolgar, 1998).

Computerized credit-scoring software is now the major determinant when it comes to the distribution of credit. This system of knowledge is heralded as rational, objective and value-free due largely to the absence of humans from the decision-making process. Prior to the 1980s, bank staff, primarily management and specialized lending officers, undertook the credit-granting process. During this time studies emerged primarily from the US, which indicated disparities in the approval rates based on race of applicants (Brown, 1992, Squires, 2003; Squires and Kim, 1995). These studies consistently indicated that the approval rates of Whites were significantly higher than those of African-Americans and Latinos even when all other factors were equal. It was clear that this process of vetting customers, which relied on the tacit knowledge embodied in bank staff, primarily European White middle-class men, was fraught with issues of power and privilege that were marked by social relations, particularly class, race and gender.

Many of the bank workers believe that because this current system is centralized and automated, it is more likely to be objective and "unbiased." However, despite the general belief in the "objectivity" and unbiased nature of this system, many bank workers question its rationality. The dilemma emerges from the contradictions around different systems of knowledge. Because of the absence of any physical being attached to this automated lending system, the decisions it renders are viewed as detached, value-free and unbiased. This system of knowledge stands in opposition to embodied knowledge rooted in experience, emotion and feeling, which is viewed as biased and irrational. This latter system of knowledge and its pedagogical value is devalued by an industry that views "financial knowledge" manifested in economic models, numbers, risk scores, and the logic of the market as rational, neutral and objective (Nazim, 2007). Many bank workers in the study expressed that they had difficulty explaining to customers why their application for credit was denied by the system when it contradicted their own knowledge, and opinions of the customer. Many of them resorted to simply saying "you don't fit the box" (Nazim, 2007).

The "box" they are referring to is really software protocols, which are kept in the background and rarely examined. The effects of these software protocols are likely to be pervasive and more insidious because they are disguised in the legitimating veneer of science, technology and "objectivity." Making these protocols transparent is difficult, largely because there has been little interrogation of those who design and write them. For example, Kohanski (1998) found that when given the task of connecting several databases of personal information, programmers rarely consider the political implications of what they're doing. In essence these protocols are dominant values and ideologies that advance a particular world-view and identities.

Knowledge and ways of knowing are rooted in power and identity and as bank workers in the study reveal, this system of credit is about the power to marginalize and exclude some more than others, notably those who are already among the most vulnerable (e.g., the poor, women, non-whites, new immigrants, disabled, and non-English speaking people).

In his work on credit-scoring, Shaoul (1989) reveals that this narrowing of identities, which benefits particular social segments of society, is methodologically structured into credit-scoring software programs.[2] The bank workers in this study brought to light many of the methodological biases that Shaoul (1989) refers to in his work on credit-scoring. They reveal how these structural biases function to privilege some social groups over others. For example, financial advisors complain about how the lending system is set up in such a way that the experiences and histories of those whose material lives have not been rooted in Canada cannot be inputted onto the system (Nazim, 2007).

The histories and values of dominant social groups structured into global computerized systems of credit are embedded in hegemonic concepts like "wealth." Essentially, the dominant definition of wealth can be defined as "the money value of the stock of assets owned by an individual at a particular point in time (excluding lifetime earning capacity or 'human capital'), minus their total debts and liabilities at that time" (Philipps, 1996:142). Generally, the government, economists, and financial industry experts use this concept of wealth to determine state and industry practices and policies. This is problematic, given that wealth is socially constructed and culturally contingent and as such is distributed more unequally than income (Philipps, 1996; Lee, 2003).

Dymski (2001) critiques the dominant economic models used to measure racial discrimination in residential credit markets in the US, arguing that it tests for discrimination from any moment in time forward, and ignores the accumulated historical disadvantage associated with minority racial disadvantage (p.2). Rather than employ the dominant economic-deprivation model to test for social inequality, Dymski suggests that researchers measure White privilege to account for racial discrimination when it comes to lending. In other words, instead of asking, "What disadvantage accrues to minority (or female) status?" the estimations done in this portion of the chapter ask, "What advantages accrue to White status?" (p.2).

Many of the bank workers in the study contend that ethnic-market staffing creates an expectation that it is the responsibility of ethno-racial staff to serve ethno-racial customers, particularly when they are from their respective ethnic communities. Besides the aspects of comfort, trust and connectedness embedded in shared identities around ethnicity and race, ethnic market staffing aims to minimize the cultural and language barriers that non-English speaking communities encounter. The assumption is that employees who speak the same languages as customers will be better able to explain the organization's products, services and practices. However, according to employees, that is often not the case. They contend that there is often resentment among staff members, including those from ethno-racial communities, towards customers who have no or limited English language skills. They argue that staff cuts, increased workload and the stress and pressure of an individualistic competitive organizational culture that rewards sales, has meant staff are less willing to spend time with customers they view as time-consuming, risky and less profitable; namely those lower socioeconomic customers with language and cultural barriers (see Nazim, 2007).

However, banks are not interested in these people, which may indicate that the practice of ethnic market staffing in a sense functions as it was intended to, which is to exclude socioeconomically disadvantaged customers from ethno-racial communities. There is an obvious need for social research to explore the experiences of marginalized segments of Canadian society who do not have access to mainstream financial institutions due to systemic barriers.

Ethnic market staffing with its emphasis on expressive notions of culture and issues around trust and belonging position ethno-racial bank workers in such a way that their connection could be utilized to attract customers from their respective communities. Bank workers in the study contend that there is an underlying expectation from ethno-racial customers that they will not encounter discrimination from ethno-racial employees or that they will understand their experiences in ways that employees from the dominant group would not and thus work harder for them. At the same time, there are limitations as to how much these employees can help ethno-racial customers who do not fit within the parameters of what the industry defines as "profitable." Many of these customers are unfamiliar with the centralization of the industry, particularly the system of granting credit. Instead, they assume that financial advisors have the same powers that lending officers once had when the system was decentralized. This belief is more prevalent among new immigrants who come from countries where this older system of granting credit still operates (see Nazim, 2007).

Like multiculturalism, ethnic market staffing posits ethno-racial communities as homogeneous and does not address the intersections of race and racism with other markers of difference. Instead, the orchestrated positioning of ethno-racial staff on the frontlines who are charged with the responsibility of carrying out exclusionary organizational practices not only distracts and disguises the ways racism operates to exclude poor ethno-racial people, but also makes it harder to name as racism. Thus, as ethno-racial employees point out, while poor White customers may resist their authority on the basis of race, poor ethno-racial customers have a harder time using race as a basis from which to challenge their authority. In some ways, ethno-racial customers tend to be somewhat more receptive to these policies if they are implemented or enforced by ethno-racial employees, who they do not associate with racism. In effect, the use of ethno-racial bank workers makes it easier for the organization to implement its exclusionary policies more smoothly and without encountering resistance or objection when a form of racism whether visible or invisible is carried out through these practices (see Nazim, 2007).

Oppression is multifaceted as is evidenced by the fact that racialized bodies are enforcing organizational practices that oppress and exclude other racialized individuals, while enabling such practices to be disguised by other organizational practices like ethnic market staffing. Given the post 9/11 world we live in, Canada's increasing social diversity and the classed, racialized and gendered structure of its political economy, risk will continue to be a salient factor in society. A financial sector that continues to restructure for profit in ways that focus on reducing "risk" will also continue to marginalize and exclude minoritized people in Canada.

CONCLUSION

Canadian financial institutions have strategically drawn on the dominant model of Canadian multiculturalism through their organizational practice of ethnic market staffing to support a global profit driven financial system that reinforces existing relations of economic and social inequality. It can be seen from the arguments of this paper that the practice of ethnic market staffing is fraught with problems and inconsistencies around issues of difference, identity, diversity and relations of power and privilege. As such, the practice of ethnic market staffing is inadequate in responding to the needs of diverse staff members and the larger communities that they represent. Rather, this organizational practice serves to disguise the oppressive and exclusionary nature of credit scoring technology in Canada and globally.

NOTES

1. The term "risk" encompasses a range of definitions in the financial services industry. Leyshon and Thrift defines eight types of risk that have gained increasing significance since the onset of restructuring of the financial services industry world-wide. However, the study only focused on two types of risk–credit risk (the assessment by credit-granting institutions of whether or not borrowers are both willing and able to repay the debit they incur) and clearing and settlement risk, have emerged as issues of growing importance.
2. Shaoul's (1989) identifies five serious methodological problems: the use of small sample sizes; errors introduced from the statistical translation of verbal information; histogram error because multiple discriminate analysis needs continuous data, not the discrete variables produced by scorecards; the use of median values to fill gaps in incomplete application forms, and the problem of "reject interference," which refers to the fact that credit-scoring does not contain information from a random sample of the population, but only from that section of the population that in the past has had applications accepted making it impossible to compare this population with any other, for such systems of analysis preclude any analysis of the applications deemed unacceptable.

REFERENCES

Abu-Laban, Y., and D. Stasiulis. (1992). "Ethnic Pluralism under Siege: Popular and Partisan Opposition to Multiculturalism." *Canadian Public Policy* XVIII(4):365-386.

ACORN. (2004). *Protecting Canadians' Interest: Reining in the Payday Lending Industry.* Association of Community Organizations for Reform Now. Available at http://www.acorn.org/.

Bair, S. (2003). "Improving Access to the U.S. Banking System Among Recent Latin American Immigrants." Amherst, University of Massachusetts: The Multilateral Investment Fund. Center for Public Policy and Administration. Available at www.IADB.ORG/MIF.

Bannerji, H. (2000). *The Dark Side of the Nation: Essays on Multiculturalism, Nationalism and Gender.* Toronto: Canadian Scholars' Press Inc.

Barnes, D., and Z. Nazim. (2004). "Diversity Management and the Legacy of Canadian Multiculturalism: Moving Towards a Critical Social Framework." *The International Journal of Diversity in Organizations, Communities and Nations* 4:1101-1114.

Bolaria, S.B., and P. Li. (1988). *Racial Oppression in Canada,* 2nd ed. Toronto: Garamond Press.

Booth, J. (2001). "A Critique of 'Cultural Fit' in Relation to the Recruitment of Indi@n Inform@tion Technologists for the Y2K Project." *International Journal of Diversity in Organizations, Communities and Nations* 4:4-16.

Bose, P. (2007). "Development, Displacement and Diaspora: Contesting Identity in a Globalized World." In A. Asgharzadeh, E. Lawson, K. Oka, and A. Wahab (eds.), *Diasporic Ruptures: Globality, Migrancy, and Expressions of Identity: Vol. 1.* Rotterdam: Sense Publishers.

Bowker, G., and L.S. Star. (1994). "Knowledge and Infrastructure in International Information Management." In B. Frierman (ed.), *Information Acumen: The Understanding and Use of Knowledge in Modern Business.* London: Routledge.

Brown, J. (1992, November). "Opening the Book on Lending Discrimination." *Multinational Monitor* 14(11). Available at http://multinationalmonitor.org/.

CCRC. (1997). *Access to Basic Banking Service: Ensuring a Right to this Essential Service.* Canadian Community Reinvestment Coalition. Available at http://www.cancrc.org/.

Clarke, G., R. Cull, M.S. Peria, and S.M. Sanchez. (2001). "Foreign Bank Entry: Experience, Implications for Developing Countries, and Agenda for Further Research." *World Bank Research Observer* 18(1):25-59.

Cloud, C., and G. Galster. (1993). "What Do We Know About Racial Discrimination in Mortgage Markets." *Review of Black Political Economy* 22(1):102-122.

Dreier, P. (2003). "Protest, Progress, and the Politics of Reinvestment." In G. Squires (ed.), *Organizing Access to Capital: Advocacy and the Democratization of Financial Institutions.* Philadelphia: Temple University Press.

Dymski, G.A. (2001). "Is Discrimination Disappearing? Residential Credit Market Evidence, 1992-1998." *International Journal of Social Economics* 28(10/11/12):1025-1045.

_____. (2004). "Credit Rationing and Financial Exclusion in the Age of Globalization." Paper presented at the Eighth International Post-Keynesian Conference, Kansas City.

Enns, R. (2005). "Immigrant Households and Homelessness." *Canadian Issues* (Spring):127-130.

Farrell, M. (2005). "Responding to Housing Instability among Newcomers." *Canadian Issues* (Spring):119-122.

Galabuzi, G.E. (2005). "Factors Affecting the Social Economic Status of Canadian Immigrants in the New Millenium." *Canadian Issues* (Spring):53-57.

Golinger, J., and E. Mierzwinski. (1998). *PIRG: Mistakes Do Happen: Credit Report Errors Mean Consumers Lose.* Available at http://uspirg.org/report/mistakesdohappen3_98.pdf.

Gravenor, K. (2001). "Redlining Redux: Canadian Banks Fight Proposal that could Invigorate Slums." *The Front,* July 26, pp.1-4.

Grint, K., and S. Woolgar. (1997). *The Machine at Work.* Cambridge: Polity.

Henry, F., C. Tator, W. Mattis, and T. Rees. (2000). *The Colour of Democracy: Racism in Canadian Society,* 3rd ed. Toronto: Thomson Nelson.

Hollis, A. (2001). "Women and Micro-credit in History: Gender in the Irish Loan Funds." In B. Lemire, R. Pearson and G. Campbell (eds.), *Women and Credit: Researching the Past, Refiguring the Future.* Oxford: Berg.

Johnson, H. (1995). *Banking Without Borders: Challenges and Opportunities in the Era of North American Free Trade and the Emerging Global Marketplace.* Chicago: Probus Publishing.

Keung, N. (2005). "Banking on Cultural Diversity." *Toronto Star,* April 17, p. A21.

Klodawsky, F., T. Aubry, B. Behnia, C. Nicholson, and M. Young. (2005). "The Panel Study on Homelessness: Secondary Data Analysis of Responses of Study Participants Whose Country of Origin is not Canada." *Canadian Issues* (Spring):123-126.

Lash, S., and J. Urry. (1994). *Economies of Signs and Space.* London: Sage.

Lee, M. (2003). "Community Reinvestment in a Globalizing World: To Hold Banks Accountable, From the Bronx to Buenos Aires, and Basel." In G.D. Squires (ed.), *Organizing Access to Capital: Advocacy and the Democratization of Financial Institutions.* Philadelphia: Temple University Press.

Li, W., and L. Lo. (2008). "People–Money Co-movement and the Ethnic Financial Sectors in Canada and the U.S." *Migracijske i etni ke teme* 24(4):301–321.

Leyshon, A., and N. Thrift. (1993). "The Restructuring of the U.K Financial Service Industry in the 1990s: A Reversal of Fortune?" *Journal of Rural Studies* 9(3):223-241.

_____. (1999). "Lists Come Alive: Electronic Systems of Knowledge and the Rise of Credit-Scoring in Retail Banking." *Economy and Society* 28(3):467-493.

LiPuma, E., and B. Lee. (2004). *Financial Derivatives and the Globalization of Risk.* Durham: Duke University Press.

Maroney, N., A. Naka, and T. Wansi. (2004). "Changing Risk, Return, and Leverage: The 1997 Asian Financial Crisis." *Journal of Financial and Quantitative Analysis* 39(1):143-166.

Nash, A. (1997). "Ethnic Entrepreneurship: The Case of Canadian Business Immigrants." *The American Ethnic Geographer 5*(1):4-5.

Nazim. Z. (2007). *Interrogating Restructuring: ACritical Ethnography of Ethno-Racial Women Workers in Canadian Retail Banking.* Doctoral Thesis. Toronto, Ontario: Department of Sociology and Equity Studies, OISE/University of Toronto.

Neal, R. (2004). *Voices: Women, Poverty and Homelessness in Canada.* Ottawa: Report of the National Anti-Poverty Organization.

Novac, S., J. Darden, D. Hulchanski, A. Seguin, and F. Berneche. (2002). *Housing Discrimination in Canada: What Do We Know About It?* Centre for Urban and Community Studies. Toronto: University of Toronto.

Philipps, L. (1996). "Tax Policy and the Gendered Distribution of Wealth." In I. Bakker (ed.), *Rethinking Restructuring: Gender and Change in Canada.* Toronto: University of Toronto Press.

Razack, S. (2002). "Introduction: When Place Becomes Race." In S. Razack (ed.), *Race, Space and the Law: Unmapping a White Settler Society.* Toronto: Between the Lines.

Rose, S. (1992). "A New Approach to Private Banking." *Journal of Retail Banking,* XIV(2):11-21.

Sassen, S. (2001). *The Global City: Strategic Site/New Frontier.* Available at www.india-seminar.com.

Satzewich, V., and N. Liodakis. (2009). *Race and Ethnicity in Canada: A Critical Introduction,* 2nd ed. Toronto: Oxford University Press.

Shaoul, M. (1989). *Ticking for the Truth: An Investigation of Credit Scoring.* Manchester: Manchester School of Management.

Squires, G., and S. Kim. (1995). "Does Anybody Who Works Here Look Like Me: Mortgage Lending, Race, and Lender Employment." *Social Science Quarterly* 76(4):823-838.

Squires, G. (2003). "Introduction: The Rough Road to Reinvestment." In G. Squires (ed.), *Organizing Access to Capital: Advocacy and the Democratization of Financial Institutions.* Philadelphia: Temple University Press.

Star, L.S. (1991). "Power, Technology and the Phenomenology of Conventions: On Being Allergic to Onions." In J. Law (ed.), *A Sociology of Monsters: Essays on Power, Technology and Domination.* London: Routledge.

Trott, D., and K. Sjogren. (1997). "Capturing the Wealthy Client." *Canadian Banker* (March/April):18-22.

Walker, B. (2008). *History of Immigration and Racism in Canada: Essential Readings.* Toronto: Canadian Scholars Press.

Woolgar, S. (1998). "A New Theory of Innovation." *Prometheus* 4:441-452.

Chapter 12

Gender and Inequality

Global Migration, Gender, and Inequality: Chinese Immigrant Women's Employment Experience in Canada

Guida Man

York University

INTRODUCTION

The prioritizing of highly educated, skilled immigrants and business personnel has historically been the objective of the Canadian state, especially since 1967, when the purportedly "non-discriminatory"[1] points system was introduced into Canadian immigration policy. With the intensification of economic globalization since the early 1980s, and Canada's participation in Canada-U.S. Free Trade Agreement (CUFTA) and North American Free Trade Agreement (NAFTA), the Canadian neoliberal state underwent rapid economic restructuring, downsizing, privatization, and deregulation in order to achieve the goal of being a "lean state" (Shields and Evans, 1998). Concomitantly, the state developed new immigration initiatives to prioritize the highly skilled as well as business immigrants to Canada. Obviously, Canada is not the only country pursuing policy changes to procure highly skilled immigrants, other post-industrial nations (notably the United States and Australia) too have undergone similar policy transformations (Boyd, 2001; Cornelius et al., 2001; Fincher et al., 1994). The selective immigration policy and the targeting of skilled immigrants has been contentious. On the one hand, the state's assumption behind the new initiatives is that highly skilled jobs are in demand in the new economic order (Shields, 1995). The strategy, therefore, is to bolster Canada's competitiveness in the global market place with a skilled, fluid and flexible labour force that would provide Canada with a "comparative advantage" (Brecher and Costello, 1994) in the post-industrial era of global competition. In such a political and economic climate, it is expected that "skilled"

This chapter is a revised version of a paper entitled "Gender, Work and Migration: Deskilling Chinese Immigrant Women in Canada," published in *Women's Studies International Forum* 27(2004):135-148.

immigrant workers, unlike their "unskilled" counterparts, would enjoy a smooth transition in reinserting themselves in the Canadian labour market. On the other hand, there is growing concern that the selective policies will exacerbate the differential and negative impact on women, particularly poor women and women of colour (Arat-Koc, 1999).

Feminist scholars have long drawn attention to the plight of immigrant women, particularly working class and refugee women in Canada (e.g., Arat-koc, 1999; Giles and Preston, 2003; Ng, 1981). In recent years, a number of studies have addressed the impact of neoliberal policies on women in general (Armstrong, 1996; Brodie, 1995; Devault, 2008; Luxton and Reiter, 1997), and on immigrant women of colour in particular (Das Gupta, 2009, 1999; Jo-Anne Lee, 1999). These studies shed light on the experience of the multiple oppressions of working class immigrant women. More recently, there is an emerging literature on immigrant women who are highly educated, skilled professionals (Iredale, 2001; Man, 2002, 2007; Mojab, 1999; Ng, Man, and Shan, 2008; Preston and Man, 1999; Salaff, 1997, 2006). These studies found that many middle-class immigrant women too encountered difficulties in finding employment commensurate with their qualifications in the new country. The Canadian immigration policy's increased emphasis on the recruitment of skilled professionals to Canada resulted in a high percentage of recent immigrants being admitted under this category. For example, in 2000, economic immigrants (comprising of business immigrants as well as skilled workers) constituted 58 percent of all immigrants coming to Canada. Since 1987, the Chinese have constituted the largest immigrant group entering Canada, the majority of them came in as skilled workers. Hong Kong was the largest immigrant source country to Canada from 1987 to 1997, with the highest number of immigrants of 130,768 coming between 1991-1995 (Guo and DeVoretz, 2005). Since 1998, Mainland China surpassed other countries to become the number one immigrant sending country to Canada. While the number of Mainland Chinese immigrants was 42,077 from 1986-1990 (Guo and DeVoretz, 2005), it soared to 181,359 between 2002 and 2006 (CIC, 2009). As a result, the 2006 Census showed a total of 1.22 million Chinese in Canada (CIC, 2009).

In this chapter, I focus on the employment experiences in Canada of middle-class Chinese immigrant women who were highly-educated, skilled professionals in their home country. I argue that contrary to the state's assertion that the new economy requires a highly skilled labour, these skilled Chinese immigrant women's opportunity in the paid labour market do not fare well in the context of a new political and economic environment. The chapter demonstrates that immigrant women's employment experience in Canada is complicated by gendered and racialized institutional processes in the form of state policies and practices, professional accreditation systems, employers' requirement for "Canadian experience" and labour market conditions. The demands on immigrant women's reproductive labour in the home also affects these women but I will not address this here.

For the purpose of this chapter, I am using the term "immigrant" women to refer to the common sense usage of the word, that is, people who are seen as immigrants by others, regardless of their formal legal status. I am also adopting the definition of skilled workers as "those with some tertiary education and in possession of skills valued in the labour market" (Raghuram 2004), and with the cognizance that skill is "mediated by the unequal distribution of power along the lines of gender, class, race, language, ethnicity, national origin and the state of the economy" (Mojab, 2000:33).

NEOLIBERAL RESTRUCTURING

From the mid-1960s to the early 1970s, the Canadian welfare state has expanded its social safety net by providing post-secondary education, established medicare, provided universal benefits for seniors, and extended social services and welfare benefits to meet the social needs of the people. However, since the

1980s, the welfare state has been drastically eroded and replaced by the neoliberal state that valorizes the private over the public (Devault, 2008; Jessop, 1993). The dominant discourse of the neoliberal state argues for the natural and inevitability of the mechanisms of globalization, structural adjustment, privatization and deregulations, thereby closing off challenges and debates for possible alternative strategies and action. Feminist scholars have asserted that restructuring is a gendered process since social welfare programs and policies affect women's material conditions, and shape gender relationships (Armstrong, 1996; Bakker, 1996; Brodie, 1995). When previously state-subsidized programs are being downsized or privatized, and people in need of treatment are being deinstitutionalized, the work of healthcare, childcare, and elderly care is being pushed back into the home and downloaded onto the unpaid work of women who are expected to be the primary caregivers due to their gender (Armstrong and Armstrong, 2006; Luxton, 2006; Luxton and Reiter, 1997). Moreover, "as services and responsibilities are shifted from the public to the private, they become differently encoded, constructed, and regulated" (Brodie, 1995:54). Given the over-representation of women as users of social and community services, as welfare recipients, and as employees in the public sector (e.g., social workers, childcare workers, and nurses), government downloading and budget cuts to these services and programs affect them much more drastically. As a result, many women are forced to leave the paid labour force or settle for low-paying part-time employment to meet these caring needs. Many women lose their jobs, or are being deskilled in a leaner and meaner work environment (Armstrong, 1996; Cranford, Vosko, and Zukewich, 2006). Those women who seek employment are being channelled into the private sector as part-time, flexible labour, with no benefits or job security.

Neoliberal restructuring has also served to marginalize immigrants (Shields, 2002). The dismantling of social support programs and the fostering of highly bifurcated labour markets undermine immigrants' ability to successfully integrate into their host society. As a result, this segment of the population becomes highly susceptible to the problems of social exclusion. In the new labour market, immigrants, and in particular immigrant women of colour are increasingly being used as "flexible" and disposable labour, suited to the demands of the globalized economy (de Wolff, 2003; Mirchandani et al., 2008; Vosko, 2006).

Despite their high levels of education and training, many Chinese immigrant women professionals in my study did not enter Canada under the "skilled worker" category. Rather, they entered as dependents of their husbands who are the principal applicants under the economic class category. This is so because "skill" is "constructed and negotiated through ideological and political processes" (Arat-Koc, 1999:284). Gender biases in definitions of education, work, and skill means that women's skills and personal qualities are either excluded or undervalued. Hence the immigration processes reproduces and structures inequality within the family by rendering one spouse (typically the wife) legally dependent on the other (Ng, 1996). This gender differentiation in immigration status (principal applicant versus dependents) indicates the structural difference between male and female immigrations with regard to their occupation and status in their home country as well as in Canada.

RESEARCH METHODOLOGY

The research methodology I employ for this chapter is known as institutional ethnography, developed by Dorothy Smith (1987, 2006). I placed the immigrant women as the subject of the inquiry, and I linked their accounts to the larger social, economic, and political processes in society in which their experiences are embedded. Instead of starting with preconceived notions, hypotheses or theories originating in the discourse, and using the everyday world of experience as a resource to support the sociological discourse, the "standpoint of women" shifts the sociological problematic from the discourse to the everyday world. This methodology has enabled me to investigate how individual Chinese immigrant women as subjects account for their situations, and to demonstrate how their subjective experiences articulate with larger social, economic, and political relations.

This chapter is also informed by the notion that race, gender and class are socially constructed relations that are integral to the formation of contemporary social life (Ng, 1993). Race, gender, and class are not distinct, unitary entities that operate separately but must be conceptualized as intersecting (Sayer, 1987), fluid and dynamic, and subject to temporal and spatial fluctuations. Thus they appear in divergent forms in different social and historical periods.

The Sample

The research data for the immigrant women from China is derived from focus group and individual interviews with 20 women who have immigrated to Canada between 1994 and 1999. The data for the immigrant women from Hong Kong has been generated through in depth interviews with thirty women who have immigrated to Canada with their families between 1986 and 1993. Five were living in Vancouver at the time of the interview, and the rest were living in Toronto. For the purpose of clarity, for the rest of the chapter, I will refer to the immigrant women from Hong Kong as HK women, and the women from Mainland China as Mainland women. I have artificially delineated women's work into the spheres of paid work and household work for investigative purposes although in actuality, these two spheres are very much interrelated.

INSTITUTIONAL AND LABOUR MARKET PROCESSES

Chinese immigrant women's employment opportunities are predicated on labour market conditions as well as gendered and racialized institutional processes. Institutional processes here refer to those policies and practices that are embedded in government, law, education, and professional systems. Such processes can engender and perpetuate social injustice in our society.

Although almost all the women I interviewed had come in as dependents of their husbands, many are highly educated, particularly, the Mainland women. Of this group, one has a master degree, 15 have bachelor degrees and 4 have tertiary diplomas. Amongst the HK women, one has a master degree, 9 have bachelor degree, 8 have diplomas, 2 have some post-secondary education and the rest have high school education. The higher education of the Mainland women could be attributed to the fact that the Mainland women came to Canada more recently than the HK women and were, therefore, subjected to even more stringent requirements by the immigration criterion. While 15 of the 30 HK women worked in professional/administrative positions or quasi-professional positions in their home country, all 20 of the Mainland women had worked as professionals prior to emigration in fields such as research, teaching, engineering, medicine, computer science, accounting, business and administration. At the time of the interviews, however, only three Mainland women were employed in professional positions none of whom had children. Of the rest, five were marginally employed, and eleven were unemployed. Among the HK women, three were employed in similar fields prior to emigration, two had managerial/supervisory positions, and the rest worked either in clerical positions, were self-employed or ran their own/husband's small business. A large number (eight) of them were housewives. Only three declared themselves as unemployed.

Within a household, the decision to emigrate necessitates the family to pool their resources. In all patriarchal societies, male education and skills are assigned more value than female education and skills. In order to maximize their opportunity for immigration admission, male family members are often designated as the principal applicant. As a result, the majority of these women came to Canada under the family immigrant status as dependents of their husbands, who are the principal applicants. The gendering of principal and non-principal applicants has far reaching consequences. As dependents, the women are treated as being "not destined for the labour market" due to institutionalized racist and sexist practices embedded in the immigration process. In fact, women in China have always participated alongside their male counterparts in productive processes (Association for the Advancement of Feminism, 1993).

While feminists have made some inroads in improving the working conditions of women, gender and racial discriminatory practices in employment continue to be prevalent (Kerr, 1996). The downward leveling effect of restructuring, privatization, and deregulation has aggravated labour market conditions by lowering wages and fostering part-time, insecure, contingent employment. This has a polarizing effect in gender, race, ethnicity and class interactions. Predictably, immigrant women's employment has been adversely affected. Numerous studies have found that immigrant women and racialized groups now face greater challenges in getting established in the job market and are increasingly located in disproportionate numbers in low-wage, contingent forms of employment especially in service, sales and production jobs (Smith and Jackson, 2002; Badets and Howatson-Leo, 2000). Minoritized women and immigrant women of colour, in particular, have a propensity to be channeled into "secondary" employment and they tend to stay in it through their working careers (Hiebert, 1997). Previous studies have also found that immigrant women have higher unemployment rates than Canadian-born women (Badets and Howatson-Leo, 2000; Boyd, 1992).

As neoliberal restructuring programs intensify, we see a drastic reduction of immigrants' earning power. In 1980, both male and female immigrant groups had earnings above the Canadian average, a reflection of the generally higher education levels of the immigrant population, but by 1996, these figures had fallen significantly below average. Female immigrant economic principal applicant earnings dropped from around $21,000 in 1980 to about $16,000 in 1996 in comparison with Canadian female average earnings which increased from just under $19,000 to nearly $21,000. Male immigrant economic principal applicant earnings also tumbled from $40,000 in 1980 to $25,000 in 1996, while Canadian male average earning remained virtually unchanged at just under $35,000 per year in 1999 (Grant and Thompson, 2000:5).

In recent years, the labour force participation of immigrant women in Canada has also fallen and is much lower than that of either Canadian-born people or immigrant men. According to Statistics Canada, between 1986 and 1996 employment rates for immigrant men aged between 25 and 44 fell from 81% to 71%, while that of immigrant women of the same age group fell from 58% to 51%. In the same period employment rates for Canadian-born women, however, rose 8% to 73% (Badets and Howatson-Leo, 1999) even though immigrant women generally have higher educational attainments than their Canadian-born counterparts. For example, Badets and Howatson-Leo's (1999) study found that recent immigrant women and men are more likely than their Canadian-born counterparts to have completed university education (31% and 36% versus 18% and 20%). Yet this does not improve their chances of employment in Canada, particularly in professional positions (Lo and Wang, 2003; Mojab, 1999; Man, 2002; Travato and Grindstaff, 1987).

The devaluation of international credentials and experience has been seen by some as rooted in the nature of capitalism (Mojab, 2000; Shields, 1996). Regardless of education and experience, immigrants are treated as a source of cheap labour and relegated to low paid, menial positions. These positions are often precarious,[2] with part-time, flexible hours, and no security or benefits and employment in these sectors is a highly gendered and racialized phenomenon (Cranford and Vosko, 2003; De Wolff, 2003; Galabuzi, 2001; Ornstein, 2000; Vosko, 2006). Li (2000) contends that the central issue is not so much a problem of individual employer decisions but of labour market discrimination. Institutionalized racist and sexist processes in the labour market discriminate against immigrants in general, and immigrant women in particular, making it very difficult for them to find employment commensurate with their credentials.

The employment opportunities for immigrant women of colour in a gender segregated, racialized, and globalized labour market are even more seriously jeopardized. Boyd (1992) found that being foreign-born, a member of a visible minority group or female has a cumulative effect such that foreign-born women of colour received the lowest wages and salaries of all workers. Immigrant women from developing countries, who do not have English or French language skills, or the "appropriate" educational background, are prone to being ghettoized in low-paid menial labour (Ng, 1993; Das Gupta, 1996).

Previous studies have found that despite their education and skills, the employment experiences of Chinese immigrant women were marred by difficulties (Man, 2002, 1997; Preston and Man, 1999; Salaff and Greve, 2005). Similarly, the 1996 census data reveal that with regard to education, although a higher percentage (17.5%) of Chinese immigrant women (foreign-born) have obtained a bachelor's degree or higher as compared to "other Canadians," both female and male (12.2% and 14%, respectively). However, fewer Chinese immigrant women have been able to enter the highly coveted managerial and professional occupations (3.7% and 8.5%, respectively) as compared to "other Canadian" women (3.8% and 9.8%, respectively) and "other Canadian" men (8.3% and 9.3%, respectively; Man, 2003:225, Table 10.3 and Table 10.4).

Comparisons between the 1986 census data (i.e., the early period of neoliberal policies) and 1996 census data (when neoliberal policies have been well entrenched) on education and occupation of Chinese immigrant women (foreign born) is even more revealing. It is found that in 1996 a much higher percentage of Chinese immigrant women have a university degree (17.5% and 12.8% respectively), yet the opportunity for Chinese immigrant women to enter professional, semi-professional and technician positions is only slightly higher than in 1986 (10.4% and 9.9% respectively; Man, 2001).

CHINESE IMMIGRANT WOMEN'S EMPLOYMENT EXPERIENCE

When asked about their employment experience, the women in my studies echoed the difficulties that other immigrant women of colour have voiced, for instance, those posed by requirement of "Canadian experience," by employers' reluctance to recognize immigrant women's qualifications and experience from their own countries and by racism in the labour market (George, 1998; Man, 1997). Several HK women became so exasperated with their job search that they gave up the idea of entering the labour force altogether. Their material conditions afforded them the choice of becoming full-time homemakers and taking care of their children, although they were unhappy with this situation. A HK woman who was a former administrator told me, "I have always worked my whole life. I enjoy working. I'm not old, I don't like sitting home and do nothing." Both the HK women and the Mainland women spoke of the monetary and emotional reasons for the need to find employment as soon as possible, particularly among the Mainland women. Although most of the HK women have brought money with them, they feared they would soon deplete their savings. They also said that they did not want to be dependent on their husbands financially, and that they needed a paid job to feel actualized. A HK woman reflected on her job search experience, "It's a catch-22. I cannot get a job because I don't have Canadian experience, and yet I don't see how I can possibly get Canadian experience without being hired in the first place!"

Another HK woman who was a social worker prior to entering Canada became self-employed after several months of being rejected by employers due to her lack of "Canadian experience" and her "foreign" degree. She contends that it was a rationale used by employers to discriminate against internationally trained immigrant women and men. Pursuing re-certification involves applying for an evaluation of her social work credentials, doing course work and accumulating at least two years of field practice.[3] Few immigrant women can afford to forgo wage work to pursue such an expensive and time-consuming process. Thus, the accreditation process deters immigrant women from practicing their professions.

The lack of recognition of immigrants' previous credential and work experience is a serious problem confronting highly educated immigrant women who are professionals (Raghuram and Kofman, 2002). In Canada, trades and professions are regulated through the governing and licensing bodies of professional associations such as the Royal College of Physicians and Surgeons, Canadian Council of Professional Engineers, and the Canadian Association of Schools of Social Work. In turn, each association has its provincial licensing bodies such as the Ontario College of Physicians and Surgeons, Professional Engineers of Ontario (PEO), Ontario College of Teachers (OCT). Currently, there are about thirty-five registered professions in Ontario (Skills for Change, 2001). The re-certification process is often costly and time consuming. There is a prolonged waiting period, and information regarding re-certification is not easily available, and often couched in vague language. It is difficult for new immigrants to navigate through bureaucratic red tape.[4]

It has been argued that professional associations and licensing bodies function as "labour market shelters" to protect and reduce competition for those already licensed by placing entry restrictions into higher-status and better paying occupations and professions (Krahn et al., 2000; Boyd, 2000). The professional licensing bodies have complete autonomy in their decision-making process and are ultimately responsible for determining the criteria for immigrants' re-entry into professions. Since many regulatory bodies have a legislated mandate for "protecting the public good," they are also in a position to "define characteristics of occupational internal labour markets which create monopolies on products and/or services by controlling labour supply" (Boyd, 2000:4). Issues such as lack of standard assessment process, lack of knowledge of comparative education systems, and arbitrary decisions without recourse to an appeal process limits immigrants' participation in the labour force (Skills for Change, 1995:27).

Immigrant women who were teachers in Hong Kong and China, in particular, found that their teaching experience and qualifications from their home countries are not recognized in Canada. In some cases, re-certification meant having to go through a minimum of one or two years of retraining. In other cases, they have to go through undergraduate education again in order to be accepted into Teacher's college. One HK woman explained why she has decided against retraining:

> I worked as an elementary teacher in Hong Kong for thirty years. The certification system there is different. I got my teaching certificate from the teachers' college in Hong Kong, that's it. Here, I have to be recertified again...At my age, I don't think I can go through another few years of schooling and still have no guarantee of getting a job later.

Since many of the Mainland women needed to make a living right away, they recognized the necessity of acquiring "Canadian experience," and took whatever jobs they were able to find. The economic recession in Canada in recent years means that new immigrants looking for work found jobs in low-pay, entry level positions, which do not utilize their skills, education, or experience. Unfortunately, the women often found that this first job experience eventually situated them in the labour market (Ng, 1993). The long working hours and the demands of their household responsibilities meant that some women were unable to retrain or attend English language courses and so found themselves unable to extricate themselves from the menial positions they are ghettoized into. A Mainland woman who was a teacher in Beijing who became a hotel cleaner in Canada exemplifies their experiences:

> The first job I had was babysitting, that was one month after I arrived. I found this job from a newspaper. My husband helped me prepare the interview. At that time, I knew very little English, but the woman hired me because she thought I have a good heart and would be kind to her children. I was very happy to get this job...I worked there for over one year. I have very good relationship

> with that family. Now I work in a hotel as a cleaner, full-time. It's hard work. My English is not good, I want to improve it, so I attended English classes in the evening at first while I was working during the day. But I couldn't keep doing so as I felt too tired. I couldn't concentrate on my study, so I have to give it up.

Feminist activists have protested against the gendered policies, which discriminate against immigrant women's opportunities in learning English. Prior to 1974, Employment and Immigration Canada offered a full-time language-training program known as the National Language Training Program (NLTP). It provides language training with a living allowance (a subsidy) to immigrants who were "heads of households," who are typically immigrant men (Boyd, 1992; Arat-koc, 1999). Immigrant women were not eligible for it, nor could they afford to forgo wage work in order to learn English. After 1974, the NLTP program was designated for those "destined for the labour market." Since immigrant women typically came in as dependents of their husbands they were, therefore, not considered as "destined for the labour market" and so deemed ineligible for the language course. Furthermore, due to racial discriminatory practices, immigrants of colour were often placed in part-time programs in community centres and local schools, while Northern Europeans were over-represented in NLTP at community colleges (Doherty, 1992).

In 1992, two programs were introduced to replace the NLTP. These are: Language Instruction for Newcomers to Canada (LINC) to provide basic communication skills; and Labour Market Language Training (LMLT) for advanced language training targeting those whose labour market skills are in demand. Unfortunately, to reduce cost, the state also eliminated the living allowance and restricted both programs to new immigrants who have been in Canada for less than a year. The elimination of a living allowance discriminates against the most disadvantaged immigrants who cannot afford to forgo wage work to attend language classes full-time. It is in this way that race, gender, and class inequalities in Canadian society are reproduced and perpetuated.

In recent years, as a cost saving measure, LMLT, together with two other employment insurance (EI) programs (Severely Employment Disadvantaged (SED), and Project Based Training (PBT)) that drew heavily on an immigrant clientele have also been eliminated. Daycare support too has been cut so that now a mother of two children is excluded from training because the childcare costs are deemed to be too expensive. Significantly, eligibility for training support is no longer universally accessible. Only those individuals that qualify for EI benefits are now granted access to EI funded training programs. Many immigrants and refugees who were not able to obtain long term appointment to fulfil the employment insurance requirements are consequently automatically excluded (Whittleton, 1999:3-4).

Without appropriate language training support, the Chinese immigrant women felt that their inadequate command of the English language specific to their professions (e.g., in engineering, accounting, and medicine) posed a barrier to employment. At the same time, most of the women found the Language Instruction for Newcomers (LINC) programme too elementary, as it did not help them in gaining the vocabulary they needed in finding employment commensurate with their qualifications.

As a result of all these factors there is a high level of unemployment or underemployment amongst Chinese immigrant women (see, e.g., Man, 2007; Preston and Man, 1999). When they do find employment, they are often overqualified. Even though some of the women did find employment, the poor condition of the work environment, the discriminatory practices, the irregular hours, and the unstable and insecure nature of the work makes it difficult for them to retain the job. The jobs they find concentrate predominantly in the retail and service sector, in the restaurant, retailing and garment industries. Many can only find work in the ethnic enclave, in Chinese businesses. These are part-time, insecure jobs with no benefits. The women work irregular and shift work, and are often paid below minimum wage as one Mainland woman explained:

> I found a job through a job agency in two months, that was a confectionery factory. The first day I worked there from 12 midnight till morning. The factory did not have good hygiene, it was dirty. My impression of it was bad. The supervisor was not friendly to us at all. I worked only one day, and was asked to pay a $20 union fee, which was supposed to be a monthly fee. But we worked only one day, then they didn't call me back to work. One week later, they called me back to work, and asked me to pay another $20 union fee. It was not fair. We felt really discriminated, exploited and bullied. My language was not good enough to argue with them. Their attitude towards us was very bad...One of my Chinese friends worked there for three days, and they only paid her for two days. When I deducted the transportation fees and union fees, I only got a bit over $20 left for a whole day's work. They paid us $7.65/hour. I worked for only two days, and I didn't want to go back there any more. My husband found a job in a mattress factory, full-time, hard work. He was paid $9.50/hour. You know we have never done this kind of work when we were in China. Now after immigration, we became labourers.

Not only was this woman underemployed, she was unfairly treated and exploited by her employer and supervisor. Thus, the Canadian labour market has been less than hospitable to workers. In the past, women have made concrete gains in paid employment through the union movement. The right to bargain collectively in large workplaces has made the most difference in improving wages and working conditions in women's paid jobs. In fact, unionization has promoted pay equity for women (Labour Canada, 1992; Luxton and Reiter, 1997). Public sector unions offer much better protection than their private sector counterparts on issues such as discrimination, sexual harassment, health and safety risks, and work reassignments. However, although unions guarantee some protection for workers, they can also exclude the most vulnerable sector of workers–the part-time, temporary, flexible labour force. First of all, it is more difficult for these workers to unionize. Besides, the neoliberal climate of structural adjustment and privatization has eroded the power of the unions, and women's participation in it. As the above example shows, the most disadvantaged are women in contingent, flexible jobs. Without seniority they feel doubly exploited by having to pay high union dues which they cannot afford, and at the same time, not reaping the benefits of union protection in terms of job security.

The Chinese women's underemployment and unemployment in the new country has undermined their sense of stability and well-being. The difficulties some of them encountered in communicating in English also exacerbate their feelings of isolation and depression. The relative affluence of the HK women did allow them more choices, affording some the option of not participating in the paid labour force. The HK women who experienced underemployment found it difficult at first. But many endured this with patience and tenacity, hoping to obtain better positions in the future. Here, a HK woman told me her difficulties:

> It was difficult for me at first because I had been working as a bank supervisor in Hong Kong, and all of a sudden, I was only a teller here. I had to learn to be supervised by other people and to learn to take their orders rather than vice versa. I stayed in that job for over two years. It is a lot better now with this position because I am now working more independently.

When they were in Hong Kong or in China, the higher education and professional skills of these women ensured that they would have secure careers. For the Mainland women, whether they had worked for the government or for businesses, they never had to worry about their livelihood. For the HK women, the booming economy in the 1980s and 1990s and the low unemployment rate in Hong Kong relative to that of Canada meant that they never had to confront unemployment. Immigration ruptured their careers.

Their immigrant status in Canada meant that they had to curtail their previous careers, thus transforming their everyday lives in the new country. Many immigrant women were frustrated by the discrepancies in their expectations and the reality of the harsh life in Canada. Here's how one Mainland woman analyzed her situation. Her analysis echoes other Chinese immigrant women's experiences in Canada:

> We thought that if the Immigration Department accepted us as "other independent" [skilled workers] class immigrants, and we got in with high points because of our profession and education, we shouldn't have difficulty in getting jobs. So it's an expectation problem.

One woman had to give up her own hope of being retrained as a teacher in order to support her husband to be retrained as a physician since his qualification was not recognized in Canada. Many foreign-trained immigrant physicians are unable to get a license to practice even after passing the Medical Council of Canada evaluation examinations and the College of Family Physician examinations because they are unable to obtain a medical residency position. To be able to obtain a license to practice, the candidate must work for at least two years in a residency program. As a result of budgetary constraints and restructuring in the healthcare system, the provincial governments have frozen the number of residency positions at teaching hospitals. Since 1999, the shortage of doctors has prompted the governments to increase the number of medical school positions, but there has been no corresponding increase in the number of residency positions. For example, in 2003, there were as many as 4,000 foreign-trained physicians in Ontario who were waiting to be re-trained and licensed, while there were only 50 to 75 spots in specific specialties. Many internationally trained physicians have had to work in menial positions to make ends meet as the re-certification process can take more than ten years (Jimenez, 2003).[5] In 2002, 670 international medical graduates passed the necessary Canadian exams to qualify for residency, but only 67 got a place (Bueckert, 2003).

CONCLUSION

As the process of globalization, privatization, transnationalization, and deindustrialization deepens, the Canadian state, in an effort to take full advantage of the fluidity and flexibility of human capital, is launching new initiatives to actively recruit skilled immigrants to the country. However, neoliberal policies and practices, mediated by accreditation requirements by professional organizations and regulatory bodies, labour market conditions, gendered and racialized discriminatory practices embedded in Canadian society, and women's responsibilities in the home, intersect in complex ways to marginalize the highly educated and skilled Chinese immigrant women.

The Canadian state's requirement for skilled labour is not being met through current institutional policies and practices. Skilled immigrants are being deskilled in Canada and this deskilling is complicated by the contradictory processes of globalization and economic restructuring, with its polarizing effects along the axis of gender, race, ethnicity, class, citizenship, and so on. For immigrant women to become equal and active participants in Canadian society, resources must be made available to them. This requires changes in state policies and institutional support for community agencies servicing new immigrants. To accomplish this, the rhetoric of neoliberalism and the hegemonic thinking about the natural and inevitable force of the market must first be unmasked. With the provision of inclusive programs and policies, Chinese immigrant women will be able to enjoy equal opportunity and outcome.

NOTES

1 For a critique of the point system, see Man (1998).

2 Precarious employment refers to "those forms of work involving atypical employment contracts, limited social benefits and statutory entitlements, job security, low job tenure, low wages and high risks of ill health" (Vosko, 2003).

3 See CASW/ACTS "Assessment of Foreign Trained Social Worker's Degree" www.casw-acts.ca/swassessment_e.htm.

4 Interview with Shauna Paull, Coordinator, Immigrating Women in Science (IWIS).

5 Many foreign-trained doctors had to take on menial jobs such as delivering pizza, working in restaurants in order to make ends meet. Ontario recently announced a clearing-house program that would allow international doctors in certain specialties to complete six-month qualifying rotations in hospitals. In Marina Jimenez, "For Sale: Prized Positions at Canada's Medical Schools," *Globe and Mail,* 1 November 2003, A1, A13.

REFERENCES

Arat-Koc, S. (1999). "NAC's Response to the Immigration Legislative Review Report: "Not Just Numbers: A Canadian Framework for Future Immigration." *Canadian Women Studies* 19:18-23.

Armstrong, P. (1996). "The feminization of the labour force: Harmonizing down in a global economy." In *Rethinking, Restructuring: Gender and Change in Canada.* Toronto: University of Toronto Press.

Armstrong, P., and H. Armstrong. (2006). "Thinking it Through: Women, Work and Caring in the New Millennium." In A. Medovarski and B. Cranney (eds.), *Canadian Women Studies: An Introductory Reader.* Toronto: INANNA Publications & Education Inc.

Association for the Advancement of Feminism (AAF). (1993). *The Hong Kong Women's File.* Hong Kong: Association for the Advancement of Feminism (Chinese language).

Badets, J., and L. Howatson-Leo. (1999). "Recent Immigrants in the Workforce." *Canadian Social Trends.* Statistics Canada, Spring, Catalogue No. 11-008.

_____. (2000). *Recent Immigrants in the Workforce. Canadian Social Trends,* 3rd ed. Toronto: Thompson Educational Publishing.

Bakker, I. (1996). *Rethinking, Restructuring: Gender and Change in Canada.* Toronto: University of Toronto Press.

Berneria, L. (1999). "Globalization, Gender and the Davos Man." *Feminist Economics* 5:61-83.

Boyd, M. (1992). "Gender, Visible Minority, and Immigrant Earnings Inequality: Assessing an Employment Equity Premise." In *Deconstructing a Nation: Immigration, Multiculturalism, and Racism in 1990s Canada.* Halifax: Fernwood.

_____. (2000). "Matching Workers to Work: The Case of Asian Immigrant Engineers in Canada." Working Paper No. 14. San Diego: University of California, San Diego, Center for Comparative Immigration Studies.

_____. (2001). "Asian Immigrant Engineers in Canada." In *The International Migration of the Highly Skilled.* San Diego: University of California, San Diego, Center for Comparative Immigration Studies.

Brecher, J., and T. Costello. (1994). *Global Village or Global Pillage: Economic Reconstruction from the Bottom Up.* Boston: South End Press.

Brodie, J. (1995). *Politics on the Margins: Restructuring and the Canadian Women's Movement.* Halifax: Fernwood Publishing.

Bueckert, D. (2003). "Medical Residents Squeezed out of Canada." *Globe & Mail,* November, A6 section.

CIC. (2009). *Facts and Figures 2009: Immigration Overview–Permanent and Temporary Residents.* Communications Branch, Citizenship and Immigration Canada, Ottawa.

Cornelius, W.A., T.J. Espenshade and I. Salehyan (eds.). (2001). *The International Migration of the Highly Skilled.* San Diego: University of California, San Diego, Center for Comparative Immigration Studies.

Cranford, C., and L.F. Vosko. (2003). "Mapping Multiple Dimensions of Precarious Wage Work." In *Precarious Employment in the Canadian Labour Market.* Montreal: McGill-Queen's University Press.

Cranford, C.J., L. Vosko and N. Zukewich. (2006). "The Gender of Precarious Employment in Canada." In *Working in a Global Era,* 99-119. Toronto: Canadian Scholars' Press.

Das Gupta, T. (1996). *Racism and Paid Work.* Toronto: Garamond.

______. 1999. "The Politics of Multiculturalism: 'Immigrant Women' and the Canadian State." In *Scratching the Surface: Canadian Anti-Racist Feminist Thought.* Toronto: Women's Press.

______. (2009). *Real Nurses and Others: Racism in Nursing.* Halifax: Fernwood Publishing.

DeVault, M.L. (2008). *People at Work: Life, Power, and Social Inclusion in the New Economy.* NY: New York University Press.

De Wolff, A. (2003). "Privatized Employment Counselling in Toronto." In *Precarious Employment: Understanding Labour Market Insecurity in Canada.* Montreal: McGill-Queen's University Press.

Doherty, N. (1992). "Challenging Systemic Sexism in the Language Training Program." In *Socio-Political Aspects of ESL.* Toronto: OISE.

Edward-Galabuzi, G. (2001). *Canada's Creeping Economic Apartheid: The Economic Segregation and Social Marginalization of Radicalized Groups.* Toronto: The CSJ Foundation.

Fincher, R., L. Foster, W. Giles and V. Preston. (1994). "Gender and Migration Policy." In *Immigration and Refugee Policy: Australia and Canada Compared.* Carlton: Melbourne University Press.

Guo, S., and DeVoretz, D. (2005). "The Changing Faces of Chinese Immigrants in Canada." Vancouver Centre of Excellence, Research on Immigration and Integration in the Metropolis, Working Paper Series No. 05-08.

George, U. (1998). "Caring and Women of Colour: Living the Intersecting Oppressions of Race, Class and Gender." In *Women's Caring: Feminist Perspectives on Social Welfare.* Toronto: Oxford University Press.

Giles, W., and V. Prestion. (2003). "The Domestication of Women's Work: A Comparison of Chinese and Portuguese Immigrant Women Homeworkers." In *Studies In Political Economy: Developments In Feminism.* Toronto: Women's Press.

Grant, M., and E. Thompson. (2000). "Immigrants and the Canadian Labour Market." In *Fifth International Metropolis Conference.* Vancouver.

Hiebert, D. (1997). "The Colour of Work: Labour Market Segmentation in Montreal, Toronto and Vancouver, 1991." Research on Immigration and Integration in the Metropolis, Working Paper Series, No. 97-02.

Iredale, R. (2001). "The Migration of Professionals: Theories and Typologies." *International Migration* 39(5):7-26.

Jessop, B. (1993). "Toward a Schumpeterian Workfare State? Preliminary Remarks on Post-Fordist Political Economy." *Studies in Political Economy* 40.

Jiminez, M. (2003). "For Sale: Prized Positions at Canada's Medical Schools." *Globe & Mail*, November 1, A1, A13.

Krahn, H., T. Derwing, M. Mulder and L. Wilkinson. (2000). "Educated and Underemployed: Refugee Integration into the Canadian Labour Market." *Journal of International Migration and Integration* 1:59-84.

Labour Canada. (1992). *Bureau of Labour Information Collective Agreement Database*. Jan. Ottawa: Labour Canada.

Lee, J.A. (1999). "Immigrant Women Workers in the Immigrant Settlement Sector." *Canadian Woman Studies/les cahiers de la femme* 19:97-103.

Li, P. (2000). "Earnings Disparities between Immigrants and Native-Born Canadians." *Canadian Review of Sociology and Anthropology* 37(3):289-311.

Lo, L., and S. Wang (2003). "Chinese Immigrants in Canada: Their Changing Compositions and Economic Performance." Retrieved Jan. 2004, from http://www.chass.utoronto.ca/~salaff/conference/papers/ChineseImmigrantsInCanada-Wang-and-Lo.pdf.

Luxton, M., and E. Reiter. (1997). "Double, Double, Toil and Trouble...Women's Experience of Work and Family in Canada 1980-1995." In *Women and the Canadian Welfare State*. Toronto: University of Toronto Press.

Man, G. (1997). "Women's Work is Never Done: Social Organization of Work and the Experience of Women in Middle-Class Hong Kong Chinese Immigrant Families in Canada." In *Advances in Gender Research*. Greenwich: JAI Press Inc.

_____. (2002). "Globalization and the Erosion of the Welfare State: Effects on Chinese Immigrant Women, Special Issue: Women, Globalization, and the International Trade." *Canadian Woman Studies/les cahiers de la femme* 21/22:26-32.

_____. (2003). "The Experience of Middle-Class Women in Recent Hong Kong Chinese Immigrant Families in Canada." In *Voices: Essays on Canadian Families*. Toronto: Thomson Nelson.

_____. (2007). "Racialization of Gender, Work, and Transnational Migration: The Experience of Chinese Immigrant Women in Canada." In S. Hier and B. Singh (eds.), *Racism and Anti-Racism in Canada*. Peterborough: Broadview Press.

Mirchandani, K., N. Roxana, N. Colomo-Moya, S. Maitra, T. Rawlings, K. Siddiqui, H. Shan, and B.L. Slade. (2008). "The Paradox of Training and Learning in a Culture of Contingency." In D. Livingstone, K. Mirchandani, and P. Sawchuk. (eds.), *The Future of Lifelong Learning and Work: Critical Perspectives*. Rotterdam: Sense Publishers.

Mojab, S. 1(999). "De-Skilling Immigrant Women." *Canadian Woman Studies/les cahiers de la femme* 19:110-14.

_____. (2000). "The Power of Economic Globalization: Deskilling Immigrant Women through Training." In *Power in Practice: Adult Education and the Struggle for Knowledge and Power in Society*. San Francisco: Jossey-Bass.

Ng, R. (1981). "Constituting Ethnic Phenomenon: An Account from the Perspective of Immigrant Women." *Canadian Ethnic Studies* 8(1):97-108.

_____. 1993. "Racism, Sexism, and Nation Building in Canada." In *Race, Identity, and Representation in Education*. NY: Routledge.

_____. 1996. *The Politics of Community Services: Immigrant Women, Class and State*, 2nd ed. Halifax: Fernwood Press.

Ng, R., G. Man, and H. Shan. (2008). "Learning to be an Immigrant: Professional Immigrant Women Navigating the Canadian Labour Market." Roundtable presentation at the Canadian Association for the

Studies of Adult Education (CASAE), 27th Annual Meeting, Uuniversity of British Columbia, Vancouver, May 31-June 3.

Ornstien, M. (2000). *Ethno-Racial Inequality in Toronto: Analysis of the 1996 Census.* Toronto: City of Toronto.

Preston, V., and G. Man. (1999). "Employment Experiences of Chinese Immigrant Women: An Exploration of Diversity." *Canadian Woman Studies/les cahiers de la femme* 19:115-22.

Raghuram, P., and E. Kofman. (2002). "The State, Skilled Labour Markets, and Immigration: The Case of Doctors in England." *Environmental Planning A* 34(11):2071-89.

Salaff, J.W. (1997). "The Gendered Social Organization of Migration as Work." *Asian and Pacific Migration Journal* 6:295-315.

_____. 2000. "Women's Work in International Migration." In *Transforming Gender and Development in East Asia.* London: Routledge.

Salaff, J.W., and A. Greve. (2004). "Can Women's Networks Migrate?" *Women's Studies International Forum* 27(2):149-162.

_____. (2006). "Why do Skilled Women and Men Emigrating from China to Canada Get Bad Jobs?" In E. Tastsoglou and A. Dobrowolskyn (eds.), *Gender, Migration and Citizenship.* London: Ashgate.

Sayer, D. (1987). *The Violence of Abstraction: The Analytical Foundations of Historical Materialism.* London: Basil Blackwell.

Shields, J. (1995). "Post-Fordism, Work Flexibility and Training." *Socialist Studies Bulletin* 41:47.

_____. (1996). "Flexible Work, Labour Market Polarization and the Politics of Skills Training and Enhancement." In *The Training Trap: Ideology, Training, and the Labour Market.* Winnipeg: Fernwood.

_____. (2002). "No Safe Haven: Markets, Welfare and Migrants." In *CSAA Conference.* Toronto.

Shields, J., and M.B. Evans. (1998). *Shrinking the State: Globalization and the Reform of Public Administration.* Halifax: Fernwood Publications.

Skills for Change. (1995). *Building Bridges: Identifying Opportunities and Overcoming Barriers to Employment and Licensure for Foreign-Trained Engineers in Ontario.* Toronto: Skills for Change.

Skills for Change and Centre for Research and Education in Human Services. (2001). *Making a Change Together: A Resource Handbook for Promoting Access to Professions and Trades for Foreign-Trained People in Ontario.* Toronto: Queen's Printer for Ontario.

Smith, D. (1987). *The Everyday World as Problematic: A Feminist Sociology.* Toronto: University of Toronto Press.

_____. (2006). *Institutional Ethnography: A Sociology for People.* Toronto: Altamira Press.

Smith, E., and A. Jackson. (2002). *Does a Rising Tide Life all Boats? The Labour Market Experiences and Incomes of Recent Immigrants, 1995-1998.* Ottawa: Canadian Council on Social Development.

Travato, F., and C. Grindstaff. (1986). "Economic Status: A Census Analysis of Thirty-Year-Old Immigrant Women in Canada." *Canadian Review of Sociology and Anthropology* 23:569-87.

Vosko, L. (ed.). (2006). *Precarious Employment: Understanding Labour Market Insecurity in Canada.* Montreal and Kingston: McGill-Queen's University Press.

Whittleton, H. (1999). "Settlement Services for Immigrants and Refugees in a Changing Environment." *Third National Metropolis Conference.* Vancouver.

Chapter 13

Crime and Deviance

Crime and Deviance in Canada

Patricia O'Reilly and Thomas Fleming

Wilfrid Laurier University

CRIME AND DEVIANCE IN CANADA

Crime is an inescapable part of our everyday lives in Canada. Some of you have, or will be victims of crime. Each day we are confronted with images of crime, both real and imagined, in newspapers, on television, in films and on the internet. Crime news is often front page in the country's papers, and comprises the subject matter of the most viewed programs on Canadian television (Ericson, Baranek, and Chan, 1989, 1991; Dowler, 2007; Dowler, Fleming, and Muzzatti, 2006). We are intrigued by the science of forensics in the investigation of crime, and the human dramas which unfold on our streets and in the courtroom. Our attraction to crime stories emerges as both a fear of the unpredictable and a fascination with the varieties of human behavior which surround us (Fleming, 1981). In this chapter we will be exploring the nature of criminal behavior in Canada. The focus will be on select issues which provide a roadmap of the nature and extent of crime in Canada to give readers a snapshot, as it were, of the state of crime in contemporary society. This is not as easy a task as might be supposed. Hundreds of thousands of crimes, in a wide variety of categories are committed in Canada each year. These acts range from threats to assault, theft, embezzlement, computer crimes, environmental crimes to the deliberate taking of human life. While we view certain crimes as more serious, and hence more "newsworthy," all crimes impact upon victims, and that impact may be profound even in a less serious crime such as mugging. Our exploration of crime and deviance in Canada commences with a consideration of what constitutes a crime in Canada and how we deal with crime through law.

WHAT IS A CRIME IN CANADA?

Crimes are acts which society has deemed must be formally written into a code for all to obey, and which sets out penalties for their infraction. In Canada, all crimes are contained with *The Criminal Code of Canada* (Greenspan, 2009). Readers may have heard of the expression, "ignorance of the law is no excuse," and indeed, this cannot form a defense to a criminal charge. However, when one considers that the *Code* is over 1,000 pages in length, then the question must arise, how can the average citizen possibly be expected to know what acts are against the law, and which are not? Given that there are also provincial regulations, and municipal by-laws by which we must abide, the number of laws, regulations and by-laws which govern our life are considerable in number. However, the majority of the acts deemed criminal in the *Code* are a matter of common sense for most citizens. There are two classes of crime, the first of which is more self evident than the second. First, there are crimes which are termed *mala in se*, "crimes in themselves." This class of crime is found in most cultures over history and includes murder, rape, assault and theft. They are often referred to as **heinous crimes**. The second category of crime is known as **mala prohibita** offenses, which are crimes that are created in this country by the Parliament, at the federal level. Possession of marijuana, tax evasion, environmental crimes, in other words, acts that may not be readily apparent to be criminalized, which have been made crimes via the legislative process. We have stated that the *Code* applies to all Canadian citizens, with one exception. No person under the age of 12 may be charged with a criminal offense. In the 1800s persons as young as 6 years could be charged with criminal offenses. Indeed, we have accounts of prisoners as young as 8 years old being whipped in Kingston Prison (Fleming, Dowler, and Ramcharan, 2008).

MURDER IN CANADA

The most serious of crimes in our criminal code involve the taking of human life. Murder "in everyday life" (Leyton, 1995) is an atypical crime, that is, there are very few murders committed in Canada each year in comparison to assaults. No crime is more reflective of desperate lives. Most murders, according to criminologist Neil Boyd (1988) involve desperate persons killing other desperate persons. Murder is classified in Canada into three categories; manslaughter, second degree murder, and first degree murder. Murder may be either *culpable* or *non-culpable*. The former refers to killing for which one is held accountable before the law. The latter refers to killing which does not constitute a crime, for example, in the case of self-defense. Manslaughter involves the taking of human life in the heat of passion with no malice aforethought (Blom, Cooper, and Morris, 2004). This form of murder accounts for about 60% of all murders committed in Canada. Since there is no element of planning involved the sentence for this crime is generally about 4 to 8 years in prison (with some notable exceptions). Uninformed observers often wonder aloud how persons who murder can receive such a "light" sentence. However, let us compare it to the other two forms of homicide. Second degree murder is more difficult for most students to understand. Essentially it falls between manslaughter and first degree murder in terms of the seriousness with which it is viewed by the court. Second degree murders are those in which the killing is still intentional but there is a lack of premeditation. First degree murder involves "planning and deliberation." This is the form of murder which makes for fascinating crime novels, television shows and movies. However, in contrast to the dramatization of murder on programs such as Law and Order and CSI Miami (and their many spin off series) only 5% of murders in this country are first degree. In other words, first degree murder is the rarest of all forms of murder.

The motives for murder have remained relatively unchanged over the course of history. Anger, revenge, hatred, sexual infidelity and greed are all repetitive causes of murder. You can probably add several motives to this list which reflect specific motivations such as arguments over "turf" by gangs, "disrespecting" someone, jealousy and so on. Motives provide us with an immediately comprehensible understanding of why someone committed murder, but they are limited in their ability to truly explain the complex decisions and interactions which underlie most murders.

While the motives and methods of murder are not uniquely Canadian, it can be argued that our country's culture has long supported resolutions to conflicts and interpersonal clashes that do not result in the killing of one person by another. Our murder rate is very low compared to our American neighbours, and this reflects our Canadian identity. We are, in the majority of cases, able to find other ways to deal with conflict other than dispatching another human being. This emerges not from the threat of a death penalty but rather from cultural messages about behavior (Leyton, 1995). Moreover, Canada has rejected the carrying and use of personal handguns as a means of deterring crime and personal protection, and has banned handgun ownership other than for peace officers and registered collectors. The active pursuit of gun dealers and illegal guns, through the activities of guns and gangs squads in police services across the country distinguishes Canada from other countries where gun ownership is permitted, often with disastrous results.

Serial and mass murders do occur in Canada, but they are very infrequent. In the past 30 years there have been three cases of serial murder reported in Canada; the Olsen, Bernardo/Homolka and Pickton cases (Fleming, 2008). Serial murderers kill more than three people over a period of days, weeks, months or years with a resting period in between murders. Canada has had very few serial murder cases in comparison to the many reported in the United States and other countries. This also applies to mass murder cases such as the Montreal massacre where over a dozen women were shot by Marc Lepine. The small number of Canadian cases has been argued to reflect our culture of mutual respect and personal control by some researchers (Leyton, 1995).

There is little evidence that murder is changing dramatically as a form of crime in this country. The rise of gang related murders can be argued to reflect a cultural gap created when young people face difficulties integrating into mainstream Canadian culture. Gangs offer a support network for young people who feel disenfranchised, alone and unable to achieve in school and broader society (Fleming, 1997). The importance of providing resources for new Canadian families is reflected in the work of Farrington (1996) and others. Resources spent in the early years, and in supporting healthy alternatives for teens can have a profound impact on participation in crime. For aboriginal young people, this sense of disillusionment has seen the rise of aboriginal youth gangs (Grekul and LaBoucane-Benson, 2008) who view their criminal actions as a rebellion against a dominant culture that offers little to them. Certainly the overrepresentation of aboriginal peoples in the criminal justice system in Canada supports their view that there are significant problems with our nation's current approach to supporting aboriginal peoples in reaching their full potential (York, 1999).

DEVIANT BEHAVIOUR

Deviance encompasses many forms of behaviour, and in an increasingly diverse and tolerant world, defining it poses some difficulties for criminologists. Howard Becker (1966) argued that deviance is defined by societal reaction to a particular behavior(s). This is a *subjective* definition. Behaviour that is normal in one era may become deviant in another, or when we move from one country to another. *Primary deviance* refers to the original act or transgression engaged in by the deviant. Secondary deviance emerges as a result of negative reaction to the behavior which convinces the deviant that there is no dividend in attempting to act "normal" and so the rewards of deviant behavior are sought as a response to the disapproval of others. We may also define deviance as conduct which varies from the norm or violates societal norms or rules. This is referred to as an *objective* definition. Historically, the use of marijuana and LSD were not criminalized in Canada until the 1960s when its use spread to a large cross section of young people (Erickson, 1980). Sexual relations between men over the age of eighteen did not become legal until very recently. Not only can a behavior which is accepted as normal in Canada be deviant elsewhere, for example, an adult drinking alcohol, it can result in arrest and imprisonment in other countries. Robert Stebbins (1988) a renowned Canadian expert on deviance developed a system for distinguishing between *tolerable* and *non-tolerable* forms of deviance. Tolerable forms are behaviors which we may not necessarily approve of, such as swinging but which we accept as the right of others to engage in, and which are not the subject of the criminal law. Non-tolerable forms receive disapproval from society and are classified as crimes. These include bestiality and sexual assault.

Deviance can be best understood as a form of undesirable difference (Fleming and Visano, 1987). Often our characterization of someone as deviant arises out of which organization or group is deviantizing the behavior. More specifically, if an individual is "sick" they are labeled as such by medical authorities, if they are "criminal" they have been labeled by the criminal justice system, if they are "sinners" they have been designated deviant by a religious organization (Fleming and Visano, 1987). Deviance can be controlled by someone's immediate family or friends, as occurs in drug and alcohol abuse control on the television program *Intervention*, or it may be controlled by the criminal justice (Fleming, Ramcharan, and Dowler, 2008) or psychiatric systems. When deviant behavior is discovered, it is first labeled as such by someone in authority to do so. The individual so labeled transfers the individual from "normal" to "deviant" status. Of course what is deviant is a matter of some discussion in Canada. What is deviant to a group of senior citizens may be perfectly normal for a group of teens and vice-versa. Our society is composed of a great number of groups constantly vying for power, and with power comes the ability to make behaviours deviant or normal (Turk, 1976). Crimes are a sub-category of deviant behavior. They are acts or actions which violate our criminal law.

CYBERCRIME: AN EMERGING CRIMINAL ACTIVITY

The advent of the internet and personal computers has provided an ideal opportunity on a global basis for criminals to engage in crimes without borders. Cybercrimes are difficult to police since they require that police services have the equipment and expertise required to be effective at locating and apprehending offenders. You are all familiar with fraud schemes which arrive daily in the inbox of your computer. Normally you are being told that someone in another country, most generally an African country, is the wife of a prominent individual who died leaving millions of dollars in a bank account. They will share it with you, and have contacted you because you are a trustworthy individual. You are asked to provide your name, address, telephone, bank name, address and account number so that the funds can be transferred to your account. If you respond to this email, you are typically asked to send a cheque for from $1,000 to $5,000 as a show of faith in order to pay off a banker or some other fictitious individual. Of course, your millions never arrive, and you simply receive more and more requests for small amounts of money because of "problems" which keep recurring until you, the "mark" in this fraud scheme realize that you have been victimized. **Identity theft** is now a major form of crime in Canada, costing victims, financial institutions and society several billion lost dollars each year. The ready availability of fake identification from a variety of sources may be familiar to students who know someone who has obtained "fake ID" in order to be admitted to a club, event or bar.

Cybercrimes can also include attempts to infect your computer, and that of millions of others with viruses designed to spy on your computer activity. These Trojans can record valuable information about your bank transactions, investments, identity and so on which can be used by criminals to siphon monies from your accounts, and more ominously steal your identity and use it either to defraud others, or to sell as bogus ID to be used in obtaining fraudulent passports and work cards. Hackers use the internet to infiltrate computer systems, attempting to steal the personal information of a company's clients. In 2009, customers of Toronto Hydro were sent a warning about their accounts having been breached. Similarly, *Winners* was hit by a similar invasion of their computer system earlier in the year, compromising the credit and Interact cards of their customers.

One of the most disturbing crimes committed via the internet is the distribution of child pornography. Canada has strict laws against the manufacture, distribution and sale of child pornography. The Metropolitan Toronto Police Service gained worldwide notoriety for its development of Project P which was instrumental in tracking down not only persons making pornographic images and movies, but in actually rescuing several children forced to appear in these media forms. However, it is difficult to pursue this issue in other countries which might have different laws and standards regarding child pornography. This became evident in the famous case of *R. v. Sharpe* where Robin Sharpe was caught in possession of child pornography consisting of pictures he had imported, as well as his own writings about having sex with young boys. He could not be convicted on the latter behavior since writing about one's sexual fantasies is protected under the *Charter of Rights and Freedoms* section concerning freedom of expression. To curtail his right to express his private ideas in writing would mean that the law could intervene in other person's freedom of expression. Law professors refer to this as "the slippery slope" concept, since disallowing Sharpe's writings would lead to more bans on what Canadians can express whether in writing, art or photography (Keegan and Lacobe, 2000).

Finally there is the crime of **cyberstalking.** In Canada, we have passed laws regarding criminal harassment, involves repeatedly harassing someone, their friends or family at their place of work, home or elsewhere. This is a serious crime and one that has been on the increase since the law was first passed in 2004. One variation of this is the use of the internet or email (and now twitter) to stalk someone. Given our level of connectedness to the world wide web, it is much easier to find someone and to use these forms of communication to harass them. An example of how this can be done is by the stalker going to an online meeting service, such as *Lavalife* or *Ashley Madison.com* and posting phony information about the victim indicating they are looking for sex partners, and providing their contact information; real name, address, telephone or cell number, and email addresses to induce others to harass them. The anonymity of the web, and the reluctance of web services to give out information on their subscribers make investigation and prosecution of cyberstalkers difficult at best.

The rapid proliferation of new technology reflected in widespread use of *Myspace, Twitter, Gmail, Hotmail* and other forms of communication has meant that Canada both contributes to and is open to victimization by cybercriminals on an international basis. Cyber criminals prey on the naivety of vulnerable users who don't recognize they are being victimized. Canada has become part of a global community. We are joined by the internet around the world. We can talk to people in other countries on *Skype* and view them at the same time on our computer's camera. Devices like the *iphone* with tens of thousands of applications not only increases our ability to connect with the world, but also increases our vulnerability to cybercriminals. Whether we bank, pay bills, pay for items on *Ebay, Amazon*, or one of thousands of other websites we are providing personal information that may be at risk of being harvested by those intent on harming us, usually financial or by stealing personal information. Thus, Canada is not independent in the cyber-universe but is an integral part of it.

Finally, the most disturbing variant of cybercrime involves the attempt by pedophiles, that is, persons who desire sexual relations with minor children, to lure them to secluded meeting places with the intent to have sex with them. Adult sex predators make a routine of visiting chat rooms for teens, posing as other teens interested in helping them with their problems, or assisting them in running away from home, or with an interest in them. They construct a fake personality to achieve their goal.

TERRORISM

Since 911, the terrorist attack on the World Trade Towers in New York, terrorism has become a preoccupation of the western world. Much of the effort of the United States and its allies has focused on al-Qaeda and the Taliban in terms of military efforts and in particular the military invasion of Afghanistan. The attack produced a tidal wave of interest in security, and in its wake amendments to the Criminal Code, Official Secrets Act and many other Acts (Macklem, Daniels, and Roach, 2001). The new omnibus bill *Canada Anti-Terrorism Act 2001*, (Bill C-36) granted the police wide sweeping authority to arrest and detain persons suspected of terrorist activity without a warrant, hold them for long periods of time, put them on trial using evidence wherein their lawyer could not question the evidence, and prohibit the media from obtaining information about investigations. These new powers were, and still are, the subject of intense criticism for their further intrusion into the civil liberties of Canadians. The question it raises is what sacrifices to our personal liberties are Canadians willing to tolerate in the "fight against terrorism?" Overall, Canadian anti-terrorism legislation has not been effective at identifying or prosecuting terrorists. In several noted cases, individuals held for long periods of time without trial, and subsequently released, are suing the Canadian government. In a well publicized case, Mahar Arar was seized at Kennedy International Airport in 2002 returning from a family trip to Syria. American authorities placed him in solitary confinement, interrogated him and then returned him to Syria (although he is a Canadian citizen).

He was subsequently tortured in Syrian prison before finally being released and returned to Canada. Mr. Arar's nightmare was caused by Canadian officials giving American authorities unsubstantiated information on his suspected terrorist activities claiming that he had links to al-Qaeda. Eventually, he sued the Canadian government winning millions of dollars in compensation (*CBC News*, January 26, 2007; *New York Times*, February 18, 2009).

Terrorism is a difficult form of crime to detect and prevent since recently the emphasis of these individuals appears to have shifted towards individual terrorists, often of the "home grown" variety, that is, persons born in the US, UK or Canada who have converted to terrorist beliefs. Examples of this would include the London Underground bombings of July 7, 2005 carried out by four Muslim men; one who was a British Jamaican citizen, and three who were British Pakistani. "Terror from within" carried out by individuals or small groups leaves little in the way of electronic "chatter" on the internet or through communication channels that would permit intelligence services to track and prevent attacks. Fifty-two people were killed in this attack, and some 700 were injured (*BBC News* Special Reports, July 7, 2005). On June 5, 2006 the RCMP arrested 17 Muslim men (12 adults aged 19 to 43 and 5 suspects under age 19) who were charged (*Associated Press*, June 5, 2006).

Terrorism can also be internet based wherein individuals attempt to invade computer systems which control finances in North American, nuclear power systems, or national security computers. This scenario comprised the plot of the movie *Die Hard IV*, although interestingly the villain was an American computer expert who had been fired by the government. Most experts argue that individual terrorists, increasingly drawn from the ranks of individuals born in countries like Canada, Britain, the United States and other "enemy" countries, will become the focus of more of our efforts to curb attacks in the future.

Canada is also viewed as a country with lax immigration laws and little control of its borders by the United States and other countries. With the longest undefended borders in the world, (including the northern borders of Canada), we are seen as a country which terrorists can easily enter, and seek to enter the United States to engage in terrorist acts. As a country which encourages and cherishes diversity we are somewhat vulnerable to those who would enter Canada with the intent to attack us or our neighbour. Our immigration controls have been the subject of considerable criticism by American terrorism experts, and this has been reflected in recent changes in entry regulations for Canadian visitors to the United States. It is now required that all Canadians show passports to enter America, whereas in the past, a driver's license would suffice.

VICE AND SEX CRIMES

In this section of the chapter we will be dealing with two very different yet often connected areas of deviant and criminal behavior. Vice is a term which is often used to refer to behavior which is considered evil, immoral or degrading, at least by some observers in society. As we discussed earlier, tolerable forms of deviance do not generally invite police interaction with participants, but the area of vice is one that often teeters on the precipice which separates the tolerable from the non-tolerable. Let's begin our exploration with the issue of having sex in a public place. The first issue which confronts us is what is a public place? Well, it is any place to which the public has a right of access. A park is a public place, and so is the street. Shopping malls, despite their appearance are not public places and neither is the inside of an automobile. An adult private club which charges a fee of admission for entrants would seem to be private but the police might not view it as such. Consider the case of the now famous Pussy Palace Raids. On September 14, 2000 police raided a lesbian event at a men's bathhouse they had rented in downtown Toronto. The facility is normally a place where gay men can go for anonymous sexual encounters with other willing adult males. During the raid the male officers spent more than an hour walking through the facility looking at the women who were in various stages of undress. No charges were laid, but 10 women had their names and other information recorded. The women, and the lesbian community in Toronto organized a fund to take the police to court, and at trial Justice Peter Hryn stated that when they entered the facility the women had a "reasonable expectation of privacy" and the women won their case (May-Chang, 2007).

But where can adults have sex outside of their homes or a hotel room in Canada? Public sex, while legal in some European countries is against the law in Canada. Sections 173 and 174 of the Criminal Code prohibit any indecent act in a public place committed in the presence of one or more persons, or intended to insult or offend any person. It is unlawful to be nude in a public place or on private property or to be "so clad as to offend against public decency or order." However, it is not illegal for a woman to walk topless in a public place. Neither is it illegal for adults to engage in swinging in a private club since the decision by the Supreme Court in December 2005. The Supreme Court, in its decision weighed the issue of the actual harm(s) caused by the behavior rather than the violation of a "social consensus." In effect the Supreme Court interpreted the actual meaning of "indecency" in the Criminal Code which had remained undefined for many decades. Following this decision several major Canadian cities have seen the development of adults only sex clubs. Wicked, for example, opened in 2006 in Toronto's west end near the club district. It is a swing club directed towards the 25-35 age range, complete with an orgy room, sex foreplay lounge, an "exhibitionist cage," VIP suites for sexual intercourse, open play areas, "sex furniture" and dancing (www.clubzone.com).Toronto also has gay bars which have catered to this new ruling by establishing "back rooms," where men can gather to engage in consensual, anonymous sexual activities.

PROSTITUTION

Surprisingly to many students there is no law against prostitution, per se, in Canada. However, this is not to say that we have not developed laws to deal with the activities associated with prostitution. Our concern is that it occurs in public. Canadians have a low tolerance for public displays of deviance (Borovoy, 1988). We want our streets to be safe, reasonably clean, and devoid of public displays of sexuality, violence, drunkenness, or unruly behavior. Thus, our legal response to prostitution has been to focus on criminalizing acts which precede a prostitute-customer exchange. Under section 213(1) of the Criminal Code it states clearly that: "Every person who in a **public place or in any place open to public view** (my emphasis)" or engages in stopping or communicating in any manner for the purpose of engaging in prostitution or of obtaining the sexual services of a prostitute or stops or attempts to stop any motor vehicle or impedes the free flow of pedestrian or vehicular traffic or prevents someone from entering or leaving premises is guilty of an offence punishable on summary conviction. If you review the previous sentence you will note that the law centers its attention more on the issue of disrupting public streets or the lives of law abiding citizens more than on the actual issue of prostitution itself. This law is extremely dangerous for sex trades workers since it means that sex trade workers are forced into alleyways and dark parking lots to negotiate with their customers rather than doing so on a well lit street.

Canada has also become a haven for the global sex trade market. Our immigration laws permit the immigration of women as strippers and domestic servants, for example, who often become unwilling participants in the sex trade industry. Unscrupulous sex entrepreneurs recruit them in poor European and Asian nations with promises of careers and good employment in Canada. Once they arrive, their passports are taken from them and they are forced into prostitution to "pay off" the "debt" they supposedly owe to the importer for getting them into Canada. Virtually confined as sex slaves, with no identity papers, limited English language skills and no friends, they can be forced to prostitute themselves. Vancouver has been cited by the FBI as the most frequent entry point for sex trade workers in North America.

In response to police activity against street prostitution the majority of prostitution now takes place through escort agencies, "massage" parlours, independent in-call and out-call services, in hotel settings, and through call girls. Free magazines like Toronto's *NOW* feature about a dozen pages of advertisements by prostitutes. The ads are for the first three of the categories listed above and may show a picture of the woman/women, list sex acts that they are open to be involved in, and in some cases they provide prices. Massage parlours offer a feeble attempt at massage typically followed by a "happy ending" involving either masturbation of the client or oral sex. Escort agencies generally offer in hotel services to visitors at an inflated price since the client must pay for the transportation to the hotel plus negotiate a fee for oral sex, full intercourse or a combination of both. Independent in-call and out-call services are provided by women out of their own condos or apartments. The customer may come to their location or they will attend at the hotel. Generally, women will not go to a private residence preferring the security offered by a hotel which requires identification for the client at check in and has patrons and security on premises. Hotel prostitutes generally position themselves in the bars of premium hotels, and pay off bar staff to let them solicit on the premises, which is a private rather than publicly owned space. Call girls are the most exclusive and highly paid of all prostitutes. They solicit clients by word-of-mouth rather than advertisement. Their clients are well-to-do and will pay thousands of dollars for an evening as compared with the $100 paid to massage workers, or the $50 or less paid to street prostitutes.

CONCLUSION

Crime and deviance are subjects which capture the public imagination and also form part of our everyday lives in society. In this chapter we have explored some of the fundamental issues which underscore our attempts to control crime and deviance within Canadian society. Canada is now connected to the world through the diverse makeup of its citizenry, and through the internet. Crimes can be committed against Canadians from almost any country using the internet. We have learned that Canada is a relatively non-violent country in comparison with its American counterpart, where our respect for others is reflected in very low rates of homicide and interpersonal violence. The diversity of persons which underscores our cultural identity has given us a country which has an overall respect amongst citizens for one another. It is a country in which the right of individiual gun ownership has been rejected in favour of the safety of all. The flexibility and adaptability of our systems of laws reflects this strength in our national character and will permit us to change to accommodate the ever changing population of our country.

REFERENCES

Becker, Howard. (1996). *The Outsiders: Studies in the Sociology of Deviance.* NY: Free Press.

Blom-Cooper, L., and T. Morris. (2004). *With Malice Aforethought: A Study of the Crime and Punishment for Homicide.* Oxford: Hart Publishing.

Borovy, A. (1988). *When Freedoms Collide: The Case for Civil Liberties.* Toronto: Lester and Orpen Dennys.

Boyd, N. (1988). *The Last Dance: Murder in Canada.* Toronto: Prentice Hall.

Chang, M. (2007). "Today in Queer History." www.pridedepot.com. Sept. 14.

Dowler, K. (2007). "Media Criminology in a Television World." *Journal of Criminal Justice and Popular Culture* 14(3):237-242.

Dowler, K., T. Fleming, and S. Muzzatti. (2006). "Constructing Crime: Media, Crime and Popular Culture." *Canadian Journal of Criminology and Criminal Justice* 48(6):837-850.

Erickson, P. (1980). *Cannabis Criminals: The Social Effects of Punishment on Drug Users.* Toronto: ARF.

Ericson, R.V., P. Baranek, and J. Chan. (1989). *Negotiating Control: A Study of News Sources.* Toronto: University of Toronto Press.

_____. (1991). *Representing Order: Crime, Law and Justice in the News Media.* Toronto: University of Toronto Press.

Farrington, D. (1996). *Understanding and Preventing Youth Crime.* London: Joseph Rowntree Foundation.

Fleming, T. (1981). "The Bawdy House 'Boys': Some Notes on Media, Sporadic Moral Crusades and Moral Panics." *Canadian Criminology Forum* 3:101-117.

_____. (1997). "Swarms, Runs and Wildings: Canadian Youth Subculture and Racism." In B. Schissel (ed.), *Youth and Deviance.* Toronto: Oxford University Press Canada.

_____. (2008). "Victims Lost: Recurring Investigative Errors in Canada's Serial Murder Mega Cases." *The Canadian Society of Criminology Conference,* October 3.

Fleming, T., and L.A. Visano. (1987). *Deviant Designations: Crime, Law and Deviance in Canada.* Toronto: Methuen.

Fleming, T., K. Dowler, and S. Ramcharan. (2008). *The Canadian Criminal Justice System.* Toronto: Prentice Hall.

Government of Canada. (2001). *Anti-Terrorism Act, 2001.* Ottawa: Department of Justice Canada.

Greenspan, E. (2009). *Martin's Annual Criminal Code.* Toronto: Canada Law Book.

Grekul, J., and P. LaBoucane-Benson. (2008). "Aboriginal Gangs and Their (Dis)placement: Contextualizing Recruitment, Membership and Status." *The Canadian Journal of Criminology and Criminal Justice* 50(1):59-82.

Katz, J. (1988). *Seductions of Crime: Moral and Sensual Attractions in Doing Evil.* NY: Basic Books.

Kegan, D., and D. Lacombe. (2000). "Scapegoat in Risk Society: The Case of Pedophile/Child Pornographer Robin Sharpe." *Law, Politics, and Society* 20:183-206.

Leyton, E. (1995). *Men of Blood: Murder in Modern England.* London: Constable.

Daniels, R.J., P. Macklem, and K. Roach (2001). *The Security of Freedom: Essays on Canada's Anti-Terrorism Bill.* Toronto: University of Toronto Press.

Stebbins, R. (1988). *Deviance: Tolerable Differences.* Toronto: McGraw-Hill.

Turk, Austin T. (1976). "Law as a Weapon in Social Conflict." *Social Problems* 23(3):276-291.

York, G. (1999). *The Dispossessed: Life and Death in Native Canada.* Toronto: McArthur and Company.

PART IV

Canadians in the Global Context

Canadians are increasingly tied to economic and cultural developments beyond the nation-state. This collection of chapters highlights how Canadians function in a time when, according to David Korton, "corporations rule the world."

Chapter 14 by Stephen L. Muzzatti shows us how pervasive and ubiquitous **mass media** is in the lives of Canadians today. Mass media ties us to global processes and practices, and yet, Muzzati provides key concepts in this area of sociology to show how we can use our sociological imagination to question corporate hegemony.

Chapter 15 by Mensah and Bridi focuses of **immigration under globalization** to help us understand issues of "the refugee" and immigration forces as Canada invites newcomers to this country. Key theories and concepts from scholars in the area of migration studies are discussed in detail.

Chapter 16 by Scott McCloud on **politics and social movements** provides us with insight into the anti-globalization movement. He effectively shows that Canada's activist community is non-hierarchical diverse. The anti-globalization movement serves as a reaction to the forces of globalization characterized by capitalism and imperialism. Globalization is all encompassing to Canadians and yet movements such "anti-globalization" ensure that corporation cannot "rule the world" without critical reactionary forces.

Lastly, Chapter 17 by Alexander Shvartz look at how **transnationalism and globalization** has given rise to Russian entrepreneurship in both Canada and the United State and that the historical belief that immigrant must "work their way to top" is questioned in this chapter. New forms of entrepreneurship are promoted by the forces of globalization and transnationalism. He demonstrates that a large portion of this change happened after 1980 and the collapse of the Soviet State giving rise to new global opportunities for Russian entrepreneurs. Shvartz questions the extent to which Russian entrepreneurs help the new immigrant community since the entrepreneurs adopt and individualist value system insofar as they are "out for themselves" and for profit.

Taken together, the chapters in this section place Canada and Canadians in the wider context of global issues and forces.

Chapter 14

Mass Media

Mass Media in the Lives of Globalized Subjects

Stephen L. Muzzatti
Ryerson University

INTRODUCTION

One of the most significant and potentially illuminating areas of sociological inquiry is the analysis of the mass media. As individuals, the way in which we interpret and understand the world is based on our experience with both direct and indirect forms of communication. Because the mass media is a vital source of indirect communication the messages we receive from it are tremendously influential in the way we think about ourselves and the world around us. These messages impact upon not only our own sense of who and what we are, but influence the interactions and relationships we have with other people and social institutions, both within our national borders and beyond. As residents of a highly technological society undergoing rapid transformations in the conduits for information, we are subject to an increasing array of options in forming our ideas about the world and our place in it. A staple assertion of introductory sociology is that our understandings of the world are formed through exposure to various forms of media, including radio, television, film, newspapers, magazines and the internet.

While the mass media are often lumped into one homogeneous category, it is important to recognize that there are many diverse forms of media ranging from chart-topping music downloads, best-selling novels, hit TV programmes and Hollywood blockbusters through political affairs news magazines, sports radio programmes and amateur internet pornography sites. There are also different types of media, defined largely if not wholly by their creators' purpose. At the first level of approximation we should consider three types of media: news, entertainment and advertising. Hence, considering the different types and forms of media, and the shape that any combination of these may take, to suggest homogeneity of any sort is simplistic. So too, we need to consider that different forms and types of media have come into existence and shaped the mediascape (Appadurai, 1990) at different historic periods. For example, Canada's first newspaper, *The*

Halifax Gazette began in 1752. While some media, such as newspaper have been in existence for several centuries, most of the media that we are exposed to daily emerged much more recently. Canada's first radio station, CFCF, began broadcasting in 1919, and advertisements, undeniably the most ubiquitous of mass media's incarnations, only began to take on their current form in the 1920s. Television, though currently in decline, but still one of the most prominent media forms is largely a product of the post-WWII boom—Montreal's CBFT first went on the air in 1952. Music videos and video games emerged in the 1980s, and while the internet has existed since the late 1950s (as an American military platform) commercial and personal websites only took off in the mid-1990s. Similarly the past decade has seen the explosion of internet radio, file-sharing sites, podcasts and social networking sites (see Lorimer, Gasher, and Skinner, 2010).

Therefore, when we speak of knowledge of ourselves and the world around us, we also have to be specific concerning the type of information we receive and the form in which this information is presented. The way Canadians access knowledge has changed dramatically in the past two hundred years, from first-hand knowledge of people and events in rural communities and small urban centres to a society in which we are inundated with so much information that it is difficult to assess what specific impact given media messages have on our ideas and attitudes.

This chapter will examine several major models for understanding the media's influence. Thereafter, it will address three different types of media; the news, entertainment, and advertising. As such, this chapter is designed to provide some requisite conceptual skills to better understand the prominence of the mass media and media narratives in the lives of globalized subjects both in Canada and elsewhere in the world.

MODELS OF MEDIA INFLUENCE

While the "sociology of the media" is a relatively recent development sociologists have studied and postulated media impacts for much of the last century. Many early researchers such as Gabriel Tarde contended that the mass media destroys the individual's capacity to act autonomously. However, subsequent scholars from Columbia University and the University of Frankfurt posited a more complex interaction between the mass media, people and society. Elevating the role of human agency, these latter works contended that individuals actively evaluate and interpret mass media narratives. Theories about media influence have evolved over the last half century from those which emphasised direct and immediate influence (a "hypodermic needle" model) and those which suggested relatively little influence through those that maintained a select influence and long-term effects. Recognizing the dynamic tension between human agency and social structure most contemporary media scholars address the media as a process, and also the relationships among the myriad elements of this process.

French sociologist Gabriel Tarde (1890/1912) was among the first to suggest that the mass media exerted a strong and direct (and often detrimental) influence on people. This "hypodermic needle" model (sometimes referred to as "direct effects" or the "silver bullet" model) assumes that the audience is largely passive, and hence easily influenced. For Tarde, media messages were the underpinnings of social trends, styles and fashions. Darkly foreshadowing our own era of narcissism and our obsession with "celebrity news," Tarde theorized that people would imitate the behaviour, argot and styles of higher status people popularized through the news. According to Tarde, while this process impacted on all spheres of social activity it was most acute in matters of transgressive behaviour and crime. Observing a pattern of attacks with straight razors, Tarde coined the term "suggesto-imitative assaults"–what we would today refer to as "copy-cat crimes." He posited that sensationalistic newspaper coverage of these crimes was contributing to their spread across the country. He wrote: "Diseases of the respiratory system are spread by air or wind. Epidemics of crime follow the line of the telegraph" (p. 87). While Tarde's ideas enjoyed a brief period of popularity, today most media scholars, and indeed most people (aside from some conservative commentators decrying the moral bankruptcy of Hollywood and the music industry, such as Nancy Grace, Charles McVety, and Bill O'Reilly) realize that the model is too simplistic and deterministic to meaningfully contribute to our understandings of the complex interrelations between mass media and society.

Considerably less deterministic in its approach is the "minimal effects" model. American sociologists affiliated with Columbia University such as Paul Lazarsfeld and Robert Merton working in the late 1940s contended that the mass media's influence was far less direct than was previously suggested. Focusing their work more on the media's news production than on its entertainment endeavours, these scholars found that interpersonal relations served to mitigate media messages. Furthermore, they found that in many instances media messages acted more to reinforce existing beliefs, values and behaviours than to change them. This, they theorized, was a result of a multi-stage process wherein opinion leaders, who themselves where drawn to the mass media, incorporated media messages they were amenable to, and then worked to promulgate them among family, friends and acquaintances. For Merton and Lazarsfeld (1948) the biggest threat from the media came from what they termed its potential "narcoticising dysfunction." In other words, a torrent of media information about a given event (such as the Haitian earthquake or the proroguing of Parliament) may actually numb audiences–essentially paralysing them into inaction.

Theorists from the German Frankfurt School such as Max Horkheimer and Theodore Adorno provided some of the earliest and most systematic analyses of the mass media's influence. According to these scholars, the media, whether in the form of news or entertainment, is a "culture industry" (Adorno, 1941/1992; Horkheimer and Adorno, 1944/1972) transmitting information to a somewhat passive audience. This model of a unified and powerful media further suggests that consumerist messages work together with political ideology to further the hegemonic designs of those in power. The general public hungrily consumes packaged media spectacles ranging from news magazines detailing the "war on terror" to prime-time television comedy-dramas on the antics of upper-middle class suburbanites who live on Wisteria Lane.[1]

In addition to the Frankfurt School's contributions, the work of C. Wright Mills (see particularly 1953 and 1963) contributed significantly to the radicalization of sociology in the 1960s and 1970s and heralded the emergence of the "agenda-setting" model of the mass media. Inspired by Mills' analysis of the elite's ability to control the kind of information that is filtered to the general public, this model recognizes the role of growing media monopolies to tell people not *what to think* but rather *what to think about.* According to this approach, the media organizes public understanding in keeping with preferred social and cultural codes. The corporately owned mass media impart cultural, political, social, and economic statements of "truth." It, as the name implies, sets the agenda. It symbolically reflects what is "important," and hence worthy of our attention (by devoting coverage to it) as well as what is "not important" (by giving it little, if any, attention). In so doing, the mass media reinforce late modernity's sets of values and relationships. As audience members we use these messages as cues to fashion our identities and relationships as social actors.

Emerging in the mid-1990s, George Gerbner and his colleagues' "cultivation model" addresses the long term cultural influence of the mass media on the people's beliefs and values. Focusing primarily on the impact of television, Gerbner and his colleagues (Gerbner, et al., 1994; Gerbner, 2008) assert that lengthy exposure to messages from the corporately owned mass media have a mainstreaming or homogenizing effect on an otherwise heterogeneous population. Hence, rather than the direct causal effect posited by some, this model contends that continuous and sustained exposure will, over time, impact upon the audience's worldview. According to this model, the cultivation factor has moved the general population politically and ideologically to the right over the course of the last two decades. Not unlike the agenda setting model, this model is particularly attentive to a shrinking media cosmos which, while on the surface appears to offer more choices (more television channels, radio stations, online resources, newspapers, and so on) actually offers a narrower perspective because of increasingly oligopolistic ownership patterns and the concomitant horizontal and vertical integration across media. Put simply, fewer and fewer massive corporations own an increasingly large share of media production and distribution. Among other issues, the following sections of this chapter on the news, entertainment and advertising media will address this concentration of ownership, and its impact on the global mediascape.

NEWS MEDIA: NO MORE BREAD

In theory at least, the news media is engaged in the business of surveillant assemblage; the gathering, collation and distribution of information about society. Sociological functionalism likens the news media to public education in that it serves unifying and informative functions. In short, it provides people with knowledge about the world in which they live so that they can make informed choice on important social, economic and political matters that impact upon their lives. Of course, there are serious questions about whether the news media actually serves (or has ever really served!) that function. The suggestion that media organizations do not simply report the news, but instead determine "the news" is a well established maxim. Sociologists of the media have long contended that what is reported by the news media is not an objective representation of reality (Cohen, 1972; Gans, 1979). As Stuart Hall and his colleagues (1978:53) point out: "'News' is the end product of a complex process which begins with a systematic sorting and selecting of events and topics according to a socially constructed set of categories." Hence, news is inherently subjective; and while reporters and editors do not make up facts,[2] they do select facts–facts to include as well as facts to ignore. The selection and exclusion of certain stories is in part a result of what has been described as "professional ideology" (Hall et al., 1978:60). The news that we the audience consumes reflects both the reporters' academic training and the hierarchical nature of their work environment. Reporters are taught to get the "scoop," providing readers with exclusive tantalizing information that will attract audience interest. Editors, whom represent the news organization's supervisory staff, serve to direct and control each reporter's contribution. This editorial control serves to homogenize news reporting (Muzzatti and Featherstone, 2007). In short, far more of any given day's events are left out of the daily news than are included. The exclusions or omissions (perhaps more so than the inclusions) reflect the hegemony of advanced capitalism. The classic example is that daily news postings, broadcasts and print medium have a "business" segment or section, but no similar coverage of "labour." So too, we regularly hear or read comments ("expert analysis") by academic authorities, corporate spokespersons and state techno-bureaucrats, but rarely from students, service workers or other "ordinary Canadians" about whom they are speaking.

The power of the news media does not lie only in what it omits; it very much commits itself to influencing public perceptions. Jacobs (1996) argues that the news media use narrative constructions in reporting stories, and in so doing directly shape the public's reactions to a particular event. Major news organizations are able to select which "news items" are advanced and how they are framed. By constructing the theme of a story the news media is able to shape and influence the way the audience (browsers, listeners, readers and viewers) interpret the events. Hence, the news media does not simply create a story out of nothing, but instead rely upon hegemonic understandings of the world to structure their framing of an event. When constructing these accounts, the media looks for a certain combination of malleable ingredients that are compatible with the preferred readings of the social world. These components are then fashioned in such a way as to reify popular narratives and fit them into the narrow grooves of institutional meaning. As part of the media's storytelling enterprise, news coverage must be constantly producing new tales once the novelty or shock of the original event begins to dissipate (Moeller, 1999). One way in which this accomplished is through saturation. This technique commonly involves the simultaneous presentation of several related news stories. Prolonging the story is most often achieved by utilizing adjoining news stories which draw upon a wide supporting cast of social actors to provide popular narratives within the rubric of preferred meanings. While this is most clearly visible in instances of media panics, such as the recent H1N1 scare (or the previous SARS crisis) the technique is applied to a wide array of news stories from street crime and celebrity break-ups to global weather patterns and wild animal attacks.

These serious problems with the news media have a great deal to do to the fact that the news business is just that–a business. With the notable exceptions of CBC/SRC, TVO, and a select few independent (usually internet-based) outlets, most of the news that Canadians consume daily (irrespective of the form of media) is simply one product line, or "division" of a large, for-profit media entity such as *News Corporation* or *Rogers Communications Inc.* As addressed in the previous section of this chapter, corporate control of the media, specifically the increasing consolidation of ownership has drastically shrunk the media cosmos, leaving audiences with fewer real choices for news as the profit motive and "cost cutting" strategies continually erode the quantity and quality of news we consume. This is not a new phenomenon, but one that has grown steadily over the past 50 years, and accelerated rapidly over the last decade. Newspapers, which up until only recently were the pre-eminent source of news for Canadians proves to be an instructive example. In 1958 three newspaper chains (*Financial Post Publications, Thomson Newspapers Company Ltd*, and *Southam Inc*) controlled a quarter of all the English-language newspapers in the country. By 1970 that control extended to over 53%, while in the French-language market two companies, *Gesca Ltée* and *Quebecor* owned almost 50% (*CBC*, 1970). Today, while "news" is distributed more widely across media forms, and there are many more outlets (i.e., TV and radio stations, and websites). The tremendous growth in horizontal integration (sometimes referred to as cross-ownership) means that a proportionately smaller number of major media companies own and control the industry. For example, *Rogers Media Inc.* owns 53 radio stations, numerous broadcast and specialty TV channels (e.g., *OMNI* and *CityTV* stations in Toronto, Winnipeg, Edmonton, Calgary and Vancouver) as well as magazines such as *Maclean's* and *Canadian Business. Torstar Corp* publishes several papers in southwestern Ontario such as the *Toronto Star*, the *Hamilton Spectator* and the *Guelph Mercury*. The company also publishes 95 community newspapers in southern Ontario, and owns a half-interest in *Sing Tao*, Canada's largest Chinese-language daily. As I write this chapter, *Torstar* is bidding to buy the newspaper assets of insolvent *Canwest Global Communications. Transcontinental Media* is Canada's second-largest publisher of local and regional newspapers and is a major publisher of consumer and specialty magazines. It owns 12 daily newspapers including the *Guardian* of Charlottetown and the *Daily News* in Halifax, and more than 200 other papers. It also publishes more than 40 magazines and specialty publications. *Gesca Ltée* owns seven French-language dailies including *La Presse* in Montreal and *Le Droit* in Ottawa. Quebecor Media owns eight dailies including the *Toronto Sun* and 200 other local and community papers. *CTVglobemedia* owns the *Globe and Mail*, the *CTV* network and its 27 TV affiliates and has full or partial ownership of 30 specialty TV channels including *CTV Newsnet* and *Business News Network* (*CBC*, 2010).

The results of these ownership patterns are significant, and are part of a move toward a national entertainment state. The term, coined by media studies theorist Mark Crispin Miller (2006, 2008) refers to a process he observed in the US media throughout the 1990s. Sadly, the same processes have become increasingly evident in Canadian news over the course of the past several years. Among the most glaring has been a greater reliance on news services resulting in considerable repetition of stories across media and less in-depth coverage. This also includes less reporting of global/international issues, the cancellation of local television newscasts and a greater use of "filler" such as entertainment or celebrity news and thinly veiled inducements to greater consumption.

ENTERTAINMENT MEDIA: CIRCUSES ABOUND

As options for "real news" shrinks our menu for entertainment grows. The same patterns of media ownership are also applicable to the entertainment media. While we can access a far wider array of specialty programming than we did even a decade ago, many of these programmes originate in the US, or are modelled directly on commercially successful American progenitors. As a form of "cultural imperialism," the colonization of the Canadian (and indeed, much of the world's) media by enormous American companies is not a new phenomenon. Hollywood supplied 65% of films worldwide by the end of WWII. Today, even with competition from India's enormous "BollyWood" industry, American films continue to generate over two-thirds of global box office receipts (Miller, et. al., 2001; MMPA, 2009). Readers will not likely be surprised that in an average year American films account for over 95% of box office receipts across Canada (McIntosh, 1988; CMPDA, 2009; MPAA, 2009).

Perhaps ironically, many of these American films (as well as many TV series) are filmed in Canada, with Toronto, Montreal and Vancouver frequently cast as Chicago, New York, Washington DC and other major US cities. Part of *The Hulk 2* (2008) was filmed on Yonge Street outside Ryerson University, and on the University of Toronto's St. George campus. *Kick-Ass* (2010) was filmed in part on Yonge Street in Toronto and Charles Street in Hamilton (as well as in locations in the UK and the US). It is not just Canadian major cities that stand in for American locations. The remake of George Romero's *Dawn of the Dead* (2004) was shot in Thornhill, Ontario with most of the film set in the closed Thornhill Square Shopping Centre. The rural Connecticut of *A Haunting in Connecticut* (2009) was in fact Winnipeg and Tuelon, Manitoba.

In a globalized world where New Zealand is Middle-Earth and Hawaii is Pandora it is little wonder that the entertainment Canadian's consume is a virtual hodgepodge of cultural infusions. While this by no means minimizes the cultural imperialism of our southern neighbours, it does add some complexity to our entertainment landscape. For example, the TV programme *Who Wants to be a Millionaire?* was developed by a Japanese team at *Sony Pictures Television International* and originally aired in the UK in 1998. It was first broadcast in Canada via the American *ABC* network a few years later. To date, the programme airs in over 100 countries worldwide, including India. *Slumdog Millionaire* (2008) is a British film based on Indian author Vikas Swarup's novel *Q & A*. The film centres around the life of Jamal Malik, a former street kid from Mumbai's Juhu slums who finds himself one correct answer away from the grand prize on India's *Who Wants to be a Millionaire?* Though it was screened at a small film festival in Colorado the week before, its true global debut came at the Toronto International Film Festival (TIFF) on September 7, 2008. The film received critical and popular acclaim, eventually winning numerous awards, including eight Academy Awards.

The case of *Slumdog Millionaire* just scratches the surface of the steady overlap among various kinds of entertainment media that has occurred over the last two decades. The expanding world of entertainment media's cross-pollination is connected to the increasing concentration of media ownership, both in Canada, and the US, and takes many forms. Indeed, even the traditional divisions amongst news, entertainment, and advertising are breaking down and the boundaries are becoming increasingly fluid. Much of this confluence is market driven, as executives from a host of cultural industries have recognized the profitability of crossover merchandizing and are devising ever more creative, some would argue insidious, ways to engage such projects.

The use of popular music in Hollywood films and the subsequent emergence of the "movie soundtrack," was one of the earliest forays. The sale of vinyl records containing songs popularized in Hollywood films has roots in the 1930s (Altman, 2001). However, it was not until the early 1970s, when Hi-Fi stereo systems became increasingly common fixtures in homes, that the sale of entire albums comprised of music from films truly began to soar. Among some of the best sellers of that decade include the soundtrack from the original *Star Wars* (1977) featuring the grand symphonic scores of composer John Williams and *Saturday Night Fever* (1977) containing such hits as the Bee Gees' "Stayin' Alive," Kool and the Gang's "Open Sesame" and "Boogie Shoes" by KC and the Sunshine Band. Throughout the 1980s a number of comedies and teen-angst films such as the *Breakfast Club* (1985), *Pretty in Pink* (1986) and *Some Kind of Wonderful* (1987) spawned hit soundtracks featuring artists like Simple Minds, New Order and Flesh for Lulu. In the 1990s, as CDs replaced vinyl, sales of movie soundtracks waned, though feature songs or title releases still were popular as CD singles. Coolio's "Gansta's Paradise" from *Dangerous Minds* (1995), The Verve's "Bittersweet Symphony" from *Cruel Intentions* (1999) and a number of releases from *American Pie* (1999), including Oleander's "I Walk Alone" are some examples of songs heavily cross promoted through film. As music went digital in the new century the trend toward singles over full soundtracks intensified, though music-film cross promotion is still a significant component of the entertainment media as the success of Leona Lewis' "I See You" from *Avatar* (2009) and Muse's "Neutron Star Collision/Love is Forever" from *The Twilight Saga: Eclipse* (2010) indicate.

Entertainment media crossovers are not restricted to film and music. Indeed, as many readers know, like the case of the above cited *Twilight* series of films, a host of teen and tween oriented fiction have been transformed into Hollywood spectacles. Chief among them are J.K. Rowling's seven Harry Potter books, which resulted in six films between 2001 and 2009. Rowling's final book *Harry Potter and the Deathly Hallows* (2007) has been made into two movies, tentatively scheduled for release in 2010 and 2011. Likewise, a wide range of heroes, anti-heroes and villains from graphic novels and comic books have sprung to life on the big screen over the last decade in films such as *Blade, Sin City*, The *Xmen, Batman, Spiderman, The Punisher, Surrogates, The Losers, Iron Man* and *Kick-Ass.* Video, PC and on-line games have as well crossed over into movies, and vice-versa. The games Lara Croft: *Tomb Raider, Resident Evil, Max Payne, Silent Hill, BloodRayne, Doom* and *Prince of Persia: The Sands of Time* have all become Hollywood films. The films that have inspired games are far more numerous, extensive and diverse, including *Ghost Busters, Mean Girls, The Chronicles of Narnia, Watchmen, Kung Fu Panda, 007: Quantum of Solace, Night at the Museum, Cars* and *Shutter Island.*

ADVERTISING MEDIA: CARNIVALS OF CONSUMPTION

Advertising is the most ubiquitous type of mass media, not only because it is present in all of media's forms, but as well because it underwrites and infiltrates both the news and entertainment media. Indeed, because of its omnipresence it is likely the single most influential agent of socialization in Canada and other late-modern societies. Its scope and impact are tied to enormous fiscal expenditures. According to the advertising industry's own calculations, spending on advertising in 2006 topped over $150 billion in the US and $385 billion worldwide, the latter predicted to exceed $500 billion by the end of 2010 (Price Waterhouse Coopers, 2008). This type of spending buys a great deal of exposure. For example, young people in Canada averaging one to two hours of television daily will see between 20 and 40 thousand commercials in a given year (*CBC*, 2008). This is, of course, in addition to the other ads they are exposed to in public spaces, on the internet, and increasingly in schools. When considered in combination with the amount of product placement they encounter in their favourite video games, films, TV programmes, social networking websites and music videos, it is not surprising that they display an intimate familiarity with between 300-400 brands and list shopping as one of their favourite leisure activities (*CBC*, 2008). For corporations the stakes are extremely high as they compete for children's markets worth $1.9 billion in Canada and $30 billion in the US; to say nothing of the estimated $1 trillion in family spending that they are estimated to influence (*CBC*, 2008).

The consolidation of ownership in media has contributed to increasing fluidity between entertainment and advertising, much the same way as it has blurred the boundaries between news and entertainment, and facilitated considerable cross pollination. One of the more recent forays in crossover spaces is what some are calling "advertainment"–the conflation of advertisement and entertainment. Unlike the infomercials that first appeared in the late 1980s, approximating a talk show or TV news-magazine format to shill kitchen wares, cleaning products, and exercise equipment, this most recent foray draws heavily upon the use of popular styles artifacts, and actors in combination with lifestyle marketing to sell everything from cars and alcohol to holiday packages and retirement funds (Muzzatti, 2008). Television ads scripted to look like serial dramas, or music videos, product placement in movies, TV shows and music videos, commercials running prior to the movie in theatres and television programmes and websites devoted to rebroadcasting TV commercials all speak to this widespread and growing trend.

While ads have been around for many years, advertising as we understand it is a relatively recent phenomenon. Beginning in the 1920s advances in mass industrialization made the production of consumer goods easier and more efficient than at any other time in history. It also lead to growing alienation in the workplace as faster production meant more work and understandably, more disenfranchisement and dissent within factories. In short, the birth of modern advertising was propelled as much by the need to create new markets for products as by the desire to neutralize the potentially incendiary mix of discontented workers and militant labour movements (Ewen, 1977).

The growth of television as a medium during the post-World War II boom provided a new outlet of previously unheralded power for advertisers. This new visual medium was extremely expensive to produce, and almost from the outset relied upon outside funding sources to underwrite it. In the early days of television, much of the outside money came in the form of "sponsorship." Companies paid to have the programme named after them. At the beginning of a program an announcer would proclaim, "Texaco Star Theater" or "The Desilu Playhouse brought to you by Westinghouse," with some musical fanfare and perhaps a tagline or slogan. The "spot commercial," an advertisement that interrupted the programme first appeared when the small cosmetics company Hazel Bishop wanted to advertise on TV but could not afford to sponsor an entire programme. The compromise struck between the company and *NBC* resulted in a 30-second message from a twenty-six-year-old Merv Griffin being inserted into the middle of "The Kate Smith Evening Hour" (1951), spawning the ubiquitous commercial spot we know today. As the spot commercial became an increasingly normalized and substantial part of TV cultures lifestyle advertising, specifically the presentation of characters that advertisers thought the audience aspired to be quickly became the staple. Television provided advertisers with considerable opportunities to dynamically link the everyday/night worlds of the audience with consumption practices.

As marketplace competition increased and the testimonials of hegemony's organizing agents (i.e., actors cast in the roles of meddling neighbours, doctors, professional chefs, mechanics, dry cleaners and other "product experts") became increasingly commonplace in television commercials, advertisers searched for ways to augment their product push. Borrowing the visual style of popular TV programmes, music videos and movies, contemporary advertising became highly symbolic, crammed with images designed to exploit cultural metaphors and metonyms. Indeed, contemporary ads are so imbued with cultural mythologies that the sales pitch is furtively hidden behind a multilayered veil of artifice, multiple *entendres* and postmodern lifestyle scripts (Muzzatti, 2008).

In the late 1980s and early 1990s advertisers began to use rock and other popular music genres in television commercials. Among the first were Nike's use of the Beatles' "Revolution" and a Levi's use of the Clash's "Should I Stay or Should I Go?" A deal between Microsoft and the Rolling Stones for rights to use "Start Me Up" in the Windows95 campaign was a watershed moment in this process. Since then, popular music has become ever more commonplace in advertising. For example, between 2002 and 2007 a series of Mitsubishi commercial cocktails feature groups of young club-goers enthusiastically navigating the night's urban landscape in their Lancers, Eclipse Spiders, and Galants to the dance beats of Dirty Vegas, Telepopmusik, The Wise Guys, and Deltron 3030. In a strange inversion of this process, Bodyrockers' "I Like the Way" was broken in 2005 a month before the single's scheduled release not on commercial radio or other traditional venues (such as MuchMusic's Much on Demand), but rather in a Diet Coke commercial. The song has subsequently been featured in ads for Diet Coke, DirecTV, Hyundai and BMW. Finally, in a surreal fusion of music, advertising and consumerism, Telus Mobility and Blackberry feature Maylee's "What's it Worth" and Grayson Matthews' "All You Need is Love" in their respective commercials. These remakes of 1960s hits are currently available to purchase and download as ringtones.

In addition to music, visual styles appropriated from the entertainment media have become increasingly prevalent in advertising. The styles range from the saccharine to the extreme (Muzzatti, 2010). For example, in the early 1990s, reborn into the roles they played in the UK in the late 1980s, British actors Sharon Maughan and Anthony Stewart Head appeared in a series of commercials for Taster's Choice instant coffee, shot in the style of a soap opera with the concomitant allusions to serendipity, affluence and illicit sexual trysts. The influence of Hollywood's extreme driving action sub-genre is evident in Mountain Dew's 2003 commercial featuring Hoobastank's "Crawling in the Dark" as a young (and at the time, relatively unknown actor) Channing Tatum races through the streets and leaps his old school Firebird over a delivery truck to retrieve a can of pop. In a similar vein, Jason Statham reprises his role in films *The Transformer* and *Death Race* by car-jacking Mercedes Benz, BMW, and Lexus drivers in unsuccessful attempts to evade his pursuers in a commercial for the 2009 Audi A6. Borrowing the visuals of a post-apocalyptic landscape seen in films such as *The Book of Eli* a commercial for Doritos' Collisions flavoured chips are representative of two ragtag armies, one in blue, the other in red, taunting each other before engaging in a final confrontation to determine the supremacy of the Red Hot Wings or Blue Cheese flavours. Also capitalizing on the blue versus red theme is Mountain Dew's 2009 commercial featuring two women metamorphosing into members of the Horde and the Alliance from the massively multiplayer online role-playing game World of Warcraft as they battle for supremacy in the check-out aisle of a grocery store. Finally, adopting and fusing elements from *Jackass*, *Punked* and other surreal-humiliation reality programmes, a series of commercials for Stride gum features unsuspecting gum chewers assaulted by a bizarre assortment of Oktoberfest-clad folk dancers, a 1970s-style wrestler and dodgy corporate running dogs.

CONCLUSION

Mass media are vital sites of cultural and economic brokerage. Over the course of the last quarter century the mass media have expanded steadily resulting in new forms of cultural pedagogy. As the mass media's omnipresence becomes more entrenched, traditional boundaries among news, entertainment, and advertising become increasingly fluid. Slick and emotional, profound and poetic, rhythmic and insistent, and most of all, never fully shut out, mass media narratives serve as conduits through which society re-presents itself in ways by which social and personal identities are articulated and disseminated.

As privileged residents of a highly globalized world, we are the major consumers of mass media. From policing practices in Toronto's Keele and Eglinton neighbourhood, Lady Gaga's latest outfit and youthful misbehaviour on the *Jersey Shore* through the malfeasance of Canadian mining companies in Ecuador, the wars in Iraq and Afghanistan and international World Cup fever, most of what we know about our communities, the nation, and the world is a result of the mass media. To wit, it behoves us to engage in thoughtful and informed analyses of these texts in an effort to uncover and explore the array of approved, fugitive and oppositional meanings. The mass media's multiple appendages provide many opportunities for those willing to use the sociological imagination to challenge corporate hegemony. The intention of this chapter, was not to provide a comprehensive assessment, nor for that matter a general overview of the literature on the sociology of the media, but rather to introduce a heuristic through which readers can intellectually and politically challenge dominant media narratives.

NOTES

1 Wisteria Lane in Fairview, USA is the fictional setting for *Desperate Housewives.* While the programme's ratings in the US have dropped since its peak in 2006, it is one of the most popular televison programmes in the world, airing in 59 countries.

2 Maybe this is too strong a statement considering the revelations that the now disgraced Jayson Blair of the *New York Times* regularly fabricated his stories.

REFERENCES

Adorno, T. (1941/1992). "On Popular Music." In A. Easthope and K. McGown (eds.), *A Critical and Cultural Studies Reader.* Toronto: University of Toronto Press.

Altman, R. (2001). "Cinema and Popular Song: The Lost Tradition." In P. Robertson Wojcik and A. Knight (eds.), *Soundtrack Available: Essays on Film and Popular Music.* Durham: Duke University Press.

Appadurai, A. (1990). "Disjuncture and Difference in the Global Cultural Economy." *Public Culture* (2)2:1-24.

Cashmore, E. (1994). *And There Was Television.* London: Routledge.

Cohen, S. (1972). *Folk Devils and Moral Panics: The Creation of the Mods and Rockers.* Oxford: Basil Blackwell.

Canadian Broadcasting Corporation (CBC). (2010). "Media Convergence, Acquisitions and Sales in Canada." Available at http://www.cbc.ca/money/story/2010/04/29/f-media-ownership-canada.html.

Canadian Broadcasting Corporation (CBC). (2008). "Pester Power: Your Child's Inner Consumer." Available at http://www.cbc.ca/health/story/2008/12/22/f-barwick.html.

Canadian Broadcasting Corporation (CBC). (1970). "How Free Is Canada's Press?" Available at http://archives.cbc.ca/version_print.asp?page=1&idlan=1&idclip=4832&iddossier=790&idcat=290&idcatpa=254.

Canadian Motion Picture Distributors Association (CMPDA). (2009). "CFTPA Profile 2009: Economic Report on the Canadian Film and Television Production Industry." Toronto: Canadian Motion Picture Distributors Association.

Ewen, S. (1977). *Captains of Consciousness: Advertising and the Social Roots of Consumer Culture.* Toronto: McGraw-Hill Book Company.

Fiske, J., and J. Hartley. (1989). *Reading Television.* London: Routledge.

Gans, H.J. (1979). *Deciding what's News.* NY: Vintage.

Gerbner, G. (2008). "Who is Shooting Whom?: The Content and Context of Media Violence." In M. Pomerance and J. Sakeris (eds.), *Popping Culture,* 5th ed. Boston: Pearson Education.

Gerbner, G., L. Gross, M. Morgan, and N. Signorelli. (1994). "Growing Up With Television: The Cultivation Effect." In J. Bryant and D. Zillman (eds.), *Media Effects: Advances in Theory and Researched.* Hilldale, NJ: Lawrence Erlbaum Associates.

Hall, S., S. Winlow, and C. Ancrum. (2008). *Criminal Identities and Consumer Culture: Crime, Exclusion and the New Culture of Narcissism.* Devon: Willan.

Hall, S., C. Critcher, T. Jefferson, J. Clarke, and B. Roberts. (1978). *Policing the Crisis: Mugging, the State, and Law and Order.* NY: Holmes and Meier Publishing Inc.

Horkheimer, M., and T. Adorno. (1944/1972). *Dialectic of Enlightenment.* NY: Herder and Herder.

Jacobs, R.N. (1996). "Civil Society and Crisis: Culture, Discourse, and the Rodney King Beating." *American Journal of Sociology* 101:1238-1272.

Lazarsfeld, P., and R.K. Merton. (1948). "Mass Communication, Popular Taste, and Organized Social Action." In L. Bryson (ed.), *The Communication of Ideas.* NY: Harper.

Lorimer, R., M. Gasher and D. Skinner. (2010). *Mass Communication in Canada.* 6th ed. Toronto: Oxford University Press.

Mcintosh, D. (2008). "Waiting for Hollywood: Canada's Maquila Film Industry." Available at www. canadiandimension.com/articles/1728/.

Miller, M.C. (2008). "Saddam and Osama in the Entertainment State." In M. Pomerance and J. Sakeris (eds.), *Popping Culture.* 5th ed. Boston: Pearson Education.

_____. (2006). *The Death of News.* In *The Nation.* Available at http://www.thenation.com/Issue/July-3-2006.

Miller, T., N. Govil, J. Mcmurria, and R. Maxwell. (2001). *Global Hollywood.* London: British Film Institute.

Mills, C.W. (1963). *The Marxists.* Harmondsworth: Penguin.

_____. (1953). *White Collar: The American Middle Classes.* NY: Oxford University Press.

Moeller, S.D. (1999). *Compassion Fatigue: How the Media Sell Disease, Famine, War and Death.* NY: Routledge.

Motion Picture Association of America (MPAA). (2009). "Theatrical Market Statistics 2009." Available at http://www.mpaa.org/resources/091af5d6-faf7-4f58-9a8e-405466c1c5e5.pdf.

Muzzatti, S.L. (2010). "Drive It Like You Stole It: A Cultural Criminology of Car Commercials." In K. Hayward and M. Presdee (eds.), *Framing Crime: Cultural Criminology and the Image.* London: Routledge.

_____ (2008). "They Sing the Body Ecstatic: Television Commercials and Captured Music." In M. Pomerance and J. Sakeris (eds.), *Popping Culture,* 5th ed. Boston: Pearson Education.

Muzzatti, S.L., and R. Featherstone. (2007). "The Culture of Fear and the Production of the D.C. Sniper Story." *Contemporary Justice Review* 10(1):43-66.

Postman, N. (1985). *Amusing Ourselves to Death.* NY: Penguin.

Price Waterhouse Coopers. (2008). "Global Entertainment and Media Outlook: 2008-2012." Available at http://www.pwc.com/extweb/pwcpublications.nsf/docid/5ac172f2c9ded8f5852570210044eea7.

Tarde, G. (1890/1912). *Penal Philosophy.* NY: Little Brown.

Chapter 15

Immigration and Globalization

Canadian Immigration under Conditions of Globalization and Transnationality

Joseph Mensah
and Robert M. Bridi

York University

I. 1NTRODUCTION

"*You know, Abraham was really the first immigrant.*" With this pithy title, Peggy Levitt (2003) drives home the point that migration is a long standing phenomenon, arguably, going as far back as humans have lived on this earth. Still, there is no denying that the phenomenon has intensified under contemporary globalization, and its attendant innovations in transportation and communications technologies, knowledge production, and electronic mediation (Allen and Hamnett, 2000; Castells, 2000). Adding to these scientific and time-space compression advancements are a host of complex socioeconomic and geopolitical factors that have helped sustain the processes of migration the world over. Political instability, violations of human rights, the growing inter- and intra-national economic disparities, environmental hazards/disasters, and the destabilizations wrought by capitalist penetration into peripheral regions via neoliberalism are among the usual culprits in this regard (United Nations, 2000; Bond, 2008; Castles and Miller, 1993).

Additionally, epochal events such as the collapse of the Soviet Union and the civil wars and ethnic cleansing in several countries (including Somalia, Rwanda, Sudan, Liberia, the Democratic Republic of Congo, Bosnia-Herzegovina, and Sri Lanka) have all fed into the recent increase in international migration. The restructuring of (inter)national labour markets is also implicated in the escalation of modern global nomadism, with migrant workers now making a significant contribution to the economies of both sending and receiving countries. The International Labour Organization estimates that in 2006 sending countries received the equivalent of US$250 billion in remittance from migrant workers, a sum larger than all overseas development assistance and foreign direct investments (ILO, 2008). Recent figures from the United Nations indicate that the global migrant stock was as high as 214 million people in 2009, of which some 128 million (or 60 percent) were in the developed world, with the remainder in developing countries. As the number of global migrants increases, so have the academic debates on the causes, consequences, and the policy implications of the processes of migration at both the local and global levels of analysis.

This chapter contributes to the burgeoning literature on international migration by examining the trends in Canadian immigration in the context of contemporary globalization. How has Canadian immigration changed since the advent of contemporary globalization? To what extent have the globalization-induced cultural trends and technological innovations impacted immigration in Canada? How have immigrants used globalizing social, economic, and cultural trends to negotiate Canadian citizenship? Has globalization undermined how the Canadian nation-state asserts its governmentality over immigrants, or not? How do immigrants balance their ethno-racial identities with their Canadian national identity under contemporary globalization? To what extent has the rise of transnationalism among immigrants affected the settlement and integration process of immigrants in Canada? How have Canadians reacted to the growing presence of visible minority immigrants in their midst? These are some of the issues grappled with in this chapter.

We start our discussion with some theoretical grounding, shedding light on the existing models of international migration and international refugee movements. Following this is a historical profile of immigration in Canada, in which we identify the key immigration policies and trends in the pre-Confederation era to about the 1960s and early 1970s. The next section then moves the discussion to the nature of Canadian immigration under contemporary globalization; after which we discuss the key socioeconomic and cultural trends that have influenced the dynamics of immigration in Canada from the 1970s and beyond. In the penultimate section, we tease out the ramifications and responses of the Canadian nation-state and Canadian citizens to the growing number of visible minority immigrants in their midst. We conclude the chapter with remarks on the need to pay more analytical attention to the debates on immigration, multiculturalism, and citizenship. While Canada remains our main focus, we are cognizant of the fact that we cannot reasonably map out the intersections of *immigration* and *globalization* in the exclusive context of Canada, given the very nature of these two processes. We, therefore, draw upon themes and examples from around the world as we weave our Canadian narrative.

2. CONCEPTUAL FRAMEWORK

Like most commonly used social science concepts, "migration" is known to almost everyone; yet, it is hard to define with any appreciable level of theoretical rigour and precision. Two main difficulties relating to distance and time are involved in this problematic: First, *how far* does one have to travel to fit the notion of migration; and, second, *how long* does one have to stay at the destination for the move to be considered one of migration? Add to these the wide diversity of axes upon which one can categorize the processes of migration—including those of *pattern* (inter- versus intra-); *scale* (local, national, international); *decision-making* (voluntary, forced); *numbers* (individual, mass); and *causes* (economic, social)—and the complexities and dialectical tensions in any theorization of migration become apparent to even the most cursory analyst. Not only that, even the flow of migration may vary, depending on how the preceding axes intersect with each other. We thus have *stepwise migration* (i.e., movement through a series of places), *chain migration* (i.e., flows determined by kinship ties), *return migration* (i.e., migrant returns to his or her origin), and *circulation,* (i.e., migration as a continuous process of circular flow) (Ogden, 1984).

With these complexities in mind, we define migration as a process by which people relocate from one place to another, either permanently or semi-permanently, and in doing so change their "activity space" (Johnston et al., 2000; Fellman, Getis, and Getis, 1995; de Blij, 1993). We all have what human geographers call an "activity space" (i.e., a space within which we enact our daily activities). Geographic literature suggests that we develop new activity spaces and shed old ones through the processes of migration (Fellman, Getis, and Getis, 1995).

Over the years, social scientists have sought to understand the dimensions of migration, with some focusing their analytical attention on the characteristics of different origins and destinations of migrants, and others probing into how migration affects the population structure and the labour markets of origins and destinations; and still others examining the factors that push and pull people into migration (Hall, 2003; Anthias, 1998; Stark, 1997; Sassen, 1988). The extent to which migration feeds into people's identity and sense of place; the problems faced by immigrants in settling and integrating into host societies; the transnational practices of immigrants; and the interconnections between migration and development have also been a fecund source of scholarly work for decades now (Moghissi, Rahnema, and Goodman, 2009; Goldring, 2004; Levitt, 1996). Notwithstanding the long-standing academic interest in this area of research, we are yet to have a well-grounded theory of migration, capable of bringing the various aspects of the phenomenon under a comprehensive and coherent theoretical framework. Noteworthy attempts have been made to draw out the theoretical and empirical connections between the relevant variables of migration, through a host of mini-narratives, suppositions, generalizations, and quasi-theories, some of which we explore in what follows.

2.1. Theorizing Inter- and Intra-National Migration

One of the very first major attempts at migration theory was by Ernst G. Ravenstein. Born in Germany in 1834, Ravenstein moved to England in 1855 where he served in the Topographical Department of the War Office. He witnessed first-hand the industrial revolution which started in England and diffused across Europe and North America, and in the process uprooted millions of people within and across various countries. To understand the migration processes and patterns of industrialization, Ravenstein (1889, 1885) formulated a series of generalization he called "the laws of migration" (Table 1), following a statistical analysis of census data from England, Wales, Scotland, and Ireland, for the period from 1871 to 1885. In his original paper in 1885, he formulated seven such "laws," most of which emphasized the relationships between distance and migration. These "laws" were later expanded into eleven in another paper in 1889. Interestingly, Ravenstein's "laws of migration" have stood the test of time, with many contemporary migration scholars still deriving their own hypotheses from them (Corbett, 2009; Tobler, 1995; Richmond, 1994; Grigg, 1977a and 1977b).

TABLE 1: RAVENSTEIN'S "LAWS OF MIGRATION"

- The majority of migrants go only a short distance.
- Migration proceeds step by step.
- Migrants going long distances generally go by preference to one of the great centres of commerce or industry.
- Each migration current produces a compensating counter-current.
- The natives of towns are less migratory than those of rural areas.
- Females are more migratory than males in their country of birth, but males more frequently venture beyond.

- Most migrants are adults–families rarely migrate out of their country of birth.
- Large towns grow more by migration than by natural increase.
- Migration increases by volume as industries and commerce develop and transport improves.
- The major direction of migration is from agricultural areas to the centres of industry and commerce.
- The major causes of migration are economic.

Sources: Ravenstein (1885 and 1889); see also Grigg (1977a and 1977b).

Another important migration theorist in the tradition of Ravenstein is George Zipf, who in a 1949 study incorporated the former's idea on the influence of distance in migration into his own theorization, couched in the Newton gravity model. In its simplest formulation, Zipf's distance/gravity model states that the migration between any pairs of places is a positive function of their populations, and inversely proportional to the distance between them. Zipf's model is intuitively appealing, as it corresponds to the notion of least effort—the idea that when people migrate, they usually prefer to travel as short a distance as possible, since the financial, psychological, and social costs of migration tend to increase in direct proportion to the distance between origins and destinations.

In contrast to Zipf, the American sociologist Samuel Stouffer (1960, and 1940) emphasized "opportunities" in explaining the spatial pattern of migration, with his notion of *intervening* opportunities. According to Stouffer, the number of movements or flows between an origin and a destination is directly proportional to the number of opportunities at that destination, and inversely proportional to the number of intervening opportunities. Thus, intervening opportunities are the attractions that serve to reduce the spatial interaction or the migration that would otherwise develop between two complementary areas. "Opportunity" here may refer to, for example, the number of jobs or the number of housing vacancies in a particular place. Furthermore, as Stouffer points out, migrants are in constant competition for these intervening opportunities, whether they know it or not.

In a 1970 paper, the prolific Nigerian geographer Akin Mabogunje used the systems approach to examine the relationships between economic, social, technological, and environmental factors, on one the hand, and migration, on the other. For Mabogunje, migration is best conceptualized as a circular, intricately intertwined, self-modifying system. For his part, the American cultural geographer Wilmur Zelinsky (1971) examined the relationships between the processes of urbanization, industrialization, modernization, and migration in what he calls the hypothesis of mobility transition which he patterned after the celebrated demographic transition model. According to Zelinsky, a transition from a relatively sessile condition of limited geographic mobility towards much higher rates of such movement occurs as a society experiences the process of modernization. This is what Zelinsky dubs "the mobility transition," which, like the demographic transition, forms part of the modernization process. Zelinsky (1971) notes that the nature, intensity, frequency, duration, periodicity, distance, and the function of migration change as societies move from the pre-modern, through the early transitional and late transitional stages, to the advanced and super-advanced stages of modernization.

Theories of international migration are routinely classified as *macro* or *micro*, depending on the level of analysis. The macro theories deal with large-scale migration, focusing on the socioeconomic and demographic characteristics of migrants in aggregate terms. These theories typically examine the broader societal causes, consequences, and ramifications of international migration. The micro theories, on their part, are concerned with the socioeconomic and behavioural factors that differentiate between movers and non-movers, and usually use the individual as the unit of analysis (Richmond, 1994). Much of this micro-level theorization has been done by social psychologists, many of whom see the decision to migrate as an individual choice, with or without consultation with family members. The basic assumption behind a number of micro analyses is the concept of economic rationality (i.e., the supposition that migration decisions are made by people with access to adequate information on which to base an economically rational decision to migrate or not to migrate, after subjectively weighing all conceivable "push" and "pull" factors).

Another useful typology deployed by Massey et al. (1997), categories international migration into *initiation* and *perpetuation* theories. *Initiation* theories include the neoclassical economic theory of migration, which attributes international migration to wage differences between nations; the new economics of migration, which sees international migration as primarily an effort by households to reduce or diversify the risks to their incomes; and the world systems theory (Wellerstein, 1974), which sees international migration mainly as a form of displacement of peasant labour by the penetration of capitalists production into peripheral and semi-peripheral regions.

Massey et al. (1997) discuss three main international migration perpetuation models: network theory, institutional theory, and the cumulative causation theory. The network theory defines networks as the interpersonal ties that people establish, based on the commonalities of background, relations, and organization. These ties constitute a form of social capital, which migrants and non-migrants rely on to gain useful insights into foreign labour markets. According to the network theory, international migration is perpetuated through interpersonal connections among migrants, former migrants, and non-migrants in both origin and destination countries. Institutional theorists, on their part, give primacy to the activities of private and non-profit organizations that aim to "satisfy the demand created by an imbalance between the large number of people who seek entry into capital-rich countries and the limited number of immigrant visas these countries typically offer" (Massey et al., 1997:265). As with the networks, these institutions serve as social capital that assists prospective migrants in their migration process. Complementing both the network and institutional theories is the notion of cumulative causation. Coined by the Swedish economist Gunnar Myrdal (1957), the theory of cumulative causation emphasizes the possible cumulative advantages, vis-à-vis migration, that the prospective migrant gains in specific geographical settings as a result of increased migration flows. It is reasoned that each migration flow changes, or improves, the social and economic context in which subsequent migration decisions are made (Massey et al., 1997). Also, the social labelling of some jobs as "immigrant jobs" in receiving countries makes these jobs unattractive to natives; this also intensifies the process of cumulative causation (Mensah, 2010; Massey et al., 1997).

As international migration intensifies under contemporary globalization, most migrants do not sever their ties with their homelands, but maintain them through a variety of cross-border relationships. The theorization of these cross-border relationships is done under the rubric of transnational migration. The pioneering research in this area is traced to anthropologists Nina Glick Schiller, Linda Green Basch, and Christiana Szanton-Blanc (1995, 1994 and 1992). As Hiebert and Ley (2003) note, until these seminal works, scholars have downplayed the transnational dimensions of international migration and, consequently, of immigrants' integration experiences. The focus was primarily on models of integration and assimilation that take the nation-state as the unit of analysis, and give primacy to issues of immigrants' containment within national borders; however, to the extent that many recent international migrants are implicated in transnationalism (Satzewich and Wong, 2006), it behoves on scholars to incorporate the dynamics of immigrants' cross-border activities, not only into theorizations of international migration, but also into debates on immigrants' integration, multiculturalism, and citizenship (Mensah, 2008a).

2.2. International Refugee Movements

The migration models identified in the preceding sub-section deal mainly with voluntary migration and have virtually no relevance to our understanding of refugee movements. Who is a refugee? What factors initiate refugee movements? As inadequate as the existing theories on voluntary migration are, there is an even greater paucity of theoretical foundation for refugee movements in the available literature. While voluntary migrants usually have a choice of *where* and *when* to migrate, by definition the opposite is true of all forced and impelled migrants. Admittedly, migration decisions of all kinds are made under some pressure, but in the case of forced migration, the pressure is so intense that prospective migrants are often impelled to move with a sense of loss of control over their own fate (Hollenback, 2008; Stalker, 2001; Richmond, 1994).

Several Western countries, including Canada, following the lead of the 1951 United Nations Convention on the Status of Refugees, define a refugee as a person with a

> well-founded fear of being persecuted for reasons of race, religion, nationality, membership of a particular social group or political opinion, is outside the country of his nationality and is unable or, owing to such fear, is unwilling to avail himself of the protection of that country; or who, not having a nationality and being outside the country of his former habitual residence as a result of such events, is unable or, owing to such fear, is unwilling to return to it. (Office of the United Nations High Commissioner for Human Rights, 2007)

A refugee claimant is accorded certain rights and protections under the United Nations convention. For example, signatories of the United Nations refugee convention, such as Canada, cannot return refugee claimants against their will without first allowing them entry and assessing the merit of their refugee claim. Also such countries are obliged to offer protection and basic social assistance, including food, shelter, and clothing, for the prospective asylum seeker. Notwithstanding these potential benefits, the "refugee" label conjures some negative connotations, often leading to stereotyping and ecological fallacy in which individual identities are subsumed under group identities (Loescher, Betts, and Milner, 2008; Hall, 2003; Boyle, Halfacree, and Robinson, 1998).

The notion of "pull factors" routinely used in the analysis of voluntary migration has little relevance in the case of refugee movement, but "push factors" (e.g., armed conflicts, geopolitical struggles, environmental hazards, and straitened economic circumstances) dominate as causes of refugee movements (de Blij, 1993). Although these push factors are behind many refugee movements, "it is no longer possible to treat refugee movements as completely independent of the state of the global economy" (Richmond, 1994:51). Internal and external social, economic, political, and environmental factors combine in different permutations with global politics and economics to produce refugee movements. In some cases, people that migrate for economic reasons are also responding to political conflicts and repression (Haddad, 2008; Richmond, 1994). Conversely, people that migrate for political reasons may also be responding to economic and material circumstances (Dowty, 1987).

3. CANADIAN IMMIGRATION: AN HISTORICAL PERSPECTIVE

Immigration has been a prominent feature of *Canadiana*. The arrival of immigrants from other countries has for centuries played an important role in the process of nation-building in Canada (Iacovetta, Draper, and Ventresca, 2002). Prior to the 1850s, Canada's demography was primarily made up of Aboriginal, French, and British people. Immigrants came from France, Britain, the United States, and north-western Europe, making Canada a white-settler society. The French and the British, or the founding nations, were responsible for defining Canada as a nation-state; Aboriginal people were for the most part treated as subordinates (Palmer, 1994). In 1867, the British colonies of New Brunswick, Nova Scotia, and Canada (then comprising a union between Canada East and Canada West) joined in Confederation to form the Dominion of Canada. In the following six years, the Canadian territory expanded further to include Prince Edward Island, the interior lands of the Hudson Bay Company, and the colony of British Columbia. The total population then was a mere 3.5 million, with people of British descent accounting for 60 percent and those of French background making up 31 percent of the population, with Aboriginal and "others" constituting one percent and 8 percent of the population, respectively (Palmer, 1994). With an expansive geographic territory, and a relatively small national population, immigration became a priority for national development. In pursuit of this, Sir John A. MacDonald, the first Prime Minister of Canada, implemented the National Policy which encouraged immigration, promoted economic growth, and subsidized the building of the Canadian Pacific Railway to facilitate the settlement of the Western provinces of Canada.

In the 1870s, the Alexander Mackenzie government (1873-1878) instituted Canada's first Immigration Act. While in theory there was an "open door" immigration policy with few restrictions, in practice Blacks and other visible minorities were not welcome. To promote immigration, the government set up immigration offices in London, Dublin, Belfast, and Glasgow. Regardless of such efforts, slow economic growth in the three decades following the Canadian Confederation discouraged immigration. Between 1881 and 1891, emigration exceeded immigration by some 200,000 people. The turnaround in the economy did not occur until the period between 1896 and 1911 when Wilfrid Laurier was Prime Minister. The Laurier government financed two new transcontinental railways, and this opened up lucrative opportunities for mining in Ontario and Québec, provided employment for thousands of people, and linked various isolated areas in the West to central Canada. With the establishment of east-west trade, and the relatively small number of people living west of Ontario (less than 10 per cent of the total Canadian population), the Laurier government began offering free land for settlement in the West (Norrie and Owran, 2002). Settlers flocked to the Prairies and British Columbia as a result of these government initiatives.

From the dawn of the twentieth century to the end of WWII in 1945, there were two main waves of immigration to Canada. The first occurred between 1903 and 1913 when more than 2.5 million people arrived in Canada. Indeed, the highest levels of immigration ever recorded in Canadian history occurred between 1910 and 1913 when Canada received nearly 1.4 million immigrants. In 1913 alone, there were 400,830 immigrants—the highest number of immigrants in one year in Canadian history. Available data indicate that as high as 72 percent of the immigrants who came in 1913 were from the United Kingdom and the United States, with the rest coming mainly from Russia, Ukraine, Italy, China, Germany, Bulgaria, and Poland (Citizenship and Immigration Canada, 2008). The main impetus for this dramatic surge in immigration was increased demand for Canada's natural resources and raw materials in the world market and a consequent rise in employment opportunity in Canada at the time. As well, prospects for a better life in Canada, relative to the drudgery of working in the factories of Britain and other European countries, coupled with growing urban decay in the industrial cities of Europe at the time fed into the growth in Canadian immigration (Palmer, 1992). According to McInnis (2000a, 2000b), this unprecedented influx of immigrants marked one of the most important episodes in Canadian history, helping to transform Canada into a full-fledged economy, capable of competing with the United States, to some extent, in the Western Hemisphere.

Despite the high levels of immigration in the early part of the twentieth century, the zeal to maintain Canada as a predominantly white-settler society remained strong, and every effort was made through immigration regulation to keep racial minorities out of this country. A classic example in this regard is the Chinese Head Tax of 1885, which imposed a fifty-dollar fee on persons of Chinese origin entering the country. This Head Tax was introduced by the Federal Government, after the completion of the Canadian Pacific Railway to restrict further Chinese immigration to Canada. Sensing that the fifty-dollar fee was not stemming Chinese immigration fast enough, it was raised to $100 in 1900 and again to $500 in 1903.

Despite the Head Tax, Chinese migrants continued to come to Canada, and the Canadian government responded by passing the Chinese Exclusion Act in 1923, which banned Chinese immigration altogether. It was not until 1947 that this Act was repealed (Chinese Canadian National Council, 2010).

The infamous *Komagata Maru* incident is yet another example of past discriminatory practice in Canadian immigration. In 1914, in an attempt to challenge Canada's "continuous journey regulation," Gurdit Singh chartered the Japanese steam-liner Komagata Maru to carry passengers from Hong Kong to Canada. The continuous journey regulation stipulated, that prospective immigrants coming to Canada were supposed to travel by way of a continuous or single journey, without a stopover anywhere. With passengers made up of 340 Sikhs, 24 Muslims, and 12 Hindus, the Komagata Maru was barred from landing in Vancouver, for breaching the continuous journey rule. This created an episodic stalemate at the harbour, and episode that ended with only 24 passengers being allowed entry into Canada, and the rest forced to return to India (Encyclopaedia of the Sikhs, 2009).

The second major wave of immigration during the early part of the twentieth century occurred in the mid-1920s, when stiff economic competition compelled Canadian businesses and industries to enlist cheap immigrant labour from abroad. The influx of immigrants engendered xenophobia and nativist reaction among many Canadians. Notwithstanding these negativities, the formation of a new Canadian society that included many other ethnic groups was already underway at this time. The "second wave" was interrupted by the Great Depression of the 1930s as well as by the WWII (Kelley and Trebilcock, 1998). Available data show that in 1929 some 164,993 immigrants (i.e., a rate of 1.9 percent of the population) were admitted into Canada, compared to 20,591 (0.2 percent of the population) in 1933. In 1942 there were only 7,576 immigrants (0.1 percent of the population) admitted into Canada—the lowest rate of immigration in Canadian history, according to available data (Citizenship and Immigration Canada, 2008).

The post-war period was one of unprecedented prosperity in Canada, with a wide range of employment opportunities across the country. For example, the construction industry boomed immensely due to increased housing developments and urban sprawl. Industrial output increased, as productivity soared due to technological advancements in manufacturing. As a corollary, wages increased, as did the standard of living for many Canadians. Quite expectedly, it did not take long for the post-war prosperity to lead to increased immigration in Canada (Norrie and Owran, 2002). For instance, between 1946 and 1962, as high as 2.2 million immigrants were admitted into Canada. Indeed, for the five-year period from 1946 to 1950 alone, some 430,389 immigrants were admitted into this country; this exceeded the number of immigrants admitted in the previous 15 years (Citizenship and Immigration Canada, 2008).

There is no denying that humanitarian considerations contributed to the increased admission of immigrants into Canada in the post-war era, especially given the atrocities, and consequent public outcries, surrounding the war. For one thing, Canada accepted some 23,000 European refugees between 1945 and 1947 (Kelley and Trebilcock, 1998). Yet, economic priorities and national identity considerations remained paramount in Canadian immigration policy then. Consequently, Canada refused to sign on to the 1951 UN Convention Relating to the Status of Refugees until 1969. Not even the human rights and anti-discrimination advocacy of the United Nations codified in the UN Universal Declaration of Human Rights of 1948—to the effect that all humans are equal regardless of colour culture, religion, sex, and so on—could dent the racism in Canadian immigration at the time (Kelley and Trebilcock, 1998).

While Canada's new *Immigration Act* in 1952 did not explicitly discriminate against ethno-racial minorities, there was little doubt that the most "preferred classes" remained Anglo-Saxons. Not surprisingly, even though the Act provided for the family reunification of Asian-Canadian citizens and their immediate overseas relatives, strict quotas were instituted. For Canadian immigrants from India, for instance, the quota was set at 150 for 1952 (and increased to 300 in 1953); the corresponding figures for Pakistanis and Sri

Lankan were 100 and 50 immigrants, respectively. Furthermore, the 1952 *Immigration Act* permitted Special Immigration Investigation Officers to deny entry to persons on the basis of their *nationality, customs,* or *unsuitability to Canadian climate or culture.* Undoubtedly, in today's terms, this stipulation passes for an explicit form of racial discrimination. While such measures allowed the French and British to maintain their dominance in Canada, the ethnic composition of the nation was already becoming progressively diverse, as a result of natural population increase and the cumulative effects of immigration. It was not until 1962 that regulations were tabled to help eliminate all discrimination from Canadian immigration. Further changes to Canada's immigration policy occurred in 1967 through a new Immigration Act, which introduced the now famous "point system" for assessing applicants on the basis of education and skills, rather than on race, ethnicity, and nationality. The obvious question here becomes: What were the impetuses for this dramatic shift? Again, that some humanitarian and altruistic concerns played part in the "sudden" abandonment of racism in Canadian immigration is undeniable. Equally indubitable is the fact that global geopolitics, the civil rights movement, and the intense competition for labour at the time were also behind this anti-discriminatory move in Canadian immigration. In 1971, four years after the promulgation of the point system, the official policy of multiculturalism was introduced. The degree to which multiculturalism has benefited immigrants is still a hotly debated matter. Still, that official multiculturalism has ushered in an era in Canadian history where immigrants are increasingly admitted from non-European countries is perhaps self-evident (James, 2005; Henry and Tator, 2009).

4. CANADIAN IMMIGRATION UNDER CONTEMPORARY GLOBALIZATION

Many believe that the concept of globalization entered popular imagination in the 1960s when the Canadian media scholar Marshall McLuhan coined the term "global village" in his *Understanding Media* (1964). As John Tomlinson (1997:22) aptly points out "in its relatively short career, globalization has accumulated a remarkable string of positive and negative connotations without having achieved a particularly clear denotation." Unsurprisingly, globalization has become "the intellectual property of no specific field," with different scholars approaching its analysis from different vantage points (Jameson, 2001:xi). For instance, globalization may be understood as an economic concept, entailing the interdependence of national economies in trade, finance, and macroeconomic policy. For Kobrin (1997:147-148), it has more to do with increased technological innovation and information flows, similar to Manuel Castells' (2000) notion of "space of flow" rather than with foreign trade and investment, *per se*. In a similar vein, David Harvey (1990) sees globalization as more or less synonymous with "time-space compression," and Roland Robertson (1992) even goes further to conceptualize globalization as both the compression of the world and the intensification of consciousness of the world as a whole. With so many interpretations of globalization, some scholars are concerned that the term risks becoming a hollow cliché, with much of what is written about it amounting to nothing but "globaloney" (Held et al., 1999; Veseth, 2005). For the purpose of the ensuing discussion, globalization is seen as "a multifaceted, dialectical process involving complex interconnections between socioeconomic groups, individuals, and institutions worldwide," the ultimate effect of which is an increased integration of societies (Mensah, 2008b:37).

Quite naturally, given the many different interpretations and perspectives to its study, it is not easy to pinpoint when the phenomenon (as against the concept) of globalization began with any appreciable degree of certainty. Still, the work of David Harvey (1990) suggests that contemporary globalization, or what he calls "time-space compression," began in the mid-1960s and the early 1970s, when the capitalist mode of production shifted from one of Fordism to post-Fordism, or flexible accumulation. Around this time, capitalism entered into an entirely "new sectors of production, new ways of providing financial services, new markets, and above all, greatly intensified rates of commercial, technological, and organizational innovation" (Harvey, 1990:147). This new mode of capitalist production, "rest on flexibility with regards to labour processes, labour markets, products, and patterns of consumptions"—hence the name "flexible accumulation" (p.147). The belief is that it is the dismantling of the Fordist regime of accumulation by the early 1970s that ushered in the present time-space compression, or globalization.

Interestingly, the shift from Fordism to post-Fordism in industrialized countries, and the emergence of contemporary globalization, or time-space compression, occurred at the time when Canada assumed an explicitly non-racist stance in immigration regulation through the point system. In fact, during the 1960s and 1970s, a host of other cultural and theoretical shifts, as well as geopolitical dynamics arranged themselves into conjunctures that give greater analytic visibility to matters concerning international migration worldwide. Notable among these were the rise of postmodern tendencies; increased refugee situations; the social upheavals of the civil rights movement; the emergence of cyber-spatial connectivity and electronic mediation, and transnationality, *inter alia*. In the years following the introduction of the point system, Canada witnessed a dramatic shift in the sources of immigrants from Western European nations and the United States to the so-called visible minority hubs of Asia, Latin American, the Caribbean, and Africa. The change in the composition of immigrants became most palpable starting around the 1980s when some 48 percent of all immigrants to Canada came from Asia and the Middle East (compared to only 3 percent prior to the 1960s). Indeed, since the 1981 census, the majority of the top ten "countries of birth" of immigrants to Canada have been visible minority countries, such as China, India, the Philippines, Pakistan, Jamaica, and Sri Lanka (Mensah, 2010:73).

A new immigration policy in 1973 allowed for the immigration of temporary workers under the employment visa program. This program, later incorporated into the 1976 *Immigration Act*, permits the use of foreign workers for short-term jobs, especially in agriculture and domestic activities, for which no Canadian citizens or landed immigrants are available (Stafford, 1992). The 1976 Act also established an inland refugee determination system for the processing of claims submitted within the borders of Canada, for the first time. Unlike the point system which focused mainly on skills and educational qualifications, the 1976 Act placed emphasis on family unification and the settlement of refugees—all of which facilitated the inflow of yet more people from visible minority nations of the global South. The leading sources of refugees in Canada continue to include many countries of the developing world (e.g., Haiti, Colombia, Sri Lanka, Nigeria, the Democratic Republic of the Congo, and Zimbabwe), where escalating ethnic and political conflicts, human rights abuses, and environmental crises have fostered various episodic refugee and forced migration situations.

Another impetus for the influx of visible minority to Canada was the targeting of "business-class" immigrants. Initiated in 1984, the business-class of immigration was used primarily to target wealthy business people from Hong Kong who were seeking avenues to diversify their investment portfolio in advance of the 1997 changeover to communist control in China. Many business people from elsewhere in Asia (notably, Mainland China, Japan, and India) joined the fray, with many of them settling in Toronto and the Lower Mainland of British Columbia. Generally, to qualify under the business-class, the prospective immigrant is required to bring/invest anywhere from $250,000 to $500,000 in Canada over; and for this the person is given high processing priority in immigration application. Available data indicate that in 1989, for instance, there was a capital inflow of some $3.5 billion from Hong Kong to Canada, of which 63 percent (or 2.21 billion) was transferred through business-class immigration (Mitchell, 2009:348). Also, as Mitchell rightly speculates, this figure may be underestimated for reasons of income tax. In 1994, immigrants from Hong Kong alone accounted for 20 percent of immigrants from all sources to Canada and 33.3 percent from all sources to British Columbia (Government of British Columbia, 1997:1). In that same year, an estimated $480 million was invested by business immigrants in Canada, with Hong Kong entrepreneurs accounting for a sizeable proportion (Wong and Ng, 1998).

A new immigration legislation introduced in 1992, Bill C-86, sought to, among other things, allow Canada to continue its commitment to family unification, to help select immigrants who are more responsive to the economic needs of the nation, and to streamline the nation's refugee determination process. Critics of the 124-page Bill are particularly concerned about its "safe third country" provision, with which the government of Canada reserves the right to refuse a refugee claim by anyone who traveled to Canada through a "safe country" where he or she could have sought asylum. The related 'transportation company liability' clause, which empowers the Canadian government to hold airlines liable for bringing in a prospective refugee with no valid visa and travel documents is equally worrisome to many critics, including Jakubowski (1997), Amnesty International Canada (1992), and Alderman (1992).

With yet another piece of immigration legislation—the Immigration and Refugee Protection Act or Bill C-11 (introduced in June 2002)—the government seeks to make immigration responsive to the labour market needs of the country by selecting immigrants based on their ability to adapt easily to the Canadian labour market. With Bill C-11, the Non-Immigrant Employment Authorization Program, instituted in 1973 and subsequently changed to the Temporary Foreign Worker Program (TFWP) in the 1990s, was revamped. From the government's perspective, Bills C-11 and C-86 are to help forge a balance between the nation's international humanitarian obligations and its changing labour market needs (Citizenship and Immigration Canada, 1993). Still, some immigration critics (e.g., Trumper and Wong, 2007; Stasiulis, and Bakan, 2005) continue to question the TFWP for its biases against women and racialized groups. According to these critics, the TFWP tends to draw its highly skilled workers from Europe and the United States and lower-skilled ones, such as farm and domestic workers, from visible minorities regions (e.g., the Caribbean, Asia, and Latin America).

5. NOTABLE SOCIOECONOMIC AND CULTURAL TRENDS SINCE THE 1970S

Clearly, since the introduction of the point system in 1967, Canada has been home to many visible minority immigrants. While several factors were behind the establishment of the point system, the decline in birth rates across Europe, and the intense advocacy for racial tolerance under the civil rights movement around that time are particularly worthy of note here. Equally significant is the increased global inter-connectedness, attributable to the time-space compression innovations of globalization. The dramatic rise in the number of visible minority immigrants in Canada has made the intersections of race, ethnicity, identity, citizenship, and multiculturalism a fertile ground for clashing views in Canadian public and academic discourse. How has Canada, as a nation-state, dealt with this situation? How have members of the White majority group reacted to the growing number of non-Whites in their midst? How have these visible minority immigrants coped with the settlement and integration challenges they face in Canada? And what are some of the socioeconomic and cultural contestations implicated in the evident shift of the centre of gravity of Canadian immigration from the traditional sources of Western Europe and United States to non-traditional sources in the global South?

Without question, international migration is a global process, with various socioeconomic situations and cultural phenomena outside of Canada impinging (in)directly on what occurs here, especially with regards to the perception and treatment of minority immigrants. Thus, it is hard to sustain any uniqueness thesis concerning Canada's exclusive involvement in international migration, in particular, and globalization, in general. For certain, there are bound to be some Canada-specific issues, but, for the most part, the manner in which the Canadian nation-state and its citizens relate to immigrants, especially visible minority ones, is invariably influenced by global trends, and, therefore, not much different from what one would find in other immigrants receiving nations in the West. It is our fervent contention that any difference in this regard, between say Canada and the United States, is one of *degree* and not of *ilk*, and certainly not of *essence*. We thus find Canadians complaining about the influx of minority immigrants, via our "broken" refugee and immigration regulations, just as Americans engage in their own vociferous public outcries over the "invasion" of Mexican immigrants, and Western Europeans enter into a xenophobic frenzy over the increasing presence of Africans and Asians in their midst, with calls for the fortification of Europe growing by the day. One can reasonably argue that Canada is unique to some extent, given its British and French colonial background, couched in the terrain of First Nations communities (Mookerjea, Szeman, and Faurschou, 2009), and given its former dominion status, which situates it in the historiography of both the *core* and *peripheral* regions of the global economy. Yet, we cannot easily discount George Grant's (2009:146-47) provocative assertion that:

> The majority of Canadians are a product of western civilization and live entirely within the forms and assumptions of that enterprise...our very form of life depends on our membership in the western industrial empire which is centered in the USA and which stretches out its hegemony into parts of Western Europe and which controls South America and much of Africa and Asia...The very substance of our lives (as Canadians) is bound up with the western empire and its destiny, just at a time when the empire uses increasingly ferocious means to maintain its hegemony.

Notwithstanding this obvious connectivity of Canada to the rest of the Western World, we still need to heed Homi Bhabha's (2004:xv) suggestion that "globalization...must always begin at home; [and that] a just measure of global progress requires that we first evaluate how globalizing nations deal with 'the difference within'—the problems of diversity and redistribution at the local level, and the rights and representations of minorities in the regional domain" (2004:xv). The key questions then become: what is the status of visible minority immigrants and visible minority citizens in Canada? Are these minorities given the opportunity, or treated in ways, that allow them to realistically see themselves as true Canadians? And what are the emergent socioeconomic and cultural contexts within which the Canadian nation-state and Canadians relate to immigrants in this country? In seeking to address these issues, our discussion will move seamlessly between global and Canadian (local) examples, as we interweave recurrent themes from contemporary socioeconomic and cultural trends, such as postmodernism, transnationalism, deterritorialization, cultural hybridity, and flexible citizenship (Bhabha, 2004; Faist, 2000; Ong, 1993; Harvey, 1990).

Perhaps no other global phenomena have impacted the "cultural logics" of international migration under contemporary globalization more than the proliferations of transnationality and postmodern tendencies since the 1970s. As Huyssens (1984) points out, it would be an exaggeration to claim that there has been a "wholesale paradigm shift of the cultural, social, and economic orders, [yet] there is a noticeable shift in sensibility, practices and discourse formations which distinguishes post-modern set of assumptions, experiences and propositions from that of a preceding period" (cited in Harvey 1990:39). In literary work, for instance, the boundary between fiction and science fiction—and, indeed, between binary opposites, in general—started to dissolve around the early 1970s (Harvey, 1990:41). Similarly, in philosophy there has been a growing denunciation of "objective truth," and abhorrence for totalizing discourse or meta-narrative (Lyotard, 1984), with many now believing that knowledge (if not truth itself) is both subjective and *fragmentary*.

In this context, we must note, as did Bannerji (2009:327; mine in parenthesis) that "Canada, with its primary inscriptions of 'French' or 'English,' its colonialist and essentialist identity markers, (and one might add, its potpourri of immigrant groups) cannot escape a fragmentary framework." With the emergent postmodern cultural logic has come a growing concern for "otherness" among many theoreticians and social movements. This concern has, in turn, yielded cultural pluralism, with a concomitant realization that erstwhile subjugated groups (or *subalterns*), such as immigrants, minorities, women, gays and lesbians, and the poor, "have a right to speak for themselves, in their own voice and have their voice accepted as authentic and legitimate" (Harvey, 1990:48). It is, therefore, not surprising that many scholars with background in the global South (e.g., Bhabha, 2004; Bannergi, 2009; Mbembe, 2001) now "talk back to the empire" from within, in what might be seen as anti-foundational and emancipatory scholarship drawing upon the seminal works of Frantz Fanon (1925-61) and Edward Said (1935-2003). For the most part, this discourse, commonly called postcolonialism, confronts the subtleties and contradictions of power, language, race, ethnicity, cultural identity, hybridity, diaspora, nationality, multiculturalism, and the dynamics of subjectivity under imperialism.

Coterminous with all these cultural and scholarly inclinations in the 1970s and beyond is a growing trend towards transnational migration—a trend which is keenly tied to the spatial diffusion of time-space compression innovations. Transnationalism is arguably as old as migration itself, but it has undoubtedly accelerated in recent years, with scholars now according it a variety of interpretations. Some see it as a conduit for global capital flow, remittance, and ethno-entrepreneurship (Portes, Heller, and Guarnizo, 2001; Wong and Ng, 2002), while other see it as a site for political engagement and cosmopolitanism (Kymlicka, 1995; Ong, 1999; Faist, 2000). Still, others see it as an avenue for socio-cultural reproduction (Lo, 2000; Nederveen Pieterse, 1997).

However, until recently, students of international migration assumed that most immigrants, especially from the "Third World," make a one way permanent move to settle in rich countries, and sever their ties with their homeland. We now know better: immigrants' entrepreneurship, identity, citizenship and many other related phenomena have gone transnational, if not global. And as Ong (1999:4) points out, in addition to denoting how migrants connect to nation-states and capital and enact their cultural identities, transnationalism "alludes to the *trans*versal, the *trans*actional, the *trans*lational, and the *trans*gressive aspects of contemporary behaviour and imagination that are incited, enabled, and regulated by the changing logic of state and capitalism."

The literature on the transnational practices of immigrant groups in Canada has been growing since the early 2000s. For instance, in a special edition of *the Canadian Geographer*, edited by the prolific York University geographer Philip Kelly (2003), we find the case studies of several Asian immigrant groups in Canada, including those of Indians living in Vancouver (Walton-Roberts, 2003); Hong Kong and Taiwanese immigrants in Vancouver (Waters, 2003); and Sri-Lankan immigrants in Canada (Hyndman, 2003). Satzewich and Wong (2006), in their edited volume *Transnational Identities and Practices* in Canada (2006) capture homologous narratives on other immigrants groups, including Caribbeans (Simmons and Plaza, 2006); Latin Americans (Goldring, 2006); Chinese (Wong and Ho, 2006); and Southern-Europeans (Aguiar, 2006). And the works of Tettey and Puplampu (2005) and Mensah (2008 and 2009) on African-Canadian transnationalism and on Ghanaian-Canadian religious transnationalism, respectively, broaden the geographic coverage of the literature on transnationalism even further.

Recurrent in these Canadian studies are some basic findings. Firstly, we now know that while historical precedence of cross-border activities exists, recent improvements in long-distance travel and telecommunications technologies have made contemporary transnationalism among Canadian immigrants faster and more extensive than its earlier manifestations (Waters, 2003; Walton-Roberts, 2003). Secondly, we now know that immigrants' transnationalism in Canada occurs not only in the sphere of economics, but also in the social, cultural, political, and other fronts (Mensah, 2008a; Goldring, 2006). Thirdly, while many immigrants engage in such cross-border connections, with little or no socioeconomic duress, others are compelled by racism and social exclusion in Canada to pursue life in the Bhabhaian *third space* (Tettey and Puplampu, 2005; Wong and Ho, 2006). Finally, from the handful of quantitative studies on transnationalism in Canada we know to our surprise that for the most part respondents' sex, education, and income have a negligible impact on their propensity to engage in transnationalism. Thus, males and females are involved in virtually the same rate, just as the poor and the rich, and the highly educated and not-so-highly educated participate at par (Mensah, 2008a; Hiebert and Ley, 2003).

As a result of the growing transnationalism among immigrants in Canada, as in other parts of the world, the tilt towards "flexible citizenship" (Ong, 1999) has become pronounced. It is not uncommon now to find immigrants travelling with relative ease between different nations, and accumulating worth and capital in response to changing socioeconomic opportunities in different countries. With the aid of electronic mediation and other communication technologies for cross-border interaction, these immigrants lead a de-territorialized lifestyle, which at once situates them within more than one identity category, or what Hommi Bhabha calls the "third space." In this space of cultural hybridity, immigrants find themselves to be "in-between" or "out-of-place" in both their homeland and their adopted country. Armed with the notion of "third space," it is not hard to see how the cultural identities of many transnational immigrants in Canada would cease to be authentically foreign and authentically Canadian; paradoxically, they become *both* and *neither* at the same time. Quite naturally, the assimilative expectations faced by these immigrants in both the homeland and in Canada compound the emotional tensions and socioeconomic burdens of life in the "third space."

Ong (1999 and 1998) demonstrates how, using the flexibility occasioned by transnationality and deterritorialization, Chinese immigrants in the United States, Canada, United Kingdom and elsewhere have developed strategies of capital accumulation that enable them to bypass, and sometimes exploit, citizenship rules to their advantage. Of course, this is hardly unique to Chinese immigrants. One can detect such manoeuvres among many other contemporary immigrants groups in Canada and other immigrant receiving nations worldwide. With multiple passports and "flexible citizenship" many transnational migrants are able to de-link themselves from government and other regulations of the nation-state in both their homeland and their adopted country, with prudent timing. Ultimately, these immigrants (re)position themselves as subjects of global trade, rather than as loyal subjects of any particular country. Under such circumstances, the Canadian passport, citizenship, or landed immigrant status become a conduit to gain access to the Canadian labour and real estate markets and the social welfare system, more so than attestations of these immigrants' patriotism or loyalty. Still, we have to be careful not to fault only the immigrants for taking advantage of the situation, as the implicit disingenuousness, if not culpability, applies to the Canadian nation-state as well. For one thing, Canada, like many other advanced countries (e.g., United States, United Kingdom, and Australia) uses its immigration regulations (notably, the point system) to cream-off the brightest minds from the "Third World," with many from that part of the world gaining legitimate access to Canada only as *homo economicus*, or as business (wo)men.

5.1. Ramifications and Responses within Canada

How has the Canadian nation-state and the Canadian majority reacted to the growing number of minorities in their midst since the early 1970s? With many immigrants pursuing transnational connections with their homeland and some even leading a de-territorialized lifestyle, what has been the reaction of mainstream Canadians? Who gets to decide what Canadian culture should be? What are some of the socioeconomic tension and cultural politics implicated in the growth of visible minority immigrants in Canada? Has the perennial fear of immigrants undermining the Canadian national identity increased or decreased in recent years? What have been the assimilative expectations of the majority for the minority in Canada? And to what extent has the majority promoted, or otherwise undermined, the integration of minorities in Canada?

Very often, in the rush to sing the praises of globalization, transnationalism, and cultural hybridity, the on-the-ground experiences of minority immigrants in host countries have been overlooked in the prevailing literatures. As Mitchell (2009:344) points out, with insights from Visweswaran (1994:109), "in an era of global capitalism, the heralding of subject positions at the margins too often neglect the actual marginalization of subjects. And positive readings of the forces of deterritorialization inadequately address the powerful forces of oppression unleashed by them." To be sure, though, in the Canadian context, the social exclusion and marginalization faced by minority immigrants have been well documented. For instance, from the works of Teixeira (2006), Murdie (2002), and Danso and Grant (2000) we know of the discriminatory practices exacted upon minority immigrants in the housing market; from the likes of Hum and Simpson (2007), Li (1998), and Henry and Ginzberg (1985) we find reliable empirical evidence of racism in the Canadian job market; and from studies by Dei (2005), Solomon (1992), and other scholars of education, we have long known of the oppressive practices in the Canadian school system. Even the Canadian law enforcement and justice systems have been found wanting in their mistreatment of racial minorities, as evidenced by the audacious scholarship of Tator and Henry (2006), Tanovich (2006), and Wortley and Tanner (2004). And the subtle and not-so-subtle Eurocentric and "white supremacist" preferences embedded in the production of knowledge and representations of culture in Canada are gradually being unearthed through the pens of such authors as Mitchell (2009) and Mackey (2009).

The adverse impacts of race-based discriminatory practices manifest themselves in myriad of ways, especially in urban centers such as Toronto, Montreal, and Vancouver where the vast majority of new immigrants reside. These manifestations often come in the form of physical and social distance between various ethnic groups, as evidenced by the emergent ethnic enclaves in Canadian cities. Add to these the prevalence of racial profiling on city streets and the race-based discriminations in housing, employment, and even sports, and one would readily appreciate the frustration of visible minorities in Canada (Mensah, 2010).

It would be decidedly disingenuous to downplay the fact that many minority immigrants have done, and continue to do, quite well in Canada by any conceivable measure. Over the years, Canada has helped improve the living standards of countless immigrants and refugees from around the globe, even giving some the taste of freedom of speech and of association for the first time. Still, it is only fair to acknowledge that for most visible minority immigrants, including Africans, Caribbeans, and Asians—it matters little whether they are born here or not, and it matters not whether they immigrated with money (as did most immigrants from pre-1997 Hong Kong), or whether they arrived with virtually no material possessions or financial resources (as did most African refugees)—it is almost impossible to escape the ubiquity of ethno-racial discrimination and the constrictions of an outsider status. And, of course, in times of economic downturn, these immigrants are blamed for "stealing" jobs from true Canadians. Perhaps, what is most astounding is the fact that if you belong to the "visible minority group" (e.g., Blacks, Arabs, and Chinese) then, you would never cease to be an immigrant in the eyes of most Canadians, regardless of your official immigration status. This is how Bannerji (2009:335) expresses this demoralizing sentiment:

> Thus for non-whites in Canada, their own bodies are used to construct for them some sort of social zone or prison, since they can not crawl out of their skins, and this signals what life has to offer them in Canada. This special type of visibility is a social construction as well as a political statement. Expressions such as "ethnics" and "immigrants" and "new Canadians" are no less problematic…

The irony compounds when one discovers that all white people, no matter when they immigrate to Canada or as carriers of which European ethnicity, become invisible and hold a dual membership in Canada, while others remain immigrants generations later.

It would be inaccurate to think that these subtle and not-so-subtle Eurocentric biases occur only in the social and economic spheres of life in Canada. Indeed, they are equally embedded in the production of knowledge and the representation of culture across the country. For instance, in the work of Mackey (2009), we read of the sophisticated ways in which cultural differences and knowledge production are articulated by mainstream Canadians to the detriment of minorities. Mackay's case study was the 1990 controversy surrounding the *Heart of Africa* exhibition at the Royal Ontario Museum in Toronto. This exhibition was eventually aborted, following intense opposition from the Coalition for Truth about Africa—a group readily formed by the members of the Black community in Toronto. The *Heart of Africa* exhibition, curated by a (White) Canadian anthropologist, was based on artefacts that colonialists had brought back from Africa. Notwithstanding the sizeable and vibrant African-Canadian population in Toronto, the Royal Ontario Museum did not give the Black community the chance to share the power to control and define the content of the exhibition. In so doing, "the exhibit," writes Mackey (2009:373), "'othered' the Africans of the colonial time, as well as African-Canadians in Toronto in 1990." And, it is exactly against the Eurocentric condescension, "othering," and race-laced dehumanization implicated in the exhibit that the Coalition protested. Unsurprisingly, the Coalition was ridiculed by members of the mainstream press and academia for what they saw as a shallow, unsophisticated, and "politically correct" approach to matters of history and cultural identity (on the part of the Black African protestors).

Mitchell (2009) uses discourse analysis to write about a similar cultural politics on the production of meaning, concerning the "monster house" phenomenon in Vancouver, just around the time that the museum controversy was making news in Toronto. Starting in the late 1980s and early 1990s, with more and more Hong Kong immigrants acquiring real estate in Vancouver, there was intense public outcry about their new big houses, many of which were built by demolishing original smaller houses bought from old residents of the city. As Mitchell (2009:350) points out:

> Many of the new houses are perceived as ugly and cheap by the older, white residents, who are drawn primarily from the rank of the upper middle class and wealthy. Although the new houses are much larger...the general neighbourhood impression of these houses is that the quality of materials is poor, the architectural style is boxy and clumsy, the landscaping is unappealing, and the entire package is non-contextual. Residents spoke of ...the loss of ambience, tradition, and heritage in their neighbourhood, bemoaning the new buildings' lack of 'character.'

Utterly unmindful of the amount of money the Hong Kong immigrants of the 1990s poured into the Vancouver economy, or more specifically into the hands of the "true" Canadians, many among the latter see the new buildings as an arrogant destruction of Canadian culture—a culture for which they are at once the foremost progenitors and custodians.

How has the Canadian nation-state reacted to the increased presence of non-Whites in this country? Have the conditions of transnationality and globalization strengthened or undermined the power of the Canadian nation-state to manage its immigration and attendant problems of race-relations in this country? What are some of the specific policies developed by the Canadian nation-state to help immigrants settle in this country? Benedict Anderson's (1994) position that the classical nation-state project to align social habits, cultural attachment, citizenship, and political participation is being undermined by modern transportation and communication innovations and transnationalism is a recurrent theme in the literature on globalization (Ohmae, 2008; Strange, 2008; Sassen, 1996). Indeed, there are indications that "the truth claims of the state that are enshrined in the passport are gradually being replaced by its counterfeit use in response to the claims of global capitalism" Ong (1999:2). Still, one has to be careful not to assume that the state is in total retreat, yielding all control over international migration, international migrants, and national borders to the forces of globalization, for what is happening on the ground is far more complicated than the *zero-sum* assertions espoused by many in this debate. A close reading of Ong (1999:3), for instance, suggests that the power realignments under contemporary globalization do not necessarily imply a win or lose situation in which nation-states lose their sovereign grip over their borders and citizens, while global capital gains control over the affiliations and behaviour of subjects.

In the specific case of Canada, we just learn that the nation-state has instituted a range of legislative and regulatory instruments to stem "fraudulent" refugee claims, and to properly correlate the flow of immigrants with the nation's labour market needs. Also, over the years, Canada has developed various policies and services to facilitate the settlement and integration of immigrants in this country. Federal and provincial government assistance in the areas of immigrant housing, education, and language training are worthy of note here. To reduce ethnic and racial discrimination, there are various human rights and anti-discrimination policies, of which the employment equity program deserves special mention. Most of these policy initiatives and support systems are placed under the umbrella of Canada's official policy of multiculturalism, first introduced in 1971 by the Pierre Trudeau Liberal government. Unfortunately, multiculturalism has elicited raucous criticisms from both the political left and right across Canada. No wonder Abu-Laban and Stasiulis (1992:337) once remarked that criticising official multiculturalism has become a pastime for many Canadians.

As the work of Mensah (2010, Chapter 8) shows, some critics allege that the policy promotes cultural relativism, commodifies ethnic cultures, and feeds into existing cultural stereotypes. Others fault the policy for allegedly undermining the cultural distinctiveness of Canada, while others insist that the policy depoliticizes social inequality in Canada. In a scathing critique of the policy, Bannerji writes that multiculturalism is an ideology of national unification and legitimation, by which Canada seeks to mediate the fissures and ruptures engendered by its French and English background, its colonialist identity, and its contemporary ethno-racial diversity. According to Bannerji, "the legacy of a white settler colonial economy and state and the current aspiration to imperialist capitalism mark Canada's struggle to become a liberal democratic state. [Contextualized as such, multiculturalism becomes] a fantastic evocation of 'unity,' which in any case becomes a reminder of the divisions [in Canada]" (Bannerji 2009:329).

In the final analysis, though, the queries surrounding Canadian multiculturalism demand a relative judgment, and it would be fallacious to assert categorically that multiculturalism is "good or bad, blameworthy or blameless, significant or insignificant. There is neither simple affirmation nor rejection of this policy" (Mensah, 2010:234-235). The issues implicated in how Canada relates to its immigrant population under contemporary globalization are not only cultural, but also socioeconomic, with tap-roots in the dynamics of class oppression. However, the adhesive overlap between class and race (and sometime space), for some immigrants groups such as Blacks in Canada, often makes it extremely hard to disentangle the specific axes of oppression in such analysis. Still, the politics of class struggle is no less significant than that of cultural identity, even among visible minority immigrants.

6. CONCLUSION

As migration becomes more dominant globally, scholars have understandably begun to situate its analysis in the context of globalization and kindred phenomena such as transnationality, de-territorialization, cosmopolitanism, and cultural hybridity. Converse to the migration trend of the sixteenth to nineteenth centuries, contemporary migration has emanated primarily from the regions of the global South to the North, with many in the latter region expressing considerable angst over the presence of ethno-racial minorities in their midst. In this chapter we have profiled the history of immigration in Canada and examined how the Canadian nation-state and Canadian citizens have reacted to new immigrants, paying particular attention to the cultural and identity politics implicated in the process. While the focus remained on the Canadian case, we took due cognizance of relevant global socioeconomic and cultural trends, now and then drawing our examples from beyond the borders of Canada. It is clear from our discussion that the Canadian nation-state was built on, and continues to be impacted by, immigration. Although the influence of the founding nations (i.e., English and French) remains dominant, there are indications that other ethnic groups are making a discernable dent into the social, economic, cultural and political fabric of Canadian life. To the extent that immigration will continue to grow in the near future, by all conceivable predictions, with visible minority constituting the lion share of immigrants, it is high time we started paying serious analytical attention to the special issues occasioned by the presence of a racial minority in a White majority nation like Canada. Indeed, as the ethnic makeup of Canada continues to diversify, the challenges posed by matters concerning race, ethnicity, visible minority status, multiculturalism, and citizenship would assume center stage in the cultural politics and class dynamics of Canada, and the time to confront these inevitable problematics is, indeed, now.

REFERENCES

Abu-Laban, Y., and D. Stasiulis. (1992). "Ethnic Pluralism under Siege: Popular and Partisan Opposition to Multiculturalism." *Canadian Public Policy* 27(4): 363-86.

Aguiar, L.L.M. (2006). "The New 'In-Between' Peoples: Southern-European Transnationalism." In V. Satzewich and L. Wong (eds.), *Transnational identities and practices in Canada.* Vancouver: UBC Press.

Alderman, H. (1992). "Editorial, Special Issue on New Amendments to *Immigration Act*, Processing Bill C-86." *Refuge* 12(2):1-3.

Allen, J., and C. Hamnett. (eds.). (2000). *A Shrinking World? Global Unevenness and Inequality.* Oxford: Oxford University Press.

Amnesty International Canada. (1992). *AI Canada's Concern with Respect to Bill C-86.* Accessed April 12, 2010 from http://www.amnesty.ca/Refugee/Bill C-86.php.

Anderson, B. (1994). "Exodus." *Cultrual Inquiry* 20(Winter):324-25.

Anthias, F. (1998). "Evaluating 'Diaspora': Beyond Ethnicity?" *Sociology* 3:557-580.

Bannerji, H. (2009). "On the Dark Side of the Nation: Politics of Multiculturalism and the State of 'Canada.'" In S. Mookerjea, I Szeman, and G. Faurschou (eds.), *Canadian Cultural Studies: A Reader.* Durham: Duke University Press.

Bhabha, H. (2004). *The Location of Culture.* NY: Routledge.

Bond, P. (2008). "Accumulation by Dispossession in Africa: False Diagnoses and Dangerous Prescriptions." In J. Mensah (ed)., *Neoliberalism and globalization in Africa: Contestations on the Embattled Continent.* NY: Palgrave.

Boyle, P., K. Halfacree, and V. Robinson. (1998). *Exploring Contemporary Migration.* NY: Longman.

Castells, M. (2000). *The Rise of the Network Society, vol. 1, The Information Age: Economy, Society, and Culture.* Malden, MA: Blackwell.

Castles, S., and J.M. Miller. (2003). *The Age of Migration: International Population Movements in the Modern World*, 3rd ed. NY: Guilford.

Chinese Canadian National Council. (2010). *Chinese immigration in Canada.* Retrieved January 20, 2010 from http://www.ccnc.ca/redress/history.html.

Citizenship and Immigration Canada. (2008). *Facts and figures 2008: Immigration Overview of Permanent and Temporary Residents.* Retrieved January 20, 2010 from http://www.cic.gc.ca/english//pdf/research-stats/facts2008.pdf.

_____. (1993). *Canada's Immigration Law.* Ottawa: Supply and Services Canada.

Corbett, J. (2009). *Ernest George Ravenstein: The Laws of Migration, 1885.* Retrieved January 20, 2010 from http://www.csiss.org/classics/content/90.

Danso, R., and M. Grant. (2000). "Access to Housing as an Adaptive Strategy for Immigrant Groups: Africans in Calgary." *Canadian Ethnic Studies* 32(3):19-43.

de Blij, H.J. (1993). *Human Geography: Culture, Society and Space.* NY: John Wiley.

Dei, G.S. (2005). "Racism in Canadian Contexts: Exploring Public and Private Issues in the Educational System." In W. Tettey and K.P. Puplampu (eds.), *The African Diaspora in Canada: Negotiating Identity and Belonging.* Calgary: University of Calgary Press.

Dowty, A. (1987). *Closed Borders: The Contemporary Assault on Freedom of Movement.* NY: Yale University Press.

Encyclopaedia of the Sikhs. (2009). *Komagata Maru.* Retrieved January 20, 2010 from http://www.sikhiwiki.org/index.php/Komagata Maru.

Faist, T. (2000). "Transnationalization in International Migration: Implications for the Study of Citizenship and Culture." *Ethnic and Racial Studies* 23(2):189-222.

Fellman, J., A. Getis, and J. Getis. (1995). *Human Geography: Landscape of Human Activities.* Iowa: W.C. Brown Publishers.

Goldring, L. (2006). "Latin American Transnationalism in Canada: Does it Exit, What Forms Does it Take, and Where is it Going." In V. Satzewich and L. Wong (eds.), *Transnational Identities and Practices in Canada.* Vancouver: UBC Press.

_____. (2004). "Family and Collective Remittances to Mexico: A Multi-Dimensional Typology." *Development and Change* 35(4):799-84.

Government of British Columbia. (1997). *Special Feature: Immigration from Hong Kong after the 1997 Handover.* Available at http://bcstats.gov.bc.ca/pubs/immig/imm971sf.pdf.

Grant, G. (2009). "Canadian Fate and Imperialism." In S. Mookerjea, I. Szeman, and G. Faurchou (eds.), *Canadian Cultural Studies: A Reader.* Durham: Duke University Press.

Grigg, D. (1977a). "Ernst Georg Ravenstein, 1834-1913." *Geographers: Bibliographical Studies* 1:79-88.

_____. (1977b). "E.G. Ravenstein and the 'Laws of Migration.'" *Journal of Historical Geography* 3(1):41-54.

Haddad, E. (2008). *The Refugee in International Society: Between Sovereigns.* Cambridge: Cambridge University Press.

Hall, S. (2003). "Cultural identity and Diaspora." In J.E. Braziel and A. Mannur (eds.), *Theorizing Diaspora.* Oxford: Blackwell Publishing Ltd.

Harvey, D. (1990). *The Condition of Postmodernity: An Enquiry into the Origins of Cultural Change.* Oxford: Blackwell Publishing Ltd.

Henry, F., and E. Ginzberg. (1985). *Who gets the Work? A Test of Racial Discrimination in Employment.* Toronto: Social Planning Council of Metropolitan Toronto and Urban Alliances on Race Relations.

Henry, F., and C. Tator. (2009). *The Colour of Democracy: Racism in Canadian Society.* Toronto: Nelson Education.

Held, D., A. McGraw, D. Goldblatt, J. Perraton. (1999). *Global Transformations: Politics, Economics and Culture.* Stanford, CA: Stanford University Press.

Hiebert, D., and D. Ley. (2003). "Characteristics of Immigrant Transnationalism in Vancouver." Working paper No. 03-15. Vancouver Center of Excellent, Research of Immigration and Integration in the Metropolis.

Hollenbach, D. (ed.). (2008). *Refugee Rights: Ethics, Advocacy, and Africa.* Washington: Georgetown University Press.

Hum, D., and W. Simpson. (2007). "Revisiting Equity and Labour: Immigration, Gender, Minority Status in Income Differential in Canada." In S.P. Hier and B.S. Bolaria (eds.), *Race and Racism in 21st Century Canada.* Peterborough, ON: Broadview Press.

Huyssens, A. (1984). "Mapping the Post-Modern." *New German Critique* 33:5-52.

Hyndman, J. (2003). "Aid, Conflict and Migration: The Canada-Sri Lanka Connection." *The Canadian Geographer* 47(3):251-268.

Iacovetta, F., P. Draper, and R. Ventresca. (eds.). (2002). *A Nation of Immigrants: Women, Workers, and Communities in Canadian History, 1840s-1960s.* Toronto: University of Toronto Press.

International Labour Organization. (2006). *Facts on Labour Migration.* Retrieved January 20, 2010 from http://www.ilocarib.org.tt/portal/images/stories/contenido/.

_____. (2008). *Global Employment Trends: January 2008.* Retrieved January 20, 2010 from http://www.ilo.org/global/lang--en/index.htm.

Jakubowski, L.M. (1997). *Immigration and the Legislation of Racism.* Halifax: Fernwood Publishing.

James, C.E. (ed.). (2005). *Possibilities and Limitations: Multicultural Policies and Programs in Canada.* Halifax: Fernwood Publishing.

Jameson, F. (2001), "Preface." In F. Jameson and M. Miyoshi (eds.), *The Cultures of Globalization.* Durham, North Carolina: Duke University Press.

Johnston, R.J., D. Gregory, G. Pratt, and M. Watts. (eds.). (2000). *The Dictionary of Human Geography.* Massachusetts: Blackwell Publishing Ltd.

Kelley, N., and M. Trebilcock. (1998). *The Making of the Mosaic: A History of Canadian Immigration Policy.* Toronto: University of Toronto Press.

Kelly, P. (2003). "Canadian-Asian Transnationalism." *The Canadian Geographer* 3:209-218.

Kobrin, S. (1997). "The Architecture of Globalization: State Sovereignty in a Network Global Economy." In J.H. Dunning (ed.), *Government, Globalization, and International Business.* NY: Oxford University Press.

Kymlicka, W. (1995). *Multicultural Citizenship: A Liberal Theory of Minority Rights.* Oxford: Clarendon Press.

Levitt, Peggy. (2003). "'You Know, Abraham Was Really the First Immigrant': Religion and Transnational Migration." *International Migration Review* 37(3):847-873.

_____. (1996). *Social Remittances: A Conceptual Tool for Understanding Migration and Development.* Working Paper Series (96.04) Cambridge, MA: Harvard.

Li, P. 1998. "The Market Value and Social Value of Race." In V. Satzewick (ed.), *Racism and Social Inequality in Canada: Concepts, Controversies and Strategies of Resistance.* Toronto: Thompson Educational.

Loescher, G., A. Betts, and J. Milner. (2008). *The United Nations High Commissioner for Refugees (UNCHR): The Politics and Practice of Refugee Protection into the Twenty-First Century.* London: Routledge.

Mabogunje, A.L. (1970). "Systems Approach to a Theory of Rural-Urban Migration." *Geographical Analysis* 2(1):1-18.

Mackey, E. (2009). "Postmodernism and Cultural Politics in a Multicultural Nation: Contests over Truth in the *Into the Heart of Africa* Controversy." In S. Mookerjea, I. Szeman, and G. Faurschou (eds.), *Canadian Cultural Studies: A Reader.* Durham: Duke University Press.

Massey, D., J. Arango, G. Hugo, A. Kouaouch, A. Pellegrino, and E. Taylor. (1997). "Migration Theory, Ethnic Mobilization, and Globalization." In M. Guibernau and J. Rex (eds.), *The Ethnicity Reader: Nationalism, Multiculturalism, and Migration.* Massachusetts: Blackwell Publishing Ltd.

Mbembe, A. (2001). *On the Postcolony.* Los Angeles: University of California Press.

McInnis, M. (2000a). "Canada's Population in the Twentieth Century." In M.R. Haines and R.H. Steckel (eds.), *A Population History of North America.* Cambridge: Cambridge University Press.

McInnis, M. (2000b). "The Population of Canada in the Nineteenth Century." In M.R. Haines and R.H. Steckel (eds.), *A Population History of North America.* Cambridge: Cambridge University Press.

McLuhan, M. (1964). *Understanding Media.* Toronto: Signet Books.

Mensah, J. (2010). *Black Canadians: History, Experiences, Social Condition.* Halifax: Fernwood Publishing.

_____. (2009). "Doing Religion' Overseas: The Characteristics and Functions of Ghanaian Immigrant Churches in Toronto, Canada." *Societies without Borders* 4:21-44.

_____. (2008a). "Religious Transnationalism among Ghanaian Immigrants in Toronto: A Binary Logistic Regression Analysis." *The Canadian Geographer* 52(3):309-330.

_____. (2008b). "Cultural Dimensions of Globalization in Africa: A Dialectical Interpenetration of the Local and the Global." In J. Mensah (ed.), *Neoliberalism and Globalization in Africa: Contestations on the Embattled Continent.* NY: Palgrave Macmillan.

Mitchell, K. (2009). "In Whose interest? Transnational Capital and the Production of Multiculturalism in Canada." In S. Mookerjea, I Szeman, and G. Faurschou (eds.), *Canadian Cultural Studies: A Reader.* Durham: Duke University Press.

Moghissi, H., S. Rahnema, and M.J. Goodman. (2009). *Diaspora by Design: Muslim Immigrants in Canada and Beyond.* Toronto: University of Toronto Press.

Mookerjea, S.I. Szeman, and G. Faurschou. (2009). "Introduction: Between Empires: on Cultural Studies in Canada." In S. Mookerjea, I. Szeman, and G. Faurschou (eds.), *Canadian Cultural Studies: A Reader.* Durham: Duke University Press.

Murdie, R.A. (2002). "The Housing Careers of Polish and Somali Newcomers in Toronto's Rental Market." *Housing Studies* 17(3):423-443.

Myrdal, G. (1957). *Rich Lands and Poor: The Road to World Prosperity.* NY: Harper.

Nederveen Pieterse, J. (1997). "Traveling Islam: Mosques without Minarets." In A. ncü and P. Weyland (eds.), *Space, Culture and Power.* London: Zed.

Norrie, K., and D. Owran. (2002). *A History of the Canadian Economy,* 3rd ed. Toronto: Thomson Nelson.

Office of the United Nations High Commissioner for Human Rights. (2007). *Convention Relating to the Status of Refugees.* Retrieved January 20, 2010 from http://www2.ohchr.org/english/law/refugees.htm#wp1037003.

Ogden, P.E. (1984). *Migration and Geographical Change.* Cambridge: Cambridge University Press.

Ohmae, K. (2008). "The End of the Nation State." In F.J. Lechner and J. Boli (eds.), *The Globalization Reader* Malden. MA: Blackwell Publishing Ltd.

Ong, A. (1999). *Flexible Citizenship: The Cultural Logic of Transnationalism.* Durham: Duke University Press.

_____. (1998). "Flexible Citizenship among Chinese Cosmopolitans." In P. Cheah and B. Robbins (eds.), *Cosmopolitics: Thinking and Feeling Beyond the Nation.* Minnesota: University of Minnesota Press.

_____. (1993). "On the Edge of Empire; Flexible Citizenship among Chinese in Diaspora." *Positions* 1(3):(Winter):745-78.

Palmer, B.D. (1994). "Upper Canada." In M.B. Taylor (ed.), *Canadian History: A Reader's Guide, vol. 1, Beginnings to Confederation.* Toronto: University of Toronto Press.

Portes, A., W. Heller, and L.E. Guarnizo. (2001). "Transnational Entrepreneurs: The Emergence and Determinants of an Alternative Form of Immigrant Economic Adaptation." Working Papers Series, Transnational Communities Program, Oxford University.

Ravenstein, E.G. (1885). "The Laws of Migration." *Journal of the Royal Statistical Society* 46:167-235.

_____. (1889). "The Laws of Migration: Second Paper." *Journal of the Royal Statistical Society* 52:241-305.

Richmond, A.H. (1994). *Global Apartheid: Refugees, Racism, and the New World Order.* Toronto: Oxford University Press.

Robertson, R. (1992). *Globalization: Social Theory and Global Culture.* London: Sage.

_____. (1996). *Losing Control? Sovereignty in an Age of Globalization.* NY: Columbia University Press.

Sassen, S. (1988). *The Mobility of Labour and Capital: The Study of International Investment and Labour Flow.* Cambridge: Cambridge University Press.

Satzewich, V., and L. Wong, L. (eds.). (2006). *Transnational Identities and Practices in Canada.* Vancouver: UBC Press.

Schiller, N.G., L.G. Basch, and C. Szanton-Blanc. (1992). "Transnationalism: A New Analytic Framework for Understanding Migration." In *Towards a Transnational Perspective on Migration: Race, Class, Ethnicity, and Nationalism Reconsidered.* NY: New York Academy of Sciences.

_____. (1995). "From Immigrant to Transmigrant: Theorizing Transnational Migration." *Anthropological Quarterly* 68(1):48-63.

Simmons, A.B., and D.E. Plaza. (2006). "The Caribbean Community in Canada: Transnational Connections and Transformations." In V. Satzewich and L. Wong, L. (eds.), *Transnational Identities and Practices in Canada.* Vancouver: UBC Press.

Solomon, P. (1992). *Black Resistance in High School: Forging a Separatist Culture.* NY: State University of New York Press.

Stafford, J. (1992). "The Impact of New Immigration Policy on Racism in Canada." In V. Satzewich (eds.), *Deconstructing a Nation: Immigration, Multiculturalism, and Racism in '90s Canada.* Halifax: Fernwood Publishing.

Stalker, P. (2001). *The No-Nonsense Guide to International Migration.* Toronto: Between the Lines.

Stark, O. (1997). *The Migration of Labor.* Cambridge: Basil Blackwell.

Stasiulis, D., and A.B. Bakan. (2005). *Negotiating citizenship: Migrant Women in Canada and the Global System.* Toronto: University of Toronto Press.

Stoufer, S.A. (1940). "Intervening Opportunities: A Theory Relating Mobility and Distance." *American Sociological Review* 5:845-867.

_____. (1960). "Intervening Opportunities and Competing Migrants." *Journal of Regional Science* 2:1-26.

Strange, S. (2008). "The Declining Authority of States." In F.J. Lechner and J. Boli (eds.), *The Globalization Reader.* MA: Blackwell Publishing Ltd.

Tanovich, D.M. (2006). *The Colour of Justice: Policing Race in Canada.* Toronto: Irwin Law.

Tator, C., and F. Henry. (2006). *Racial Profiling in Canada.* Toronto: University of Toronto Press.

Teixeira, C. (2006). "Housing Experiences of Black Africans in Toronto's Rental Market: A Case Study of Angolan and Mozambican Immigrants." *Canadian Ethnic Studies* XXXVIII(3).

Tettey, W.J., and K.P. Puplampu. (2005). "Border Crossing and Home-Diaspora Linkages among African-Canadians: An Analysis of Transnational Positionality, Cultural Remittance, and Social Capital."

In W.J. Tettey and K.P. Puplampu (eds.), *The African Diaspora in Canada: Negotiating Identity and Belonging.* Calgary: University of Calgary Press.

Tobler, W. (1995). "Migration: Ravenstein, Thornthwaite, and Beyond." *Urban Geography* 16(4):327-343.

Tomlinson, J. (1997), "The Myth of Development: A Critique of Eurocentric Discourse." In R. Munch and D. O'Hearn (eds.), *Critical Development Theory: Contributions to the New Paradigm.* NY: Zed Books.

Trumper, R., and L.L. Wong. (2007). "Canada's Guest Workers: Racialized, Gendered, and Flexible." In S.P. Hier and B.S. Bolaria (eds.), *Race and Racism in 21 Century Canada.* Peterborough, ON: Broadview Press.

United Nations. (2000). *International Migration and Development: Report of the Secretary General.* Retrieved January 20, 2010 from http://www.un.org/esa/population/publications/ittmigdev2002/SG_REPORT_58_98.pdf.

Veseth, M. (2005). *Globaloney: Unravelling the Myths of Globalization.* MD: Rowman and Littlefield.

Visweswaran, K. (1994). *Fiction of Feminist Ethnography.* Minneapolis: University of Minnesota Press.

Walton-Roberts, M. (2003). "Transnational Geographies: Indian Immigration to Canada." *The Canadian Geographer* 47(3):235-250.

Waters, J. (2003). "Flexible Citizens? "Transnationalism and Citizenship amongst Economic Immigrants in Vancouver." *The Canadian Geographer* 47(3):219-234.

Wong, L., and C. Ho. (2006). "Chinese Transnationalism: Class and Capital Flows." In V. Satzewich and L. Wong (eds.), *Transnational Identities and Practices in Canada.* Vancouver: UBC Press.

Wong, L.L., and M. Ng. (1998). "Chinese Immigrant Entrepreneurs in Vancouver: A Case Study of Ethnic Business Development." *Canadian Ethnic Studies* 31(1):64-85.

_____. (2002). "The Emergence of Small Transnational Enterprise in Vancouver: The Case of Chinese Entrepreneur Immigrants." *International Journal of Urban and Regional Research* 26(3):508-530.

Wortley. S., and J. Tanner. (2004). "Discrimination or 'Good' Policing? The Racial Profiling Debate in Canada." *Our Diverse City* Spring:197-201.

Zelinsky, W. (1971). "The Hypothesis of Mobility Transition." *The Geographical Review* 61(2):219-249.

Zipf, G.K. (1946). "The P1P2/D Hypothesis: On the Intercity Movement of Persons." *American Sociological Review* 11: 677-686.

_____. (1949). *Human Behaviour and the Principal of Least Effort.* Massachusetts: Addison-Wesley.

Chapter 16

Politics and Social Movements

Mapping out the Movement: Understanding the Ideological Framework of Canada's Anti-Globalization Community

Scott MacLeod

Simon Fraser University

'I've heard its nothing,' the prime minister said when asked if he'd seen the protesters. 'A couple hundred? It's sad.' Bush looked over his shoulder and smiled when asked the same question, but remained silent and walked with the prime minister into the building.

~Prime Minister Stephen Harper and US President George W. Bush reacting to reporters' requests for their impressions of the street protests that greeted the 2007 North America Leader's Summit, in Montebello, PQ. (Alexander Panetta, "PM Welcomes Bush; Dismisses Summit Protest as Sad Spectacle," *The Guardian*, August 21, 2007, p. A1.)

INTRODUCTION

This chapter is divided into three sections: **Setting the Stage**, **Mapping the Movement** and **Meeting the Movement.** Appropriately, in "Setting the Stage," the discussion begins by acquainting the reader with the Canadian anti-globalization activist community. The next section, "Mapping the Movement," contextualizes the ideological character of activists from said community with the help of Michael Freeden's analytical mapping technique that enables ideologies to be understood as a hierarchical arrangement of core, adjacent and peripheral concepts. Finally, in the last section, "Meeting the Movement," Freeden's framework is applied to the Canadian activist community to reveal three anti-globalization democratic ideologies—*Anti-capitalism, Economic Nationalism*, and *Green Activism.* Though hardly an exhaustive portrayal of the various democratic ideologies that defines Canadian anti-globalization activism, what follows nonetheless is intended to serve as a touchstone to encourage further interest and/or future research into the subject of anti-globalization activism either in Canada or elsewhere in the world.

SETTING THE STAGE

If the mark of a truly transnational movement is its ability to leave few corners of the planet untouched, then anti-globalization activists could easily live up to their global billing based upon sheer worldwide numbers alone. Yet for all the countless examples of individuals and groups all over the world who are engaged in some form of opposition or resistance to globalization on a daily basis, it is the Canadian activist community that makes for a particularly compelling starting point for furthering our sense of the movement's ideological roots. Naturally, as an extension of the much broader transnational resistance movement, the character of anti- globalization activism in the Canadian context is really not that different from what is typical of activist resistance in other parts of the world. For instance, as is the case with the larger movement, Canadian activists openly question the authority of the global governance regime that channels the phenomenon of globalization through institutions such as the World Trade Organization, the World Bank, and the International Monetary Fund and multilateral trade blocs like the North American Free Trade Agreement (NAFTA). Secondly, like their counterparts throughout the movement, Canadian activists also contest the growing influence that "rootless" multi-national corporations wield over domestic policy making institutions. Third, many in the Canadian activist community also stand in solidarity with their peers throughout the wider movement who blame globalization for the growing discrepancy between rich northern industrialized countries and poor developing states. Finally, in terms of structure, much like the overarching global movement, Canada's activist population is also both non-hierarchical and diverse in that it too encompasses a multitude of issue-oriented non-governmental organizations, environmentalists, labour unions, students, church groups, anarchists, fair trade proponents, anti-war factions and nationalists (Carroll, 2003:35-55; Clarkson, 2002; Ayres, 2004; Cox, 1999; Conway, 2004).

However, what makes the Canadian anti-globalization activist community the intriguing case study that it is, is perhaps not that it conforms to the conventional narrative of anti-globalization activism so well, but rather for its perspective on globalization that is unique to the Canadian experience. Simply put, as a mid-sized state with a diverse political culture, a history of constitutional instability, a fragile national identity and a fundamental economic reliance on the resource and commodities trade—particularly with the United States—Canadian anti-globalization activists readily contend that Canada is especially vulnerable to many of the leveling effects often associated with globalization (Kingwell, 2000:5-6).

Perennially dependent upon international trade and foreign investment, it is fair to say that Canada's political economy has never truly known a period in which its existence did not rely on exports and staples. More importantly though, this ongoing dance between economic autonomy and economic security has proved to be anything but delicate—particularly in regard to Canadians' enduring anxiety over its trading relationship with the United States. To be sure, while the Progressive Conservatives' victory in the contentious 1988 election ushered in the pre-NAFTA Canada-US Free Trade Agreement (CUFTA), Brian Mulroney was hardly the first prime minister to ask Canadians to approve of such a treaty as two such similar propositions had previously been considered and subsequently rejected by voters in 1891 and 1911 (Salutin, 1989:266).

Even so, if the Mulroney government's success at the ballot box in 1988 did indeed prove that the "third time" would be a charm for proponents of free trade with the US, there was little danger of the Conservatives' triumph translating into a final curtain call for the activists and organizations who were dogmatically opposed to the implementation of CUFTA. In fact, not only would the anti-free trade campaign go on to rank as an exceptional, if not an abnormal event in the history of Canadian politics, it would also come to be seen as a preview of what would eventually follow in the anti-free trade activists' "second act." For with the passage of time, the specter of the free trade revolt of 1988 has grown to represent something much more than simply a collection of like-minded voters who gathered together in an attempt to derail a key policy ambition of the Mulroney era. It was in the end, much more of a manifestation of a populist-organized, yet politically sophisticated effort that until the "free trade election" of 1988 had been a rarity in the Canadian electorate. As author Rick Salutin observed at the time, "the anti-free trade movement had this capacity to mould different constituencies into a political force. It was unlike other coalitions, which centre on a single issue like daycare or missile testing. It was, in its way, about *all* issues: a way of life" (Salutin, 1988:14).

This emergence of a provocative anti-free trade "political force" would certainly rank as a noteworthy occurrence in the history of Canadian democracy if only for its role in challenging the order of the status quo at the time. But despite failing in its initial cause to thwart the adoption of CUFTA, the anti-free trade coalition that arose in opposition to the agreement would in retrospect prove to be anything but a political anomaly, as its advent would instill within activists a legacy of grassroots activism that continues to blossom to the present day and thus stands as perhaps *the* most transformative political moment in contemporary Canadian collective action circles (Ayres, 1998; Falconer, 2001:43-44, 98). And herein lies what is undoubtedly the most enticing feature of the Canadian anti-globalization movement: its storied heritage, for as William Carroll (2003:48) argues, "activists in Canada got a head start in the politics of globalization compared to those in capitalist democracies and in this regard may be further along in the learning curve."

To the extent that the Canadian activist community is a combination of the common elements of the transnational movement and the distinctive geo-political and historical dynamics that give Canadian activism its unique flair; to truly round out this story, an account that contemplates the ideological character of activists is in order. What follows in this chapter is just such a commentary in the sense that it proposes to address the nature of anti-globalization activists' ideological pedigree by offering a representation of the Canadian activist community's ideological family tree. The resultant family tree was crafted from source material that was primarily drawn from a series of interviews with a number of Canadian anti-globalization activists of varying degrees of notoriety and was further supplemented with contributions from the movement's discourse that covered a range of alternative press, online blogs and pamphlets. With the data collection complete, Michael Freeden's approach to mapping ideologies was then employed to sort through the interview responses and movement paraphernalia and create a detailed account of the way in which democratic concepts and principles are arranged within the movement's ideological framework. From this process came the conclusion that much like traditional complex ideologies á la socialism, liberalism or conservatism; anti-globalization constitutes a varied—though small—ideological family that consists of three distinct anti-globalization democratic ideologies: Anti-capitalism, Economic Nationalism and Green Activism.

Mapping the Movement: Conceptual Morphology

To a skeptic, the notion that anti-globalization activism displays distinctive ideological qualities may seem to be a bit of an analytical reach—for the obvious counter claim to such an argument is that if anything, the movement already belongs to, or at least channels, traditional ideologies such as socialism, liberalism and in some instances, conservatism. To be sure, anti-branders, trade unions, environmentalists, ecclesiastical groups, human rights organizations, anarchists, students and various other globalization resistors may make for an intriguing cultural, political and social cocktail. Still, the question remains: can the anti-globalization movement's efforts seriously be characterized in distinctive ideological terms on par with the sort of "macro" ideologies that produce actual schemes for the just distribution of scarce and vital goods?

Here is where Michael Freeden's understanding of the nature of ideologies can be particularly instructive. In other words, although Freeden suggests that ideologies may serve as collections of the ideas, fundamental concepts, symbols and units of political thought that constitute a legitimate political argument "in a necessarily constrained version of their infinitely possible modes of meaning" (Freeden, 2003b:4); they by no means need to be overly ambitious in scope to qualify for ideological status. Ideologies, then, come in more than just one size in that they can be macro or "thick" à la socialism or liberalism, but they can also be "thin" and still exhibit a dynamic conceptual arrangement. Thus, even if anti-globalization activism may deviate from the mission of traditional "thick" ideologies by speaking to rather than addressing the time honoured political questions of who gets what, when, and how; Freeden's analytical standard suggests that it is still possible to envisage anti-globalization activists within a cohesive—albeit thin—ideological milieu of their own making.

However, while it is clear that anti-globalization activism seems to display enough ideological flair to be consistent with Freeden's definition of an ideology, before going any further, another question is in need of additional consideration—i.e., does anti-globalization sentiment and activity constitute a "family" of ideologies or does it simply amount to a single umbrella-like democratic ideology? Perhaps the simplest way to respond to such a question is to pose another question along the lines of: if it is true that globalization boasts the sort of conceptual density that continues to produce multiple theoretical iterations, can one assume that resistance to globalization is a varied and complex enterprise in its own right? For Freeden (1996), there would be no need to answer the first question as his response to the second would without hesitation be a resounding "yes," as "ideologies are the bridging mechanism between contestability and determinacy" (pp. 77-77). In other words, given that the activist community often seems as conflicted with itself as it is united in its resistance to globalization, the fact of the matter is that there is far too much fragmentation and diversity at work within the movement for there to be only one branch on the anti-globalization ideological family tree.

Central to Freeden's approach is the proposition that an ideology is a fluid collection of core, adjacent and peripheral concepts. In this arrangement, core concepts are the most essential component as they are the primary organizing principles that define an ideology's political agenda. Although the core functions as the philosophical engine room of an ideology, core concepts are not abstract or ethereal notions that are based only on ideals and occur irrespective of experience. Because it is difficult for ideologies to survive on a single concept, the core is typically a crowded place as concepts cluster together to form the ideology's foundation. Alternatively, the core can also be a place of competition as concepts are eliminated, introduced, and modified as they interact with one another (p.84). However, it is this conceptual volatility that enables ideologies to ultimately exist as semantic fields where concepts engage one another and are eventually defined or as Freeden would say "decontested."

Thus, just because a concept happens to occupy an ideological core, it does not mean that it is universally revered, used or for that matter understood in the same way. For instance, the notion of "revolution" is a central feature of many anarchist *and* Marxist-inspired critiques of globalization, yet the idea of revolution means drastically different things to different people. It can be for some activists, a very sincere or literal goal, whereas for others, "revolution" may simply just be a metaphorical principle that informs their state of mind. Whatever the case, for activists who believe that globalization is a hyper-accelerated form of capitalism that must be completely dismantled; the concept of revolution remains intrinsic in their arguments even if its application depends upon one's personal belief system.

Situated next to the core, are adjacent concepts that are in a sense more precise expressions of the basic normative commitments of core concepts. Often, it is this interaction between specific core and adjacent concepts that lends definition and distinction to ideologies as they are "essential to the formation of an ideology" (Freeden, 1996:78). Adjacent concepts are those concepts that are logically and culturally adjacent to the ideological core. Oftentimes within the ideological schema, both the core and adjacent concepts can intersect one another as they form "mutually influential relationships" and networks with one another that do much to give an ideology its distinctive character. For instance, for many anti-globalization activists, social democracy ranks as a core concept that defines their resistance to globalization. Frequently underscored by activists in their expression of this core concept though, is the adjacent concept of social justice.

Finally, the ideological map becomes complete with the inclusion of the peripheral concepts that occupy the outer realm of an ideology. Peripheral concepts add "a vital gloss to the ideological core," but do not affect the overall structural integrity of the ideology. Peripheral concepts include the perimeter concepts that serve as "the specific ideas or policy-proposals rather than fully fledged concepts, lacking the generalization and sophistication associated with a concept." In such capacity, they essentially provide a metric by which to judge the political relevance of ideologies, for it is the peripheral concepts that represent the "interchange between ideas and practice" (Freeden, 2003b:3-4). For the anti-globalization movement, peripheral concepts cut across the core and adjacent concepts that differentiate activists from one another as they cover a number of identifiable hallmarks of activist behaviour ranging from "direct action" activities such as "culture jamming" to street protests to the use of alternative media to promote the movement's message.

MEETING THE MOVEMENT—THE 3 ANTI-GLOBALIZATION IDEOLOGIES

Anti-Capitalism

> *Globalization is capitalism with the gloves off. It basically is the same structures that have always had peoples' lives at least in jeopardy as far as their worth.*
>
> ~Macdonald Stainsby, social justice activist
> (Interview, May 2007)

In some small way, anti-capitalist resistance to globalization has always embodied what one might call a "Rouseauian" spirit. In other words, just as Jean-Jacques Rousseau's critique of the modernity of his time was premised on the notion that humanity's relentless pursuit of material wealth and "amour propre" had denigrated the concept of democracy and devolved society into a callous free-for-all; anti-capitalism's grim appraisal of the globalization era strikes a similar chord, thanks to its depiction of a global population enraptured by the temptations of mass consumerism and is in turn, largely alienated from the public sphere, shell-shocked by militarism and oblivious to the injustices of imperialism. That anti-capitalists respond to what they see as the excesses of globalization with such visceral spirit is a testament to the tremendous philosophical authority of the two concepts that sit within anti-capitalism's core—anarchism and Marxism. As two significant theoretical traditions that share a long history of ideological rivalry, the presence of both anarchism and Marxism in the heart of the same anti-globalization ideology can sometimes make for a precarious coexistence. Nevertheless, because both Marxist anti-capitalists and anarchist anti-capitalists tend to believe that the phenomenon of globalization represents an ideological struggle of far greater importance than whatever one that has historically existed between their respective philosophical camps; solidarity in resistance to globalization must take precedence over their own internal philosophical debates. All things considered, in the minds of anti-capitalist activists, it is capitalism—an economic system that has long been a target of derision of both Marxist doctrine and much of the anarchist canon for its emphasis on perpetual growth for the betterment of the few, at the expense of equality of all—that is the real culprit behind globalization (Slingshot, 2001; Barnes, 2006; Stephanie Gude, 2007).

This reading of globalization as the latest manifestation in the ongoing worldwide class struggle against capitalism is further evident in anti-capitalism's embrace of both *equality* and *social justice*—two of the adjacent concepts that circle this ideology's core (Hunter, 2007; Walia, 2007; Sharpe, 2007). One example in which both of these adjacent concepts intermesh with one another in this ideology is in anti-capitalists' response to what they see as one of the great myths of globalization—i.e., the phenomenon's promise of a world premised on open borders. For their part, anti-capitalists willingly embrace a "borderless world" vision of globalization, so long as it is one that celebrates social, cultural and technological exchanges and unfettered migration rather than one that amounts to little more than a pathway to the irrelevancy of the nation-state via a hyperactive, liberalized international trade regime. For in the words of the first "demand" from *No One is Illegal*–Vancouver's "Dismantle Fortress North America" agenda, the grassroots anti-colonial, immigrant and refugee rights collective states:

> Canadian borders are becoming increasingly open to capital, while at the same time restricting the movement of those who have been displaced by free trade policies. Government policies to open borders to profits while closing them to human beings are being negotiated and signed in complete secrecy with great consequences for the environment and basic human rights. (*No One Is Illegal*)

Finally, given anti-capitalism's categorical rejection of the established order of the current economic and political system, anti-capitalist activists are in turn able to draw upon an almost infinite number of peripheral concepts in the form of tactics and strategies to serve as the "outward" expressions of their ideology's core and adjacent principles. Activist reliance on alternative media, be it blogs, "zines" or social networking is of course one obvious peripheral concept that is pivotal to the dissemination of anti-capitalists' message. But, it is perhaps "direct action" be it in the form of civil disobedience, demonstrations, radical cheerleading, teach-ins or—depending on the political temperament of individual activists—targeted property vandalism that best embodies the nonconformist values of anarchy and Marxism that occupy the ideology's core (Rovics, 2009; Philadelphia's Defenestrator Collective, 2000; Gelderoos, 2004).

Economic Nationalism

> *The period we are living in now is probably best characterized by the French when they call it L'américanisation, in which they label it directly what it is. And it is very much an Americanization process—especially for a country like Canada which is in such close proximity of the United States and has such well advanced American control of our country.*
>
> ~David Orchard, activist, farmer, and politician
> (Interview, September 3, 2007)

If ever the essence of economic nationalism was most succinctly put, it would likely be in the words of Maude Barlow, who once articulated the Council of Canadians' position on the international trade regime by claiming: "We're not opposed to trade, and we're not opposed to globalization in any form. But these rules are not going to be written by a group of faceless bureaucrats and lobby groups" (Coyne, 2001). Taken at face value, Barlow's comments no doubt epitomize the kind of stern rebuke of the contemporary global governance regime that has come to resonate within the minds of activists throughout the anti-globalization movement. However, also underlying Barlow's sentiment is something much more tangible to economic nationalists than mere frustration or disillusionment with the actions of supranational institutions, and that is one of this ideology's key core concepts–*sovereignty*.

Considered by practically every modern state in the world to be *the* most important norm of the international community, sovereignty is the concept that symbolizes a nation's territorial integrity. In short, sovereignty is what gives a nation the freedom to do whatever it wants within its own recognized boundaries. But, for Canadian economic nationalists who generally view globalization as part of a largely American-driven enterprise that includes the added possibility of a continent-wide, enhanced economic and security relationship based on the nebulous concept of "deep integration," the notion of sovereignty is much more than an abstract international custom. For economic nationalists, sovereignty embodies the very essence of Canada's mortality (Canadian Action Party, 2006; Duncan Cameron, 2006).

Though economic nationalists consider sovereignty to be crucial in safeguarding Canadian autonomy from the designs of supranational institutions and multinational corporations, it is the second core concept of *social democracy* that enables activists to envision an alternative economic and political paradigm to the current one of globalization (Common Front on the World Trade Organization, 2000). So central is social democracy to the ideological character of economic nationalism, that aside from a sprinkling of traditional "Tory" elements, the majority of economic nationalists are typically self-identified social democrats. It is thanks to the presence of these social democrats and their commitment to "time-honoured Canadian values" of a robust social safety net, multiculturalism and a strong central government that plays the primary role in setting the country's economic agenda that gives economic nationalism much of its intellectual spirit (Barlow, 2006; Ducharme, 2007; Mora, 2007).

The fact that economic nationalists are so convinced of globalization's potential as an existential threat to Canada's economic and political independence is not surprisingly derivative of a critical thread in the narrative of the broader movement that insists that the supranational institutions that typically drive the phenomenon—i.e., the WTO, the G8, multinational corporations, and so on—exhibit a pathological obsession with meeting or functioning under a deliberate shroud of secrecy. If true, such behavior on the part of the global governance regime cannot help but give the impression to the outside world that while their agendas may be meant for public consumption, they are not designed with public consultation in mind. Hence, even if globalization is a much less nefarious enterprise than the movement often assumes, economic nationalists claim that it is impossible to ever really be sure of the intentions of its proponents because there is no tangible fiduciary relationship between a trade regime or a supranational institution or a multinational corporation and the average citizen (Hargrove, 2007; Bakan, 2007; Hurtig, 2007). To quote Yves Le Fort, "we've always known that business has had the ear of the government in a way that ordinary citizens and civil society groups do not" (Le Fort, 2006). And thus lies the adjacent concept of *accountability*—a vital supporting principle to economic nationalism's ideological core, and "a key component of democracy" (MacCuish, 2006).

In light of Canada's participation in NAFTA, it goes without saying that much of the rhetoric that frames economic nationalism's critique of globalization reflects a deep anxiety among activists over the prospect of even further continental integration down the road. However, while such unease may be prompted by economic nationalists' fear of what is to come, it is shaped in large part by the wariness with which they view Canada's historical asymmetrical relationship with the United States. In fact, so dubious are economic nationalists of Canada's long standing, lop-sided bilateral rapport with the US that they believe that if Canadians are ever going to credibly shield themselves from the tide of globalization, they must first re-evaluate the country's current and future relations with its neighbor to the south. This push for such rumination is most succinctly articulated in the form of one of economic nationalism's most fundamental adjacent concepts—*reverse integration.* To some degree, the drive to have Canada scale back, if not completely disengage from its formal associations with the United States is somewhat rooted in an undercurrent of anti-Americanism in Canadian political culture that dates back to the late 1700s when the first Loyalist settlers fled the American revolution for the more monarch-friendly climes of British North America. For the most part though, the strategy of reverse integration is simply a reflection of economic nationalists' belief that if past examples of integration between the two countries (i.e., the Canada-US Free Trade Agreement, NAFTA, North Atlantic Treaty Organization (NATO), the SPP) are any indication, what Canada typically loses in terms of political and economic autonomy far outweighs what it gains in any political cache with Washington or economic share of the US market (Dobbin, 2008).

Lastly, as with anti-capitalism, the core and adjacent elements of economic nationalism's ideological framework also spawn a number of peripheral concepts that help activists try to put their ideas into practice. Some of these concepts include fair trade, as well as certain forms of direct action. But if there is one peripheral concept that is aimed to assuage economic nationalists' belief that globalization in its current form either creates or exacerbates a democratic deficit at all levels of government (i.e., sub-national, national and transnational) it is in activists' ambition to address that perception within Canada's domestic political institutions by calling for the reform of the electoral process. Hardly a notion that is exclusive to the anti-globalization movement, the proposition that Canada's democratic system is in dire need of some type of *electoral reform*—be it proportional representation or campaign spending limits or referenda or some other proposal—has long captured the attention of Canadian voters from across the political spectrum. As a peripheral concept for economic nationalists though, the prospect of electoral reform holds particularly special meaning in that it would restore the electorate's faith in the democratic concept of representation by assuring *all* voters that their voices in the political process could no longer be ignored, overlooked or neglected. Furthermore, it could conceivably bring greater accountability and transparency to the country's legislatures. Most of all though, economic nationalists contend that by truly giving citizens a legitimate say in the political process, Canada's houses of government would begin to reflect the legitimate will of the people and thus make the kind of choices that would preserve Canada's political and economic independence as opposed to perpetually embracing the economic, political and cultural temptations of the US, all while further acquiescing to the seductive lure of globalization.

Green Activism

> *What we need is a marketplace where the price of every product tells the ecological truth; that is one of the really big fundamental changes that has to happen to the global economy to basically create a global market regime of true-cost markets.*
>
> ~Kalle Lasn, Adbusters Founder and Editor in Chief
> (Interview, February 13, 2007).

Just as anti-capitalism and economic nationalism constitute unique anti-globalization democratic ideologies that share some similarities, but are ultimately quite different from one another, so too can the same be said of green activism. However, while both anti-capitalists and economic nationalists essentially adhere to a similar view that globalization is best understood as a complex economic paradigm, green activism distinguishes itself from both of its ideological cousins by looking at its impact through a much broader environmental prism. This is not to say that green activists reject the conclusion of many economic nationalists and all anti-capitalists that globalization is essentially a capitalism-driven enterprise. It is just that if other movement activists' conceptions of globalization are rooted in the "big picture," the green perspective's picture just happens to be quite a bit bigger (Koleszar, 2007; Guerin, 2007; Broderick, 2006). It is bigger in the sense that although green activists acknowledge that globalization can be a significant destabilizing influence on a variety of contemporary political, social, cultural and economic institutions and relationships, what truly animates the green anti-globalization democratic ideology, is its perception of the phenomenon's long term effects in the form of unfettered migration, built-in product obsolescence, unbridled consumerism and of course, global warming (Green Peace, 2006; Herbert, 2007).

That green activists are so motivated by what they see as globalization's long term consequences, is certainly indicative of the significance of two of the ideology's fundamental core concepts—*equality* and *intergenerational social justice*. As well, it also reveals the reality at work inside of green activism's ideological core in which both concepts interact with one another to create this holistic perception of globalization. Most importantly, it speaks to the unique meaning that green activism attaches to the concept of equality which is based on activists' contention that because human beings do not possess a monopoly on moral worth, neither they nor the planet's ecosystem are considered to be mutually exclusive of one another. Hence, green activists' message to the rest of the anti-globalization movement—and for that matter, the entire world—is that if the international community is ever to achieve a truly fair and just system of global governance, it has to be one that recognizes all life-forms for their intrinsic moral value rather than for whatever their instrumental merit may represent to human beings (Green Party of Canada, 2006; Canadian Environmental Network, 2006; Labchuk, 2007).

Complementing green activism's revision of what typically passes for equality in a democracy is the other aforementioned core concept that is particularly germane to activists' assessment of globalization and that is intergenerational social justice. Characterized by philosopher Brian Barry (1997:107) as "a sort of shorthand for justice between the present generation and future generations," in so far as no future generation should ever have to find itself worse off due to the actions of the present one, green activists look to this concept as further rationale for resisting globalization, particularly in light of its penchant for economic excess.

In challenging the philosophical orthodoxy of how concepts like equality and social justice are typically perceived in modern democracies, green activists do so in the hope that they might also provoke the average voter/citizen/consumer to begin re-evaluating the economic—and by extension, environmental—choices they make in their everyday lives. One way in which activists hope to influence such present and future choices is expressed in the adjacent concept of *true-cost economics*. A clear reflection of green activism's core concept of intergenerational social justice, the purpose to taking a "true cost" approach to economics is to compel human beings to appreciate that capitalism in its current context does not offer an accurate accounting of the real "costs" of the goods and services it produces. For instance, at present, when an individual purchases an automobile from a car lot, its price tag reflects only a rough approximation of the manufacturing cost. But, according to the logic of true cost economics, the *true* cost of that car should also include its lifetime maintenance, the resource extraction costs for the car's materials, health care costs due to exhaust pollution and of course, whatever recycling fees are incurred upon its disposal. All told, the *true* cost of that car should reflect not only how much of a financial burden it imposes upon its owner at the point of sale, but more significantly, the total environmental toll that the car's production and usage will exact upon the planet. Applicable to almost any manufactured goods and numerous services, green activists consider the true cost approach to be a most effective counter point to many of what they see as globalization's most environmentally destructive attributes, whether it is the pursuit of perpetual economic growth, the encouragement of mass consumption, or the increase in intercontinental mass mobility (Lasn, 2007; Schmidt, 2007).

A second means by which green activism channels its ideological core is through the adjacent concept and counterpart to that of true cost economics—*sustainable development*. Premised upon the goal of sustainability, which Barry (1997:106) suggests essentially amounts to "the conservation of what matters for future generations," sustainable development is often envisioned as a check upon capitalism's pursuit of infinite economic growth without requiring the complete abandonment of the current economic system. It seeks to find a "happy medium" (i.e., an ideal symmetry) between economic growth and the capacity for the Earth's ecosystem to accommodate the human activity that produces that growth. Championed by many activists in the movement and increasingly embraced by the corporate world, sustainable development is in simple terms, the perfect marriage between theory and practice in that it allows economic development to remain profitable so long as it is first and foremost, "sustainable" (May, 2007; Danaher, 2006; *Taking it Global*, 2006). For green activists, though, who situate themselves on the left of the political spectrum—as a democratic ideology, green activism encompasses a wide variety of political orientations from right to left—it is not always clear how the concept of sustainable development can be squared with the reality of an "ecological debt" that has been racked up by an industrialized west that has spent decades appropriating a disproportionate share of the planet's resources both at the expense of the developing world and to the detriment of future generations. In other words, how does the developed world sell the concept of sustainable development to rising economic powers like China or India; both of whom seem to be increasingly embracing the fossil-fueled, throwaway, consumer-based globalization model that appears to be working fine for them at the moment?

Like its ideological brethren, green activism relies on a variety of peripheral concepts to put a "public face" on its ideology—the most obvious of which one being direct action. As part of a broader environmental tradition with its own long history of direct action, green activists are obviously well versed in the art of the sit-in, the rally, the march and even the use of abseilers to stage "guerilla-style" banner hangings in public places. In fact, in anticipation of the December 2009 Climate Summit in Copenhagen, some in the anti-globalization movement claimed that the meeting had generated so much interest in mobilization that it had the makings of the next "Battle in Seattle" (White, 2009; van der Zee, 2009). One creative peripheral concept though that may lack the cache of a street protest, but possesses an edginess all its own and stands as a reflection of intergenerational social justice and equality via true cost economics and sustainable development is *Buy Nothing Day*. Dating back to 1992 when it was conceived by Vancouver cartoonist Ted Dave, Buy Nothing Day is now most often associated with the Adbusters Media Foundation, that for one day a year—typically the last Friday in November before the start of the Christmas shopping season (aka "Black Friday)—appeals to everyone in the world to refrain from shopping for one continuous 24 hour period (Conner, 2008, EW19). In keeping with green activism's holistic view of globalization, Buy Nothing Day is pitched as an opportunity to at least once a year, "take a stand against the consumer culture that is killing our world"(Adbusters, 2009).

CONCLUSION

Globalization marches on.

~Noam Chomsky—linguist, activist and philosopher.
(March 26, 2010)

Given the constraints of time and space— not to mention the complex nature of the movement itself— this discussion could obviously never be considered the definitive word on Canadian anti-globalization activism. In truth, even though great effort was spent in analytically unpacking the three democratic ideologies on display here—anti-capitalism, economic nationalism and green activism—there are quite conceivably many more real and possible core, adjacent and peripheral concepts than could theoretically or realistically be revealed here. For that matter, there could even be one or two other distinct anti-globalization democratic ideologies besides the aforementioned three. What this chapter does hopefully demonstrate though is that there is a unique reward for observing the anti-globalization movement up close rather than from afar, as such an approach offers indisputable proof that there is much more to the ideological character of the movement than what can often appear to be an incoherent rehashing of traditional political philosophy. Lastly, while both the approach used here and the subsequent findings underscore the point that activists harbour very palpable feelings of frustration towards globalization for what they perceive as its leading role in creating a democratic vacuum in the realm of global governance; such sentiment undoubtedly pales in comparison to the sense of aggravation activists express towards globalization for what they see as its role in contributing to the perception of a democratic deficit within their own domestic political institutions.

REFERENCES

Adbusters. (2009). "Buy Nothing Day Wrap-up." Accessed December 8, 2009 from https://www.adbusters.org/.

Ayres, J.M. (1998). *Defying Conventional Wisdom: Political Movements and Popular Contention against North American Free Trade.* Toronto: University of Toronto Press.

_____. (2004). "Framing Collective Action against Neo-liberalism: The Case of the 'Anti-Globalization' Movement." *Journal of World-Systems Research* X(1):11-34.

Bakan, J. (2007). *Personal Interview.* (June 12, 2007).

Barlow, M. (2006). Council of Canadians. *Personal Interview.* (December 20, 2006).

Barnes, D. (2006). Freedom Socialist Party. *Personal Interview.* (March 27, 2006).

Barry, B. (1999). "Sustainability and Intergenerational Social Justice." In A. Dobson (ed.), *Fairness and Futurity: Essays on Environmental Sustainability and Social Justice.* NY: Oxford University Press.

Broderick, L. (2006). PEI Network of Activists against GE Foods. *Personal Interview.* (September 1, 2006).

Cameron, D. (2006). Rabble.ca. *Personal Interview.* (February 20, 2006).

Canadian Action Party Globalization and the Death of Democracy. (2006). *The Canadian Action Party.* Accessed February 16, 2006 from www.canadianactionparty.ca.

The Canadian Environmental Network. Building a Strong Network for a Sustainable Environment. (2006.) *The Canadian Environmental Network.* Accessed March 13, 2006 from www.cen-rce.org.

Carroll, W.K. (2003). "Undoing the End of History: Canada-Centered Reflections on the Challenge of Globalization." In Y. Atasoy and W.K. Carroll (eds.), *Global Shaping and its Alternatives.* Aurora: Garamond Press.

Slingshot. (2001). "Invisible Hands: The Cell." *Slingshot.* 71(Spring). Available at http://slingshot.tao.ca/index.php.

Chomsky, N. (2010). "Globalization Marches On: Growing Popular Outrage has not Challenged Corporate Power." *The New York Times Syndicate.* Accessed March 30, 2010 from www.commondreams.org.

Clarkson, S. (2002). *Uncle Sam and US.* Toronto: University of Toronto Press.

Common Front on the World Trade Organization. (2000). "A Better World is Possible: Developing common Security Through Fair Trade." (Pamphlet). *Common Front on the World Trade Organization.*

Conner, S. (2008). "Buy nothing Day Spawns Debate: Anti-consumerism Protest takes place during Economic Downturn." *The Vancouver Courier,* (November 28): EW19.

Conway, J.M. (2004). *Identity, Place, Knowledge: Social Movements Contesting Globalization.* Halifax: Fernwood Publishing.

Cox, R.W. (1999). "Civil Society at the Turn of The Millennium: Prospects for an Alternative World Order." *Review of International Studies* 25(1):3-28.

Coyne, A. (2001). "Free Trade's Democratic Deficit." *National* Post, (April 18). Accessed August 12, 2003 from www.andrewcoyne.com.

Danaher, K. (2006). Global Exchange. *Personal Interview.* (March 20, 2006).

della Porta, D., and M. Diani. (2004). "'Contro la guerra senza se né ma': le proteste contro la guerra in Irak." In V. Della Scala and S. Fabbrini (eds.), *La Politica in Italia.* Bologna: Il Mulino.

della Porta, D. (2005). "Making the Polis: Social Forums and Democracy in the Global Justice Movement." *Mobilization: An International Journal* 10(1):73-94.

Dobbin, M. (2008). "Americanize Me? No Thanks *The Tyee.*" Accessed May 1, 2008 from www.thetyee.ca.

Ducharme, P. (2007). Public Service Alliance of Canada. *Personal Interview.* (August 7, 2007).

Dunkley, G. (2004). *Free Trade: Myths, Reality and Alternatives.* Black Point: Fernwood Publishing.

Evans, P. (2005). "Counter Hegemonic Globalization: Transnational Social Movements in the Contemporary Global Political Economy." In T. Janoski, R.R. Alford, A.M. Hicks, and M.A. Schwartz (eds.), *The Handbook of Political Sociology: States, Civil Societies and Globalization.* NY: Cambridge University Press.

Falconer, T. (2001). *Watchdogs and Gadflies: Activism from Marginal to Mainstream.* Toronto: Viking/Penguin Books Canada.

Freeden, M. (1996). *Ideologies and Political Theory.* NY: Claredon Press.

Freeden, M. (2003a). *Ideology: A Very Short Introduction.* NY: Oxford University Press.

_____. (2003b). "Editorial: Ideological Boundaries and Ideological Systems." *Journal of Political Ideologies* 8(1):3-12.

Gelderoos, P. (2004). *What is Democracy?* Tucson: See Sharp Press.

Gills, B.K. (2000). "Overturning Globalization: The Politics of Resistance." In J. Dragsbaek Schmidt and J. Hersh (eds.), *Globalization and Social Change.* NY: Routledge, Taylor & Francis Group.

The Green Party of Canada. (2006). "Platform 2006: the Green Party Vision." *The Green Party of Canada.* Accessed March 13 2006 from www.greenparty.ca.

Green Peace. (2006). "Encourage Sustainable Trade." *Green Peace International.* Accessed March 13, 2006 from www.greenpeace.org.

Guerin, G. (2007). Sustainability Solutions. *Personal Interview.* (June 4, 2007).

Gude, S. (2007). Ontario Coalition against Poverty. *Personal Interview.* (July 24, 2007).

Hargrove, B. (2007). Canadian Autoworkers Union. *Personal Interview.* (July 31, 2007).

Herbert, Y. (2007). The Dominion. *Personal Interview.* (July 5, 2007).

Hunter, A. (2007). Anti- Poverty Committee. *Personal Interview.* (May 26, 2007).

Hurtig, M. (2007). *Personal Interview.* (May 19, 2007).

Kingwell, M. (2000). *The World We Want.* Toronto: Penguin Books Canada.

Koleszar, A. (2007). *Personal Interview.* (September 25, 2007).

Labchuk, S. (2007). Earth Action. *Personal Interview.* (September 17, 2007).

Lasn, K. (2007). Adbusters. *Personal Interview.* (February 13, 2007).

LeFort, J-Y. (2006). "Harper gets by with a Little Help from his (Corporate) Friends: Cancun Summit welcomes CEOs to the Table." *Canadian Perspectives* (Summer 2006).

MacCuish, D. (2006). Social Justice Committee. *Personal Interview.* (April 28, 2006).

May, E. (2007). Green Party of Canada. *Personal Interview.* (September 8, 2007).

Mullard, M. (2004). *The Politics of Globalization and Polarization.* Northampton: Edward Elgar Publishing.

No G8 Halifax. (2010). "About." Accessed May 9, 2010 from www.nog8halifax.ca.

No One Is Illegal. (2009). "What We Demand: Dismantle Fortress North America." Accessed September 22, 2009 from www.nooneisillegal.org.

Orchard, D. (2007). Citizens Concerned about Free Trade. *Personal Interview.* (September 3, 2007).

Panetta, A. (2007). "PM Welcomes Bush; Dismisses Summit Protest as Sad Spectacle." *The Guardian*, August 21, p. A1.

Philadelphia's Defenestrator Collective. (2000). "Direct Action & A New World." *The Defenstrator* (October, 2000).

Rovics, D. (2009). "The Police are Rioting: Reflections on Pittsburgh." *Songwriter's Notebook.* Accessed September 27, 2009 from http://www.songwritersnotebook.blogspot.com/.

Salutin, R. (1989). *Waiting for Democracy: A Citizen's Guide.* Toronto: Viking/Penguin Group.

Schmidt C. (2007). Work Less Party. *Personal Interview.* (May 28, 2007).

Sharpe, E. (2007). Founder, Fernwood Publishing. *Personal Interview.* (April 28, 2007).

Stainsby, M. (2007). *Personal Interview.* (May 17, 2007).

Starr, A., and J. Adams. (2003). "Anti-globalization: The Fight for Local Autonomy." *New Political Science* 25(1):19-42.

Taking it Global. (2006). "Poverty & Globalization." *Taking it Global.* Accessed March 13, 2006 from takingitglobal.org.

van der Zee, B. (2009). "Naomi Kelin Kick-Starts the Activism at Copenhagen with Call for Disobedience." *The Guardian/UK.* Accessed December 10, 2009 from http://www.guardian.co.uk/.

Walia, H. (2007). *No One is Illegal. Personal Interview.* (June 13, 2007).

White, A. (2009). "The Movement of Movements: From Resistance to Climate Justice." *Share the World's Resources (STWR).* Accessed December 10, 2009 from http://www.stwr.org/.

Chapter 17

Transnationalism and Globalization

Russian Transnational Entrepreneurs in Toronto: How the Global Capitalist Economy Influenced Entrepreneurship

Alexander Shvarts

University of Toronto

INTRODUCTION

One of the most interesting results of the collapse of the former Soviet Union is the emergence of successful cosmopolitan entrepreneurs from former Soviet republics who have immigrated to countries, such as the United States and Canada, settling in metropolitan areas like Toronto and making millions establishing businesses in their new host countries.

This chapter considers how globalization, transnationalism and experiences in a transitional economy affect the role of human capital, financial capital, and social capital in establishing businesses in Canada. It looks at the effects of globalization and transnational business linkages, which are unique to Russian immigrants. While the unique historical, economic and political environment of the former Soviet Union provided favourable conditions for entrepreneurship, the emergence of Russian entrepreneurs, under the forces of globalization and transnationalism, did not contribute significantly to new immigrant communities. Rather than helping new immigrant communities, the entrepreneurs adopted an "individualist" value system insofar as they are "out to profit."

This chapter focuses on successful cosmopolitan entrepreneurs from the former Soviet Union because this group comes from a place where the free market economy did not exist before the 1980s. How did people who grew up in a context where entrepreneurship was forbidden and there was no privatization prior to the 1980s (Gold, 1995:xii), develop entrepreneurial skills and how they could transfer these skills to establish successful businesses in the modern context of market capitalism in Toronto?

According to Statistics Canada, at the time of the 2006 Census, there were 20,920 recent Russian immigrants in Toronto. Many researchers have noted that in the US and Canada there is an overrepresentation of the foreign born in the business population and some groups have entered business ownership in numbers disproportionate to their group's size (Chan and Cheung, 1985:143; Aldrich and Waldinger, 1990:112). Despite their numbers, there has been relatively little research on this group (Gold, 1995:x). In Canada there has been very little systematic research which focuses on immigrant entrepreneurs from the former Soviet Union, and no studies have explored the effects of transnational business linkages between Russians in major immigrant receiving countries, such as Canada and in their sending countries.

This research is based on qualitative data derived from face-to-face in-depth interviews with 32 immigrants from the former Soviet Union who became entrepreneurs by starting private companies/businesses in Toronto. Two large cohorts of immigrants were identified from the former Soviet Union, those who immigrated to Toronto in the late 1970s and early 1980s and those who arrived in the late 1980s and 1990s. It is hypothesized that those who immigrated in the late 1970s and early 1980s came to Toronto with virtually no entrepreneurial experience and no financial capital because they came before the market transition in the former Soviet Union, making them more likely to use networks within their ethnic community in Toronto to establish businesses within the enclave economy or to rely on networks to access the mainstream Canadian economy. It is also hypothesized that those who immigrated in the late 1980s and 1990s were more likely to come with entrepreneurial experience and financial capital because they lived in the former Soviet Union during the market transition; they will be more likely to use networks and connections formed during the transitional Russian economy of the 1980s and 1990s to establish transnational businesses in Toronto.

To address how Russian immigrants have established businesses in Toronto, I will examine how social capital, financial capital, human capital, and home country experience, specifically experience in the transitional economy have affected Russian entrepreneurs at each stage of business development in Toronto. I approach these four factors through the two following critical lenses: ethnic and class dimensions of entrepreneurship and transnationalism. I use the central postulates of each of the two approaches to determine how these major factors influenced and shaped business practice and success in Toronto for the two cohorts of Soviet immigrants. I focus on two phases of entrepreneurship and the founding of a business: (1) Pre-Start-Up - Motivation and Idea Development and (2) Start-Up - Planning and Organizing the Founding of a Firm. As has been noted elsewhere, these phases are important to entrepreneurship (Greve, 1995: 3; Carter et al., 1996; Kamm and Nurick, 1993).

GLOBALIZATION LEADING TO CREATION OF MEDIUM AND LARGE BUSINESSES BY IMMIGRANT ENTREPRENEURS

In contrast to past research, which believed that medium and large businesses are run by native-born Canadians and established immigrants who have worked their way to the top, my research demonstrates that as a result of globalization, the immigrants I interviewed from Russia established not only small businesses, family-owned ethnic businesses in an enclave market where they provide retail goods and services to co-ethnic or minority consumers (see Bates, 1994; Razin, 1992; Lo and Wang, 2007:65), but also medium and large businesses. The latter generate a yearly revenue of over one million dollars in a diversity of industries, many of which have transnational links to Russia.

Global political and economic restructuring and the international population movement of the last two decades have drastically altered the market. Contemporary ethnic economies, which include medium-sized and large firms, go beyond retailing and ethnic enclaves to command transnational networks (Li, 1998, in Lo and Wang, 2007: 65). In the past, medium and large businesses were mainly the territory of native-born Canadians and well-established immigrants. More recently, global movements of ideas and technology, and people and resources, have created a very different scenario. Many immigrants now come with human and financial capital, as well as management experience and business knowledge (Fong and Luk, 2007b:65). The Russian immigrants I interviewed all came with a great deal of human capital; most of the second cohort who immigrated in the late 1980s and 1990s came with financial capital, management experience and business knowledge. My findings suggest that for my interviewees, self-employment represents an opportunity for economic advancement.

UNIQUE MARKET TRANSITION IN THE FORMER SOVIET UNION

The conditions in the transition era were unique. Market transition can be implemented at different speeds and through a wide variety of policies. In Russia, a series of radical institutional reforms dismantled the system of far-reaching state control over the economy, leading to the rapid rise of private ownership and the market-based allocation of resources and consumer goods (Gerber, 2002:631). Russia experienced a recession in the 1980s, which contrasts starkly with the strong growth experienced in China after the introduction of market reforms (Gerber, 2002:633). However, the Russian transition differed from European countries, such as Hungary. For one thing, Russia retreated to primitive barter relations and a subsistence existence, while Hungary consolidated its money economy. Russia criminalized the economy, while Hungary had an emergent rule of law. In Russia, there was a huge concentration of power in oligarchs; Hungary had a diversified economic structure, where small producers began producing goods and offering services on price-regulating markets in agriculture, the service sector, the construction industry, and some industrial branches (Eyal et al., 1998:177; Burawoy, 2001:1109). Unlike other European countries, Russia chose unlimited "voucher" privatization that allowed mediated participation as a method of property transformation (Laki and Szalai, 2006:324, 340). In Russia, Ukraine and most other CIS countries, new laws allowing free enterprise coexisted for many years with Soviet-period laws and were considered illegal until the mid-1990s (Havrylyshyn, 2006:35).

After the 1980s, the state sector downsized; many state firms entered into contracts with foreign companies, and new opportunities for entrepreneurship emerged. Official control was completely withdrawn, so people could now start private businesses and control the entire budget of their business. By the time the USSR had collapsed at the end of the 1980s, the second economy shifted an ever-expanding proportion of the benefits of economic activity away from the state into private hands, paving the way for self-employment to grow unimpeded in Russia for the first time. The success of Russian entrepreneurs in cities like Toronto was likely influenced by these unique historical circumstances. In particular, Russian immigrants who lived in Russia during the transition or who returned to Russia from Toronto at that time took advantage of privatization schemes and developed networks with state officials, former managers of state enterprises, and new Russian entrepreneurs (known as "New Russians"). They were then able to use these contacts to develop businesses in Toronto.

LITERATURE REVIEW

This chapter draws upon two bodies of literature, specifically the ethnic and class dimensions of entrepreneurship and transnationalism approach, to examine how social capital, financial capital, human capital, and home country experience, specifically experience in the transitional economy affected Russian entrepreneurs at each stage of business development in Toronto.

I selected these two approaches because individual-level explanations which focus on a certain kind of personality and competence are inadequate in explaining the founding and success of a business. Because of their similar backgrounds, individual level explanations may lead to the expectation that new Russian immigrants are prime candidates for ethnic entrepreneurship, but personality and culture do not explain how people who grew up in a similar environment in the former Soviet Union have different rates of entrepreneurship after immigrating to Toronto. I also selected these two approaches because past studies of ethnic businesses have not paid enough attention to the context of the country of origin and the role of the global economy on facilitating the setting up of businesses and the successful running of businesses in the host country.

According to the *ethnic and class dimensions of entrepreneurship approach*, the inclination toward business and the relative success of entrepreneurial efforts by immigrants is a balance of class and ethnic resources (Light, 1984; Waldinger et al., 1990). All groups possess class resources, which include financial, human, and cultural capital and ethnic resources, but the balance varies from group to group. *Ethnic resources* are socio-cultural features of a group which co-ethnic entrepreneurs actively utilize in business or from which their business passively benefits. Typical ethnic resources include relationships of trust, ethnic-derived social capital, native language fluency, a middleman heritage, entrepreneurial values and attitudes, rotating credit associations, multiplex social networks, sojourning orientation, social networks and other characteristics based in group tradition and experience that connect the entire group (Light and Gold, 2000:102-105). Ethnic resources contribute to economic survival and achievement among groups lacking class-based endowments of skill, education, or capital (Light and Gold, 2000:106). Ethnic resources include social networks, and these help to start, develop and run businesses, and further entrepreneurship (Salaff, Greve, and Wong, 2001:12). Newcomers intending to do business can draw on social networks for advice, information about business opportunities, access to credit, and customers, which are central to entrepreneurship during pre-start (motivation and idea development) and start-up (planning and organizing the founding of a firm) (Aldrich, 1999; Light, 1972, 1992; Salaff et al., 2007:102). *Class resources* include financial capital, human capital and professional or entrepreneurial experience (Ley, 2006:745). Money and wealth are the two main forms of *financial capital* (Light and Gold, 2000:84-5). Education and work experience are the basic forms of *human capital*. Evidence shows that among all ethno-racial groups and categories, human capital increases rates of entrepreneurship (Light and Gold, 2000:87). Human and financial capital do not guarantee optimal entrepreneurship. Nor do money and human capital explain intergroup differences in entrepreneurial responsiveness. Therefore, it is necessary to look at the internal characteristics of groups to explain persistent intergroup differences. *Cultural capital* refers to the skills, knowledge, attitudes, and values required to succeed in entrepreneurship which are transmitted in the course of socialization (Light and Gold, 2000:92). The ethnic and class dimensions of entrepreneurship approach focuses on how local social networks impact entrepreneurship and business development and does not fully address the role of transnationalism. Some networks cross borders and draw on business communities back in their home country (Salaff et al, 2001:13). In recent decades, studies documenting the importance of the direct and indirect impact of transnational linkages on ethnic business operation have shown how products, clients, and employees are recruited from either the sending countries or the receiving countries (Kyle, 1999; Landolt, 2001; Fong and Luk, 2007a:11). Growing numbers of migrants are participating in the political, social, and economic lives of their countries of origin, even as they put down roots in their host countries (Levitt, 2001). Such processes are likely to give rise to new structures and forces that determine ethnic entrepreneurship (Zhou, 2004:1054). Therefore, I will turn to the transnationalism approach to demonstrate how immigrants draw on business communities from their home country and from the receiving country–transnational networks–to become successful entrepreneurs in their new host country.

According to the transnationalism approach, immigrant entrepreneurs are increasingly engaging in transnational business practices conducting business between their home and receiving countries (Wong, 2004:143; Fong and Luk, 2007a:10). Immigrants who are bilingual and who have international social networks have serious natural advantages in trade promotion (Collins, 1998:vol 2, 398-99; Lever-Tracy et al., 1991:xi, 113; Light, 2007:90). They more easily notice the business opportunities that cultural frontiers generate and have the international social capital that supports international business (Fukuyama, 1995; Walton-Roberts and Hiebert, 1997; Wong, 1998:95; Light, 2007:90). Immigrants often draw on business communities from their home country and the receiving country. These transnational entrepreneurs reinvest in firms back home while remaining abroad. Other migrants may return to their original country, bringing with them new business connections (Salaff, et al., 2007:100). Immigrant transnational entrepreneurs promote bilateral foreign trade with their homelands, so their businesses are not limited to local markets of the host society (Light, 2001:59; Levitt, 2001). Individuals with more extensive and diverse social networks will be in a better position to initiate and sustain transnational enterprise (Kyle, 1999; Poros, 2001).

In the empirical section which follows, I demonstrate how human capital, social capital, financial capital, and home country experience influenced the path taken to entrepreneurship. These paths represent opportunity structures linked to the structural problems faced by all new immigrants, including these particular immigrants from the former Soviet Union. I also look at the influence of institutional arrangements after the transition to a market economy in Russia, using the central postulates of each of the two theoretical approaches (ethnic and class dimensions of entrepreneurship and transnationalism) to explain the factors that influenced business practice and success in Toronto for the Russian immigrants I interviewed. I will discuss these factors by looking at two phases of entrepreneurship and the founding of a business (see Wilken, 1979): (1) pre-start-up–motivation and idea development and (2) start-up–planning and organizing the founding of a firm. I will compare how these two cohorts learned entrepreneurship skills; where they got ideas about business in Canada; where they learned about getting capital for their business, and how they established or took over existing firms.

PRE-START-UP–MOTIVATION AND IDEA DEVELOPMENT

In the first phase of entrepreneurship and the founding of a business someone is motivated to start a business. The business idea is developed and social support is sought through discussions with other people (Greve, 1995:3). The main incentives for startups include: gaining a better economic position; preventing unemployment; attaining higher social status (Radaev, 1997:33). In the pre-start-up stage, potential entrepreneurs look for advice, financial resources, and moral support from families, friends, and business associates, usually exploring possibilities within a small circle of close contacts. They contact others to test initial ideas, develop a business concept and get further support (Kamm and Nurick, 1993). This section discusses the influence of class and ethnic resources, the transitional economy, and transnational linkages on the pre-start-up stage of an immigrant business in Toronto. It considers where entrepreneurs get motivation and ideas for a business. Unlike Western entrepreneurs for whom the inclination toward business and the relative success of entrepreneurial efforts is influenced mainly by class and ethnic resources within the city where they start their business, immigrant entrepreneurs look to their financial, human, social, and cultural capital acquired elsewhere, in this case, the former Soviet Union.

CLASS RESOURCES: FINANCIAL CAPITAL, HUMAN CAPITAL AND PATHS TO ENTREPRENEURSHIP

Immigrant entrepreneurship success is partly determined by the amount of financial/material resources that immigrants bring with them (Zhou, 2004:1046). Since the Soviet government limited the amount of money and goods that émigrés could take out of the country (only about $100 in Rubles was permitted)

(Gold, 1995:22), the majority of the immigrants came to Toronto with virtually no financial resources. They had also earned low wages in rubles in the state-run economy. A few came with financial resources because they had worked overseas, or had earned money while immigrating through another country to Canada. For example, Leon was allowed to work in Iran, where he was the manager of all construction sites for an Iranian construction company and was in charge of 5000 employees. He worked there from 1975 to 1978, making $10,000 a month; when he immigrated to Toronto in 1978, he had financial capital.

On the other hand, over 40% from the second cohort came with a significant amount of financial resources from businesses they ran in Russia after the transition. The relative absence of constraints on asset appropriation due to a period of regime instability and a privatization program that occurred rapidly and in an unregulated manner and no institutional framework created a new propertied and corporate elite with greater opportunities to maintain control of public assets as they were privatized or to obtain personal ownership of assets and enter the emerging market economy with large business advantages (Walder, 2003:907-8). For example, Victor G., who is a property investor in Toronto, ran several businesses in Russia, and came to Toronto with millions that he made from property investment in Russia.

Both cohorts had considerable human capital, coming to Toronto with a high education and skill sets. The majority of both cohorts had more than three years of work experience in the former Soviet Union before coming to Toronto; about half of the second cohort left state-sector jobs to work in other professional fields or to open up businesses. Those who worked in jobs in other countries before immigrating to Toronto accumulated financial capital and acquired valuable knowledge.

Opportunity theory suggests that when immigrants are working in salary jobs and an opportunity comes up to start a business, they may decide to do so (Aldrich and Waldinger, 1990:114, 116; Cooper, 1986:156). Russian immigrants who took this path to entrepreneurship found opportunities within the organization where they were working and decided to open a business. Over half the immigrants from the first cohort and nearly half from the second cohort found business opportunities within their field or an allied field. Alex started his own business because an opportunity opened up within a field closely related to his field of expertise after developing close connections with a businessman who had good connections in Russia sourcing steel. Alex, an immigrant from the first cohort, decided to quit the company that he was working for in Switzerland after he met someone from Belgium who was a steel trader, and he became his partner in the steel business, and they decided to form a company together in 1992 called Transstall. Alex decided to start the steel business with his friend because he believed that this transnational business would be an effective means of maximizing his human capital returns and expanding his middle-class status through higher earnings and would give him more economic independence. As a result, human capital, in terms of his experience in the labour market in Switzerland and Russia, and social capital came together in a successful venture. Some of the highly educated immigrants, such as Alex, quit their salaried jobs to pursue entrepreneurship because they thought they could better utilize their skills, bicultural literacy, and transnational networks to reap material gains.

Some Russian immigrants started by working for a firm owned by a co-ethnic or a Canadian firm; while working here, they found out about an opportunity to open up a business from their co-ethnic friends, and if they had the necessary resources and capital requirements, they decided to do so. Thirty percent of the immigrants from the first cohort and about twenty percent of the immigrants from the second cohort talked to friends and were convinced by them to leave a salaried position and start a business. Leon, an immigrant from the first cohort, talked to friends while he was working in a salaried job that was within his field of expertise. They mentioned a business opportunity, and he decided to leave his well-paying salaried job to start a business with them. Thus, his social capital was important. The chance encounter with friends from the Russian community who were in the process of opening up a business led Leon to leave his salaried position. Leon believed that this transnational business would be an effective means of maximizing his human capital returns and expanding his middle-class status through higher earnings and would give him more economic independence.

Business Background theory suggests that immigrants who have business experience outside of North America or in their country of origin are more likely to use their business experience to establish businesses in their host country (Light, 1984; Bonacich, 1973; Portes and Bach, 1985). This path to entrepreneurship is consistent with the transitional economy approach (Pontusson, 1995:119; Nee, 1991:267), which states that the immigrants who were present during the transition to a market economy are more likely to set up businesses and come to Toronto with business experience and financial capital.

Victor G., as mentioned previously, opened a construction company and started building apartments and malls throughout Russia after the transition; he had no work experience in Toronto before starting a similar business.

Before his immigration, Boris opened a furniture business where he manufactured furniture cheaply and sold it for a large profit in Russia, Europe and Israel. When he moved to Toronto he continued to operate his furniture business in Russia. He had also opened a business in Brazil where he produced vodka and sold it to various countries; he also produced vodka in Russia. Boris came to Canada with business experience from Russia and financial capital from his businesses in Russia and Brazil.

ETHNIC RESOURCES: ETHNIC SOCIAL NETWORKS AND SOCIAL CAPITAL

The established community of earlier Russian immigrants in Toronto, a form of social capital in the host country, did not provide any information to the immigrant entrepreneurs from either cohort regarding the business climate or the types of enterprises that would be feasible in Toronto.

Some immigrant entrepreneurs drew upon their ethnic resources. For example, Alex, an immigrant from the first cohort, met his current partner, Edward, a fellow Russian, who was working as a head representative for a Hong Kong-based steel trading company. Edward knew all the general directors in Russia, and he knew the steel business inside out. Alex convinced Edward to become his partner, telling him he would be given freedom to operate and much more authority in their new company, Midland. Alex also offered to finance it. He took the capital that he needed from his old company, Transtall, which eventually stopped operating. In this case, Alex used his ethnic resources to enhance his business.

START-UP - PLANNING AND ORGANIZING THE FOUNDING OF A FIRM

In the second phase of entrepreneurship entrepreneurs start planning the business in detail; they work on financing the business, setting up business deals, agreements, and finding a property for their business (Greve, 1995:3). In the start-up stage they establish their companies, reaching out to partners, staff, buyers, and suppliers. At this point, entrepreneurs need to mobilize a larger social network (Carter et al., 1996). The two theoretical approaches, ethnic and class dimensions of entrepreneurship and transnationalism, help explain how various factors, including financial, human, social, and cultural capital influenced the start-up. I maintain that while their class resources came into play, their ethnic resources were much less important.

CLASS RESOURCES: HUMAN CAPITAL

Some Russian immigrants from the second cohort obtained entrepreneurial experience by setting up business after the transition to a market economy in Russia or by going to other countries, and they used this experience to set up businesses in Toronto. One-third of the immigrants from the second cohort came to

Canada with business experience and financial capital, already knowing they were going to do business. One such entrepreneur is Misha K., an immigrant from the second cohort, who has an MA in electro-mechanical engineering from the Technical University in Haifa, Israel. When he came to Toronto in 1998, he planned to continue in the telecommunications industry, where he had business experience opening companies in several countries. He opened a telecommunications company in Toronto three years after arriving, with the intention of providing international long distance services for mostly the Russian community.

In this case, Misha K. came to Canada with international business experience and financial capital, already knowing that he was going to do business. Although he had little work experience in Toronto, he drew upon his human capital, in terms of his expertise and experience in the international telecommunications industry, his social capital, in terms of his connections to providers around the world, and his financial capital.

CLASS RESOURCES: FINANCIAL CAPITAL

The choice of financing source shows that human capital, in the form of years of education, work experience and high occupational skills, was recognized by the banks and the government. As a result, the majority of the immigrants obtained financing from traditional sources of capital, such as banks, or from a combination of sources, such as banks and private investors to start businesses in Toronto. The immigrants from the second cohort who came to Canada with human capital, business experience and financial capital intending to open a business obtained financial capital from their own financing and/or from a variety of sources. Misha K. had financial resources that he accumulated from several international telecommunications and project management companies that he opened in several countries. He used this to open a telecommunications and international project management business in the field of mechanical and electrical engineering, and he also got a loan from the bank.

ETHNIC RESOURCES: ETHNIC SOCIAL NETWORKS AND SOCIAL CAPITAL

Ethnic groups regularly provide their members with financial capital through personal loans, which rely on reputation and enduring relationships as collateral (what Light and Bonacich (1988) call ethnic facilitation), but this was not the case for my entrepreneurs. The Russian ethnic community did not provide the majority of the entrepreneurs with any business advantages. Possibly they had adequate financial means already, or they had social capital in terms of education to obtain resources in Toronto. At any rate, none of the immigrants knew anyone in Toronto before they arrived. As a result, the majority of the entrepreneurs turned to banks and private investors for seed capital.

These entrepreneurs began to network through mainstream and formal channels (i.e., professional associations and specific trade organizations), rather than joining ethnic associations or organizations. Igor A., an immigrant from the first cohort, went to various fishing and hunting, sporting goods, and outdoor shows in the United States, Canada and Europe, such as ISPO where he found many of the distributors and chain stores that are now selling his fishing rods.

Some of the entrepreneurs came with their own financial capital which they used to open up their business. Gabe worked in Moscow as an institutional equity salesman for a U.S-Russian investment bank called UFG (United Financial Group), and he made so much money in Moscow that he didn't need to borrow any money when opening his investment company in Toronto. Michael T. used the money that he made in construction jobs to open his company; he has a branch in the Ukraine which manufactures patented concrete reinforcers, and sells them to the construction industry across North America.

The success of 13% of the entrepreneurs from the first cohort and 33% of the entrepreneurs from the second cohort was dependent upon their ability to utilize ethnic resources. These entrepreneurs targeted their businesses to the Russian ethnic community, hired co-ethnic employees, and used co-ethnic suppliers to buy their products. Paul, an immigrant from the first cohort, knew nothing about the grocery business, but together with a few people from his Russian ethnic group, he formed a food importing company called S&F Foods. Paul and his partners imported food from Europe and Russia and sold about 70% of their products to an ethnic network of delicatessens across Toronto. Valera, an immigrant from the second cohort, started the first Russian ethnic television channel in Toronto with his wife. The channel, called Russian Waves, is targeted exclusively to the Russian community. All journalists are Russian. This network combines reports on Russian immigrants in Toronto and programming from Russia, including news and entertainment. Misha K. targeted his Toronto telecommunications company to his ethnic community, providing international long distance services for mostly the Russian community.

The majority of the immigrants from both cohorts did not target their businesses to the Russian enclave community or eventually expanded to other communities because they believed that they could make more money selling their products in a variety of different communities. Arkady, an immigrant from the first cohort, says his company, Eurotrade, imports a variety of food products from Russia. Some of his salespeople are Russian, and they sell many products in Russian meat and deli stores, but over time he expanded to stores across Ontario.

The majority of the immigrants did not target their businesses to the Russian enclave community because they were concentrated in mechanical and technical fields where they manufactured and sold products to anyone in their field. For example, Paul, an immigrant from the first cohort, owns a software company called pVelocity, which sells software to companies all over the world. Ilya, an immigrant from the first cohort, owns ITS Technology, which provides satellite communication technology for the military and satellite industry in Canada and other countries.

CLASS RESOURCES: CLASS-SPECIFIC CULTURAL CAPITAL

Russian immigrants obtained cultural capital, in the form of skills, knowledge, attitudes, and values required to plan and organize the founding of their business in Toronto from experience in the Toronto labour market and from the market transition economy in Russia.

ENTREPRENEURIAL EXPERIENCE DEVELOPED IN THE LABOUR MARKET IN TORONTO OR OUTSIDE TORONTO THAT HELPED ENTREPRENEURS START BUSINESSES IN TORONTO

Since the first-cohort immigrants had limited access to relevant home country business experience Canadian business experience is vital to the success of their enterprises. However, entrepreneurs from both cohorts, regardless of their path to entrepreneurship, all said their experience in the labour market in Toronto helped them develop the skills, knowledge, experience, and contacts required to eventually start their own businesses.

Ilya, an immigrant from the first cohort, arrived with human capital and worked in his field for a few years. Because of his social capital, he found a business opportunity within his field, and decided to leave his salaried job. Ilya says he gained experience to start his own company while working as a salaried employee. Ilya started his company, ITS Technology, after working for Malco and Associates in the United States and Canada for four years. At Malco he brought technologies purchased from Advancetech to Canada for the defense and satellite industry. While working at Malco, he realized that there were no longer any companies that were providing the services required by the military and satellite industry in Canada–in short, he discovered a niche.

Another entrepreneur from the first cohort who worked in his field for a few years and because of his social capital, found a business opportunity within his field, and decided to leave his salaried job, but who received all his education and job experience in Canada is Paul. He obtained training and experience at IBM and at a software company, Unitech, which he later used to start his own software company.

When second-cohort member Misha K. arrived in Toronto, he had human capital, business experience, and financial capital and knew he was going into business. He had gained work experience in international telecommunications and project management companies that he opened in several countries before coming to Toronto. His past experience helped him to open Lorotel, his telecommunications and international project management business in the field of mechanical and electrical engineering.

ENTREPRENEURIAL SKILLS AND TRANSNATIONAL ETHNIC NETWORKS DEVELOPED DURING THE TRANSITION ECONOMY IN RUSSIA THAT HELPED ENTREPRENEURS START TRANSNATIONAL BUSINESSES BASED IN TORONTO OR RUSSIA

An important form of immigrant economic adaptation is the practice of transnationalism. The likelihood of establishing transnational businesses for both cohorts of immigrants from the former Soviet Union depended to some extent on the alliances forged at the beginning of the transition process between these immigrants and (a) state elites; (b) financial sector elites; and (c) Russian entrepreneurs. It was important for these immigrants to have connections to former managers of public enterprises who emerged as modern corporate executives, freed of the restraints of the command economy, as they acquired the majority of shares in most of the privatized and privatizing firms and assumed control of capital intensive firms. These firms required large capital investments to develop (often from abroad); some immigrants took advantage of this and established Toronto companies which entered into contracts with these state firms and provided the capital investment that they needed. About 35% of the immigrant entrepreneurs from the first cohort and the second cohort were able to develop businesses in Toronto with links to Russia because they had connections to elite insiders in the former Soviet Union.

Abe began to do business in the former Soviet Union during the transition because business was slow in Toronto. In 1993, Abe began building overseas when he established connections with people who came to Toronto from the former Soviet republics. Opportunities started to emerge as a result of the changes going on in the former Soviet Union. Abe's extensive and diverse social networks in Canada and Russia helped him to initiate and sustain a transnational enterprise.

Abe built commercial office buildings, shopping malls, retail, and high rise residential buildings in Russia, Kazakhstan, Ukraine, Lithuania, and Latvia. He was able to deal with government regulations because he spoke the language and could speak directly to the people in the government when he needed building and construction permits. He obtained supplies and construction material from Canada because it was cheaper to bring the supplies from Canada or the US. For the most part, he was hired by private companies and individuals. One of his biggest customers was a Pension Fund company, New Century Holdings, based in New York; this company was a big investor in the former Soviet Union, and the money came from companies such as General Motors, Kodak, etc. Then he got contracts in Almata, Kazakhstan, and Riga, Latvia.

Jacob, an immigrant from the first cohort, got involved in Russia and the Ukraine by organizing space conferences. After developing contacts at these conferences he decided to introduce his company, Integrity Testing Laboratory, which tests and produces materials for aerospace applications, to space researchers in the Ukraine and Russia. Jacob says that his business opportunities emerged as a direct result of the market transition:

> Before the transition happened, they didn't allow me to go to the Soviet Union to attend space conferences, which I was invited to, but couldn't attend because I was never given a visa to enter the country. The fact that you were now able to go and do business there is a direct consequence of the transition.

Igor S. is an immigrant from the first cohort, became successful by acting as an intermediary between a buyer in the Ukraine and a supplier in India. He established a trading company that supplied some medical goods that were in short supply in the Ukraine during the transition. He could do so because of his connections:

> It came through networking. A friend of mine was already doing business with Ukraine in construction materials. He told me that there are opportunities there; they still don't have a lot of medical supplies, and they can't afford the high-priced American goods. He had a relationship with someone high in the ministry of health, so it was very easy for us to follow all of the government regulations.

Alex, an immigrant from the first cohort, because of his connections, was able to establish a company, Midland, which sourced steel from Russia and the Ukraine for low prices and sold it all over the world for large profits. Alex established his first connections in the former Soviet Union by working for companies doing business there. He moved with his family to Switzerland to work in a global steel trading company that was doing business in Russia. When he met a steel trader from Belgium, they decided to form a company together in 1992 called Transtall. They saw it as an opportunity since Alex had contacts in Russia and would be able to source the steel. Alex initially obtained steel by bartering and trading. He and his partner didn't need a lot of capital because these companies were willing to give up their steel based on trust. Many foreign companies took advantage of this trust and made millions. But Alex and his partner decided not to break the relationship they had built up, and this gave them an advantage over other foreign companies.

Initially Alex and his Belgium partner made money by trading goods for steel (bartering). Later, they decided to concentrate only on selling steel. Alex and his partner had an advantage because the company directors had no knowledge of how to operate in a free market global economy.

When the transition proceeded, the economic climate began to change and companies in the former Soviet Union were no longer willing to conduct business with foreign companies based only on trust; they now wanted prepayment for their products. Around 1993, the director of the steel mill in the Ukraine started requesting money upfront. Once again, Alex and his partner had an advantage over other foreign companies.

Then the steel mills began to have problems with the companies producing the raw materials. For example, the coal mine would not release coal to the steel company because it already owed them too much money. The whole system collapsed; more specifically, the supply chain collapsed because of the large debts between the companies producing the raw materials and the steel mill. Transtall mended the supply chain and the payment orders. Because they had good connections with the companies producing the raw materials Alex and his partner had a new opportunity.

In 1993, Alex met his current partner, Edward, who was working as a head representative for a Hong Kong based steel trading company. Edward had great contacts. He knew all the general directors in Russia and the Ukraine and he knew the steel business inside out. Alex and his new partner decided that to beat out all the foreign competition, they had to buy the largest steel mill in the Ukraine. Alex claims that they were successful in buying the steel mill because other foreign companies weren't willing to take the risk.

Alex's insider information and contacts in large scale state and private ventures bestowed credibility on his efforts. Drawing on transnational ties for social capital, Alex pieced together resources from many institutional fields. His networks bridged core industries in several countries. In network terms, he linked networks and created opportunities by spanning structural holes (Burt, 1992). He got ideas from different contacts and combined resources in novel ways, which is essential to starting profitable businesses (Burt, 1992; Salaff et al., 2007:101). Alex's ethnic background and Russian and Canadian networks legitimated him among the Russian players. His brokering role is atypical of enclave businesses, in that his role is more like any other importer or exporter of goods and services. But at the same time, his ethnic background enables his business ties. Like many other enclave and mainstream businesses he depends on transnational links, and his links were activated through his migration to Canada.

Sam, another immigrant from the first cohort, established contacts on a business trip to the Ukraine for his former employer during the transition in 1995; he met the manager of a plant that manufactures Carbon Black. He discovered there was a demand for Carbon Black in the rubber and tire industries in Canada and the US, so he formed a partnership with the director of the company and is now part owner of the company in the Ukraine. He established a company, Sunrock, which imports synthetic chemicals:

> On one of my business trips to Russia for my former employer, I accidentally met a manager of a factory that produces Carbon Black at a Russian restaurant. At the time, I didn't even know what Carbon Black was. He told me about the industries which use Carbon Black, and he asked me if I could help him export Carbon Black into the US and Canada. So, upon my return to Toronto, I did a lot of research, and I found out that there was a large demand for Carbon Black in Canada and the US, but at a much lower price than it was currently being sold at. I found a customer in Canada who bought a rubber plant and he was looking for suppliers of Carbon Black, so we made a business out of it, and he is now my main buyer. Then I found out about other companies that were also in the market for Carbon Black. In 1995, I went 10 times to the Ukraine and Russia before I started Carbon Black because first I had to prove that the product was good. I traveled to several plants in Russia and established connections with the plant managers. I agreed to buy it from them for a price that was considerably lower than the global market price and sell it in North America. They agreed to give me the exclusive rights to sell Carbon Black from their plants to North America. We started with Carbon Black; today we have synthetic rubber and chemicals.

Michael T., another first-cohort immigrant, went to Russia and the Ukraine during the transition in 1990 to find material that he could manufacture in Russia or the Ukraine at a fairly low cost and then sell it to the construction industry in Toronto. He established contacts with local partners and directors of construction companies in the Ukraine and Russia, patented this construction equipment, and started exporting it from the Ukraine to Canada.

The enterprises established by immigrants like Sam, Alex, and Michael T. involved the production of goods at low prices which they could sell overseas for a large profit margin. Alex used his links in Russia and Ukraine to obtain a license from the government (not granted to everyone) to export steel at still-low Soviet prices to Canada and the US or anywhere else where it fetched a higher price, so he was able to make a lot of money very quickly. Some time elapsed between legalization of private activity and the elimination of government regulations, creating a gap between market prices and official prices and setting up opportunities for the new capitalists in Russia and Toronto, such as Alex, Sam, and Michael T., to maximize profits.

Leon, an immigrant from the first cohort, initially started Luxan Shoes with a few partners in 1980; they manufactured Italian shoes for major retail stores in Canada. Then they decided to expand to Moldova and the Ukraine in 1991. They were able to build successful shoe manufacturing plants in the former Soviet Union during the transition because he had good connections to former managers of state enterprises and to government officials. Leon had to close down the factories in Moldova and the Ukraine in 1997 because of legal changes and the dangers of doing business in the former Soviet Union

Mark, who is currently the President of NEOS, an affiliate of E. H. Harms Company, is an immigrant from the first cohort who also established contacts during his business trips to Russia during the transition in the 1990s, and because of his connections he was able to set up businesses in Russia.

Like the other entrepreneurs, he found that he had good profit margins doing transnational business –but again, this was based on his connections.

Boris, an immigrant from the second cohort, was able to set up a furniture manufacturing plant and store in Russia that sold furniture in Russia, Europe, and other markets in the world because he had connections and because there was a large demand:

> When I came back to Russia it was a new country and everything started to grow. In 1995, I decided to open a furniture business. My partner and I had connections to the government to deal with logistics and people at the border to let some of our parts arrive from Germany with having to pay high tariffs. We built our own factory and we manufactured the furniture in Russia and Germany and sold it in Russia, Israel, Europe, and Canada. When we opened our first shop, the next morning we sold all our furniture exhibition. There was a huge line up all day. There was nothing in Russia at all, so people were starving for anything.

After a few years of successful sales, he decided that he didn't want to spend most of the year in Russia watching over his business while his family lived in Toronto, so he moved back to Toronto and opened Sunca Hardwood, which imports hardwood floors from a manufacturer in Russia and Brazil; he sells it to individual customers and private contractors in Toronto. He also exports hardwood from Brazil to Russia and Kazakhstan, and from Brazil and Russia to Spain.

The people who became successful entrepreneurs in Russia during the transition to a market economy, such as Sam, Michael T., Mark, Abe, Leon, Igor S., and Alex, were double entrepreneurs (Yang, 2002). They were innovative and creative in identifying and creating new markets to export the goods that were manufactured in the state-run economy before the transition and discovering what goods were in demand and therefore should be imported from the West to Russia. They were talented in making use of and manipulating institutional rules, such as government regulations; this was valuable when the government introduced laws to promote the establishment of private enterprises. Because these entrepreneurs had connections with people who knew members of the government or had personal connections with members of the government, they could manipulate the new laws.

Immigrant entrepreneurs do not merely react to structural disadvantages they face in their host countries but actively look for opportunities and market niches beyond the national boundaries of the receiving countries, utilizing their bicultural skills and binational ethnic networks. Drawing on transnational networks to their country of origin, some Russian immigrant entrepreneurs mobilized resources for their businesses that were not available locally. Those with extensive and diverse international social networks, such as Alex, Sam, Michael T., Mark, Igor S., Leon, and Abe, were in a good position to initiate and sustain transnational entrepreneurship. They better understood the cultural aspects of business practices, the government regulations in the former Soviet Union, and the language, and were able to link up easily with distributors and retailers in Toronto. This constituted a form of "insider advantage."

As transnational entrepreneurs, Sam, Michael T., Mark, Igor S., Abe, Leon, and Alex, are part of the elite in their communities; from their activities they make higher-than-average incomes. These transnational entrepreneurs travel frequently between their permanent homes in the West where their families stay and their business in their country of origin. Alex travels every month to the Ukraine to his steel company to conduct business, while his family stays in Toronto.

CONCLUSION

The success of immigrant entrepreneurs in the two phases of entrepreneurship (pre-start-up and start-up) is influenced by a combination of the following factors: 1) social capital, 2) financial capital, 3) human capital, and 4) home country experience. To understand how the above four factors influence the success of immigrant entrepreneurs in the two phases of entrepreneurship, it is necessary to use a multi-level theoretical approach which includes the following perspectives: ethnic and class dimensions of entrepreneurship and transnationalism. Rather than seeing class and ethnic resources as competing, when we use longitudinal analysis we can see how both class and ethnic resources are important at different times and stages of business development.

The experience of Russian immigrants from the former Soviet Union casts light on our understanding of contemporary immigrant entrepreneurship, reminding us that we cannot glibly generalize about all immigrants–each case has its own unique qualities. Since the collapse of the Soviet Union, immigrants from the former Soviet republics have immigrated to countries such as the United States and Canada, and settled in metropolitan areas like Toronto. They have made millions establishing businesses in their new host countries. This research was the first systematic study done in Canada to focus on these immigrant entrepreneurs.

This chapter focuses on the emerging phenomenon of immigrants arriving with a lot of human capital, and some with a great deal of financial capital, establishing medium and large businesses. The Russian immigrants interviewed all came with human capital; most of the second cohort had financial capital, management experience and business knowledge. In contrast to past research showing that medium and large businesses would be run by native-born Canadians and established immigrants who had worked their way up, my research demonstrates that as a result of globalization, the tendency of the immigrants interviewed was to establish not only small businesses in an enclave market, but also medium and large businesses in a diversity of industries, many with transnational links to Russia.

Both cohorts of immigrant entrepreneurs embodied considerable human capital, coming to Toronto with a good education and excellent skill sets. They had technical and professional degrees and had graduated from university, many with higher degrees. This seems to indicate that those with significant amounts of human capital may make more effective entrepreneurs. Overall, the degrees they attained corresponded to the business they established.

Some first-cohort immigrant entrepreneurs accumulated financial resources and business experience in other countries before coming to Canada; they worked at various jobs or opened businesses. About half of the second cohort came with a significant amount of money they made in business after the transition.

The second cohort came to Toronto after the transition to a market economy in Russia; therefore, they were more likely to have entrepreneurship experience in the former Soviet Union and to come with enough financial capital to start a business. They were also more likely to arrive knowing that they wanted to do business. Since the first cohort immigrated without any entrepreneurial experience in the former Soviet Union, most found jobs where they worked for over 5 years before starting a business.

Second-cohort immigrants who lived in Russia during the transition and those from the first cohort who returned to Russia at that time obtained valuable cultural capital. They were likely to have built up transnational social networks, connections with state enterprise directors, state elites and business groups, which they used to good effect in Toronto.

The transnational entrepreneurs derive higher-than-average incomes. They succeeded because they actively looked for opportunities and market niches beyond the national boundaries of the receiving countries. They had a distinct advantage in forming transnational businesses with republics in the former Soviet Union because they understood how to conduct business there, the government regulations, and the language, and they were able to link up with distributors and retailers in Toronto. The entrepreneurs with extensive and diverse international social networks were in a better position to initiate and sustain transnational entrepreneurship. They set up new joint private firms with entrepreneurs and managers of enterprises in Russia, who could take advantage of the combination of legalization of private businesses and the continued government regulation of prices, export, import and internal trade licensing.

In the case of the Russian immigrant entrepreneurs, transnational entrepreneurship does not financially benefit the ethnic community, as these entrepreneurs seem to be only concerned with making millions for themselves.

REFERENCES

Aldrich, H. (1999). *Organizations Evolving*. Thousand Oaks: Sage.

Aldrich, H., and R. Waldinger. (1990). "Ethnicity and Entrepreneurship." *Annual Review of Sociology* 16:111-135.

Bates, T. (1994). "Social Resources Generated by Group Support Networks May Not be Beneficial to Asian Immigrant-Owned Small Businesses." *Social Forces* 72(3): 671-689.

Bonacich, E. (1973). "A Theory of Middleman Minorities." *American Sociological Review* 38:583-594.

Bonacich, E., and J. Modell. (1980). *The Economic Basis of Ethnic Solidarity: Small Business in the Japanese-American Community*. Berkeley: University of California Press.

Burawoy, M. (2001). "Neoclassical Sociology: From the End of Communism to the End of Classes." *American Journal of Sociology* 106(4):1099-1120.

Burt, R. (1992). *Structural Holes: The Social Structure of Competition*. Cambridge: Harvard University Press.

Carter, N.M., W.B. Gartner, and P.D. Reynolds. (1996). "Exploring Start-Up Event Sequences." *Journal of Business Venturing* 11(3):151-166.

Chan, J., and Y-W. Cheung. (1985). "Ethnic Resources and Business Enterprise: A Study of Chinese Businesses in Toronto." *Human Organization* 44(2):142-154.

Collins, J. (1998). "Cosmopolitan Capitalism: Ethnicity, Gender and Australian Entrepreneurs," Vols. 1 and 2, PhD diss., University of Wollongong.

Cooper, A.C. 1986. "Entrepreneurship and High Technology." In D.L. Sexton and R.W. Smiler (eds.), *The Art and Science of Entrepreneurship*. Cambridge: Ballinger Publishing.

Eyal, G., I. Szelenyi, and E. Townsley. (1998). *Making Capitalism without Capitalists*. London: Verso.

Fong, E., and C. Luk. (2007a). "Introduction." In E. Fong and C. Luk (eds.), *Chinese Ethnic Business*. NY: Routledge.

_____ (2007b). "Conclusion." In E. Fong and C. Luk (eds.), *Chinese Ethnic Business*. NY: Routledge.

Fukuyama, F. (1995). "Social Capital and the Global Economy." *Foreign Affairs* 74:89-113.

Gerber, T.P. (2002). "Structural Change and Post-Socialist Stratification: Labor Market Transitions in Contemporary Russia." *American Sociological Review* 67:629-59.

Gold, S.J. (1995). *From the Workers' State to the Golden State: Jews from the Former Soviet Union in California.* Massachusetts: Allyn and Bacon.

Greve, A. (1995). "Networks and Entrepreneurship–An Analysis of Social Relations, Occupational Background, and Use of Contacts during the Establishment Process." *Scandinavian Journal of Management* 11(1):1-24.

Havrylyshyn, O. (2006). *Divergent Paths in Post-Communist Transformation: Capitalism for All or Capitalism for Few?* NY: Palgrave Macmillan Press.

Kamm, J.B., and A.J. Nurick. (1993). "The Stages of Team Venture Formation: A Decision Making Model." *Entrepreneurship: Theory and Practice* 17(2):17-27.

Kyle, D. (1999). "The Otavalo Trade Diaspora: Social Capital and Transnational Entrepreneurship." *Ethnic and Racial Studies* 22(2):422-446.

Laki, M., and J. Szalai. (2006). "The Puzzle of Success: Hungarian Entrepreneurs at the Turn of the Millennium." *Europe-Asia Studies* 58(3):317-345.

Landolt, P. (2001). "Salvadoran Economic Transnationalism: Embedded Strategies for Household Maintenance, Immigrant Incorporation, and Entrepreneurial Expansion." *Global Networks* 1:217-242.

Lever-Tracy, C. et al. (1991). *Asian Entrepreneurs in Australia.* Canberra: Australian Government Publishing Service.

Levitt, P. (2001). *The Transnational Villagers.* Berkeley: University of California Press.

Ley, D. (2006). "Explaining Variations in Business Performance among Immigrant Entrepreneurs in Canada." *Journal of Ethnic and Migration Studies* 32(5):743-764.

Li, P.S. (1998). *The Chinese in Canada*, 2nd ed. Toronto: Oxford University Press.

Light, I. (2007). "Globalization, Transnationalism, and Chinese Transnationalism." In E. Fong and C. Luk (eds.), *Chinese Ethnic Business.* NY: Rouledge.

_____. (2001). "Globalization, Transnationalism and Trade." *Asian and Pacific Migration Journal* 10(1):53-79.

_____. (1992). *Immigrant Networks and Immigrant Entrepreneurship.* Los Angeles: Institute for Social Science Research, University of California, Los Angeles.

_____. (1984). "Immigrant and Ethnic Enterprise in North America." *Ethnic and Racial Studies* 7(2):195-216.

_____. (1972). *Ethnic Enterprise in America: Business and Welfare among Chinese, Japanese, and Blacks.* Berkeley: University of California Press.

Light, I., and S.J. Gold. (2000). *Ethnic Economies.* San Diego: Academic Press.

Light, I., and E. Bonacich. (1988). *Immigrant Entrepreneurs: Koreans in Los Angeles, 1965-1982.* Berkeley: University of California Press.

Lo, L., and S. Wang. (2007). "The New Chinese Business Sector in Toronto." In E. Fong and C. Luk (eds.), *Chinese Ethnic Business.* NY: Routledge.

Nee, V. (1991). "Social Inequalities in Reforming State Socialism: Between Redistribution and Markets in China." *American Sociological Review* 56:267-282.

Pontusson, J. (1995). "From Comparative Public Policy to Political Economy: Putting Political Institutions in Their Place and Taking Interests Seriously." *Comparative Political Studies* 28(1):117-147.

Poros, M.V. (2001). "The Role of Migrant Networks in Linking Local Labour Markets: The Case of Asian Indian Migration to New York and London." *Global Networks* 1:243-60.

Portes, A., and R.I. Bach. (1985). *The Latin Journey: Cuban and Mexican Immigrants in the United States.* Berkeley: University of California Press.

Radaev, V. (1997). "Practicing and Potential Entrepreneurs in Russia." *International Journal of Sociology* 27(3):15-50.

Razin, E. (1992). "Paths to Ownership of Small Businesses among Immigrants in Israeli Cities and Towns." *The Review of Regional Studies* 22:277-296.

Salaff, J., A. Greve, and S.L. Wong. (2007). "Business Social Networks and Immigrant Entrepreneurs from China." In E. Fong and C. Luk (eds.), *Chinese Ethnic Business.* NY: Routledge.

_____. 2001. "Professionals from China: Entrepreneurship and Social Resources in a Strange Land." *Asian and Pacific Migration Journal* 10(1):9-33.

Timmons, J.A. (1986). "Growing Up Big: Entrepreneurship and the Creation of High-Potential Ventures." In D.L. Sexton and R.W. Smiler (eds.), *The Art and Science of Entrepreneurship.* Cambridge, MA: Ballinger Publishing.

Walder, A. (2003). "Elite Opportunity in Transitional Economies." *American Sociological Review* 68(6): 899-916.

Waldinger, R., H. Aldrich, R. Ward et al. (1990). *Ethnic Entrepreneurs: Immigrant Business in Industrial Societies.* Newbury Park: Sage.

Walton-Roberts, M., and D. Hiebert. (1997). "Immigration, Entrepreneurship, and the Family: Indo-Canadian Enterprise in the Construction of Greater Vancouver." *Canadian Journal of Regional Science* 20:119-140.

Wilken, P.H. (1979). *Entrepreneurship: A Comparative and Historical Study.* Norwood: Ablex.

Wong, B. (1998). *Ethnicity and Entrepreneurship: The New Chinese Immigrants in the San Francisco Bay Area.* Boston: Allyn and Bacon.

Wong, L L. (2004). "Taiwanese Immigrant Entrepreneurs in Canada and Transnational Space." *International Migration Review* 42(2):113-152.

Yang, K. (2002). "Double Entrepreneurship in China's Economic Reform: An Analytical Framework." *Journal of Political and Military Sociology* 30(1):134-148.

Zhou, M. (2004). "Revisiting Ethnic Entrepreneurship: Convergencies, Controversies, and Conceptual Advancements." *The International Migration Review* 38(3):1040-1074.

_____. (1992). *Chinatown: The Socioeconomic Potential of an Urban Enclave.* Philadelphia: Temple University Press.

PART V

Future Trends

The last section of this anthology concerns future uses of sociology in a changing society such as Canada.

In Chapter 18, our co-editor, McCauley is concerned with the broad concept of **social change**. He discusses the varieties of theories and paradigms available to assist students in the questioning of the nature of social change given the processes and practices of globalization.

Chapater 19 by Andrews, Pete and Paul on **education** presents issues of contemporary Canadian education as it engages with the globalizing 21st Century world. The authors argue that the true promise of Canadian education lives in how local school jurisdictions undertake responsibilities, enhance learning, empower diverse learners, and encourage professional development of teachers in concert with the demands of social control and social reform and within the context of local and global tensions.

Chapter 20 by Crosby and Parkins introduces us to the new sub-field in **sociology known as environmental management**.The authors show that Canada faces a number of environment concerns in the 21st Century including water pollution, soil degradation and waste management. These are concerns for Canadians in an global environment and it provides suggestions for future policy directives and sociological research.

Lastly, in Chapter 21, Heather Garrett provides an excellent summary of **research methods** and their theoretical uses. Garrett shows the relationship between qualitative and quantitative research methods to assist students in their production and consumption of sociological studies.

In summary, the section on future trends assists students of sociology to understand the ways in which globalization has affected, and will continue to affect, Canadian society into the second decade of the 21st Century.

Chapter 18

Social Change

Social Change in a Global Framework: Theories and Paradigms for Canadian Sociologists

Timothy P. McCauley

York University

INTRODUCTION

The objective of this chapter is to examine the significance of social change in relation to Canada in a global framework. For the purposes of this discussion, I define social change as

> alterations in institutions, cultural values and norms, technology and material conditions as society moves forward in time.

It is argued here that social change is a key concept in both classical and contemporary theories of human society. Social change to structural functional scholars is adaptive; social change to Marxists is dialectical; while social change to the symbolic interactionist reflects the rationalization of human society. All of the perspectives above differ from post-modern theorists who contend that social change is fragmented and chaotic. Moreover, by examining social change with respect to the paradigms above, we attempt to show how they may assist Canadian sociologist interested in globalization.

The first classical theory of human society is Durkheim's functional approach developed within his *Division of Labour in Society* (1893) and *The Elementary Forms of Religious Life* (1912). In each of these studies, Durkheim finds that social change is slow and incremental and it is an adaptive process. To Durkheim, social change in human society moves gradually from mechanical to organic solidarity. Mechanical solidarity occurs within tribal cultures and to some extent in traditional communities prior to industrialization. This form of solidarity is deemed "mechanical" in that its members do not think about the nature of the ties to the social group; solidarity happens mechanically through key symbols such as the totem. Primitive man does not reflect upon group life insofar as it is *a-priori* and *sui-generi*. In contrast, human communities in the modern world are characterized by organic solidarity. Organic solidarity is maintained through collective consciousness. Ties are weaker and more abstract, and yet, they nevertheless sustain the integrity of group life on a large scale. For example, Robert Bellah's concept of *Civil Religion* (1963) is an example of how American society is held together through civil religious symbols such as the flag, the eagle, the Lincoln Memorial, Arlington Cemetery and the Washington Monument. Bellah supports Durkheim's contention that the movement from mechanical to organic solidarity is an adaptive process: Gradually group life becomes more differentiated and more organic, yet collective bonds remain constant in the modern framework (Bellah, 1963:12). Thus, social change to Durkheim and Bellah, the functionalists, is indeed adaptive, and although some scholars describe structural functionalist as static and ahistorical, social change is an element of this approach.

For example, another key structural functional theory is generated by Talcott Parsons in his work on *The Social System* (1951). Parsons argues that over time, institutions characterized by norms and rules grow increasingly diverse and differentiated. Gradually, the differences between the political, economic, religious institutions grow more pronounced. Institutional change is at the heart of the Parsonian view of the social system. Over time, and only through gradual adaptive processes, institutions in society produce increasing structural differentiation. The family, school, church, economy, and the media are each compartments of a highly differentiated modern social system and yet, they are held to together by a collective consciousness as Durkheim has shown.

A key Canadian structural functionalist in support of Durkheim and Parsons was S.D. Clark, a Professor at the University of Toronto in the 1950s. Clark sought to demonstrate that Canadian social integration is both similar and different from American civil religion through the differences in religious practices in the two countries. Canada produced the "Social Gospel" on the Prairies during the Great Depression, and it was through leftist ideology in Saskatchewan that Canada pushed further left on the political spectrum compared to America. The Social Gospel, initiated by J.S. Woodsworth, eventually became part of the political ideology of the CCF (later termed the NDP). The Social Gospel stood for the right of every individual, rich or poor, to have basic necessities cared for by the Canadian state system. It held that government should support collective ideals insofar as social responsibility overrides individualism. An expert on The Social Gospel, Richard Allen holds that:

> The Social Gospel rested on the premise that Christianity was a social religion, concerned, when the misunderstanding of the ages was stripped away, with the quality of human relations on this earth.

Thus, Clark showed that regional politics and religion in Canada are unique elements of Canadian social behaviour. Collectivism on the Canadian prairies helped to create a unique political economy in Canada (Clark, 1961). And like Parsons in the United States, Clark showed that Canadian social change is adaptive and part of the functioning of the Canadian model or social system.

A radically distinctive theory of social change was developed by Karl Marx and maintained by Marxist scholars for over a century. Marx utilized the Hegelian dialect to show that the development and demise of capitalism was inevitable. The Hegelian dialectic was a means of understanding how ideas are questioned and argued to promote revolutionary social change. The pattern to Hegel involved movement or progress through *thesis, antithesis* and *synthesis*. Through this process, social change occurs as conflicting ideas are transformed or eradicated. To Hegel the "idealist," any system had the potential to "sow the seeds of its own destruction." More importantly, beginning in 1847, Marx used Hegel's notion of "the dialectic" and applied it to an analysis of mankind's material life. Marx's theory of "historical materialism" holds that every human society and mankind itself is fundamentally about production. History has generated a variety of modes of production such as tribal, ancient communal, feudalism and capitalism, and each has contained class conflict: Each will eventually sow the seeds of its own destruction. To classical Marxists then, social change is revolutionary. Social change is not about adaptation but rather it involves revolutionary social transformation.

An example of contemporary Marxist scholarship is evident in the works of George Lukas (1923), Herbert Marcuse (1933) and Raewy Connel (1995). First, Lukas was a contemporary of Marx who sought to explore the role of ideology and false consciousness in the operations of capitalism. Following Marx, he argued that as the contradictions of capitalism become increasingly apparent over time, capitalists become more and more skillful in defending the system through ideology. Notions such as "the cream rises to the top," "any man can become President" and "hard work alone produces success" is proven increasingly false and ideological. Like Marx, Lucas maintained that capitalism will "sow the seeds of its own destruction" as the proletariat grows more aware of their role in history (Lukas, 1979). Second, Marcuse expanded upon Marx's concepts of *objectification, reification* and *alienation*. Marcuse found that industrialization and capitalism increasingly alienates workers from their products to such an extent that the workers de-humanize themselves. Marcuse writes:

> The people recognize themselves in their commodities; they find their soul in their automobile, hi-fi set, split-level home, kitchen equipment. (1964:13)

Thus, Marcuse showed how objectification is inevitable in capitalism as the products of the process take on a "life of their own." Lastly, Connel (1987) demonstrates that the proliferation of mass media is important in understanding how objectification operates. To sell their stories and entertain the public, advertisers and film makers increasing teach the public to "objectify" the self. For example, over time, males in the media demonstrate "hegemonic masculinity" while females are portrayed in terms of "expressive or emphasized femininity." Thus, the contemporary Marxists follow Marx's notion of dialectical materialism; they support Marx's conclusion that capitalism will be eventually transformed in the interest of all. Their view is indeed an "ought" perspective compared to the functionalist "is." Contemporary Marxists foresee capitalism's revolutionary transformation over time.

The third type of theory of social change is developed initially by Max Weber and eventually extended by symbolic interactionists of the Chicago School. Max Weber's thesis was that social change reflects the rationalization of human society in terms of its values, beliefs and behaviours. Weber first developed this theory in his famous text, *The Protestant Ethic and the Spirit of Capitalism* (1904). In his study of religious values of Protestant entrepreneurs, he found that their ideas and beliefs were rooted in a particular type of Protestant theology known as Calvinism. Unlike any other religion in human history, John Calvin's theology introduced to the world the notion of *predestination*. Calvin maintained that each individual has been predestined to a certain fate at birth and this predestination cannot be changed insofar as was pre-determined by God. Thus, the only way Calvinists could find relief from this loneliness and fate was by proving themselves worthy to God through hard work, mundane labour and an internal focus on the afterlife. Moreover, these sets of Protestant ideas Weber called "inner-worldly asceticism." Weber found that inner-worldly asceticism was a key component of the early Protestant entrepreneurs who helped to develop capitalistic society in the late eighteenth century. Weber utilized the sayings of Ben Franklin, a descendent of early Calvinists, to prove his point. Ben Franklin maintained that "time is money" and "early to bed, early to rise makes a man healthy wealthy and wise" (Weber, 1904). In other words, the eighteenth century Protestant emphasis on mundane labour and rational bookkeeping and prudent business practices were rooted in the ideas of Calvin in the sixteenth century. Moreover, Weber's thesis regarding the *Protestant Ethic and Spirit of Capitalism* was his foundation for his later works on the "Great Religions of the World" including Judaism, Islam, Christianity, Hinduism, Buddhism and Confucianism (Gerth and Mills, 1946). Weber finds that each of these religions promoted particular economic orientations to the world, but none of the above displayed inner-worldly asceticism quite like Calvinism. Calvinism was unique and, therefore, while capitalism moves societies towards rational conduct, capitalism was given an added boost by the Protestant Ethic.

The key element in Max Weber's theory of social change is his concept of rationalization. Although he would agree with Marx that social change is about various modes of production; the ideas within these systems are not simply ideologies perpetuated by the ruling class; rather ideas are part of the consciousness and value systems of all of members of capitalistic society as they move human societies forward in time. Weber showed through his focus on "The Protestant Ethic," that social change occurs not simply through changes to material conditions but rather through value orientations in relation to economic behaviour across the globe. Weber believed that all systems move toward economic rationalization through time. Each of the "Great Religions of the World" contained an ethos for social conduct. The Christian, the Jew, the Hindu, the Buddhist and the Muslim all provided unique orientations to conduct through their signs, symbols and language. But for Weber, only Calvinistic Protestantism provided capitalism with an added stimulus that led to the increasing rationalization of the world in the form of bureaucracy. Weber maintained that bureaucrats utilize the same formal rules of conduct that was once the substantive rationality of early Protestant entrepreneurs. Capitalism required "a Spirit," and this Spirit permeates modern culture through formal rationality that imprisons man "like an iron cage." In other words, Weber is a liberal sociologist and a pessimist who believes that formal rationality encapsulates modern man and that it will only be transformed by the "Charismatic rebirth of new Gods" (Weber, 1904:271).

In summary, all of the perspectives above (structural functional, conflict and symbolic interaction) can be deemed as modernist in their approaches. All of these key sociological paradigms equate social change with progress and modernization. Humankind improves over time through social change and society evolves onward and upward. This notion of progress then is a way to differentiate the three paradigms from post-modernism.

Michel Foucault is considered the initiator of the post-modern perspective, which holds that social change, beyond traditional and tribal communities, *does not* improve societies. Societies of the modern world *are not* improved constructions of past epochs; rather they are merely new reflections of the old. Foucault is highly critical of all modernist theorizing found in constructs such as those developed by Durkheim, and in contemporary theories such as Lenski and Lenski (1999). Lenski and Lenski, for example, classified human societies as: hunting and gathering, horticultural, agricultural and industrial, and it was from their modernist typifications that Daniel Bell (1973) generated the concept of "post industrial society." Post- industrial society differs from industrial society through the use of knowledge and whereas the industrial world of the mid-twentieth century emphasized the factory and the eight-hour day, post industrialism functions through social capital- technology, communication and education. Thus, Lenski and Lenski and Bell are contemporary theorists of social change who stand opposed to Foucault and his critique of modernization theories.

Post-modernism is a sociological paradigm rooted in critical theories that do not accept grand narratives of historical change such Lenski and Lenski and Bell. Post-modern theorists believe that historical accounts of social change emphasizing modernization are problematic and rooted in discourse. Consequently, Foucault is critical of all discourses and his intent is to critically evaluate all theories that identify the trends and processes of modernization through language such as structural differentiation, dialectical materialism and rationalization. Each modernist theory constructs trends that may be as limiting as they are illuminating. To Foucault, they are limited constructs created only through language and discourse. Thus, whereas symbolic interactionism is about social constructionism, post-modernism is concerned with deconstructionism. Foucault shows that language is powerful, and the use of language is limited to knowledge communities, or particular types of social constructionism. All paradigms for Foucault must be critically deconstructed insofar as "there are no universals" in a post-modern view of social change. As such, societies *are not* moving onward and upward, rather human history is chaotic and goes round and round (Foucault, 1961).

Therefore, in general, sociology has four main theories of social change namely, *functionalist, Marxist, symbolic interactionist* and *post-modernist.* Any one of these paradigms can help to direct contemporary theorization about social change in the era classified under the heading of globalization. Some theorists describe globalization as an adaptive process, others as dialectical, still others as rationalization, while other describe it in terms of fragmentation.

Three interesting theories relating directly to globalization include McLuhan's concept of the global village, Warren's notion of vertical community, and Ritzer's notion of McDonaldization. For example, in many respects, McLuhan's global village concept supports Foucault and post-modernism. McLuhan was a "renegade scholar" at the University of Toronto in the early 1960s. McLuhan is famous for his "Laws of Media" that demonstrates how technology extends the human senses, and yet, does not generate progress but rather turns the world round and round, backward toward "the village" of primitive man (McLuhan, 1964).

He developed the "Laws of Media" by using the concepts of *enhance, retrieve, reverse* and *obsolesce.* He argues that each new piece of technology such as the television, the radio, the computer, extends human senses in some way. A valuable piece of technology then initially *enhances* human society. The new technology then helps man *retrieve* his own past and enables each new generation to appreciate time and history. Eventually, however, the limits of the new technology become apparent, and the machinery *reverses* on itself. McLuhan wrote: "the speed and beauty of the new car loses it luster as soon as it leaves the 'commercial.'" Thus, eventually a new technology will emerge to show the limitations of previous technology and vice versa. Clearly then, McLuhan's theories of the Laws of Media and Global Village reflects the post- modern tradition. McLuhan is highly critical of man's improvements in technology, and the "medium *is* INDEED the message."

In the 1920s and 30s, William F. Ogburn proposed a very interesting structural functional theory of social change relevant to studies of globalization in Canada. Ogburn (1922) holds that social change involves unbalanced changes to material and non-material culture. He developed his theory by looking at the functions of human family. His essays entitled "The Seven Functions of Family" (1933) and "The Social Characteristics of Cities" (1937) were novel for their day. They showed how five of the seven institutional functions initially performed in the family itself are absorbed by the city. They include: political, economic, religious, protective, and recreational. Social change means that only the affective and reproductive functions remain within a modern, urban family. Ogburn, in consult with Nimcoff, argued that as societies move from agricultural to become more urban and industrial, they produce changes in the family and a loss of basic family functions (Ogburn, 1938). Thus, through his analysis, Ogburn arrives at his famous concept of cultural lag, which is still applicable to an analysis of current globalization and change.

Ogburn argues that cultural lag occurs as changes in the material culture initiate changes upon non-material culture. For example, the introduction of the mass-produced automobiles, such as the Model-T in the 1920s, created massive changes to dating patterns in the family. No longer was the young man required to meet his date inside the girl's family home. Rather, the young man might honk his horn in the driveway and expect the girl to run out and meet him. They could be alone and "go parking" away from the peering eyes of the extended family as a result of the car–a new technology (Ogburn, 1955). Thus, in this example, the non-material culture is forced to adapt and keep up with material changes–the automobile. And, in this case, parents who themselves dated during the Victorian Age were shocked by social change and the behaviour of their daughters. Thus, they suffered from cultural lag in the same way parents today struggle with their children interacting on computers. Clearly, Ogburn's theory is functionalist in that it illustrates how non-material cultures must adapt to changes in material culture. It is useful for sociologists today to observe how cultural lag occurs as a result of global technologies such as the internet, the Blackberry, the iPOD and the MP3 player. People struggle to keep up with new technology. Non-material culture does indeed lag behind changes to material culture.

Roland Warren (1963) is another contemporary theorist of social change. In his book, *Community in America*, he describes concepts such as "the great change" and the "decline of community." These notions assist in understanding how community changes as a result of technology, transportation and communication in the latter stages of the twentieth century. Warren argues that social change affects the very nature of community itself by turning social integration from "horizontal" to "vertical." Older communities, he argues were tied together horizontally. Within any small town, one would find a "cast of characters" or unique individuals performing a number of occupations usually for the community itself. Small towns across America included the local doctor, barber, sheriff, mechanic, and town drunk, and the ties between the community members were holistic and multidimensional. Within any local pub, coffee shop or restaurant, one would find these characters interacting on a daily basis. However, improvements to transportation, greater communication and technology produce great change and the decline of local communities.

Although Warren's book was first produced in 1963, his concept of "vertical relationships" produced by technology become increasingly apparent into the twenty-first century. The computer contributes to the decline of community by generating vertical community. Through the forces of the internet, there is more specialization in social relations. Doctors can communicate with other doctors across broad spaces. Lawyers, teachers, and community activists are increasingly tied by specialized relationships. Vertical community thus generates the decline of local communities and globalization is an extension of Warren's model of community. Individual community members then become alienated from their neighbours in their own small town since they are increasingly pre-occupied with networks across the globe via the computer and the internet. Thus, Warren's concepts of vertical and horizontal community are developed using both a functionalist and interactionist view of social change. He describes social relationships within communities while utilizing notions of adaptation and rationalization within his analysis.

The final contemporary theory of social change relevant to Canadian globalization is Georg Ritzer's now famous thesis on McDonaldization. Ritzer subscribes to the "Weberian Thesis" regarding the rationalization of the world and the "iron cage" of bureaucracy. Ritzer examines the McDonald's corporation–a billion dollar, multinational, corporation that emerged from a small hamburger outlet in California in 1955. He demonstrates that McDonald's grew exponentially as a result of its organizational processes that model any bureaucracy. McDonald's success was the result of main processes, namely efficiency, calculability, predictability and control (Ritzer, 1993:150). McDonald's Corporation is *efficient* in the way it chooses the optimal method of producing their product. McDonald's then carefully *calculates* how to quantify the product for sales over taste. McDonald's then uses *predictability* to satisfy customer demands (the restaurants are uniform and consistent wherever the customers find them). Lastly, McDonald's ensures that operations and employees are *controlled* to ensure overall effect. Ritzer suggests that the spirit of McDonald's corporation circles the globe and can be found in any small community or in any large urban center. The process called McDonaldization has also been deemed Coca Cola-ization, and Standardization. It is a thesis depicting a "Homogenized New World Order" built upon capitalism and conformity. More importantly, the global system is both rational and irrational according to Ritzer. He supports Weber's pessimism about the rationalization of human societies when he states:

> Most specifically, irrationality means that rational systems are *unreasonable* systems. By that I mean that they deny the basic humanity, the human reason, of the people who work within or are served by them. (Ritzer 1994:154)

Thus, Ritzer's position on social change follows his predecessor Weber and his critique of rationalization. Ritzer believes the direction and intensity of current social change produced by globalization imprisons humans like Weber's notion of the "iron cage."

In summary, the study of social change through the twentieth century helps us understand current levels of social change in Canadian society. Social change is a key unit of sociological investigation. All sociologists examined above adhere to some notion of social change and its affects upon human society. Durkheim, Parsons and Ogburn each generate structural functional theories of social change. Marx, Lukacs, Marcuse and Connel support the dialectical approach of Hegel. Lastly, Weber and the Chicago School believe that social change is about the rationalization of human society. This perspective influences Georg Ritzer's contemporary theory of rationalization and bureaucracy. All of the theorists above may be deemed modernists in that their theories view society as longitudinal upward progression. In contrast, post-modernists such as Foucault and McLuhan refute modernization by arguing that social change is fragmented and chaotic. Thus, all of the contrasting theories above are useful to Canadian sociologists as they continue to ponder Canada's place within a global framework.

REFERENCES

Allen, R. (1971). *The Social Passion.* Toronto: University of Toronto Press.

Bell, D. (1973). *The Coming of Post Industrial Society.* NY: Basic Books.

Clarke S.D. (1961). *Urbanism and the Changing Canadian Society.* Toronto: University of Toronto Press.

Connel, R. (1987). *Gender and Power: Society, the Person and Sexual Politics.* London: Allen and Unwin.

Foucault M. (1972). *The Archaeology of Knowledge.* England: Routledge Classics.

Lenski, G., J. Lenski, and P. Nolan. (1999). *Human Society: An Introduction to Macro Sociologyy*, 9th ed. NY: McGraw- Hill.

Lukacs, G. (1971). *History and Class Consciousness: Studies in Marxist Dialectics.* London: Merilin Press.

Marcuse, H. (1964). *One Dimensional Man: Studies in Ideology.* London: Routledge Kegan Paul.

McLuhan, M. (1964). *Understanding Media.* NY: McGraw Hill.

Mulhern, F. (1992). *Contemporary Marxist Literary Criticism.* California: Longman.

Ogburn, W.F. (1938). *Social Change.* NY: Viking Press.

Ogburn W.F. (1955). *Technology and the Changing American Family.* NY: Basic Books.

Parsons, T. (1951). *The Social System.* Free Press.

Ritzer, G. (1993). *The McDonaldization of Society.* Toronto: Pine Forge Press.

Weber, M. (1904). *The Protestant Ethic and The Spirit of Capitalism.* Translated by Talcott Parson. NY: Charles Scribner's Sons.

Weber M. (1948/1991). "Social Psychology of World Religions." In *From Max Weber.* Translated by H.H. Gerth and Wright Mills. London: Routledge.

Warren, R. (1963). *Community in America.* NY: University Press of America.

Chapter 19

Education

Globalization, Internationalization and Canadian Education:

Educating Today while Preparing for Tomorrow

Jac J.W. Andrews, University of Calgary
David Peat, Rocky View Schools
and Jim Paul, University of Calgary

INTRODUCTION

> *Everything is the way it is because it got that way.*
> ~D'Arcy Wentworth Thompson, 1860-1948, British biologist, *On Growth and Form*

This chapter presents perspectives concerning the issues pertaining to and readiness of contemporary Canadian education as it increasingly engages with the manifestations of a globalizing 21st Century world. We propose that the true promise of Canadian education lives in how local school jurisdictions undertake their responsibilities to enhance the learning and empowerment of diverse learners as well as the professional development of teachers in concert with the demands of social control and social reform and within the context of local and global tensions. This chapter will *unpack* this past-present-future pedagogic relationship by presenting how the Canadian educational system through utilizing internationalization educative perspectives, approaches and practices is both ready and able to engage the forces of globalization today and tomorrow within the 21st Century.

Part One of this chapter begins with an overview of the formation of Canada's education system. **Part Two** presents ideas about why and how the education system in Canada is responding to current local, provincial, national and global trends. **Part Three** offers a brief case-study of one Canadian school jurisdiction's attempt to pedagogically and practically bridge the educational present into a realizable future whereby today's Canadian learners may become tomorrow's mid- and late-21st Century global citizens.

PART ONE: OUR CONSTITUTIONAL HERITAGE OF YESTERDAY ENABLES EDUCATIONAL CAPACITY FOR PEDAGOGIC CHANGE TODAY

Those who cannot remember the past are condemned to repeat it.
~George Santayana, 1863-1952, *The Life of Reason*, 1905, from the series Great Ideas of Western Man

How does Canada, as a contemporary democratically developed nation, currently move forward in the early 21st Century with an appropriately effective, efficient and realizable and sustainable education system? Interestingly enough, Canadians seem to share a relatively high level of satisfaction with education across the nation. That is, most feel Canada, as a nation, is relatively well situated, educationally, to compete in the world. However, in contrast to this general "comfortable" feeling about education in the nation-state, many Canadians also seem to believe that there is more improvement required at their local school, school district and provincial government education system levels. In these micro-macro public opinions live some truths about Canada's educational system. In this regard, it is important to note that public education in Canada was not developed as a national, federalist system; rather it is a provincially and territorially constituted right and responsibility. Canadian education has been and will continue to be (unless there is a constitutional change), a system developed from our forefathers' and foremothers' understandings of our emergent geographic, linguistic and spiritual identity, of our local and national socio-economic connectivity, and of geographies of thought alive in our political determinism framed by continuous liberal-conservative negotiations. As such, the beginnings of Canada's educational system come from The *Constitution Act - 1867*, formerly known as the *British North America Act - 1867*. With respect to education, this is the first Canadian constitutional core document. Embedded in this Act, and later confirmed by The *Canada Act - 1982* that the British Parliament passed for the purpose of transmitting the *Constitution Act - 1982* to Canada, there are undeniable constitutional guarantees to Canadian citizens regarding language, regionalism, governance and education. Hence, in Canada's formation, conditionally and constitutionally, education is deemed a provincial right and responsibility.

Canadian Schooling Unpacked

Across Canada, at the provincial and territorial level, education is actually located within school systems in local municipalities. These municipality school systems and their schools operate according to a main statute or law, called a "schools act," or an "education act," or a "public schools act" established by their respective provincial (territorial) governments. These statues or laws determine how the schools will be established and operated. Provincial ministries or departments of education and school boards are the responsibility of the Minister of Education. The Minister of Education is the provincially elected head of the ministry and he or she has formal responsibility for the department / ministry and its staff. Generally, the minister delegates many responsibilities to ministry staff, especially the deputy minister. The deputy minister is an appointed, non-elected, civil servant and he or she often remains in his or her position across changes of provincial governments. Even though provincial ministries seem frequently to change organizational structures, deputy ministers of education provide some consistency and continuity across time. The largest units of a department are usually called divisions. These divisions are headed by associate or assistant deputy ministers. Often, divisions are divided into branches, which are headed by executive directors or directors. Across Canada, some common ministry divisions and branches are: curriculum and instruction, programs, policy, operations, planning, teacher registration / certification, finance and budgeting, buildings and facilities, regional services and school board services. In many provinces, some divisions or branches are further reduced into categories such as: preschool and/or kindergarten, elementary or primary, secondary, college, university, and adult or continuing education. In some cases, there is further break down into curricular subject matters such as science, mathematics, English, language arts, social studies, French and second languages.

In Canada, departments and/or ministries, to various degrees, mandate the curriculum through programs of studies, guides, authorized textbooks and/or learning materials. Moreover, mandated curriculums are typically linked into a system of provincially prescribed grade and/or subject specific learner examinations. In most provinces, the ministry and/or department of education is responsible for accrediting and licensing teachers. Therefore, most education ministries or departments are connected—formally and/or informally—with post-secondary teacher preparation faculties. Since provincial governments are assigned education powers by the Canadian constitution, school districts and/or jurisdictions and subsequently their school boards exist because they legislate their existence and assign them specific powers. In every province, the province retains full control over school jurisdictions (districts) and school boards. All provinces have some system of financial-operational grants for their school systems' boards. In some cases, these grants supplement monies generated by school boards from local municipal property taxes, or in other cases, the grants provide almost all the revenue. These grants normally contain fiscal accountability checks and balances regarding budgeting procedures.

With respect to school boards, the term "school district" is more common than "school division" or "school jurisdiction." In a province with denominationally-defined or linguistically-defined school boards, some geographical areas are served by two boards; be they public and separate, or Anglophone and Francophone. In some instances, particularly in urban centers, two distinct boards may operate and serve citizens in the same geographical area. School boards are normally elected by the municipality's public. Even though school board members or trustees are elected, in Canada today, school boards are envisioned as corporations. School boards are legally defined and constituted entities. Therefore, boards may enter into contracts, and legally sue, and be sued, but most benefit from limited liabilities. Boards, then, exist independently of those elected individual board members and yet all school board employees are responsible to the board as a legal and corporate unit. In all provinces, school boards manage the local schools. Boards employ teachers and assign their school placements and responsibilities. Boards often define how teachers are promoted and are assigned duties. Boards employ support staff, secretaries, custodians, and teacher aids and others.

Most provinces provide elementary and secondary schools for learners. Normally, the elementary level is the first six years of schooling, and the secondary level is the second six years. The elementary level may be divided into two divisions: division one, which consists of grades one, two and three; and division two, which consists of grades four, five and six. In secondary school, the divisions are: junior high school, division three, which consists of grades seven, eight and nine—and high school which is division four consisting of grades ten, eleven and twelve. An alternative pattern to this traditional grade arrangement is the middle school concept. Middle schools often combine an upper grade or two of the elementary level with one or two grades of junior high school. An alternative schooling pattern emergent in Canada recently is an elementary level that ends after grade five, a middle level of three years (grades six, seven and eight), and a senior high level of four years (grades nine to twelve).

Social Change, Social Control and the Canadian School

Hargreaves (1994, 1998, and 2003) and Hargreaves and Shirley (2009) write about waves of educational reform that flood over Canadian education. Despite attempts by Canadian school systems to provide learners with equal learning opportunities, there tends to be unequal achievement outcomes. What most citizens ask, then, is: *How will my local school and/or local school system balance opportunities and outcomes for our children*? Again, Hargreaves (1994, 1998, 2003) and Hargreaves and Shirley (2009) remind us that Canadian citizens' strong commitment to balance public goods (societal needs) and private goods (individual needs) is always played out contextually, locally and interpretively. In Hargreaves' (2003) opinion, educational reforms seeking to provide public and private balance have two embedded tensions. First, there are the local economic tensions and, second, there are the tensions between the school as a place of societal social control and the school as a place of opportunity for educational reform. *How relevant is the school in balancing today's and tomorrows' societal need to conserve its traditions and its need to reform its traditions in order to evolve meaningfully as a learning society?* Parents, school administrators, educators, corporate managers, politicians and futurologists are attempting to envisage schooling and schools for the mid- to late-21st century, but they often overlook the centuries-old, deep-seeded tensions between social control and social reform embedded in most school cultures.

Berger and Luckmann (1966) indicate that societal and cultural institutions are often resistant to large-order change due to a process referred to as the "social dialectic." Social dialectic refers to the working discourses that are well established in an institution. These discourses take on an institutional life of their own. Hence, these discourses establish expected patterns of being and doing for that institution's members. The institution actually communicates "what is real" regarding what it is, what it does, and how one must be present in that institution to be considered "normal." Thus, an institution constructs the "normal individual" within a "normal community." In this social control situation, the institutional norms environment then frames a person's understandings of change. Still, an institutionally-constructed person may feel as if he or she is an agent of change. However, that is why, perhaps, in terms of educational reforms, people inside the institution think about reform or change as a process of improving what already exists. History has shown that few people from inside the institution have advanced new or radical or novel ideas for educational transformation. Perhaps, this also speaks to why most schools and school systems focus on making accommodations to outside change or reform initiatives, rather than initiating radical reform and change from the inside.

Eisner (1998) in an analysis of the contemporary school and the issues of educational change and reform suggests that resistance to change in schools is deeply embedded in the structures, functions and discourses of the school itself. Historically, the school is a traditionalist-focused, change-resistant cultured institution. In a response to why educational reforms are so difficult to achieve and sustain, Eisner (1998) points out a number of factors that make it very difficult to overcome traditional normalizing practices of schools. For example, (1) teachers, in their assigned roles adhere to the images of who they are expected to be as teachers and most teachers strive to conform to those normalizing images; (2) teachers, as societal and cultural representatives and as role models are often required to adopt rigid, conformist and enduring standards for appropriate community-sanctioned values and behaviors; (3) teachers feel, experience, and tend to come to represent the deeply conservative societal expectations embedded in schools; (4) teachers often experience artificial curricular barriers between real-world disciplines and school subject matters, and often struggle to make their content relevant to learners and applicable to the worlds of learners; and, (5) teachers become jaded over time with "piecemeal flavor of the month" efforts at reform, and as these efforts often fail, the next time a reform is suggested, teachers may retreat to a "wait and see" position or adopt resistant discourses and practices.

Eisner (1998) along with Hargreaves (2003), Hargreaves and Fink (2006), Fullan (1993) and Goodlad (1991) suggest that if meaningful school reform is to take hold, schools and school systems must begin with a significant and honest understanding of the school's often contradictory culture as a social control and social reform site. Eisner (1998) presents five dimensions of schooling that must be considered in order to think about educational reform: (1) The *Intentional Dimension*: What are the necessary, viable, and enduring educational values and understandings we require of learners and of our society?; (2) *Structural Dimension:* How will the structures and functions of the school be organized to ethically and pedagogically honor and strengthen sustainable personal relationships?; (3) *Curricular Dimension*: What demonstrable and enduring knowledge, skills and attributes will learners be engaged with?, (4) *Pedagogical Dimension*: How will curriculums (ideal, mandated, planned, taught, learned, assessed) be harmonized with a variety of instructional and assessment practices?; and (5) *Evaluative Dimension*: How will achievement as authentic demonstrable performance outcomes be assessed, evaluated, valued and reported? These intentional, structural, curricular, pedagogical and evaluative dimensions of schooling collectively constitute a kind of cultural ecology of the school. Recognizing this ecological character of schools and facing up to the magnitude of the task of educational reform in an institution grounded in social control are important beginning efforts for any serious school reform. Nevertheless, schools and school systems do change, often dramatically. *How is it possible for schools to change*? According to some theorists (Gadamer, 1989; Caputo, 2000; Bernasconi, 1995; Derrida and Vattimo, 1996; Vaterling, 2003) there is a human reflexive concept and practice called "alterity." Alterity is that precarious (re)positioning of self in relation to otherness (and the world) such that at any given moment, when **"this"** happens, it could have been possible for (alternatively) **"that"** to happen. Since, everything is ultimately defined in contrast to "*what it is not*"; there is an alteric invitation for each and every event. So, in every institution, where individuals are normalized, there is the possibility to be and become "alternative," "otherwise," or not of that institution. Therein lives the possibility for change.

PART TWO: CANADIAN SCHOOLS AS RESPONSIVE LEARNING ORGANIZATIONS

> *The schools ain't what they used to be and never was.*
> ~Will Rogers, 1879-1935, American Entertainer

Globalization, Internationalization and Canadian Schools

Smith (2003) writes that there are three basic, yet inter-connected, forms of globalization operating in the contemporary world. *Globalization One* reflects the political, social, technological, and economic forces arising from what may broadly be called the revival of neo-liberalism and neo-conservatism. This form of globalization dates back to the 1980s and the western political administrations of Ronald Reagan (American president; 1980-1988), Margaret Thatcher (British prime minister, 1979-1990), and Brian Mulroney (Canadian prime minister; 1984-1993). *Globalization Two* represents the various ways people around the world have been and are responding to the West's *Globalization One* through acts of accommodation and/or resistance (Fanon, 1965; Nandy, 1983; Bhabha, 1994; Said, 1994). *Globalization Three* reflects those emergent forms of local and global dialogue regarding persons' and communities' capacities for responding to *Globalization One* and as such they are generating possibilities for sustainable human futures in a new world order that is technology-economic-globalization oriented.

All Canadian schools have experienced Smith's (2003) *Globalization One*, and some are participating in *Globalization Three*. The dialogical response to globalization is becoming known, in the West, as *internationalization*. Gunew (2004) writes, "'Internationalization' could perhaps be reserved for the ways in which each nation state (and smaller groupings) chooses to respond to globalization, as far as possible, on its own terms" (p.54). For example, in Canadian schools, the trend towards interacting with the new worlds of mega-business / multi-corporate / techno-economic border-crossing globalism is just emerging. As such, for those schools turning to engage with globalization, there is a tendency to get caught up in globalizing capitalistic-based economic-managerial trends. Thus, many schools and school jurisdictions are exposed to seductive pressures to become an "*edu-corporate*" entity. A school, then, acting within its teaching, learning, citizenship and service mandates and missions, needs to consider that its predominant defining drive is **not** to be global-corporate in nature or function. Rather, internationalization is actually about focusing teachers, learners and administrators on those school features that shape the realization of educators' and learners' internationalist perspectives. An internationalist perspective should be understood as an ethical-pedagogic consciousness or an awareness raising process requiring a dialogical and enlightening engagement that fosters openness towards diverse and complex local and global worlds. This awareness, and subsequent openness to complex and different (and often difficult) self-other-world relationships, should be present in all the organizational and functional mandates / practices of a school's response to globalization. Recognizing the necessity of internationalization as an internal transformative engagement actually prepares the school site to act more directly, purposefully, intentionally and responsibly within a range of diverse and shifting local and global landscapes. Without such a reflexive-oriented perspective, (shaped dialogically through complex and compelling conversations about what a 21st Century academic and skill learning institution is and should be), the school might be seduced into assuming an "*edu-corporate*" model.

Neo-Liberalism, Neo-Conservatism and Canadian Schools

In the 1960s, across much of the Western World, and especially in North America, there erupted cultural "revolutions." These revolutions refocused societal awareness on civic responsibilities, global awareness, media, music, race, gender, family values, fashion, science, technology, economics and politics, within demographic and social structures. They also influenced our perspectives about, for example, nature, war, justice, capitalism, legal systems, religion, spirituality, sexuality, and property. As political and business establishments struggled to address these "revolutions," school systems also became sites of contested value and behavioral applications. Schools were shown to be quite conservative in their structures and functions in the face of massive social change. In the face of significant attempts at massive cultural and societal changes, at that time, most schools and most educators clung to conventional curriculums and traditional instructional practices.

In the late 1960s and early 1970s, schools were beginning to feel the full effects of the post World War II baby boom. During this time, a largely urban and suburban middle-class "New Left" emerged. These new neoliberal ("new left") citizens ignited radical student-activist movements that in some ways defined the 1970s. Within a few years, these movements had created a culture, a style, and a set of tactics that launched effective protests against the Vietnam War, racial, sexual, and personal discrimination, as well as social-economic-environmental advancements. Across North America, in school systems (as well as in the public), as a response to the social revolutions, there were significant debates emergent about what should count as schooling and what the purposes of schools should be. For example, are schools about advancing intellect, social adjustment, or skill training? Although there were people located in each camp, the majority of citizens seemed to locate themselves in a middle position and sought general agreement that the goals of education should emphasize critical thinking, good citizenship, social competence, and employability skills. Of course, then, the debate shifted to the degree of emphasis with respect to each goal. This focus on school purpose and goals was complicated in the late 1970s and into the early 1980s with the emergence of a social, economic and political backlash against what had happened in the 1960s and early 70s (especially the neo-liberal agenda of advancing individual freedoms). In response to a perceived national neo-liberal agenda from the 1960s until the late 1970s, the evoked response became known as *neoconservatism.* Although both "*ism-sides*" focused on understandings of individualism, the realization of what that individuality actually meant was radically different. Neo-liberalism was based on individual freedoms of choice. Neo-conservatism was based on a political ideology of preservation and a returning to traditional values enabling an individual the freedom to be capitalistically successful. In order to control the importance of preserving the past, respecting and honoring all free market capitalistic traditions, neo-conservative governments, (which became all the rage in the 1980s and 1990s) claimed a need to protect the privileges associated with the traditional (capitalist, parochial, patriarchal) social order. Thus, in the face of neo-liberalist calls for more individualistic freedoms and for more choice, the neoconservatives stressed the importance of returning to and preserving traditional family values, the Church, the military, the legal system, private property, the free marketplace, and patriotism. Neoconservatives then sought to prioritize the privatization of national assets while forcing deregulation of the marketplace or industries in order to encourage business and corporate growth. Neoconservative governments also sought to reduce anything that might be seen as impediments to free market-based business growth.

The impact of the neoliberal and neoconservative tensions, then, on education in the United Kingdom, United States of America and Canada has been dramatic (Apple, 2004, 2006). As an example within Canada, Alberta became a province in 1905 and has had a far-to-middle right conservative (political) orientation. So, in a way, the neoconservative agendas emergent in the 1980s across America found receptive and fertile ground in Alberta, and the "Progressive" Conservatives emerged as a political power house. In the 1980s and 1990s through Premiers Peter Lougheed (premier, 1971-1985), Don Getty (premier, 1985-1992), and Ralph Klein (premier, 1992-2006), the Alberta Progressive Conservative governments provided a series of systemically ideological "correctives" targeting learners, teachers, schools, school boards and the provincial education system itself. These governments demanded through deficit/debt reduction and elimination statutes and laws that any monies spent on the provincial education system would be declared as wasteful unless these monies could be shown to efficiently and effectively enable the province's learners to compete locally and globally in the new economic order fronted by globalization. Accordingly, the mandate was for students to become global knowledge-broker entrepreneurs and free market capitalists and their worth—educationally—was to be judged against the extent to which they gained the knowledge, skills and attributes needed to be effective and competitive producers and consumers in local and global marketplaces. Thus, the metaphors applied to education were those of the corporation and of the capitalistic marketplace; as such, parents were consumers, learners were clients, and businesses were education's primary stakeholders.

As a result, *Outcomes Based Education* was mandated as the curriculum model of choice. Parents must have educational market choices: public, separate, and charter, and/or private schools or homeschooling options. Schools were encouraged to link themselves to business and industry. Education, then, as a system was modeled on the business world and every school needed to take a more technocratic, managerial and performance driven view of teaching and learning. An example of this economic-managerial-business to education connectivity in Alberta may be seen in the re-working, in the mid-to-late 1990s, of the K-12 English Language Arts curriculum. In 1990, the Conference Board of Canada published a set of employability knowledge and skills for the then pending 21st Century Canadian and global worker and citizen. When the Alberta government's ministry of education began re-structuring the province's English Language Arts (ELA) curriculum, the Conference Board knowledge and employability skills document (focusing on Academic Skills, Personal Management Skills, and Teamwork Skills) was used as a structural framework for designing the new K-12 ELA Alberta curriculum. The politically conservative / neoconservative Alberta educational officials believed that all literacy, numeracy, and the sciences and information computer technologies curricular areas must be connected to employability and/or academic standards in order to raise literacy standards within schools and prepare learners for the 21st Century.

Thus, beginning in the 1980s, there emerged the birth of the current education reform movements still sweeping across North America most of which are driven primarily by neoconservative political and economic agendas. In the United States of America, the reform movement was linked to a 1983 publication of the report called *A Nation at Risk: The Imperative for Educational Reform* (1983). This report outlined the weak state of affairs within America's K-12 schools and the Report documented everything from low basic literacy standards, to high failure and dropout rates, to curriculum and instructional disconnects. *A Nation at Risk*, in America and other similar studies across Western nations, became the "call to arms" for educational and political administrators and policy makers. At the core of the reform changes initiated in the 1980s was a desire, by governments, to address the value tensions between what was taught and what was being demonstrated as learned. Thus, governments, neoconservative or not, including Canadian provincial governments, called for the "standardization" of, or "standards" movement, in curriculum, learning, teaching and assessment. That meant, school systems and, therefore, schools had to demonstrate that they were attaining higher standards of learning.

Adding to the standardization movement, in late 1990s and early 2000s, Fullan (1993) and Hargreaves (1994) suggested that if any educational reforms were to become sustainable, there had to be understandings advanced about "systemic reform." Systemic reform involves an interlinking of three levels attentive to schooling. First, governments must make sound, reasonable and across-the-board changes / reforms through educational legislation via statues or laws. Second, school systems and schools must use these statues and requirements as outcomes to be met and establish them as such for their local schools. Finally, reforms must be realizable at the local levels of school systems and schools, through inviting educators into the reforms / changes with significantly relevant, job-embedded professional development. Fullan (1993) and Hargreaves (1994) further suggested that if educational reforms are to succeed, they require significant and purposeful interactions between educators and the local school/community, the district/region boards, and the government (Ministry of Education).

Outcomes Based Education and Backward Design

During the early 1980s, an accountability-based curricular design and planning movement emerged. This movement, called *Outcomes Based Education* (OBE), reinforced the neoconservative desire to move the school towards greater standardization of curriculum design, planning and implementation and assessment. OBE focused school systems on how to evaluate the learner and learning outcomes of educational instruction. These outcomes are held accountable as investment returns made in education. Calls for accountability were a major reason for the rapid spread of various forms of OBE in countries such as United States of America, Australia and New Zealand during the 1980s and 1990s. Likewise, during this time, in Canadian schools, OBE emerged as a preferred method of curriculum design and teaching. OBE as a curriculum outcomes based model focuses on what students can actually do (i.e. demonstrable performance / accomplishment) after they are taught. OBE addresses the key questions: *What do you want students to learn? How can you best help students learn it? How will you know what they have learnt?* How does OBE work—technically? The desired learning achievement / demonstrable / performance outcomes are first selected. Then working educators evoke a planning strategy called "backward design" (Wiggins and McTighe, 2005, 2007), the curriculum content, instructional materials and learner assessments are created or gathered together to achieve the intended learning outcomes (Spady, 1988, 1993). All curriculum and teaching decisions are based on how best to facilitate the desired final learner outcomes. Towers (1996) listed four points to the OBE system that are necessary to make it work: (1) what the student is to learn must be clearly identified, (2) the student's progress is based on demonstrated achievement, (3) multiple instructional and assessment strategies need to be available to meet the needs of each student, and (4) adequate time and assistance need to be provided so that each student can reach the maximum potential.

Inclusive Education Movement

Over the past few decades, developments occurring contemporaneously in the social-political and educational fields (extending from the revolutions and evolutions noted above and including the realities of the new generation of learners to be discussed in the following section of this chapter) have culminated in the decrease of segregation among people in North American society, and increased the integration and inclusion of people in all aspects of society (for example, the desegregation laws and statutes enacted in the United States and Canada following the Civil Rights Movement of the 1960s ensuring equal opportunities for all citizens and the Federal education laws in the United States [i.e., Public Law 94-142] and Provincial laws in Canada [i.e. school acts] ensuring the integration of all students in schools). In terms of education, the most significant and challenging reform in Canada has been with respect to the values-based inclusive education movement of the 1990s, a unified educational system and a partnership between special education and regular education to provide collaborative and adaptive instruction to all students in order to meet all their learning needs (Andrews and Lupart, 2000). According to Andrews and Lupart (2000), the success of inclusive education depends on educators' abilities (through training and professional development), positive attitudes, beliefs, and values as well as the presence of enabling conditions (i.e. resources, administrative leadership and support) in order to foster lifelong learning, provide educational quality and equity, facilitate independent learning and thinking, promote home/school partnership, encourage learning and living in a community, and develop the academic and social competence of all students now and in the future. What has set the *inclusive education movement* apart from previous educational reform initiatives is the fact that it is based on the concept of restructuring and unifying the educational system for all students. The current challenges of inclusive education are the same as they have been over the past decade which are how to enrich teachers' competencies and their capacity to assess, evaluate, plan, manage, instruct, and maximize the learning potential of all students (including students with diverse needs) in their classrooms. As well, teachers must understand how to ensure that all students (without discrimination based on race, national or ethnic origin, color, religion, sex, age, or mental or physical ability) are able to adapt to and prosper from the experiences they will have in the 21st Century.

Emergence of 21st Century Learners

In 1980, something remarkable happened that had never occurred before in human history. On January 1, 1980 the first member of the "Millennial Generation," or the "Digital Native Generation," or "Generation Y" was born. At the time, this event passed without much notice. Still the birth of that child meant that eighteen to twenty years later (eighteen to twenty years equals a generation) the world would be different from anything other human beings had experienced before. For the first time in human history, there are now four generations (*Traditionalists*, *Baby-Boomers*, *Generation X* and *Generation Y*) living and interacting within the same society. *Generation Y* (or, at times, referred to as "Gen M" or "Millennials" or "Digital Natives" or "Echo Boomers" or "21st Century Learners" or the "Net Generation") are those people born between 1980 and 1995. Indeed, a Millennial / Digital Native is a person, in North America, who has always known a life with electronics, in particular, computers, the Internet, electronic and digital toys, GPS systems, personal communication devices, social networking sites, and so on.

Whereas a few teachers are *Traditionalists*, most teachers are of the *Boomer Generation*, which begins with births in 1943 and runs through to 1960. Many teachers are of *Generation X* which begins with births in 1961 and runs through to 1983. In addition, a few teachers are of the Millennial Generation; however, the vast majority of students in public schools in Canada are of the Millennial Generation. Although it is impossible to generalize accurately and describe each individual in a group of people (never mind a generation), generational attitudes may be generously discerned and characterizations may be made. In general, the Millennial or Digital Native Generation or Gen Y is economically conservative. Most members have experienced family stress, across their formative years, when their parents faced difficulties with economic boom and bust cycles of the 1980s and 1990s. Therefore, most *Gen Yers* prefer not to rely on institutions or corporations for their long-term security. Rather *Gen Yers* believe in investing in their own development rather than investing time and energy and talent in organizations or corporations. While other generations may call the *Gen Yers* selfish or disloyal to "the company," *Gen Yers* are actually just being cautious about investing themselves in traditional boss-worker relationships. *Gen Yers* know what happened to their parents—a person works hard and makes major sacrifices for the company and then that person is "down sized," or "terminated," or "made redundant." Still, *Gen Yers* have clear life and work goals and they prefer to manage their own time and solve their own problems rather than having their time, issues, or lives managed, or mismanaged by others. In addition, they value complete and unrestricted access to information. Moreover, they seek out as much information as possible whenever they can. They require continuous (and normally positive) feedback, because most *Gen Yers* have been told they are "beautiful winners" since birth (due to the fact that everyone on every team got a ribbon or medal). *Gen Yers* use the feedback they receive to manage new situations they encounter; hence, they are typically quick learners. This generation understands and needs ubiquitous technological flexibility. They are highly adaptable and they work hard to find quicker and more efficient ways of working. In doing so, *Gen Yers* seek to balance work and life responsibilities. They know the perils of being a workaholic and/or not having work. It is only now, ten years into the 21st century that educators are beginning to recognize how these changing demographics are effecting the learning-teaching-assessment environment.

Active Learning in the 21st Century

Active learning is a significant trend in Canadian schooling that grew out of the 1980s and 1990s rise of outcomes based education, constructivist teaching methods, ubiquitous technology, inclusive education, and the neoconservative demands that education be standardized and held accountable economically and pedagogically. Certainly, active learning is not a new idea. There are references to active learning that may be traced back to the Ancient Greeks (for example, the Socratic Method) right through to John Dewey (for example, Progressivism). When the student or learner is at the center of the educational teaching process, then the student / learner is an "active learner." Today, because of seemingly unlimited information, expanding knowledge-bases, engaging learning materials, inviting teaching methods, and ubiquitous technologies those who advocate active learning believe traditional teaching and learning methods (for example, memorization or rote learning or lecturing) are archaic. Moving away from the full-frontal lecture and rote learning exercises, the student-centered active learning experience utilizes highly constructivist, collaborative and cooperative learning approaches as well as strategic learning and teaching, reciprocal learning and teaching, and inquiry learning and teaching. The active learning theorist and/or practitioner believes that what students know when they graduate from school is not nearly as important as what they are capable of learning, unlearning and relearning. Thus, there is a shift in education, currently underway in the early

21st Century classroom, towards learner meta-cognitive skill sets, critical thinking, problem solving, critical analysis, and inquiry—research based skills. These active learning knowledge, skill and attribute sets enable learners to engage in empowering ways with local and global environments throughout their rapidly evolving contexts. So, for the first time in Western history, across educational institutions, educators are faced with teaching a range of ages, a range of abilities, a range of skills sets, a range of perspectives, and a range of learner intentions. What is becoming a very salient question is: *Within an inclusive education environment that has specific curriculum outcomes, backward design planning, constructivist teaching methods, ubiquitous technologies, and an emerging radically different type of learner, what educator knowledge, skills and attributes are required in order to teach effectively in a values-based, technologically-connected, increasingly globalizing world?*

Cross (1996) in a keynote address at a conference on Teaching and Learning in the Next Century held at the United States Military Academy at West Point stated that, "Active learning lies at the very heart of modern learning theory." Cross (1996) points out that the learning environment for the "digital" learner must be: (1) *Interactive*: Content and instructional approaches selected for learners must motivate and challenge learners such that they respond by creating mixed-media textual representations of their and others' learning and use informational and social media as a way to express their identity and creativity through the creation of increasingly sophisticated and appropriate user-generated content and processes; (2) *Student-Centered*: There needs to be a shift in learning responsibility to the student. In this regard, the teacher needs to be able to guide instruction and model ways forward in understanding. In addition, the teacher needs to be able to clear cognitive, emotional or technological roadblocks for learners by providing them with the resources needed to develop their own learning processes; (3) *Authentic*: Learning and knowledge acquisition takes place only when situated in a social and authentic context and, therefore, teachers must design learning spaces where technologies, information and social media is experienced by learners in authentic and meaningful ways; (4) *Collaborative*: Learning, teaching and assessing are socially constructive activities, and learners learn best through observation, collaboration, intrinsic motivation and from self-organizing social systems comprised of peers within an active and engaged local-national-international learning community, and (5) *On-Demand*: Learners can multitask and handle multiple streams of information concurrently and, therefore, learners need to be engaged with learning.

Obviously, teaching and learning are "two sides of the same coin." In a sense, in 21st Century inclusive/active learning classrooms, the teacher can no longer be the "*sage on the stage*" nor may he/she abandon learners to do their own learning with the teacher serving only as "*nervous host.*" Rather, the teacher must be an open and active learner. This open learner agency for many teachers is often hard to achieve. And, one may ask: *Why do most educational reforms fail to make substantial improvements in learning or teaching?* A major reason is that reform planners, designers and implementers typically have not understood the teaching-learning transaction in schools (Andrews, 2004; Berends, 1992; Fullan 1993). To restructure and to reform does not always mean successful re-culturing. It is often the reformers' failure to recognize that the teaching-learning transaction is about linking teachers' ways of teaching with learners' ways of learning so that learning becomes authentic, meaningful, and enriching (Andrews, 2004).

On to the Future

Given the unrelenting presence of globalization, the emergence of digital learners, the need to be inclusive of all diverse learners, and the workings of neoconservative marketplace economics, as well as the entrenchment of western rugged—often nihilistic, hedonist—cultural individualism, and the rapid infusion of inclusionary active learning strategies and the rampant diffusion of technology during the past thirty years, simply building, technically better learners, cannot really work. Certainly, there are some "Camelot" or "lighthouse" educational sites where innovation has been remarkable, but they seldom last and usually these sites result from superhuman efforts of a few magnificent educators. School systems and schools, then, must understand how to develop learners who have mutating dexterities needed to live, learn, and work successfully in an ever-expanding universe of globalizing technologies. Perhaps, that means all citizens of a school must acquire an internationalist perspective, and work towards understandings of what it means to live well, ethically and productively in the sustainable tensions between public and private, large and small, and local and global tensions. Given the realities of accelerating societal change, it is obvious that what students learn, as well as how and when they learn and who they learn from and with must change. Therefore, policymakers and educators and learners must work together, top down and bottom up, towards clearly defining what it means to be "an educated learner" and "local-global citizen" in a Digital Age. To realize fully the educational opportunities that 21st Century active/inclusive learning may offer all learners and all citizens, educational leaders must formally incorporate 21st Century learning into the current ecological dimensions of schools. They must address the "neoconservatism" and "neoliberalism" natures embodied in educators and in school culture and work to playfully set free educators as learners and learners as educators from the cultural constraints of the traditional structures and functions of 20th Century schools/schooling.

In Canada, we are realizing that we have schools and school jurisdictions ready to be understood as organizational adaptation sites. That is, Canadian schools are, for the most part; ready to become 21st Century "learning organizations" as was originally characterized by Schon's (1983) work on reflective practitioners and Senge et al. (1994) work on generative school organizations. Schools facing globalization pressures must link the understanding of what it means to be a meritorious educational site, in academic, social, and pragmatic contexts, with actions that increase each site member's awareness of the need for connected, relevant and pertinent local and global inclusive/active learning and teaching. Simply, sustainable societies, institutions and organizations, throughout history, have succeeded because they remained open to a continuous dialogical process of micro-transformations and macro-transformations. The key to such transformational sustainability is that people and organizations must be able to shape and manage all sorts of current and future transformations in relation to a grounded, valued and sustainable set of beliefs and principles. Agency in this process is dependent on member and organizational awareness, development of, and a commitment to their capacity for undertaking critical, reflexive, and adaptive audits of their current situation and in their learning of how to respond to changing and mutating local-global situations. Such a learning facility must know it is a teaching-learning organization with a rich and important connectivity to its community. It is here where a Canadian school system's evolutionary synergy lives and thrives. It is here where the local school system has been constitutionally defined by boundaries that, in fact, were negotiated. The local Canadian school system is a living historical enterprise socially constructed to be adaptable. As such, Canadian schools have in their lifeblood the ability to adapt, change and re-constitute themselves accordingly to any number of changing social, economic, or politically emergent trends.

PART THREE: A BRIEF CASE STUDY ILLUMINATING A SCHOOL JURISDICTION'S PREPARATION OF 21ST CENTURY GLOBAL CITIZENS

Well done is better than well said.

~Ben Franklin, 1706–1790, American author, diplomat, inventor, physicist, politician and printer

Throughout Canada, there are many schools and school jurisdictions that are proactively implementing educational approaches responsive to emergent diverse student needs and shaped by the social, cultural, technological and generational trends in Canadian society as described in previous sections of this chapter.

As well, in numerous classrooms in Canada there are examples of exemplary pedagogy utilizing active learning and cutting-edge technology to support and enhance learner achievement. Indeed, such practices may be found in many classrooms around the world (Trilling and Fadel, 2009). However, there are few examples, in the literature, of what has been learned when an entire Canadian school jurisdiction, as compared to individual local or international schools, has conceptualized, planned for, and implemented pedagogic change directed toward the educational preparation of global citizens for the 21st century. The case example of one such school jurisdiction is Rocky View Schools, Alberta.

Rocky View Schools—A Description

Rocky View Schools is a medium-sized jurisdiction with about 17,000 students that geographically surrounds, on three sides, the city of Calgary, Alberta. The Rocky View School's thirty-nine schools are located in diverse rural, urban and suburban sites. As well, Rocky View Schools is diverse in terms of size—for example, there are one-room Hutterite Colony schools, large comprehensive high schools, and Christian schools. However, what is interesting about Rocky View Schools is that the jurisdiction, over the past three years, has intentionally, as a responsive and adaptable learning organization, embarked on a voyage "*towards*" 21st Century teaching in a 21st Century school learning environment.

The impetus for this transformational direction lives in the jurisdiction's history of readiness to adapt and change its learning organization orientations and progressive leadership. In this regard, the jurisdiction is receptive to and actually seeks out stakeholder feedback. Also, the jurisdiction is attentive to current and innovative pedagogic theory and practice, and open to learning, teaching and curricular possibilities embedded in applications of new technologies. What follows is a concise overview of how this school jurisdiction not only designed, but implemented, a local response to what they foresaw as global issues facing their learners.

Divisional Planning Processes

Rocky View Schools is mandated, as are all Alberta school jurisdictions, by the provincial education ministry (called Alberta Education) to produce a rolling three-year educational plan. Normally, these plans result in a jurisdictional action plan document which states divisional learning-teaching-curricular-assessment goals and outcomes. These goals and outcomes of jurisdictions are held accountable to priorities derived from Alberta Education's standardized assessment measures. In 2007, as initiated by the Superintendent of Rocky View Schools, and supported by the Board of Trustees, a decision was made to develop a responsive three-year education plan relative to local and global issues and that was based upon the systematic gathering of information from the school jurisdictions' stakeholder focus groups. Core to the stakeholder communities' feedback was a clear mandate for the jurisdiction to assure that their children be numeracy, scientific, reading and writing literate, and also be schooled as global citizens who were knowledge generation and dissemination literate. These stakeholders believed that technologies (information and communication technologies) were the medium through which their children would be able to compete in the new world orders emerging as a result of globalization. Hence, this consultation process provided a baseline for the jurisdiction's "*Three Year Educational Plan, 2008-2011*" (Rocky View School Division, 2008, 2009).

The Plan contained action-oriented principles, performance goals, demonstrable outcomes and accountability measures regarding a jurisdiction-wide movement to 21st Century learning and teaching. However, at the heart of the desire to attend to globalization locally within the schools, Rocky View's leadership quickly realized that a concrete, explicit conceptualization of what might actually be considered as 21st Century knowledge, skills and attributes needed to be formulated and articulated throughout the Division. To guide this developmental process, the most comprehensive sources of information regarding 21st Century knowledge, skills and attributes were provided by the Metiri Group (Lemke et al, 2008) through work commissioned by the North Central Regional Educational Laboratory (NCREL). The information provided to the school jurisdiction was ideal for their learning organization adaptation purposes. This research provided a common understanding of what was called "*enGauge 21st Century Skills*." Essentially, the Meteri Group provided Rocky View with the opportunity to formulate a locally, contextually appropriate plan that served and acted "as a platform for the shifts in school policy and practices necessary to give our students the education they require in a knowledge-based, global society" (Lemke et al., 2008). The Meteri Group not only clearly articulated what 21st Century knowledge, skills and attributes are, but the Group also provided continua of demonstrable progresses characterizing, for example, what each skill looks like in learning and teaching practices. Such a pragmatic formulation of 21st Century learning provided Rocky View administrators with clear criteria by which to gauge student achievement and progress. An overview of the enGauge 21st Century Skills framework is provided in Figure 1.

Figure 1: enGauge 21st Century Skills Framework for Academic Achievement

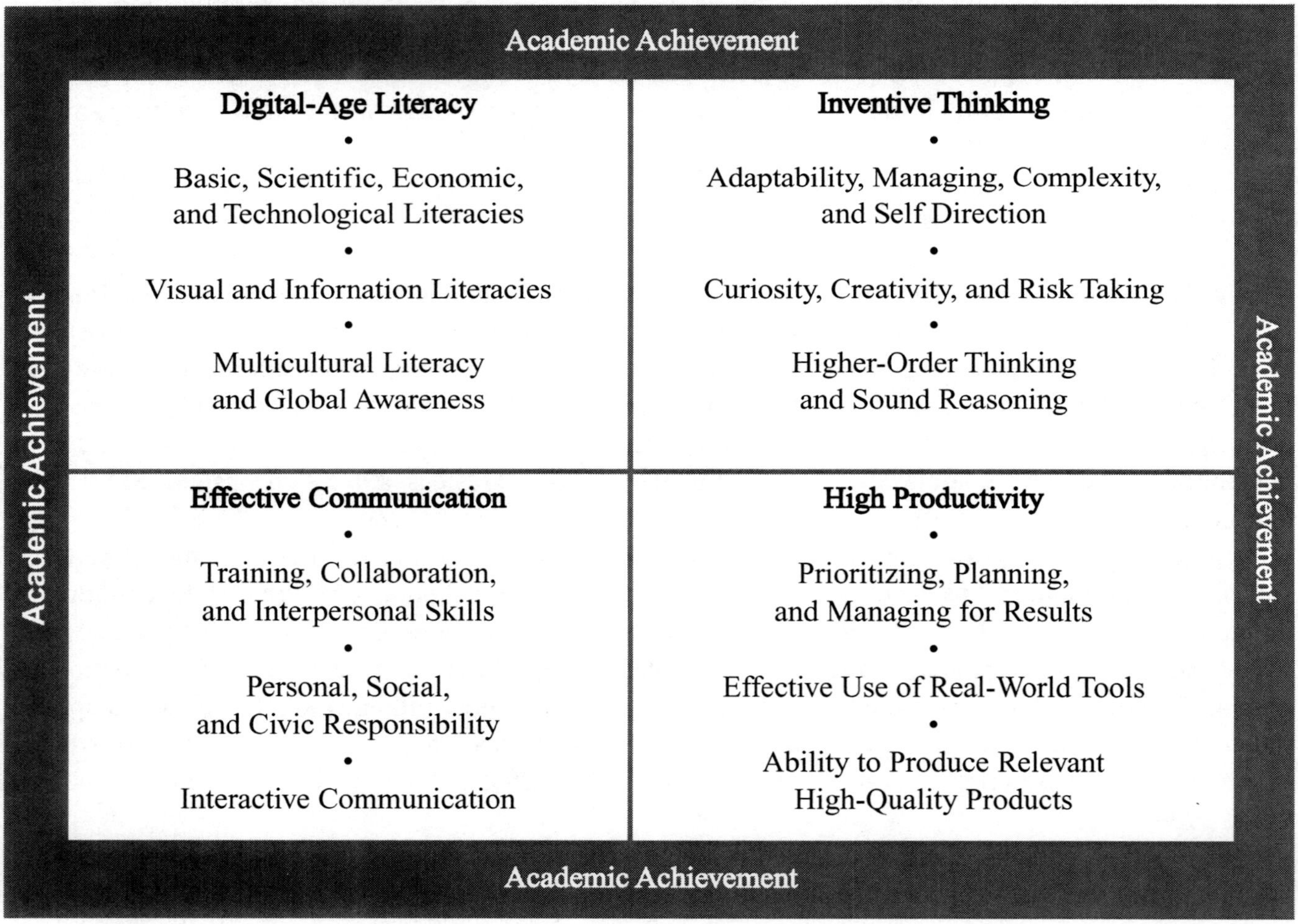

Academic Achievement

Digital-Age Literacy	**Inventive Thinking**
Basic, Scientific, Economic, and Technological Literacies • Visual and Infornation Literacies • Multicultural Literacy and Global Awareness	Adaptability, Managing, Complexity, and Self Direction • Curiosity, Creativity, and Risk Taking • Higher-Order Thinking and Sound Reasoning
Effective Communication	**High Productivity**
Training, Collaboration, and Interpersonal Skills • Personal, Social, and Civic Responsibility • Interactive Communication	Prioritizing, Planning, and Managing for Results • Effective Use of Real-World Tools • Ability to Produce Relevant High-Quality Products

Academic Achievement

Academic Achievement

Academic Achievement

The Importance of System Alignment

Waters and Marzano (2006) indicate that there is a significant positive and correlative relationship between the quality of a school district's leadership and a district's student achievement. However, this relationship exists only if and when there is collaborative goal and outcome setting with all relevant school and community stakeholders. This collaborative venture must result in the development and articulation of common and achievable system-wide learning outcomes that must be fully articulated, supported and aligned throughout a school district. This perspective framed Rocky View Schools' *Three-Year Educational Plan*, 2008-2011.

Therefore, operationally, at the Rocky View divisional office, the drafting of the "Plan" was supported by all of the Division's departments: finances, curriculum and instruction, technologies, human resources, facilities, transportation, and so on. Pragmatically, at the school level, administrative and instructional staff discussed the Division's draft Plan, and committed to infusing the Division's Plan with the "School Education Plan." And, within each school all administrative and instructional staff aligned their own "Individual Professional Development Plans" to the school's plan and Division's plan. This alignment meant that "culturally" all levels of the school system were working toward common goals and outcomes. Moreover, internally and externally, a strong message was sent to all educational stakeholders (teachers, students, parents, community agencies, local businesses and corporations, and local and provincial politicians) that Rocky View schools were 21st Century learning and teaching oriented. Thus, an entire school system demonstrated, at governance, operational, resource, and instructional levels, an orientation and commitment to results-based demonstrated accomplishment evident in 21st Century learner achievements.

21st Century Learners / Teachers and Classrooms

In order to move a school distinct, its schools and the school's classrooms towards an educational outcome that prepares students for the early and mid-21st Century, more is needed than just agreeing on systematic and systemic coordinated "planned" intent and directionality. That is where the Rocky View case becomes interesting and noteworthy. Rocky View, through its leadership, was not satisfied with predictions regarding what knowledge, skills or attributes might enable local learners to eventually actualize themselves as authentic global learners and citizens. In this regard, it was understood that although there is a strong "epistemological" component to learning (that is, a learner needs content and needs to know what they do and do not know) it is how a person holds his or her learning and actualizes it that constitutes authentic learning. This "ontological" component of learning, when properly engaged in, uncovers who a person is becoming and invites a learner into knowing "why" he or she must pedagogically engage globalization and all its manifestations. As such, Rocky View Schools consciously began an articulation of not only what counts as 21st learning and teaching, but as importantly, what does it mean to be and become a 21st Century learner and teacher?

As such, Rocky View adopted a 21st Century learning-learner model. In Figure 2, the Rocky View model is illustrated.

Improved learning for each and every learner is the core commitment of Rocky View's learning-teaching model. As such, surrounding, supporting and inviting learner improvement, as shown above, the second ring advances three inter-connected educational elements. These elements ground, foster and frame (1) educational **planning**: planning attentive to *Understanding by Design* (Wiggins and McTighe, 2005), (2) educational **accommodation**: learning design attentive to *Universal Design for Learning* (Rose and Meyer, 2002, Tomlinson and McTighe, 2006), and (3) educational **enhanced assessment**: assessment and

Figure 2: 21st Century Learning and Learners in Rocky View Schools – A Model

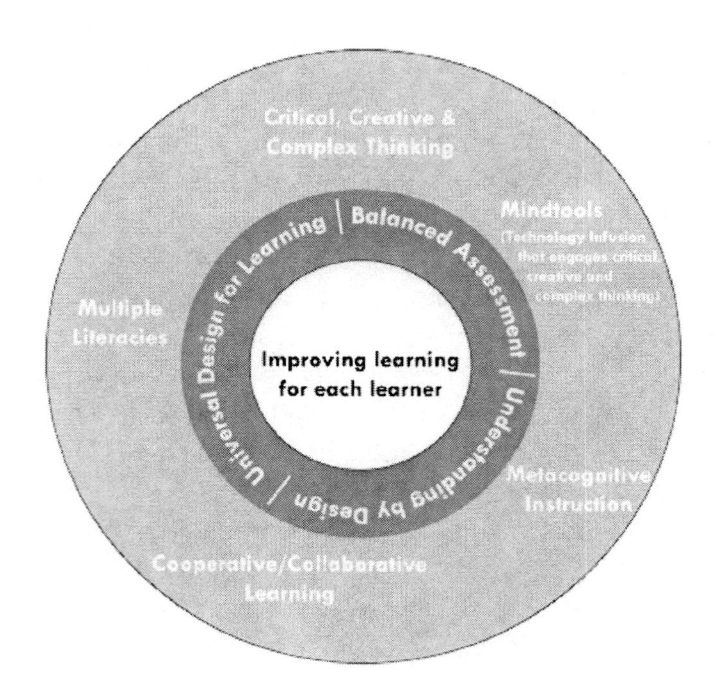

evaluation based upon demonstrable learner accomplishment as noted in *Balanced Assessment* (Davies, 2000, 2004a; www.AnneDavies.com). Hence, in Rocky View Schools, the articulation, integration and implementation of these three elements have become transformational mechanisms to advance learner and teacher growth and improvement.

Still within the learning-learner model, the outer ring is referred to as an "*informing ring.*" This informing ring represents the key three elements of the second ring. The informing ring names five current, relevant, and doable research-based pedagogical approaches to learning and teaching. All of these approaches reinforce that what is *most* important in Rocky View's schools: simply, 21st Century understandings of learning, teaching, curriculum and assessment; as well as, the practices and pedagogic use of technologies to support and enhance 21st Century learning and teaching. For example, *Mindtools* (Jonassen, 2000) is a leading edge practice that infuses learning and technologies such that learners engage in critical, creative and complex thinking. The depth, breath, scope, richness and integrative nature of the outer ring's pedagogic practices are grounded in the second ring's principles of elemental learning and teaching. Both of the outer rings revolve around the advancement of a core learner-centered value and a systematic commitment to preparing active, engaged and competent 21st Century learners (Peat and Allan, 2008).

Divisional Transformational Action Plan

If Rocky View's schools, teachers and learners were to improve their achievement outcomes, instructional practices, knowledge, skills and attributes respectively, then, at every level of the Division, a clear perspective of the operational 21st Century learning model was absolutely essential. It is important that the model be one that can be consistently implemented throughout the Division. Rocky View selected a communication-demonstration approach for implementing the learning model. Pragmatically, the Division used, in its diverse schools, "embedded coaching teams." These teams were comprised of members from the District's three central office branches of the Learning Department: Technology for Learning, Learning, and Professional Learning. These teams sought to model for the Division's schools and its teachers, students and community stakeholders that all the resources of the Division were jointly and collaboratively in the service of the Division's one primary 21st Century outcome to improve learning for all students and instructional practices for all teachers. Therefore, these leadership teams embedded themselves within and across the schools and began with teachers the supported first step of establishing "key understandings" about each teacher's disciplinary subject area. This curricular audit process utilizes an *Understanding by Design* approach that gets teachers to think about: *What is it that you really want the students to understand?* When teachers articulate what it is, from their subject matter and instructional perspective, that learners must know and be able to do, then the Division team assists the teachers to develop an action learning planning process that works "backwards" from the identification of learner "key understandings." This teacher re-education process encourages teachers to think, in depth and critically, about their subject matters, and invites them to "uncover" what is truly significant, important and worthwhile as learning within each government prescribed program of studies. It is the embedded teams that then "teach" teachers as active learners to change their curricular, instructional and assessment practices. How is this done?

The embedded transformational team works fully with school-based teachers who are organized, themselves, in teams. Both teams model for each other 21st Century learning and teaching by taking diverse teacher subject matter, treating themselves as diverse learners, and developing generative inquiry topics. The Division teams and the school teams co-develop the transformational curriculums, but the Divisional teams usually have a person who has a strong knowledge base in assistive technologies, a person with a working knowledge of student diversity (including learner special needs) and a person who is a subject matter curriculum specialist. The role of these Divisional teams is to model a learning-inquiry process, and a backward design instructional process. Importantly, they attend to 21st Century learner needs and diversity, and all the instructional processes of design, implementation and assessment while integrating cutting-edge technologies. Throughout this learning-teaching process teachers are honored as authentic learners.

Core, then, to this teamed approach to changing educational practices is the trust in a 21st Century active learning model. By using "job-embedded" professional development, teachers experience what it is the Division requires of them concerning their own 21st Century knowledge, skills and attributes. This learning and re-learning process guides and facilitates teachers to see that similar pedagogic practices are transferable to their students. The results of the transference process should mean that each school, with its learners, teachers and community, becomes alive with interdisciplinary investigations and enquiries based around essential and worthwhile knowledge, skills and attributes, open-ended questions lead by students, and learning attentiveness that is to key understanding and addressing local, provincial, national and international perspectives and issues. Moreover, this process should result in engaged learning and teaching with demonstrable accomplishments that vibrate literally and metaphorically with deep and rich understandings and applications of what it means to be a continuous learner as a local and global citizen. Essentially, schools transform their 20th Century teaching practices into 21st Century learning practices through wide spread understanding and utilization of *Understanding by Design, Universal Design for Learning* and *Balanced Assessment.* This transformative learning commitment enables learners to be and become, again and again, continuously engaged with their own learning—locally and globally—and to demonstrate their learning. This perspective about learning became Rocky View's working definition of 21st Century pedagogic success.

To summarize, Rocky View Schools, in order to address the presence locally of globalization, consciously and purposefully, shifted away from teacher-centric instructional-assessment models to a learner-centric active learning model. The Division deemed it essential that learning be active and learners be agents in their own learning and that they use all the resources available to them, locally and globally, to understand that if they are to become 21st Century competent persons, who have learned well in a transformative oriented 21st Century classroom, they would know how to engage—individually and as a member of a team or community—with the local, provincial and national manifestations of globalization.

Embedded in each Canadian school jurisdiction is both the constitutional right and responsibility to be responsive to changing learner needs. In the case of Rocky View Schools, the Division quickly and intelligently, as a responsive learning organization, addressed the tensions between social control and social reform. The Division, system-wide, perpetuated the understanding that diverse learner populations absolutely required teachers, with a 21st Century active learning pedagogic perspective, to structure a learning environment that is inquiry-based, curriculum generative, knowledge, skill and attribute focused, and where achievement is demonstrable, and learners become ontologically-grounded and supported by ubiquitous technology.

To enter a typical Rocky View school today, an observer would witness learner and teacher teams working collaboratively on-line and face-to-face within inquiry-based environments rich in technology with learner access served on a "24/7" basis. The classroom face-to-face and on-line work spaces reflect the world of digital learners who possess dexterity with technology that is rampant "in the *real* world." Yet, these learning spaces are secure, pedagogic and adult-attended. There are provisions within Rocky View's school learning communities for on-going opportunities for learners to interact with each other, and with others around the world, as well as, to access multiple sources of information (Attwell, 2007; Peat and Allan, 2008). The schools are alive with linked *plone sites* (Plone is a digital secure content management system that invites non-technical people to create and maintain information for a public website or an intranet using only a web browser), which allow the creation of blogs, wikis, on-line conversations, the co-creation of learner-learner position papers, photo/image sharing with accompanying discussions, and so on. Teachers post questions that are current, relevant and connected to topics of curriculum. This allows all curricula, teaching and learning to be "continuously current." Students can go home and on line reflect on these curricular invitations and continue debates or conversations that began face-to-face in school. In other words, students are provided with numerous inquiry opportunities and publishing environments, where the power of learning is open to students and the students themselves add to their and others' subject knowledge and skill base. Throughout the classroom experience, students access Podcasts and use laptops or studio spaces. They move in or out of these spaces, listening to documents, or downloading audio or video versions which they may load onto their *iPods*, *iPads* or other media devices for continuous access. Classrooms are structured with major tasks that students are working through; these tasks include knowledge gathering through the internet and knowledge building under the guidance of a teacher (for example, through a "mini-lesson" about a particularly difficult concept that the student needs to learn). Classrooms are "blended environments" where teachers provide lessons on topics, where students explore and gather information through viewing and/or listening to devices, then take the time to reflect and analyze information, finally coming to the stage where they have discussion and debate around their positions. There are multiple means to access information and multiple ways to present it back (Peat and Allan, 2008).

In this case, Rocky View Schools used its heritage as a responsive local learning provider to enable its teachers, learners and community to engage with the increasing manifests of globalization. The Division initiated a transformational process, because it could and needed to, by formulating and implementing a 21st Century learning-teaching model that simply opened up its learners—individually and collectively—to the perspective that even here, in this local time and place, any pedagogic orientation, via internationalization, empowers learners—as a critical inquiry thinker and doer, a conscientious citizen, and as an always learning committed person.

CONCLUSION

> *The keys for success are within us; once we find them, all we need to know is when and where to use them. (*Andrews, 2011)

Globalization is a multi-faceted, seeming continuously mutating and slippery predatory amalgam of manifestations evident across our individual and collective human histories. That is, globalization, at any given moment, today, evokes the complete and incomplete presences of tribalism, nationalism, expansionism, imperialism, colonialism, neo-colonialism, corporatism, consumerism, dominionism, euro-centrism, feudalism, Fordism, regionalism, individualism, institutionalism, positivism, liberalism, conservatism, socialism, fascism, Marxism, materialism, and mercantilism and on and on. Through time and space, local and national citizens have always been positioned and re-positioned by "**the**" resource production and consumption activities here and there and locally and internationally deemed necessary to ensure human survival. Again, that "resource" may be food, land, water, access, natural resources, human resources, technologies, knowledge, skills and so on. We believe, as educators, that it is, and always has been, education—formal and informal—that consciously seeks to invite individuals and collectives, through instructive narratives and response-leading learning models, to understand and to have agency with whatever manifestation the globalization "virus" takes. As every local community and/or nation attempts to understand and manage its core survival enterprises, it is education that delivers the possibility to advance a diversity-aware, educationally-responsive capacity development model to formulate individual and community scholarly, pragmatic and pedagogic responses to the forces of globalization. Remember earlier in the chapter Gunew (2004) wrote, "Internationalization could perhaps be reserved for the ways in which each nation state (and smaller groupings) chooses to respond to globalization, as far as possible, on its own terms." (p.54). Internationalization, then, and the realization of an internationalist-global citizen perspective must be understood as an ethical-pedagogic consciousness that invites and requires a dialogical and culturally-socially-intellectually diverse enlightening process that engages and activates the concept of academic and scholarly, pragmatic, technological and ethical self- and other-awareness. Simply, such self-awareness fosters openness towards a diverse and complex world locally and globally. This awareness and subsequent openness to complexity and the differences otherwise possible in self-other relationships must be present in all the activities and organizational and functional mandates / practices / outcomes of an internationalist-oriented educational institution itself.

Finally, what we have proposed in this chapter is that, educationally, through forethought, the constitutionally established Canadian school system that is authoritatively decentralized, and thus locally "owned and operated," is a wonderfully receptive and responsive cultural, social and intellectual institution. Now this being said, it does not necessary mean that every school jurisdiction across Canada exercises its right and responsibility to act thusly so. However, there are few structural, functional, or operational borders preventing each and every school jurisdiction from moving from social control to transformative social reform. It is in the "local" community where recognizing the necessity of internationalization as a necessary learning transformative engagement sparks to life. Still, we believe, as proposed in Part 1 and 2 of this chapter, and illustrated in Part 3 in the case of Rocky View Schools, that a person's, and his or her community's, survival, today and tomorrow, depends on how a nation-state actually constitutes what its educational institutions are capable of doing and, in turn, must do.

We believe the educational field will take on more of a lead in fulfilling the lifelong learning needs of people and enabling them to deal with the developments and challenges in the future social, commercial, political, and technological arenas. The world is becoming an increasingly complex place in which to live and work and is therefore creating a need for its citizens to develop, maintain, and extend learning / helping networks. We anticipate that more schools will adopt "bottom-up" rather than "top-down" decision making practices where much more collaboration between professionals within and outside the school will emerge. Teacher's practice will shift from knowledge disseminator to facilitator of learner knowledge creation. Our students' future learning and success in the world will be dependent on their ability to learn and to unlearn and to relearn differently in order to understand and be a part of the global network requiring an increased focus on citizen responsibility and engagement with his or her own and others' learning and teaching processes.

REFERENCES

Accessibility Suite. (2008). "Premier Assistive Technology." Retrieved February 23, 2008 from http://www.readingmadeeasy.ca/AccessibilitySuite.php.

Andrews, J. (2004). "Teaching Effectiveness." *Encyclopedia of Applied Psychology* 3:535-539.

Andrews, J., and J. Lupart. (2000). *The Inclusive Classroom: Educating Exceptional Children*, 2nd ed. Scarborough, Ontario: Nelson Thompson Learning.

Andrews, J. (2011). "Guiding Principles for Parenting and Working with Children." In J. Andrews and P. Istvanffy (eds.), *Exceptional Life Journeys: Stories about Childhood Disorder.* Manuscript in preparation. Elsevier, Burlington, MA, USA.

Apple, M. (2004). *Ideology and the Curriculum*, 3rd ed. NY: Routledge Falmer.

______. (2006). *Educating the 'Right' Way: Markets, standards, God, and Inequality*, 2nd ed. NY: Routledge Falmer.

Attwell, G. (2007). "Personal Learning Environments–The Future of eLearning?" *eLearning Papers* 2(1):1-9. Retrieved February 12, 2008 from http://www.elearningpapers.eu.

Berends, M. (1992). "A Description of Restructuring in Nationally Nominated Schools." Paper presented at the Annual Meeting of the American Educational Research Association, San Francisco.

Berger, P., and T. Luckmann. (1966). *The Social Construction of Reality: A Treatise in the Sociology of Knowledge.* NY: Doubleday.

Bernasconi, R. (1995). *The Specter of Relativism.* Edited by Lawrence Schmidt. Evanston, Ill: Northwestern University Press.

Bhabha, H.K. (1994). *The Location of Culture.* NY: Routledge.

Caputo, J. (2000). *More Radical Hermeneutics.* Bloomington: Indiana University Press.

Cross, K.P. (1996, September). "Teaching and Learning in the Next Century." In *National Teaching and Learning Forum: The Newsletter for Faculty by Faculty.* Conference paper. United States Military Academy at West Point. Retrieved from http://www.cidde.pitt.edu/teachingtimes/2000_march/active_learning_in_the_21st_century.htm.

D'Arcy, W. T. (1917 /1961). *On Growth and Form.* Abridged. Cambridge. Cambridge University Press.

Davies, A. (2004a). *Making Classroom Assessment Work.* Courtney, BC: Connections Publishing.

______. (2004b). *Finding Proof of Learning in a One-to-One Computing Classroom.* Courtney: Connections Publishing.

Davies, A., and K. Busick. (2007). *Classroom Assessment—What's working in High Schools? Book Two.* Courtney: Connections Publishing.

Derrida, J., and G. Vattimo. (eds.). (1996). *Religion.* Stanford: Stanford University Press.

Eisner, E.W. (1998). *The Kinds of Schools We Need: Personal Essays.* Portsmouth: Heinemann.

Fullan, M. (1993). *Change Forces: Probing the Depths of Educational Reform. London: Falmer Press.*

Fanon, F. (1965). *The Wretched of the Earth.* NY: Grove Press.

Gadamer, H-G. (1989). *Truth and Method.* Translated by J. Weinsheimer and D. Marshall. NY: Crossroad Press.

Goodlad, J. (1991). "Why We Need a Complete Redesign of Teacher Education." *Educational Leadership* 49(3):4-10.

Gunew. S. (2004). *Haunted Nations: The Colonial Dimensions of Multiculturalisms.* London: Routledge.

Hargreaves, A. (1994). *Changing Teachers, Changing Times: Teacher's Work and Culture in the the Post-modern Age.* London: Cassell.

______. (1998). *Fundamental Change: International Handbook of Educational Change.* NY: Kluwer Academic Publishers.

______. (2003). *Teaching in the Knowledge Society: Education in the Age of Insecurity.* NY: Open University Press.

Hargreaves, A., and D. Fink. (2006). "Sustainable Leadership." *Journal of Educational Change* 7(1-2):109-111.

Hargreaves, A., and D. Shirley. (2009). *The Fourth Way: The Inspiring Future for Educational Change.* Thousand Oaks: Corwin Press.

Jonassen, D.H. (2000). *Computers as Mindtools for Schools: Engaging Critical Thinking.* Columbus: Prentice-Hall.

Lemke, C., E. Coughlin, V. Thadan, and C. Maratin. (2008). *EnGauge 21st. Century Skills: Literacy in the Digital Age.* Lost Angeles: Metiri Group. Retrieved January, 2008 from http://www.metiri.com.

Nandy, A. (1983). *The Intimate Enemy: Loss and Recovery of Self Under Colonialism.* Oxford: Oxford University Press.

Peat, D., and B. Allan. (2008). "A Conversation about 21st Century Learning." T*he College of Alberta School Superintendents (CASS). Connection* Fall:14-21.

Rocky View School Division. (2008). *Engaging 21st Century Learners: Rocky View School Division Three-Year Plan (2008-2011).* Available at http://rockyview.ab.ca.

Rocky View School Division. (2009). *Engage, Enrich, Empower…Rocky View Schools Three-Year Plan (2009-2012).* Available at http://rockyview.ab.ca.

Rose, D., and A. Meyer. (2002). *Teaching Every Student in the Digital Age: Universal Design for Learning.* Alexandria: Association for Supervision and Curriculum Development.

Said, E. (1994). *Orientalism.* NY: Random House.

Schön, D. (1983). *The Reflective Practitioner. How Professionals Think in Action.* London: Temple Smith.

Senge, P., A. Kleiner, C. Roberts, R. Ross, and B. Smith. (1994). *The Fifth Discipline Field book: Strategies and Tools for Building a Learning Organization.* NY: Broadway Business.

Smith, D. (2003). *Teaching in Global Times.* Edmonton: Pedagon Press.

Spady, W. (1988). "Organizing for Results: The Basis of Authentic Restructuring and Reform." *Educational Leadership* 6(2):4-8.

Spady, W. (1993). *Outcome-Based Education.* Belconnen, ACT: Australian Curriculum Studies Association.

Towers, J.M. (1996). "An Elementary School Principal's Experience with Implementing an Outcome-based Curriculum." *Catalyst for Change* 25:19-23.

Trilling, B., and C. Fadel. (2009). *21st Century Skills: Learning for Life in our Times.* San Francisco: Jossey-Bass.

Tomlinson, C., and J. McTighe. (2006). *Integrating Differentiated Instruction + Understanding by Design: Connecting Content and Kids.* Alexandria: Association for Supervision and Curriculum Development.

Vasterling, V. (2003). "Postmodern Hermeneutics? Towards a Critical Hermeneutics." In Lorraine Code (ed.), *Feminist Interpretations of Hans-Georg Gadamer.* State College: Pennsylvinia State Press.

Waters, J., and R. Marzano. (2006). *School District Leadership that Works: The Effect of Superintendent Leadership on Student Achievement–A Working Paper.* Denver, CO. Mid-continent Research for Education and Learning (McREL).

Wiggins, G., and J. McTighe. (2005). *Understanding by Design,* 2nd ed. Alexandria: Association for Supervision and Curriculum Development.

_____. (2007). *Schooling by Design: Mission, Actions and Achievement.* Alexandria: Association for Supervision and Curriculum Development.

Websites

http://www.AnneDavies.com
http://www.elearning papers.eu
http://www.metiri.com
http://www.readingmadeeasy.ca/AccessibilitySuite.php
http://www.rockyview.ab.ca

Chapter 20

Sociology and the Environment

Responsibility and Environmental Governance: Exploring the Changing Social Relations in Developing Sustainable Forestry in Canada

Wayne Crosby and John R. Parkins

University of Alberta

INTRODUCTION

Unlike many other disciplines, sociology's interest in environmental issues is a relatively recent endeavor beginning around the 1970s. Since this time, a proliferation of different topics of study, approaches, and theories have emerged into what is now the prominent sub-field of environmental sociology. In general, this sub-field examines the reciprocal interactions between our social world and the physical environment with a focus on a range of topics that include environmental governance, social construction of nature, environmental attitudes, beliefs and values, and social dimensions of natural resource management. This chapter adopts an environmental sociology approach to better prepare for anticipated future trends in globalization as they relate to the complexities of environmental issues in Canada.

Canada faces a range of domestic and international environmental challenges that include greenhouse gas emissions and climate change, air and water pollution, species extinction, land and soil degradation and material waste from production and consumption. Environmental issues are inherently complex because they are simultaneously local and global, they often transcend political jurisdictions, and they often involve high degrees of uncertainty regarding ecosystem processes and future impacts. Moreover, economic growth and industrial activities related to extracting and processing natural resources (e.g., forestry and mining) are often cited as key sources of environmental concern in Canada. Governments and industry have attempted to address these concerns by endorsing agreements such as the Convention on Biological Diversity and adopting sustainable development initiatives such as the National Forest Strategy.

When it comes to the management and extraction of natural resources in Canada, provincial government agencies and departments have constitutionally determined jurisdiction over resources such as forests and the responsibility to ensure environmental protection by formulating, implementing and enforcing policies and regulations. As such, governments hold legal and moral responsibility for protecting the environment and ensuring it remains viable for future generations.

In spite of this historically defined state-centric model of natural resource management in Canada, the mechanisms and institutions for natural resource management are beginning to change. This change involves a proliferation of domestic and international non-state actors (e.g., third-party certification schemes, rural communities, and environmental organizations) now influencing, to varying degrees, domestic policy towards sustainable resource management. This in turn links Canada at times to a network of social actors outside the domestic sphere as well as actors that may or may not be democratically accountable.

This chapter examines the idea of responsibility within this evolving policy landscape by drawing upon Pellizzoni's (2004:546) typologies of responsibility and a particular emphasis on two themes: accountability and responsiveness. To ground our discussion, we examine the changing social relations of responsibility in relation to third-party certification organizations–Forest Stewardship Council (FSC), Canadian Standards Association (CSA) and Sustainable Forest Initiative (SFI)–that are now influencing what has traditionally been an exclusively state-centric mode of governance in forest policy development. Although these social relations are playing out in all parts of Canada, this chapter maintains a focus on the province of Alberta, where contemporary issues of natural resource management are particularly contentious. Canada's linkage to global processes are reflected in the influence of international non-state actors over domestic environmental policy development and this situation raises interesting questions about the globalization of domestic environmental policy development.

FROM GOVERNANCE TO ENVIRONMENTAL GOVERNANCE

Often perceived in terms of government, "governance" can be understood as the actions or processes that facilitate decision-making. The Government of Alberta defines governance as "the processes and practices through which an entity achieves its mandate, including the structures and procedures for decision-making, accountability, control and codes of conduct. It includes legislation, board of director policies and by-laws and informal norms" (2010, under "Frequently asked questions"). However, while Alberta's definition represents a good example of a conventional view of governance, important today is also the need for governance to better address environmental issues and mitigate ecological degradation.

Environmental governance is defined as "attempts by governing bodies or combinations thereof to alleviate recognized environmental dilemmas" (Davidson and Frickel 2004:471). It represents the need to embed the environment or biophysical world into all levels of decision-making processes from the local to the global. It challenges conventional governance by requiring, for example, institutions, policies, and legislation, that the environment carries equal weight with other dimensions such as social or economic needs. Conventional governance gives greater weight to economic development as the primary objective in society to increase, for example, revenues for governments to fund social services, employment and the gross domestic product in Canada. It is often believed that only after economic growth has reached a certain level that other factors such as ecological issues can then be better addressed such as creating or even enforcing existing environmental regulations. An example of this way of thinking is evident in discussions pertaining to the development and exploitation of the Oil Sands (or Tar Sands) in Alberta.

Conventional governance in Alberta upholds a strong commitment to developing the Oil Sands as a key economic activity in the province. This form of development entails a surface mining (or strip mining) process whereby the upper layers of the earth's surface (i.e., soil and rocks) are removed to access a lower layer that contains a mix of sand/clay, water and bitumen. This mixture is then processed to separate the bitumen with the use of hot water and caustic soda. For the Government of Alberta, the oil sands are the second largest source of oil in the world after Saudi Arabia (2010, under "Oil Sands").

However, the government has also received considerable criticism from various groups and concerned citizens (e.g., Aboriginal, environmental, social and natural scientists) that are questioning the scale and impact this project has on local communities and surrounding ecosystems (e.g., land degradation including forest removal, water quality and availability, and the effects of greenhouse gas emissions on climate change). Oil sands production in Alberta offers an excellent example in illustrating the primary commitment to economic growth by the province while the known and unknown effects of this form of development on the environment remain secondary concerns. Giving the environment equal weight in this example could include questioning the rate and scale of this development and accounting for environmental issues before any further expansion of production. For production currently underway, stricter environmental regulations could be created and/or enforced on various aspects related to mining bitumen such as the effects of tailing ponds (large ponds containing the waste product of separating bitumen from the sand mixture) on the flora, fauna and water quality of surrounding ecosystems.

In the end, the emphasis on giving the environment equal weight challenges the traditional conception of nature as an externality or as a dimension that can be incorporated into existing decision-making processes. The need for this type of transformation is said to be motivated by the recognition for the need to better manage, use, or protect degrading ecosystems throughout the world that not only provide life sustaining attributes for all species on the planet, but act as a source of natural resources for human use. While the process of incorporating environmental issues into political decision-making systems is beyond the scope of this chapter, what is of particular interest is the growing number and influence of non-state actors now involved and what this means for traditional social relations of responsibility over environmental challenges in Canada.

The environmental governing landscape in Canada consists of the state and non-state actors now involved in the process of addressing environmental issues. To remind ourselves of the traditional role of the state in the Western world, we can reflect on a number of *a priori* perspectives that are often associated with state authority. These include maintaining the conditions for the accumulation of capital (Rueschemeyer and Evans, 1985:44; O'Connor, 1973:6), having responsibility over the distribution of wealth, which more recently includes addressing the distribution of ecological "goods" and "bads" such as pollution (Meadowcroft, 2005:4), as well as maintaining nation-state sovereignty over its territory. In general, the state is often assumed to hold the primary responsibility for addressing environmental problems, usually in terms of reactive and/or proactive strategies because of its historical precedence over responsibility for its citizens and territory. State actors include government ministries and agencies whose mandates foster environmental objectives. However, for some, the legitimacy of our political, economic and scientific institutions to produce effective environmental policy is declining (Pellizzoni, 2004:551) while the state is believed to be losing its legitimacy and effectiveness in producing sustainability within the domestic sphere (Vogler, 2005:229). Meanwhile, we can observe the increasing role of domestic and international non-state actors in dealing with the complex nature of environmental challenges.

Non-state actors include a range of domestic and international organizations (e.g., North American Free Trade Agreement) and institutions such as third-party certification, environmental organizations, and environmental agreements/declarations. Non-state actors are located within but more often outside the sovereign jurisdiction of the nation-state and are increasingly playing a significant role in influencing domestic decision-making and policy formation. For example, Howlett et al. (2009:72) argue that developing a national forest policy in Canada has become a very complex undertaking for domestic policy makers. This is the result of competing conceptions of forests where on the one hand domestic actors (e.g., the state) see the economic value of timber extraction while on the other hand non-state actors (e.g., domestic and international environmental treaties and third party certification organizations) advocate for competing alternative uses of forestlands (e.g., recreation and conservation).

These competing perspectives over what a forest is and how they "could" or "should" be used reveals the socially constructed nature of environmental issues (Hannigan, 2006:63; Jones, 2002:247). In other words, the "environment" is a human construct that carries with it potentially contending perceptions such as economic versus conservation values highlighted above. Different stakeholders conceive, talk about and ultimately use the environment in potentially different ways (Macnaghten and Urry, 1998:3), which reveals how there is no single "environment" but instead how it represents various symbolic meanings we attach to the physical world (Jones, 2002:247). However, also debated is the degree the environment is constructed versus having a "real" physical and material existence with "real" degradation. While this chapter is unable to explore the contours of this debate, we take the position that the environment does have a physical and material existence, but how we understand and address environmental issues is socially constructed. As such, different social actors within environmental governance can have potentially different or contending perspectives over what, for example, forest landscapes entail (e.g., timber, trees, habitat, viewscapes, sacred sites) and how they should be used (or not).

The proliferation of a range of actors and the emergence of environmental governance can be attributed to at least two possible explanations. The first may be the increasing acknowledgement of the complex nature of environmental problems today. In other words, local environmental problems have global implications and every global problem has local implications. There is interconnectivity between local and global levels and, therefore, it will take a range of actors to account for the diversity of environmental problems we face collectively, and the contested nature of developing solutions to overcome these challenges (Gore and Stoett, 2009:3). Another explanation points to the proliferation of actors that are linked to various political and economic factors. For example, concerns have risen over how government departments or key actors within the overall decision-making context (locally and/or globally) shape resource and environmental policy-making within economies driven more by market principles than government intervention (Hessing et al., 2005:51). This shift in policy-making to market principles runs parallel with the pervasive "neoliberal ideology" that is said to be reconfiguring institutional arrangements through which society-nature relations are governed (Himley, 2008:433).

In understanding the contemporary socio-political landscape for environmental management in Canada, several other concepts are germane to this discussion. Neoliberalism is an abstract concept that generally entails a widespread philosophical, economic, social and political strategy associated with the internationalization of capital since the late 1970s (Harvey 2005:165). It is an ideology described by some whereby, for example, the state's role as welfare state is "rolled back" and replaced with new objectives of privatization, deregulation and trade liberalization (e.g., North American Free Trade Agreement) while turning to the "market" to manage society's affairs (Jessop, 2002:454; Peck and Tickell, 2002:385). Neoliberalism is said to be transforming the basis of governance guided by political and social values whereby governance is now shaped by normalized market values as universal values, which also promotes active participation of society in the reproduction of life and of our species on the basis of this market normalization (De Angelis, 2003:16-25). It favours what Polanyi (2001:3) refers to as the "self-regulating market," which corresponds to shifts towards a minimalist role of the state in society and the increase emphasis on the value of individuals motivated by self-interest (Jessop, 2002:454). Its ideology locates market exchange in our thoughts and practices as an ethic in itself that can guide human action, which in turn replaces previously held ethical beliefs (Harvey, 2005:165).

Distrust in market systems alone to direct human action has been expressed historically by, for example, Karl Polanyi who argued that, "to allow the market mechanism to be sole director of the fate of human beings and their natural environmental, indeed, even of the amount of purchasing power, would result in the demolition of society" (2001:76). As such, what makes neoliberalism interesting is how it offers the "promise of political emancipation through economic growth, increasing prosperity, and market mediated social relations" (Heynen, 2007:6). Important to note though is that while this discussion presents the state and markets in dichotomous terms, the reality is that we generally find that governance includes a blend of both government intervention (e.g., environmental regulations) and market forces that include various economic characteristics such as supply and demand, comparative advantage, cost-benefit analysis, price instruments designed to account for environmental services and economic incentives for the valuing and protection of a range of forestry-related products and services. Third-party forest certification raises questions in terms of the degree markets alone are driving the formation and/or enforcement of environmental regulations in the forest sector, what this means for how forests are valued and managed in Canada, and who is actually dictating those values (e.g., domestic or international actors). In other words, it appears that the traditional social relations in developing sustainable forest policy in Alberta that has consisted of the provincial government and industry is now turning to "market(s)," especially global markets (and corresponding global consumers of wood productions) to play a greater role in developing sustainable forest policy in Alberta and Canada overall.

What all of these global processes and patterns mean for addressing environmental issues in Canada links directly to the immediate question of the state's ability and responsibility to address environmental issues. For some, the authority of the state is compromised because of the proliferation of non-state actors now implicated in the process of environmental governance (Hessing et al., 2005:237; Shaw, 2004:374; Spargaaren and Mol, 2008:350). This includes analysis of the degree of diffusion of authority into voluntary third-party certification regimes (Cashore, 2002:503; Pellizzoni, 2004:553). Others describe the position of the state not in terms of declining but in terms of a hybridization of authority with other actors whereby the state's role is being renegotiated by being recentered and decentered within the governance landscape as opposed to being displaced (Conca, 2005:181). Other authors remain committed to the state apparatus, despite the need for change, because it holds the greatest means for addressing the complexity of environmental challenges (Eckersley, 2005:172). In other words, "the appeal of the state is that it stands as the most overarching source of authority within modern, plural societies" (Eckersley, 2005:172).

In the end, all of these global processes and patterns raise questions over how we are to make sense of responsibility over environmental challenges and whether we can continue to assume the state is the appropriate or only actor to be held responsible for environmental stewardship and sustainable development. Are forest certification schemes affecting the social relations of responsibility within the process of achieving sustainable forestry in Alberta? What is the state responsible for and are there constraints that limit the state's responsibility? To explore these questions, we will first develop an understanding of the concept of responsibility based on Pellizoni's (2004:546) conception of responsibility.

TYPOLOGIES OF RESPONSIBILITY: ACCOUNTABILITY AND RESPONSIVENESS

Although we often use the concept of responsibility in deliberations over who should address environmental problems (i.e., governments, individuals, corporations), the concept itself has received limited scholarly attention. In addressing this concept directly, Pellizzoni (2004:546) provides a useful typology of responsibility that entails four dimensions: care, liability, accountability and responsiveness. Two of these dimensions are of particular interest to this discussion.

Accountability is often regarded as a core principle of "good governance" and represents the recent tendency towards "promot[ing] forms of verification, evaluation, control and review" that is associated with audits (Pellizzoni 2004:550). Through accounting frameworks, the state can be held accountable for the intended or unintended consequences of its actions. As a critique of this approach to responsibility, Pellizzoni (2004:549) argues that the *caring* state has been overtaken by the arrangements within governance that are fixated on liability and accountability. This in turn reveals changing social relations of responsibility whereby the tendency towards "auditing" is linked to increased technical expertise coupled with growing complexity of choices available within social contexts. This context of expertise and complexity, in turn, puts institutional and corporate authority and trustworthiness into question because the general public has limited capacity to understand and hold the state or governments accountable for good governance. To address the challenge of uncertainty requires building relations of responsiveness that better addresses complexity in decision-making processes.

Responsiveness speaks directly to complexity within the democratic political system and refers to the need for a "receptive attitude to external inputs to help in deciding what to do" (Pellizzoni, 2004:557). In contrast to the "unresponsive" nature of current policy processes whereby individuals or organizations hold reactive, assimilative attitudes, responsiveness calls for the need to include *and* evaluate participatory processes needed in the face of growing uncertainty. It is this dimension that Pellizzoni (2004:557) argues is neglected in the debate on governance and in particular in relation to growing radical uncertainty that results in declining legitimacy of political, economic and scientific institutions. In the section to follow, we will explore these dimensions of responsibility within the context of forestry and environmental governance in Alberta.

ACHIEVING SUSTAINABLE FORESTRY IN ALBERTA

In a province where the economy is driven by oil and gas production, forestry is ranked third behind agriculture, and plays an important role in Alberta's economy by generating $11 Billion annually and 47,000 jobs (Government of Alberta, 2007:20). Forestland covers nearly 60% of the landmass and 87% of the forests are on crown land. Public forests are managed under a tenure system whereby the government grants specific rights and responsibilities to manage forests and harvest timber as opposed to outright transferring ownership rights. Tenure rights in general are awarded on either a short or long-term basis, and most commonly through area-based or volume-based agreements.

The forest industry in Alberta and within Canada in general can be characterized as an export-oriented staples economy. A staple (e.g., timber) is a "raw, unfinished bulk resource commodity sold in the market" that is subject to a minimal amount of processing (Hessing et al., 2005:28). For example, processing a log into lumber or plywood only requires milling, planning and/or kiln drying. In our globalized world, the export-oriented economy translates into Alberta's dependence on international markets for exporting their forest products and, therefore, subject to the uncertainty and volatility of boom/bust cycles in global commodity markets.

Provincial legislatures have jurisdiction and responsibility for developing regulations and policies for forestry and non-renewable resources such as oil and natural gas. The Federal Parliament of Canada on the other hand has constitutional jurisdiction for making laws on natural resource extraction in the three northern territories (Yukon, Northwest Territories, and Nunavut), and has the exclusive authority to make laws that regulate trade and commerce as well as the sea coast and inland fisheries (Hessing et al., 2005:62). Therefore, the Government of Alberta has political jurisdiction and responsibility for forestlands in the province and the Ministry of Sustainable Resource Development (SRD hereafter) has embraced this responsibility with a commitment to ensure sustainability in the forest landscape (which includes a forestry division that oversees forest management in the province). At the heart of Alberta's forest management strategy is its commitment to sustainable forestry. The sustainable forest management strategy characterizes sustainability in terms of a "checks and balance" system between the approved allowable cut and regeneration rates so that the province does not harvest more than what can be grown.

FOREST CERTIFICATION

Sustainability is also characterized in ways that extend beyond sustainable timber harvest levels. Within the forest sector of Alberta, sustainability is "the state in which we can be confident that the forest resources and all its values will be available to us not just today, but also tomorrow" (Alberta Forest Legacy, 1997:1). It is this broader conception of "values" or "multiple use values" (e.g., timber harvesting, recreation, and conservation) that guides and ultimately reveals the increasingly complex nature of forest management in Alberta. The role of SRD is to create the conditions (i.e., policies and regulations) for industry and individuals to utilize forests in a manner that remains consistent with these broader sustainability objectives.

Included in provincial strategies for achieving sustainable forestry is an interest in adopting market-based instruments to assist in managing forests. In general, forest certification schemes are voluntary, involve third-party auditors, and rely on market-based tools for the purpose of achieving forest conservation. There is a range of schemes available (e.g., FSC, CSA, and SFI), all with varying requirements or criteria that must be fulfilled before a company can obtain a "stamp of approval." In essence, forest certification is a process of "green labeling" that offers consumers some assurance that forest products are produced in a sustainable fashion, and it also offers some assurances to forest companies that access into consumer markets will be maintained. These forest certification schemes represent a new and influential non-state actor in the management of Canada's forests. Combined with international environmental campaigns, this evolving and elusive policy landscape offers an opportunity to explore the globalization of responsibility within the forest sector and the shifting context of environmental governance in particular.

By some estimates, forest certification since the early 1990s has been the leading example of non-state, market-driven governance systems (Cashore, 2002:503). These governance systems are based outside of state-centered authority and draw from market systems that rely upon the private sector to voluntarily comply with one of several competing sets of standards (Cashore et al., 2003:3; Eisner, 2004:145). In a move to use the marketplace as a means to press the state and forestry corporations for change, several international environmental organizations initiated the Forest Stewardship Council (FSC) system of third-party certification. This system established highly prescriptive national and sub-national performance standards to which applicants must adhere in order to become certified. In response to this move by the environmental community, industry and governments in North America rushed to develop national certification schemes that were arguably friendlier to their own interests.

Within Canada, the national alternative to FSC is the Canadian Standards Association (CSA) Sustainable Forest Management (Z809) (2003:2). Unlike the performance standard of the FSC system, the CSA performance standard is more flexible and is based on a dialogue between the applicant (a forest company) and a broad cross section of local community representatives who constitute local stakeholders. Within this system, the principal role of local stakeholders is to work with the forestry company, in advisory capacity, to develop a local sustainable forest management standard. Within this context, local forestry companies and the local public advisory committee are largely responsible for establishing a certification standard that will define sustainable forestry within the region. This local performance standard then forms the basis for third-party audits and CSA certification. Within the United States, an alternative to FSC is called the Sustainable Forestry Initiative (SFI). This initiative was developed initially by the American forest industry, but in recent years it has become quite similar to the Canadian standard (CSA), and in fact many Canadian forestry companies are seeking out SFI certification to maintain market access in the United States. Figure 1 illustrates the extent of forest certification throughout Canada from the three dominant certification systems.

FIGURE 1. MILLIONS OF HECTARES CERTIFIED TO A SUSTAINABLE FOREST MANAGEMENT STANDARD IN CANADA, 2009

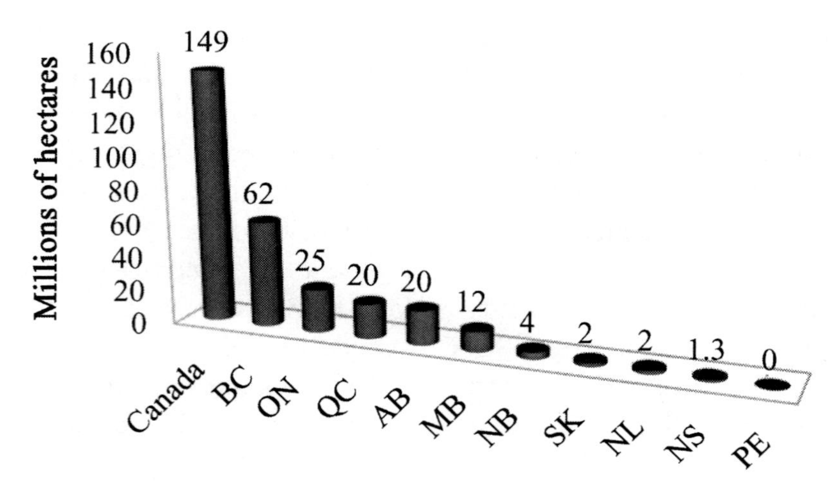

Source: Forest Products Association of Canada, Ottawa, ON.

CERTIFICATION AND RESPONSIBILITY

After describing these forest certification systems in some detail, it is possible now to step back from the details and offer an analysis of these changes in environmental governance. A common strategy within conventional policy approaches includes turning to voluntary regimes such as forest certification as an innovation in environmental governance. Voluntary regimes are seen as both beneficial (e.g., take advantage of business expertise, develop networks promoting operation and technology transfer, promote accountability and participation) and problematic (e.g., lack transparency, free riding, self-accounting and questionable effectiveness) (Pellizzoni, 2004:14). More concerning though is how voluntary regimes may be perpetuating the unresponsiveness of current policy regimes in ways that are not immediately apparent. They achieve this because they "entail to various degrees a self-referential, self-validating definition of goals and evaluation of results" that "take for granted the autonomy of economic and technical choices from public scrutiny, measuring accordingly the appropriateness and pertinence of claims and concerns" (2004:558). Pellizzoni (2004:558) argues that a way to test for responsiveness is to examine how voluntary regimes rearrange social relations and in turn result in potentially perpetuating the exclusionary and unresponsive conditions of current policy approaches. Responsive approaches are needed that include different "participatory" processes to account for answerability and public scrutiny in governance. As a result, responsiveness raises questions of democracy and looks at the effectiveness of state action by employing a more inclusive approach before action is taken. This might involve attention to other forms of knowledge (e.g., local) along side dominant scientific and technological discourses, or more diversity in public values that are incorporated into a forest policy process.

At first glance, the CSA certification system does seem to offer an advantage in terms of Pellizzoni's notion of responsiveness. First, the establishment of local performance standards is a reflection of forest ecosystem complexity and the complexity of forest values that must be identified and incorporated into a local forest management system. Given new knowledge of forest ecosystem diversity, non-equilibrium dynamics, and the diversity (and often contradictory nature) of public values, it makes little sense to establish provincial or national standards for forest management. In an ideal sense, this notion of responsiveness to environmental complexity and values complexity seems to be a positive dimension of forest certification. Second, local performance standards have a democratic tone about them in the way that local forest users, residents of forest communities, can play a role in developing these standards. These innovations in environmental governance, through forest certification, seem to offer a remedy for more responsibility in forest management through concepts of accountability and responsiveness.

Yet there are troubling dimensions here that require some attention as well. First, questions quickly emerge in regards to who specifically is responsible for environmental stewardship within a context of forest certification. In a real sense, recent changes in the forest sector involve a major shift here away from state-centric responsibility toward market-centric responsibility, and international markets in particular. Within a globalizing market economy for timber, the consumers of forest products in the United States and Europe become the social and economic force by which environmental performance standards are maintained in Canada. In other words, through market-based certification systems consumers of Canadian wood products (e.g., lumber for housing industry or individual consumers looking to renovate homes) in locations outside the political jurisdiction of Canadian provinces are able to express how they value forests when they shop at their local lumber stores by choosing certified lumber (or not).

Before the arrival of certification schemes, domestic or international consumers in general had very little influence (if any) in the process of developing forest policy in Canada and simply purchased available wood products from their local lumber dealers. In today's globalized world, consumer preference and behaviour in international markets such as the United States and countries in Europe play a much greater role influencing the way forests are valued and managed in Canada, which government policies and forest company behaviour must adhere to if they want to export Canadian forest products into those markets. This means that through certification schemes, decisions over sustainable forest management strategies now include a consumer class whose perception of forests and how they "should" be exploited could potentially differ from and in turn challenge how governments in Canada value forests, despite Canadian governments having constitutionally entrenched responsibility and authority over their forestlands. In this case, third-party certification schemes appear to be displacing the responsibility of achieving forest sustainability away from provincial governments towards including actor(s) located outside the political jurisdiction of provinces in Canada. The increase in turning to market mechanisms to assist in developing sustainable forestry in Canada brings us back to an earlier comment by Polanyi (2001:3, 76) about market mechanisms as the sole director of human activity and the ideological dimensions of market mechanisms that are so pervasive in contemporary culture. Additional concerns include questions pertaining to what this means for the sovereignty of provincial governments as well as and how much power of influence certification schemes bestow upon consumers over how forests are managed in Canada. This evolving context from which sustainable forest policy is developed is further complicated by the idea that values and perceptions of forests can not only vary throughout local and global actors, but that they are not static and, therefore, subject to change over time.

Moreover, as forest certification systems step forward and raise the bar for environmental performance in Canada, provincial governments become sidelined. Provincial governments are free to leave their legislated standards for forest management at substandard levels, knowing that forest certification systems will drive standards higher. And this situation leaves government off the hook in terms of forcing higher environmental standards on unwilling corporate actors. The upshot of this situation for the state is avoided, or shifted, responsibility in the context of a globalized, consumer oriented system of environmental governance.

Important to keep in mind is that consumer behaviour influencing decisions over how commodities are produced is a normal process in economics, but what makes this case unique is that it raises questions related to the effects market instruments have on both developing sustainable forest management policy in Canada and the effects they may have on forest ecosystems in Canada and beyond. If we find that markets play a greater degree than governments in determining forest management practices in Canada, what assurances or safeguards are in place beyond market mechanisms to ensure that they, for example, protect ecosystems, preserve biodiversity and facilitate the inclusion of local or national values? Will governments play the role of safeguarding forest ecosystems? If this is the case, what will this entail in terms of sustainable forest policy?

Canadian forests provide important economic, cultural and ecological attributes for local forest communities, the nation as a whole and the planet overall. Canada's 407 million hectares of forests and wooded areas constitute 10% of the world's forest cover. Interconnected with global ecosystems in general, Canada's forests provide essential life supporting features for humans and other species on the planet. For example, they provide and protect an important source of the world's scarce fresh water supply, are habitat to a range of species of flora and fauna and offer a source for carbon storage to address climate change. As such, forest management strategies in Canada can have direct or indirect global ecological implications, which the Government of Canada appears to recognize in their support for sustainable forest practices whereby harvested forests can store carbon while they regenerate and grow as a means to address climate change (Government of Canada, 2009, under "Greenhouse Gas Emissions and Canada's Forests"). As such, while forest certification schemes enable international consumers to influence sustainable forest management in Canada, how forests are managed on the ground can have a direct effect on global ecosystems and their life-sustaining attributes for the planet.

Second, according to Pellizzoni (2004:557), responsiveness means breaking down the exclusionary discourses around forest policy development, opening the process to a more diverse set of social actors, and working toward more inclusionary discourses of environmental governance. With regard to the CSA brand of forest certification, there are strong democratic impulses in this standard, with a view to placing local social actors at the centre of the standards development process. Yet, there is ample evidence from recent research that public advisory committees within the CSA process are far from democratic in several ways. First, these committees are composed largely of older males, with relatively high education attainment levels, and high employment incomes (Parkins et al., 2006:10). In this demographic sense, the average public advisory committee in the forest sector does not resemble the average Canadian, and women in particular are conspicuously absent from these processes (Reed and Varghese, 2007:523). Second, and arguably more problematic, there is consistent evidence that when diverse voices are represented (where there is an appearance of inclusion) these voices are systematically shut down in favour of dominant local discourses of production forestry and scientific forest management (Parkins and Davidson, 2008:193). In this sense, the appearance of responsiveness is in fact just that, an appearance. And what remains in place is a more elaborate version of discursive retrenchment around the ideas of neoliberalism and dominant economic interests in forest-dependent communities.

CONCLUSION

Through the lens of environmental governance and the idea of responsibility more specifically, this chapter addresses recent developments in the governance of forestry in Alberta. Changing social relations of responsibility involve attention to a shift in responsibility from state-centric actors to international consumers through mechanisms of forest certification. These movements in environmental governance are innovative in one sense, because there are ways in which ecosystem complexity and the diversity of public values can be effectively addressed through these flexible systems of governance. Yet there remain real concerns about the displacement of responsibility from nation-states to international consumer classes, and the possibilities of avoided responsibility for state actors with constitutional responsibility for stewardship in particular. Also, when deeper inquiries are made about the local-level mechanisms of environmental governance (such as the development of local forest certification standards) they are often found to offer little emancipator potential. Instead, dominant interests remain firmly entrenched within these newer forms of governance. So to add another term to Pellizzoni's typology of responsibility, perhaps we need to think more about the idea of authenticity; a hybrid concept between the idea of care and responsiveness that is part of his current formula. Authenticity places even greater attention to the meaningfulness and the quality of our environmental governance systems and the possibilities of meaningful change that is required for more sustainable futures.

REFERENCES

Alberta Forest Legacy. (1997). "The Alberta Forest Legacy–Implementation Framework for Sustainable Forest Management." Retrieved February 4, 2008 from http://www.srd.gov.ab.ca/forests/managing/default.aspx.

Canadian Standards Association (CSA). (2003). "Sustainable Forest Management: Requirements and Guidance." CAN/CSA-Z809-02. Mississauga, ON.

Cashore, B. (2002). "Legitimacy and the Privatization of Environmental Governance: How Non-State Market-Driven (NSMD) Governance Systems Gain Rule-Making Authority." *Governance: An International Journal of Policy, Administration, and Institutions* 15(4):503-529.

Cashore, B., G. Auld, and D. Newsom. (2003). *Governing Through Markets: Forest Certification and the Emergence of Non-State Authority.* New Haven: Yale University Press.

Conca, K. (2005). "Old States in New Bottles? The Hybridization of Authority in Global Environmental Governance." In J. Barry and R. Eckersley (eds.), *The State and The Global Ecological Crisis.* Cambridge: MIT Press.

Davidson, D., and S. Frickel. (2004). "Understanding Environmental Governance: A Critical Review." *Organization and Environment* 17(4):471-492.

De Angelis, M. (2003). "Neoliberal Governance, Reproduction and Accumulation." *The Commoner* 7:1-27.

Eckersley, R. (2005). "Greening the Nation-State: From Exclusive to Inclusive Sovereignty." In J. Barry and R. Eckersley (eds.), *The State and the Global Ecological Crisis.* Cambridge: MIT Press.

Eisner, M.A. (2004). "Corporate Environmentalism, Regulatory Reform, and Industry Self-regulation: Toward Genuine Regulatory Reinvention in the United States." *Governance* 17:145-167.

Gore, C.D., and P.J. Stoett (eds.). (2009). *Environmental Challenges and Opportunities: Local-Global Perspectives on Canadian Issues.* Toronto: Emond Montgomery Publications Limited.

Government of Alberta. (2007). *Land Use Framework.* Retrieved February 29, 2008 from http://www.landuse.gov.ab.ca/.

Government of Alberta. (2010). *Frequently asked Questions*. Retrieved February 22, 2010 from http://www.alberta.ca/home/734.cfm#2.

Government of Alberta. (2010). *Oil Sands*. Retrieved June 12, 2010 from http://www.energy.gov.ab.ca/Our-Business/oilsands.asp.

Government of Canada. (2009). *Greenhouse Gas Emissions and Canada's Forests*. Retrieved February 22, 2010 from http://www.climatechange.gc.ca/default.asp?lang=En&n=E0BE5ABD-1.

Hannigan, J.A. (2006). *Environmental Sociology*. London: Routledge.

Harvey, D. (2005). *A Brief History of Neoliberalism*. NY: Oxford University Press.

Hessing, M., M. Howlett, and T. Summerville. (2005). *Canadian Natural Resource and Environmental Policy Political Economy and Public Policy*. Vancouver: UBC Press.

Heynen, N., J. McCarthy, S. Prudham, and P. Robbins (eds.). (2007). *Neoliberal Environments: False Promises and Unnatural Consequences*. London: Routledge.

Himley, M. (2008). "Geographies of Environmental Governance: The Nexus of Nature and Neoliberalism." *Geography Compass* 2/2:433-451.

Howlett, M., J. Rayner, and A. Wellstead. (2009). "National Forest Planning and Sustainability Concerns." In C.D. Gore and Peter J. Stoett (eds.), *Environmental Challenges and Opportunities: Local-Global Perspectives on Canadian Issues*. Toronto: Emond Montgomery Publications Limited.

Jessop, B. (2002). "Liberalism, Neoliberalism and Urban Governance: A State-Theoretical Perspective." *Antipode* 34(3):452-472.

Jones, S. 2002. "Social Constructionism and the Environment: Through the Quagmire." *Global Environmental Change* 12:247-251.

Meadowcroft, J. (2005). "From Welfare State to Ecostate." In J. Barry and R. Eckersley (eds.), *The State and the Global Ecological Crisis*. Cambridge: MIT Press.

Macnaghten, P., and J. Urry. (1998). *Contested Natures*. London: SAGE Publications.

O'Connor, J. (1973). *The Fiscal Crisis of the State*. NY: St. Martin's Press.

Parkins, J.R., and D.J. Davidson. (2008). "Constructing the Public Sphere in Compromised Settings: A Case Study of Environmental Decision-Making in the Alberta Forest Sector." *Canadian Review of Sociology* 45(2):177-196.

Parkins, J.R., L. Hunt, S. Nadeau, M. Reed, J. Sinclair, and S. Wallace. (2006). "Public Participation in Forest Management: Results from a National Survey of Advisory Committees." *Northern Forestry Centre Information Report NOR-X-409*, Edmonton, AB.

Peck, J., and A. Tickell. (2002). "Neoliberalizing Space." *Antipode* 34:380-404.

Pellizzoni, L. (2004). "Responsibility and Environmental Governance." *Environmental Politics* 13(3):541-565.

Polanyi, K. (2001). *The Great Transformation: The Political and Economic Origins of Our Time*. Boston: Beacon Press.

Reed, M.G., and J. Varghese. (2007). "Gender Representation on Canadian Forest Sector Advisory Committees." *Forestry Chronicle* 83:515-525.

Rueschemeyer, D., and P.B. Evans. (1985). "The State and Economic Transformation: Toward an Analysis of the Conditions Underlying Effective Intervention." In P.B. Evans, D. Rueschemeyer, and T. Skocpol (eds.), *Bringing the State Back In*. Cambridge: Cambridge University Press.

Shaw. K. (2004). "The Global/Local Politics of the Great Bear Rainforest." *Environmental Politics* 13(2):373-392.

Spaargaren, G., and A.P.J. Mol. (2008). "Greening Global Consumption: Redefining Politics and Authority." *Global Environmental Change* 18:350-359.

Vogler, J. (2005). "In Defense of International Environmental Cooperation." In J. Barry and R. Eckersley (eds.), *The State and the Global Ecological Crisis*. Cambridge: MIT Press.

Chapter 21

Research Methods

Becoming a Critical Consumer and Producer of Research

Heather L. Garrett

York University

INTRODUCTION

We are surrounded by research throughout our daily lives. Whether we are aware of it or not, most of us are exposed to some type of social research at various points during our day. We come across research in the media by reading the newspaper, listening to the radio, surfing the internet or watching television. A glance at the newspaper or a popular magazine over your morning cup of coffee provides many articles, columns or editorials that are based on interviews with people about local matters such as changes to the minimum wage or some form of available data produced by an institution or government on global issues related to poverty. You may also find advertisements in newspapers for companies looking for volunteers to participate in pharmaceutical studies and focus groups for marketing products when you are checking the sports results. While listening to your favourite radio programme when you get dressed or when you are on your drive to and from work you might hear about some research findings on a current global, national or local topic of interest. Listeners may be asked to phone in or text their opinions on global issues such as terrorism, war or environmental degradation, national issues such as the elimination of the long-form census or local topics such as increased property taxes, bullying in their neighbourhood school or the increase in gun violence among youth in the downtown core. At work, school or during your leisure time when you log on to your internet browser there are links to current research results you can view to find out about the results of investigations on issues such as health and wellness, the environment, technological advances or Canadian identity. Tuning into the evening news on the television provides you with another opportunity to see and hear about research results from polls undertaken by your local or national government or experimental findings on new medical treatments to eco-friendly products and commodities. Making sense of all of the research studies, methods, techniques and findings you are exposed to can seem overwhelming and constraining. This does not need to be the case.

Although research influences your life on a daily basis, as a social researcher, you have the volition to use your sociological imagination to make intelligent decisions about the research findings, methods and studies you read about to become a more critical producer and consumer of social research about Canadian society. In fact you are already both a "consumer" and a "producer" of research in your daily life as a sociology student, worker and a Canadian citizen. As a student you have probably researched which university to attend, which courses to take and, once you were enrolled in your first introductory sociology courses, you most likely used the results of prior research to be a producer of your own research papers, reports and assignments. You may even subscribe to online forums, blogs and RSS feeds to keep up to date on the results of the recent research findings in your field of study. In the future, you might use the results of research to choose your career, find out which economic sectors and industries are booming or information on employers and companies that provide a safe and healthy working environment. As an ordinary Canadian citizen you might read current research on new medical treatments for cancer, diabetes or stroke if you or someone close to you is diagnosed with a chronic illness.

An analysis of sociological literature or the current media suggests that there is more than one way to do research and to collect and analyze data whether you are interested in local Canadian issues or global cross-cultural issues. A variety of themes of Canadian nationalism and identity described in the literature include the preoccupation with endurance and survival due to geographic and regional differences, the two solitudes of English and French identity, multiculturalism, being different from Americans and civility in terms of peace, order and good government (Cormack, 2008; Harrison and Frieson, 2010). Critical consumers and producers of research keep in mind that just because two events or phenomena are related, it does not mean that one event caused the other to occur. Correlation does not necessarily equal causation. It is also important to remember that conclusions drawn by researchers are as good as the data on which they are based. Positivists would argue that it is necessary to question data not collected using the "scientific method," however, even though the scientific method may have been employed by a social scientist, it is crucial to be a critical consumer of any research that you read by being wary of simple answers and absolute truths.

When you engage in the research process yourself to study Canadian society, it is also necessary to become a critical "producer" of research. When you hear, see and read about local problems and global concerns, use your *sociological imagination* to raise questions and seek answers. An informed critical consumer and producer of research understands that research conclusions are not absolute. They are always tentative and are open to further interpretation and discussion. For example, when reviewing research studies and findings on Canadian society it is important to ask yourself a variety of different questions. What research method is utilized? Who or what is being studied? Why has this research been conducted? How is the study portrayed? Who or what is the source or the author of the research? Who would benefit from this particular research study and, who would not? What is this research actually telling me and, most importantly, what appears to be missing? If you already use your sociological imagination to raise these types of questions when considering the research on Canadian society that you have come across, you are well on your way to becoming a social researcher.

If you are new to doing sociological research and just starting out, the purpose of this chapter is to assist you as you develop the skills to become a more critical producer and consumer of research in general and, more specifically, of research on topics and issues relevant to the study of Canadian society. Throughout this chapter, doing research is viewed as a social process involving active decision making by the researcher. This guiding principle is grounded in the critical sociological framework of Mills (1959) and the historical sociology of Abrams (1982). Both perspectives suggest that social change involves the interaction of structural forces and volition. It is based on Mills' (1959) assumption that, as a social researcher within the field of sociology you are an active member of society working towards social change. Abrams' (1982) perspective adds the notion that the relationship between structure and agency is a matter of *process* in time that can be viewed within its historical context.

Challenging your own personal commonly held beliefs, norms, values and ideologies and those of others by designing and carrying out a research project, you as a researcher play a key role in participating in the process of social change. Recognizing inequality and diversity in society by understanding the transformation of personal troubles to social issues empowers you as a researcher to choose the research design and methodology most suitable for creating a society at the local or global level that critically assesses taken-for-granted assumptions faced by members of a diverse world. If you think you hold all of the power in this process, think again, because you do not. All members of societies from ordinary Canadian citizens and participants in the global economy to social researchers and students face structural constraints and must use their agency to overcome challenges, confront roadblocks, and deal with the consequences of their actions. There is always hope, however. Developing your sociological imagination and engaging in social research on Canadian identity from a sociological perspective empowers you to critically assess and better understand that other researchers struggle with the same troubles and issues that you do.

One of the many decisions you as a researcher make is how to study the social issue that is of interest to you. Making intelligent decisions about different research methodologies, understanding, evaluating and interpreting prior research, becoming aware of the implications of a prior body of research and the possible biases inherent in how data are gathered to create your own unique research study can be challenging. All researchers face similar challenges during a research study. In this chapter you will learn about making research decisions that best suit your research interests and research approaches and orientations for designing a research study about Canadian society as a critical consumer and producer of research. Some of the main problems and constraints researchers can encounter while engaging in research will be addressed throughout. Several resources and examples of research on Canadian identity and topics of interest to the study of Canadian society within the Canadian and international context will be suggested. Before this can be undertaken, however, it will be necessary to consider how research as a social process in time links theory and method. Given the scope of this textbook, it is not feasible, nor do I attempt to cover all of the minute details and aspects involved in measurement, sampling, and data analysis. For these topics and other specific methodological details, a list of current suggested readings on research methods is provided at the end of this chapter.

THEORY AND METHOD

Theories are derived from systems of logic to aid researchers in explaining the observations that they find in the social world. Theories are more specific than the paradigms upon which they are based. Paradigms provide an ideological framework or model that forms how we organize and understand what we observe when we do our research. Paradigms that you are already familiar with as a sociologist, include the Positivist paradigm, the Interpretive paradigm and the Conflict paradigm. Structural Functionalist theory tends to provide more positivist macro-level societal explanations. The Symbolic Interactionist and Ethnomethodological perspectives tend to provide an interpretive micro-level individual explanation. Other theoretical frameworks such as Conflict theory and the Feminist theories can be categorized as either micro- or macro-level and use the conflict perspective to explain social phenomena. Theories generally explain why things happen. They link the causes of a specific phenomenon to an effect or specify certain conditions and situations under which an event is likely to occur. This enables the researcher to predict events and phenomena by testing a hypothesis derived from the theoretical model under different conditions and situations.

For example, a conflict theorist might start with the basic assumption or theory that there is inequality in society and hypothesize that owners of the means of production are more likely to have a higher income than workers. The inequality concept in this case is measured as a dependent variable in terms of income. Different research methodologies are then employed to test whether the basic theoretical proposition of inequality measured as income differentials holds in specific situations and conditions. A survey or interview might be used to collect data about income levels or, using a different research methodology, institutional records regarding pay rates of employees and owners could be analyzed to test the theory. This macro-level analysis of inequality based on the Conflict paradigm can be applied by researchers to other populations across Canada using individuals or institutions as the unit of analysis to make regional comparisons. When different studies are undertaken from Halifax to Toronto and Lethbridge to Vancouver, using the basic theoretical assumptions of the model, and the same observations are found and generalized to the population the more likely the model is to become accepted within the discipline. The theory can also be tested globally. A feminist researcher might start with the basic assumption or theory that there is inequality in society and hypothesize that men are more likely to have a higher income than women. Sex is the independent variable as inequality in this case is measured in terms of income differentials between the two categories of the variable sex, male and female. Similar research methodologies could then be used to test whether the revised theoretical proposition concerning inequality measured as gender-based income differentials holds in specific situations and conditions and the body of research will be expanded on the topic.

Theories are tested using the traditional scientific model by developing a research hypothesis. A hypothesis is a testable statement about a variable that predicts an observable outcome. Variables are derived from theoretical concepts through the process of conceptualization. They can be independent or dependent. Their indicators or values vary, hence the term variable. For example, income levels vary. You can have different incomes at different stages of your life and you can have a different income compared to others such as someone else at your job, your friend, a relative or a stranger living somewhere in Africa or Newfoundland. One of the decisions a researcher must make when linking theory to research is how to operationally define variables to move from a theoretical construct such as inequality in an abstract theoretical model to a specific variable such as income that can be tested. When you define your variables, you specify how you will use them in your research. Independent variables are the presumed cause and dependent variables are the presumed effect in such a relationship. For the inequality example noted previously, the variable sex with the indicators male and female would be the independent variable as the hypothesis derived from feminist theory posits that the independent variable sex will result in variations in the dependent variable of income.

At this point several questions may be coming to your mind. You may be thinking, I do not know much about theory and I only want to find out more about my research topic or I want to develop my own theory rather than test a theory. You may also be wondering how you can possibly distinguish between independent variables, hypotheses and concepts let alone figure out which research method you will choose to study your research topic. First and foremost, congratulations on beginning to develop your sociological imagination. Other researchers have also grappled with these same questions. Second, keep in mind that engaging in research is a continuing process and it takes time to develop a research approach and methodology. Before you can find answers to these questions, start thinking about your research orientation and approach. Familiarize yourself with the various types of studies you can design by comparing the differences between a qualitative and quantitative approach and the various constraints you may encounter. To become a critical producer and consumer of research it is therefore necessary to review the literature.

CHOOSING YOUR RESEARCH APPROACH AND ORIENTATION

Scientific theory and research are linked through the logic of deduction and induction. When you test a theory you are using a deductive mode of reasoning. Quantitative explanations of events tend to be based on deductive logic. Hypotheses are derived from general theoretical principles and tested by making observations using research methods that enable you to generalize your findings from the general theory to the specific population you are studying. This is the process discussed above. In a Canadian study, questionnaire data was used to analyze the underemployment of immigrants in Canada (Grant, 2008). Research hypotheses were derived from a theoretical model to predict whether skilled immigrants in Canada who are experiencing credentialing problems protest discriminatory treatment. In reality, the research process alternates between the inductive and the deductive modes of reasoning. When you develop theory, you are using inductive reasoning. Qualitative explanations of events tend to be based on inductive logic. Rather than starting with a specific theory, you begin by collecting your data and then you analyze your particular empirical observations to develop grounded theory from them. General principles, themes and patterns are inferred to theorize about events and phenomena under study. If you then want to test your theory you would move back to the deductive mode of reasoning to develop a hypothesis and test it. This does not mean that if you want to test theory you must use a quantitative research approach and if you want to develop theory you must use a qualitative research approach. Weber (1905) and Durkheim (1897) both used an historical comparative method to develop theory, however, Durkheim's work on suicide was informed by the positivist tradition whereas Weber's work on Protestantism was informed by the interpretive tradition.

The approach that you choose to conduct your research is also linked to your research orientation. To decide which research approach to use, think about what exactly it is that you want to do and what research questions you have in mind. The three main purposes or research orientations are exploration, description and explanation. With explanation you can predict events and assess or evaluate social change based on the theoretical model you have tested or implemented. You may already have a research question in mind. For example you may be interested in studying identity and what it means to be Canadian or you may want to find out how Canada as a society differs from other nations. If you are interested in finding out about what is happening in regards to a specific event, person or entity your research orientation will be either descriptive or explanatory. Exploratory research enables you to come to a preliminary understanding of what is going on in relation to a specific phenomenon. Either qualitative or quantitative research methodologies can be used for exploratory research, however, exploratory research usually tends to be qualitative. For example, Creese and Ngene Kambere (2003) used focus groups in an exploratory study of African immigrant women in Canada and found preliminary results regarding how a "Canadian English" accent is used to shape and reproduce who is "Canadian" and who is "Other."

Once you have examined exploratory research on your specified topic, and have an initial understanding of a certain event or situation, descriptive research can be carried out to provide a detailed account of trends and characteristics for a given population or phenomenon. Again, either qualitative or quantitative research methodologies can be used. Other questions that can be answered using these two orientations begin with how, when or where. For instance, Thomas (2005) examined data from the Canadian censuses of population to understand how the number of people reporting "Canadian" for ethno-cultural ancestry increased. Assessing social change is also usually comparative in nature and involves the evaluation of the effects of social interventions such as in action research where the researcher is involved in bringing about social change and assessing its impact on a specific group of people or an institution. In the research by Thomas (2005), changes to the measurement of the ethnicity variable is one reason given for the increase in the number of people describing themselves as Canadian. Theoretical paradigms may be used as an analytic framework for both descriptive and exploratory studies without actually testing any theories or hypotheses.

Asking a why question enables you to explain events and social phenomena and to further test a theoretical perspective. As noted above this type of explanatory approach would involve deductive reasoning. Predictions can be made to answer what might occur under given conditions. The purpose of predictive research assumes that a quantitative approach has been utilized. Qualitative research methodologies can also be used for explanatory purposes as is commonly used in the grounded theory approach. Themes, patterns and similarities are subjected to the constant comparison method to generate theory from the data. In many cases, a researcher can decide to combine an exploratory and descriptive orientation or a descriptive and explanatory orientation with other research orientations such as prediction and the evaluation of change depending on the specific topic under investigation. Similarly, either a qualitative, quantitative or a combined research approach can be utilized.

QUALITATIVE AND QUANTITATIVE RESEARCH METHODOLOGIES

The main difference between a qualitative and a quantitative approach is that the data generated and analyzed using a quantitative approach is numeric whereas with a qualitative approach the data is non-numeric. Quantitative methods include surveys and questionnaires, structured interviews, experiments, the analysis of secondary data, and content analysis. A nomothetic approach and deductive reasoning enable quantitative researchers to identify the main factors related to a specific phenomenon, action or situation in quantitative research. Surveys, questionnaires, and structured interviews can be used to describe demographic characteristics of a population. The results from surveys and polls can be used to explain and predict the relationship between two or more variables and to study self-reported opinions, attitudes and beliefs. Cross-cultural comparisons are facilitated by comparing survey data. In different approaches to the study of Canadian beliefs and values survey data has been compared to the United States (Adams, 2009; Bean, Gonzalez, and Kaufman, 2008). For example, Adams (2009), of the Environics Research group uses the social values research method to study the values of Canadians and Americans. A number of dimensions of values reported in surveys conducted over the past several decades in Canada and the United States are mapped to reveal that Canadians and Americans have differing values on social issues such as the family, authority and religion. Bean, Gonzalez, and Kaufman (2008) employed the multi-methods of surveys, interviews and the historical comparative analysis approach to analyze differences in political and religious identity.

While a researcher coding the manifest content of social artefacts such as diaries, newspapers, government documents and other primary and secondary sources can easily change a coding scheme to incorporate another indicator measuring a dimension of a variable throughout the research process, if you decide to collect your data using a survey or an experimental method you do not have this option. If you choose an experimental or survey design, reactivity is another constraint you will need to take into consideration in terms of your own role in the research and your research subjects' role. This is not such a problem if you choose an unobtrusive research methodology where the unit of analysis is a social artefact rather than an individual.

Experimental designs provide researchers with the opportunity to isolate cause and effect relationships by precisely measuring the independent and dependent variable and controlling all aspects of the research process. Precise measurement is one of the characteristics of quantitative research. The variables used in quantitative research to test theory should also be tested to make sure they are valid and reliable. Reliability is the stability or consistency of an operational definition of a variable. There are two general ways to check if a measure is reliable. To check the stability of a measure, ask yourself if the same results are obtained repeatedly each time the measurement technique is applied. To check for the equivalence of a measure ask whether or not the same results are obtained when a slightly different measure is used. Developing reliable and valid measures is time consuming and requires a lot of skill and effort.

The analysis of secondary data from surveys collected by other researchers is useful for cross-cultural comparisons within a global context. A constraint you may face while analyzing another researcher's data is that the reliability and validity of their measures may not meet your research needs. The way that variables are measured in the Canadian census can also be a problem as the question wording may change over time (Thomas, 2005) or questions may be dropped from the census instrument. This can also be a problem when you are analyzing available data obtained from government statistics or a census from different countries. Government agencies such as Statistics Canada provide very specific and detailed accounts of their data collection and sampling techniques. If you plan to analyze official documents from governments around the globe, you may find that you will experience difficulties. The data you may want to analyze may not be available. Moreover, there may be restrictions involved in accessing the actual data you require. When studying international communities and applying your research design at the global level, the reliability of a measure may come into question due to the way in which language is used. A measure which may be considered to be reliable in the developed world may not be in the social context of the developing world. The use of data collected by organizations such as the United Nations Development Programme can include missing data (Desai, 2010; Neumayer, 2010) making cross-cultural comparisons problematic. Some nations may not report the data or the data may not have been collected or reported during the time period under study. While the quantitative approach is criticized as being reductionist given that it is objective, structured, inflexible and does not take into consideration a research participant's individual subjective, lived experience the data generated are very highly reliable and can be generalized from the sample to the population from which they are drawn.

Data for quantitative research is obtained either by administering a research instrument such as a survey or experimental stimulus to a representative sample of individuals from a population or by analyzing a sample of social artefacts using available data. Whether data is collected about individuals, institutions, groups or things probability sampling is used. Simple random sampling is the basis of the sampling procedures and techniques available to researchers such as systematic sampling, stratified sampling and cluster sampling. Based on the logic of probability theory and the central limit theorem, the purpose of sampling is to select a representative set of elements from the population that you want to study. It is assumed that the sample you draw is representative of the population. This means that your sample has the same distribution of characteristics as the population from which it is selected. Sampling is much more cost effective in terms of time and resources than studying the entire population. As each element in a random sample has a known chance or probability of being selected, conscious or unconscious error can be avoided. You can collect much more data and your findings can be generalized to your target population. The main difference between sampling using a qualitative or a quantitative approach is that the data for a qualitative research study comes from individual case studies and can not be generalized because probability sampling is not used. Non-probability sampling techniques used in qualitative research include accidental sampling, availability or convenience, snowball quota, and purposive/judgmental sampling. In oral history research, for example, a specific number of persons who have experienced a similar event such as being Francophone teachers in English-speaking Ontario during the 1940s and 1950s are interviewed (Majhanovich, 2006). In ethnographic studies and field research studies of small groups, very often a whole group is studied as a case study and therefore sampling is not needed. For example, Collings (2009) observed an Inuit community in the Canadian Arctic.

Qualitative methods include participant observation, field research, ethnography, in-depth interviews, focus groups and oral history. In qualitative research designs, inductive reasoning and an idiographic approach enable researchers to identify in great detail all of the possible causes of a particular phenomenon, situation or action. A qualitative approach tends to be more subjective, flexible, holistic and less structured than a quantitative approach. Data analysis and data collection occur throughout the research process. One way to analyze the data is to look for similarities and differences. Applying the constant comparative method after coding and memoing the data you have transcribed from your in-depth interviews, oral history notes, focus group recordings or field notes is another way. This enables the qualitative researcher to be reflexive and be more aware of the importance of context. The research findings are rich in meaning and therefore are highly valid as they reflect the true meaning of the variables and concepts they are measuring. There are two main types of validity assessment you can use to test the goodness of fit of your measures. To check subjective validity, ask yourself whether an operational definition of a concept measures the concept that it is intended to measure. In order to assess criterion-related validity ask yourself whether or not the result you have obtained using your measure are related to some other variable to which it should or should not be related. While the validity of qualitative research is very strong, the reliability is weak. This is because it is not always possible for research to be replicated as no two research situations will be exactly the same.

Qualitative methods can be used on their own (Cormack, 2008; Sharma, 2001). They can also be combined with other qualitative or quantitative methods (Majhanovich, 2006) to provide context and develop theory by generating new insights and concepts in order to expand on the meaning of social concepts (Bean, Gonzalez, and Kaufman, 2008). They can also be used to corroborate and validate other research findings (Clary-Lemon, 2010) and document the voices of the silenced. Despite the opportunities they provide researchers with to explore topics in depth, deciding to use these methods can also lead to challenges and constraints. There may be difficulties accessing the field and making contacts with people in positions of power who can provide you with access to research participants (Collings, 2009). In the field, your presence as a researcher can influence the very behaviour and events you are studying as this type of research approach is very obtrusive. Similarly, there are differences between the spoken and written word not only for the research participants but also for the researcher. Language barriers can hinder your attempts to observe or interview any individuals or groups you plan on studying whether your research is on a local Canadian topic or a more global topic. While you record your notes in the field or during an in-depth interview or focus group, you may impose meaning which was not intended by your research subject. You may encounter situations which make you feel uncomfortable depending on the observer role you adopt to do your research. Your observer role can start out as a non-participant role and change over the course of your study to a semi- or full-participant role. It is important to reflect on your role as a researcher while engaging in qualitative research as you may become so involved in your role in the field that you forget your role as a researcher and overstep boundaries. Similarly you may consciously or unconsciously impose your own cultural interpretations on the lives of those you are studying when undertaking research studying diverse populations not only within Canada but also in other global locales.

While interviewing your research subjects or conducting an oral history interview, you might find that the account given is inaccurate when you compare your data to other sources. This could be related to constraints inherent in a qualitative research approach. Memories fade not only for participants in a research study but also for the researcher. Your subjects may impose a narrative structure on the details they provide to justify their own identity (Majhanovich, 2006) or they may have a specific underlying reason for divulging or not divulging certain information. There may also be self-serving motives or a hidden agenda. It is, therefore, very important as a researcher to take detailed field notes and analyze them throughout the research process so that you can follow up on inaccuracies by raising questions and seeking answers. Finally, it is important to be aware as a critical producer and consumer of research that there can be power relationships between an interviewer and interviewee that affect what and how events are reported. This can also occur when a quantitative researcher conducts a survey or experiment. Regardless of which research questions you want to answer and the research approaches you will ultimately use, as a critical producer of research on Canadian society, all research should be designed with ethical guidelines in mind.

Figure 21.1 provides a summary of the characteristics of qualitative and quantitative research approaches to aid you in assessing which type of research approach and methodology you should consider to frame your research and collect your data. Figure 21.1 is not meant to force you to choose one approach over another. Rather, it should be used as an analytic tool to make informed decisions about the research approach that best suits your own personal situation and research interests. Perhaps the methods you decide on will combine different research orientations and approaches as you become open to new ways of viewing social issues. As your sociological imagination and critical standpoint develop and you begin to engage in the research process to produce your own research about Canadian society, your own way of doing research will start to become evident to you. Keep in mind that although you have the volition to choose your own research approach, your decisions will be made within the context of the structural constraints of your lived experience. Questions you should consider concern resources such as time and money. For example, can you afford to travel to collect your data from a government agency in another country? Do you have two to three years to spend in the field?

FIGURE 21.1. COMPARISON OF QUANTITATIVE AND QUALITATIVE APPROACHES

Quantitative Approach	Qualitative Approach
"hard"	"soft"
numeric data	rich data, (words and images)
positivist	interpretive
structured	flexible
objective	subjective
generalize findings	can not generalize findings
reliability strong	validity strong
large samples	small case studies
random samples	non-random samples
deductive	inductive
nomothetic	idiographic
reductionist	holistic
tests theory	develops theory (grounded theory)

REVIEWING THE LITERATURE AND NARROWING THE RESEARCH TOPIC

When reviewing the literature and refining your research topic stop throughout the process to remind yourself about what you have learned about becoming a critical producer and consumer of research and ask

FIGURE 21.2:
TYPOLOGY FOR REVIEWING THE LITERATURE BACKGROUND AND STRUCTURE

Background and Structure*:

1) Who is the author?
2) What date was it written?
3) What is the full bibliographic information given?
4) What is the library call number/URL in case I have to find it again?
5) Is there an abstract?
6) Is there an appendix?
7) Is there a reference section?

*Note: Record this information; it is not necessary to include it in the literature review

Type of Study / Introduction:

1) Is it qualitative/quantitative/both?
2) What is the purpose of the study?
3) What is the research orientation?
4) What is the research question?
5) Is there a review of the literature?
6) Is there a hypothesis or hypotheses?
7) Is there a theoretical framework?
8) Describe the content of the study in 1 sentence or phrase for points 1-8.
9) Does anything seem missing, biased or inaccurate?

Research Design and Method:

1) What research method(s) are used?
2) Is there triangulation of methods?
3) How exactly are the data collected?
4) What steps are followed?
5) Are there any problems with the method: does anything seem missing, biased or inaccurate?

Sampling Technique:

1) Is the technique probability or non-probability?
2) What technique(s) is used?
3) Who or what makes up the sample?
4) How many are in the sample?
5) Are there any problems with the sample design, size, frame, etc.?
6) Are there any specific biases?

Measurement of Variables:

1) What is the main independent variable?
2) What level of measurement is used for the IV?
3) What are its attributes?
4) What is the main dependent variable?
5) What level of measurement is used for the DV?
6) What are its attributes?
7) Are there other variables mentioned?
8) Are the variables related to the hypotheses?

Reliability and Validity:

1) Are the IV and DV measures valid?
2) Does the article mention validity assessment?
3) Are the IV and DV measures reliable?
4) Does the article mention reliability checks?

Ethics:

1) What ethical concerns are addressed?
2) What ethical concerns are not addressed but should be?

Data Analysis, Findings and Conclusions:

1) How are the data analyzed?
2) How are the data presented?
3) Are statistics used?
4) What are the main findings?
5) What are the main conclusions?
6) Any problems with the data analysis / findings/conclusions?
7) Are there any policy implications?

Strengths and Weaknesses:

1) What were the main strengths?
2) What were the main weaknesses?
3) How could I build on this research?
4) What would I do differently in future research?

yourself the following questions. What is my research question? What is my research orientation? How does my research orientation link to the purpose of my study? How does this topic link to the literature and theory? The research topic and question you decide to study should be interesting to you and relatively easy for you to research given your personal circumstances. Depending on your research approach it could be related to a personal trouble that you already know about and you want to know more about. It could be based on a social issue you have experienced in your life as a Canadian citizen. As research surrounds us it could be based on current global issues, events or social trends.

When reading an empirical article for your literature review you should be aware of the aspects of the article outlined in Figure 21.2. Keep in mind, however, that you may not be able to find everything depending on the theoretical paradigm, research orientation or research approach the author has used. Reviewing the literature and refining your research topic can at times appear to be very overwhelming. To help frame your review of the literature, use your original research question as a guide. This will help you to stay on task.

A review of the literature presents the current state of research findings in order to outline and summarize the direction of research on a topic. It is based on the assumption that knowledge accumulates and that we can learn from and expand on what other researchers have found in the past. In a concurrent literature review, key points, main conclusions and methodological aspects of a variety of different empirical research studies are integrated. Connections and comparisons between research studies are made.

The different research questions, theoretical perspectives, research hypotheses, measures, variables, research methodologies and findings are described and analyzed. Limitations, agreements, disagreements, and/or conflicting or inaccurate results within the body of research are assessed. The information that is presented in a literature review is critically evaluated with an eye toward pointing out where major research questions remain as well as directions for future research.

Having read the literature you may discover that what you originally wanted to study is feasible but the body of research has not adequately taken into consideration a specific variable. Perhaps the variable you are interested in has been measured or defined in many different ways. For example, in a review of the literature on Canadian identity, identity was found to be defined generally by terms such as culture, ethnicity or race and more specifically in terms of socio-cultural contexts from ethnic, racial and aboriginal identities to national and regional or religious and linguistic identifications (Rummens, 2001). Even though your topic may already have been studied, it may not have been studied using a certain research methodology from a certain theoretical perspective. You may also find that new research questions you had not even considered start coming to mind and, using your sociological imagination, you take some time to reflect upon them. How does this new research question relate to my research orientation? What gaps and limitations in the literature can be addressed? What is the purpose of my study? What variables should I include? What research methodologies could I use? Can a qualitative and a quantitative research approach be included in my study? Can a topic specific to regional differences in Canada also be applied in a global context? Welcome to the world of social research, you are well on your way to becoming a critical producer and consumer of research.

REFERENCES

Abrams, P. (1982). *Historical Sociology.* NY: Cornell University Press.

Adams, M. (2009). *Fire & Ice: the United States, Canada and the Myth of Converging Values.* Toronto: Penguin.

Bean, L., M. Gonzalez, and J. Kaufman. (2008). "Why doesn't Canada have an American-Style Christian Right? A Comparative Framework for Analyzing the Political Effects of Evangelical Subcultural

Identity." *Canadian Journal of Sociology* 33(4):899-943.

Clary-Lemon, J. (2010). "'We're not Ethnic, We're Irish!': Oral Histories and the Discursive Construction of Immigrant Identity." *Discourse & Society* 21(1):5-25.

Collings, P. (2009). "Participant Observation and Phased Assertion as Research Strategies in the Canadian Arctic." *Field Methods* 21(2):133-153.

Cormack, P. (2008). "'True Stories' of Canada: Tim Horton's and the Branding of National Identity." *Cultural Sociology* 2(3):369-384.

Creese, G., and E. Ngene Kambere. (2003). "'What Colour is your English?'" *The Canadian Review of Sociology and Anthropology* 40(5):565-573.

Desai, M. (2010). "Hope in Hard Times: Women's Empowerment and Human Development." Human Development Research Paper 2010/14. NY: United Nations Development Programme. Retrieved September 01, 2010 from http://hdr.undp.org/en/reports/global/hdr2010/papers/HDRP_2010_14.pdf.

Durkheim, E. (1897/1951). *Suicide.* IL: Free Press.

Grant, P.R. (2008). "The Protest Intentions of Skilled Immigrants with Credentialing Problems: A Test of a Model Integrating Relative Deprivation Theory with Social Identity Theory." *British Journal of Social Psychology* 47(4):687-705.

Harrison, T.W., and J.W. Frieson. (2010). *Canadian Society in the Twenty-first Century An Historical and Sociological Approach,* 2nd ed. Toronto: Canadian Scholars' Press.

Majhanovich, S. (2006). "Pondering Priorities: Reflections on the Careers of Three Francophone Women Teachers in Ontario." *Resources for Feminist Research* 31(3-4):67-86.

Mills, C.W. (1959). *The Sociological Imagination.* Oxford: Oxford University Press.

Neumayer, E. (2010). "Human Development and Sustainability." Human Development Research Paper 2010/05. NY: United Nations Development Programme. Retrieved September 01, 2010 from http://hdr.undp.org/en/reports/global/hdr2010/papers/HDRP_2010_05.pdf.

Rummens, J. (2001). "Canadian Identities: An Interdisciplinary Overview of Canadian Research on Identity." Ottawa: Canadian Heritage (Multiculturalism). Retrieved September 01, 2010 from http://canada.metropolis.net/events/ethnocultural/publications/identity_e.pdf.

Sharma, N. (2001). "On Being Not Canadian: The Social Organization of 'Migrant Workers' in Canada." *Canadian Review of Sociology and Anthropology,* 38 (4) 415-439.

Thomas, D. (2005). "I am Canadian." *Canadian Social Trends* 76(Spring):2-7.

Weber, M. (1905/1958). *The Protestant Ethic and the Spirit of Capitalism.* Translated by Talcott Parsons. NY: Scribners.

SUGGESTED READINGS

Babbie, E.R., and L. Benaquisto. (2010). *The Fundamentals of Social Research,* 2nd Canadian edition. Toronto: Nelson.

Blaikie, N. (2010). *Designing Social Research,* 2nd ed. Cambridge: Polity Press.

Bouma, G.D., R. Ling, and L. Wilkinson. (2009). *The Research Process.* Canadian edition. Don Mills: Oxford University Press.

Bryman, A., J.J. Teevan, and E. Bell. (2009). *Social Research Methods,* 2nd Canadian edition. Don Mills: Oxford University Press.

Jackson, W., and N. Verberg. (2007). *Methods: Doing Social Research,* 4th ed. Toronto: Pearson Canada Inc.

Neuman, W. L., and K. Robson. (2009). *Basics of Social Research*: Qualitative and Quantitative Approaches. Canadian edition. Toronto: Pearson Education Inc.

Palys, T., and C. Atchison. (2008). *Research Decisions: Quantitative and Qualitative Perspectives,* 4th ed. Toronto: Nelson.

Sociology Writing Group. (2007). *A Guide to Writing Sociology Papers,* 6th ed. NY: Worth Publishers.

Swift, J., J.M. Davies, R.G. Clarke, and M. Czerny. (2003). *Getting Started on Social Analysis in Canada.* Toronto: Between the Lines Press.

Tenson, B.L., and K. Hampson. (2010). *Mastering Digital Research: A Guide for Students.* Toronto: Nelson.

Index

CPSIA information can be obtained at www.ICGtesting.com
Printed in the USA
241813LV00002B/2/P

9 781897 160305